THE SHAH-NAMAH OF FARDUSI

The Shah-Namah of Fardusi

Translated from the Original Persian by
Alexander Rogers

Low Price Publications

Low Price Publications
2013

First Published 1907
Reprinted in **LPP** 1995, 2002, 2010, 2013

ISBN 10: 81-7536-507-2
ISBN 13: 978-81-7536-507-0

Published by
Low Price Publications
A-6, 2nd Floor, Nimri Commercial Centre,
Ashok Vihar Phase 4, Delhi 110052 (INDIA)
tel.: +91.11.27302453 fax.: +91.11.47061936
url: www.LPPindia.com e-mail: info@LPPindia.com

Printed at
Salasar Imaging Systems, Delhi

PRINTED IN INDIA

Dedication.

DEAR SIR MANCHERJEE,—

In giving me your valuable co-operation in the production of my rendering of the great Epic of your fatherland by the immortal Fardúsi, I believe you are inspired by that love for Persian literature and ardour for the physical well-being of your race, which your late father manifested by his life-long study of the Persian language and by founding in 1857 the Gymnastic Institute at Bombay, the first of its kind in India. These are laudable national sentiments which a better knowledge of the Shah-Namah is well calculated to foster, and in the fervent hope that my work may prove helpful in this way to the descendants of those whose chivalrous deeds are perpetuated in it,—

I DEDICATE THIS TRANSLATION

OF THE SHAH-NAMAH

TO THE MEMORY OF

Merwanjee Nosbirwanjee Bhownaggree.

Yours sincerely,

ALEXANDER ROGERS

London, 10th October, 1907.

SIR MANCHERJEE MERWANJEE BHOWNAGGREE, K.C.I.E.,

ORDER OF THE LION AND THE SUN, PERSIA,

196, *Cromwell Road, S.W.*

Preface

THE rendering into English couplets of the major portion of Fardúsi's great epic is a fitting culmination to Mr. Alexander Rogers' Oriental studies in the course of his long and strenuous career in India. All who know him will share a fervent hope that he may be spared to give his countrymen other examples of the Persian classics. But the SHAH NAMAH must necessarily remain his *magnum opus.* It is the work of several years, and the result of sixty years' study of Persian. Not only is it the fullest version yet produced in English form, but it is the most faithful in its adherence to the original. Mr. Rogers has not sought to impose his own individuality upon the work of another, after the manner of other Oriental scholars. He has been satisfied to interpret the thoughts, the expression, and the style of Fardúsi as closely as the exigencies of a foreign medium would permit. The crudities and obscurities of the poem, alike with its beauties, have been retained. It is necessary to appreciate this singleness of purpose in judging the work, for the tendency is always to hold the translator responsible for the shortcomings of the original. Mr. Rogers might have gained more credit if he had embellished, elucidated, and generally modernised the work, but he would not have given us Fardúsi. He has moreover added to the difficulties of his task by this uncompromising fidelity, whilst he has thereby placed every student of Oriental literature under an obligation and has established his position as one of the most profound Persian scholars of the present day, for the method which he has followed will enable students of Fardúsi to master the peculiarities and intricacies of the original through the medium of this translation. The arduous duties of an official career in India are so exacting that such an instance of sustained Oriental research as Mr. Rogers has provided is rare, if not unique, and deserves both recognition and encouragement. Such literary pursuits are not only of value, when they put forth results like those embodied in this volume, to the mere student of Eastern languages, but they serve a truly Imperial purpose by establishing a congenial medium of intercourse between the peoples of the Eastern dominions of the British Crown and those of its representatives who are sent out among them to carry on the work of administration. In perusing the final proofs of these pages, this feature of Mr. Rogers's learned labours has struck me very forcibly, and I am confident that it will make a similar appeal to his readers.

EDWIN OLIVER.

Introduction

THE following is the most extensive rendering of the Shah Námah that has ever been made into the English language, and the material portion of it has been designedly made in the original ten-syllabled metre, and as literally as possible, in order to present to the reader a fair idea of the conception of the poem. As it would have been the work of almost a life-time to translate in such a manner the whole of the 50,000 to 60,000 couplets of which it is composed, the plan adopted has been that of taking the introduction, with a portion of the history of the earliest kings of Persia in the mythical and pre-historic ages, and following these with prose translations of the reigns of the best-known monarchs and with various celebrated episodes, such as that of the fight of the hero Rústam and his son Suhráb, and from those epochs down to that of Yazdagírd, about A.H. 411 (A.D. 1020), with whose reign the epic ends. Between these there has been inserted an epitome of the history of the intervening periods in prose, so that the whole conveys a full impression of the entire poem. The Persian text followed has been that of the Calcutta edition by Col. Turner Macan in 1829, considered to be about the best in existence owing to the great care with which the finest MSS. from many different quarters were collected in compiling it. With the reasons for objecting to some of these or accepting others the readers of this translation need not be troubled. Suffice it to say that this version is probably as correct as any we are at all likely to see produced, and that to all intents and purposes it contains the poem as first written by Fardúsi.

Fardúsi, whose real name was Abul Kávím-i-Mansúr, was born in the village of Shádáb, in the district of Tús and Province of Khúrásán, about the year of the Hejira (Hijri) 320 (A.D. 932), and took the name of Fardúsi, either because his father was the gardener of a garden called Fardús (Paradise) or from the exclamation of Sultán Mahmúd, when he visited the Court of the latter at Ghazni, on hearing some extemporised verses he recited in praise of Ayáz, a favourite slave of the Sultan: "Thou hast made my Court as resplendent as Fárdús." There appears to have been nothing very remarkable in his early career until he went to Ghazni, whither he was probably attracted, although other reasons also are assigned for the step, by the Sultán's fame as a patron of letters. The Sultán, who had been making a collection of the ancient chronicles of Persia, delighted with Fardúsí's poetical genius, desired the collection to be made over to him to be versified, and promised to pay him 1000 *miskáls* of gold, equivalent to about £670, for every thousand couplets that he wrote. Fardúsí unwisely preferred to be paid on the completion of his work, but when he had accomplished it, Mahmúd sent him in place of about £40,000, which he should accordingly have received, 60,000 silver dirhams, or about £2,600. It is related that he was at the time in a public bath, and that, enraged at the Sultan's breach of faith, he gave a third to the keeper of the bath, a third to the messenger who brought the money, and the remainder to a man who brought him some *sharbat* This being reported, probably in an exaggerated form, to the Sultan, Mahmúd ordered him to be trampled to death by an elephant, but relented on Fardúsi's throwing himself at his feet. The latter, however, enraged at his treatment, determined to flee from Ghazni, and did so, leaving with Ayáz what was said to be a panegyric on the monarch, but was in reality a spirited satire on him. Managing to escape, the poet wandered about to Herát, Baghdád, and other places, pursued by Mahmúd's spite, until he at last returned to his own home. The Sultan at last relented and ordered the sum originally promised to be sent to him. It was too late, however, for the messenger entered one gate of the town whilst Fardúsi's body was being borne out of the opposite gate for burial.

Mahmúd acknowledged that the epic was worthy of renown. Singers sang portions of it and made them known to all the world, to its admiration and delight. Earlier in this reign there came to Court a young man with a ready tongue, great eloquence, and a brilliant mind, who announced his intention to put the whole into verse. This was the poet Dakíki, who was shortly afterwards murdered by a slave and died, leaving the poem incomplete. Fardúsi obtained possession of the book through a friend, said to have been one Muhammad Lashkari, and having been brought to the notice of Mahmúd of Ghazni, as already related, composed this remarkable epic which, from various particulars given in the course of the poem, appears to have occupied him for from 30 to 35 years.

Not wishing to increase the size of this work, the translator refrains from commenting at any length on its merits or demerits as a history, for the real details of which the reader must go elsewhere. Its many defects in this respect are palpable, especially in the matter of its chronology, and the slight notice taken of the wars of Persia with the Greeks. He has looked on it merely in the light of a great epic, which, considering the vast period (about 3620 years) it is supposed to embrace, and the wonderful purity and delicacy of its style is hardly equalled, and certainly not surpassed, by any other ever written in the world.

ALEXANDER ROGERS.

Contents

THE SHAH NAMAH

In the name of Allah, the Merciful, the Compassionate

GREAT Lord of Life and Wisdom! In thy Name
Which to transcend no flight of thought may claim,
The Lord of honour, and of place and pride,
Who gives our daily bread and is our guide,—
The Lord of Universe and rolling sphere,
Bright in whom Nahid,* Sun and Moon appear,
Our highest ideals doth He all excel,
Painter supreme of every gem as well !—
You the Creator who now fain would see,
Trouble your eyes not, for it cannot be.
No anxious care to Him its way may find,
All dignity and fame Him lag behind.
Words that this excellence would pass beyond,
These nor in soul nor wisdom may be found,
The soul and wisdom only would he weigh,
Nor cares he wordly riches to assay.
None knows to praise Him as He truly is,
Thy service with girt loins is duly His,
For if intelligence had words to choose
For things that it could see alone 'twould use.
With means and sense that life and soul afford.

*The planet Venus.

How of creation shall we praise the Lord ?
It needs that thou His being should'st confess,
And not in speech with useless words transgress.
Worship Him therefore and attend His way,
And His commands, however hard, obey.
Whoever learning has, he, too, is strong :
On knowledge rest the hearts of old and young.
Beyond this screen there is for speech no place,
The path to Him our thoughts can never trace.

Discourse on the Praise of Wisdom

If thou would'st wisdom's value truly know,
'Tis fitting here in words its worth to show.
Speak what of wisdom thou mayst have to bring.
That listeners' ears may profit by the thing.
Best of all gifts that God on thee conferred,
To justice e'en its praise may be preferred.
The crowns that on their heads all monarchs place,
Of all renowned ones, wisdom is the grace.
Wisdom as life eternal thou may'st know,
The very source of this our life below.
Opening the heart, and on our road the guide,
For both worlds wisdom will thee aid provide.
From it is gladness and from it is pain,
From it is decrease and from it is gain.
With wisdom darkened, though man's soul be clear,
No joy is found in any region here,—
What has that skilful one of wisdom said,
By whose words wise men are to profit led?
"Before whose eyes is wisdom aye not borne,
By his own deeds his heart is ever torn."
A madman him will designate the wise,—
Stranger he seems in his own kinsmen's eyes.

Possess it and the world seems ever fair:
With wisdom gone, thy foot's in bondage there;
The soul's true eye is wisdom must thou know;
Thou joyous one, that world do not forego.
First of creation do thou wisdom see,
The soul's own guardian, prayer's own guard to thee,
Thy prayer to thee is eye and ear and speech,
Through these both good and evil will thee reach.
To soul and wisdom what strains can I raise?
And if I could, who, then, would hear and praise?
As there is none, what need to speak, O sage?
Hereafter show to us creation's page.
Open and secret all before thee laid,
By the world's Maker thou thyself wast made.
Do thou to wisdom ever hold secure,
Of both worlds cast off what may be impure.
Wait ever on the sayings of the wise:
Go round the world and every man apprise.
To every knowledge if thou wilt attend,
Thine ear to learning never cease to lend.
Of words the branch if thou should'st ever see,
Thou'lt know to knowledge that no end can be.

Discourse on the Creation of the World.

'Twere well that to enquire thou should'st begin,
Of all the elements the origin.
For God from nothing everything has made, . . .
So that His power might be thus displayed:
The essence of four elements was wrought,
And without labour into being brought.
First when the fire from motion came to flame,
From its heat dryness into being came.
With this at rest, cold must itself unfold,
And humid moisture issue from that cold.

And when these elements, the four, combined
A resting place fit for themselves to find,
And as the four thus into union blent,
Began to raise its head each element.
This swiftly moving sphere then came to view,
Displaying wonders ever fresh and new.
As the Lord for twenty-seven days appeared,
To take its fitting place each then prepared.*
Justice and generosity grew bright,
And to the learned were gifts given aright.
The heav'ns, together shaken, union knew,
And all together tow'rds each other drew.
As sea, as mountain, and as sloping height,
The earth was manifest a shining light.
The hills were raised, and rivers first did flow,
And vegetation, too, began to grow.
For land to raise itself there was no room,
It was a black sphere of a darkening gloom.
The stars in all their beauty came to light
And on the earth itself increased the light.
Like to a fire, soon as the wave wént down,
To circle round the earth began the sun.
The grass with many kinds of trees then grew,
And fortune brought their heads below the view
To grow: It had beside no other force,
It took not, runnerlike, all ways its course.
When after this a movement stood confessed,
It brought all growth beneath itself to rest.
It did not bend its head down as a tree,
Behold how hard a thing this is to see!
And sleep and rest was all that 'twould require
And for its life was what it would desire.
No intellect to see, to speak no tongue,
Nurture it gained but stones and straw among.

*Seven planets.

Evil and good it knew not. At its hand
No service the Creator would demand,
So powerful is He, and as just as wise,
And has no virtue hidden from men's eyes.
So will the world's affairs come to an end :
Open or hid, to know this none pretend.

The third Section deals with the writing of the work, with regard to which Fardusi passed many days in making enquiries from all quarters, keeping the matter secret in the meanwhile. At last a friend, whom he describes thus :

> A friend there was in our town very kind,
> So near that both in one skin you might find,

brought him a manuscript written in Pahlavi and urged him to proceed with the work. On this :

> When I obtained the manuscript I thought,
> Into my darkened soul a light was brought.

The next three Sections are devoted to the praise of Bu Mansur, son of the Muhammad, son of the Sultan Mahamúd, and of Amir Nasr, his brother. It does not seem necessary to enter into the details of these, and it need only be noticed that the actual work appears to have been commenced under the patronage of Mahamúd of Ghazní himself.

We now come to the historical portion of the Shahnámáh in an account of the reign of the first king of Ajm, Kayumúrs, who is said to have ruled for 30 years and to have been envied by the Dív, or demon, Ahriman :

What eloquent Dehkán first to record brought
The name of him on earth who greatness sought ?
Who was it placed upon his head a crown ?
None from of old has brought the memory down,

But he to whom his father told, the son,
Who tells his father's stories one by one,
The name of greatness forward who first brought,
And than the great a higher station sought.
He who the Bástán-námáh searched of old,
That stories of the Pahlavans has told.
He said: "The customs of the throne and crown
First Kayumúrs when he was king laid down.
To the Ram's constellation when the sun
Entered, the earth with brilliant splendour shone.
From the Ram's constellation he gave light.
So that the earth became all young and bright.
When Kayumúrs was master of the land.
In the hill country first he took his stand.
His throne and fortune overtopped the hill.
Yet all of panther skins wore clothing still.
For all advancement give to him the mead
Men knew not how to dress or how to feed.
For thirty years, when he the crown had won,
Well ruling, he was brilliant as the sun.
Just as the full moon on the cypress tall,
He from his lofty throne shone down on all,
And the wild beasts that came within his ken
Were at their ease with him and rested then.
Bending, they sat down there, his throne beside;
His wondrous glory thus was magnified;
In act of supplication near they drew,
And in that place alone their faith they knew.
One son, Siámak, fair of face and name,
Sought virtuously, like his father, fame.
Handsome in face, of genial temper, too,
Kayumúrs' heart rejoiced with him in view.
Looking on him, the very earth was glad,
Good root and many a fruitful branch he had.
Seeing him live, he wept of joy the tear,

And of his absence had a boding fear.
Such is the way in which the world goes on;
A father gains fresh vigour in his son.
After this manner some time passed away;
The King's prosperity was bright and gay.
Of enemies upon the earth he'd none,
But secretly the impure Ahriman,*
And Ahriman, on evil deed intent,
To seize upon him envy's counsel lent.
He had one son, as a fierce wolf he grew,
And he was brave, with a large army, too
Gathered his host, he took tow'rds him the way,
As for Kay's throne and crown in wait he lay.
To that Dív child the world was very black,
Of King Siámak's fortune for the lack.
To all around his secret to unfold,
Throughout the earth his strident voice he rolled.
And Kayumúrs, how knew he of the thing,
For his great throne there was another king?
A heav'nly messenger came sudden in,
In Paris' † form, clothed in a panther skin,
And said: "From door to door let all men know
What tow'rds thy son now contemplates thy foe."

The going of Siamak to fight the Dív, and his being killed by him.

When to Siámak's ear the word was brought
Of deeds done by foul Dív of evil thought,
The Prince's heart grew hot such things to hear,
He gathered troops and opened wide his ear.
Upon his form a panther's skin he bore—
In warfare then the breast plate no one wore.

* Pronounced "Ahrimun."
† Pronounced "Purris."

Now when the armies face to face were set,
Eager to fight, the aspiring Dív he met.
Naked in body, Siámak came on.
And held on to that son of Ahriman.
The black Dív's claw struck him in backward blow,
The two together fell, the Prince below.
Down to the earth that princely form he bent,
And with his claw his royal loins were rent.
Siámak of his life, by Dív bereft,
Died, and his host without a lord was left.
Of his son's death the monarch was aware,
And black to him became the world through care.
He beat his back and hands, with wailing moan;
Tearing his side he came down from his throne,
With bleeding cheeks, his heart with sorrow burned.
Hard on himself he thought that fate had turned.
Up from the host arose a wailing shout,
As the king's gate they close their ranks about.
Their garments all were stained with purple dye,
Wine-hued their cheek, and full of blood their eye.
The beasts and birds and game assembled there,
Wailing and mourning to the hills repair.
Mourning, in pain, in sorrow for their woes,
From the king's palace a great dust arose.
A year they sat, their hearts with grief aflame,
Until a message from their Maker came.
Propitious greeting then an angel brought,
"Recall your senses; do not wail for nought,
Form now an army; my command obey,
From that assembly raise a dust this day,
Clear ye from off the earth that demon base,
And from your hearts these thoughts of wrath efface."
To the sky raised his head the noble king,
And vented curses on that evil thing.
By the great name of God on him he cried,

From the king's eyelash then the tear was dried,
Siámak to avenge he went in haste,
And sought not day or night repose and rest.

The going of Húshang and Kayumúrs to fight the Black Dív: his being killed, and the death of Kayumúrs.

Happy Siámak had an only son,
Dastúr's place to his grandsire who had won,
Of sterling worth. Now Húshang was his name:
Thou'dst said: "To ev'ry virtue he had claim."
And in the memory of his father blessed,
His grandsire held him closely to his breast.
His grandsire looked upon him as his son,
And seeing him for other eye had none.
When he set war with vengeance in his heart,
Worthy Húshang he summoned then, apart,
Repeated to him all he had to tell,
His secrets all revealed to him as well.
"An army will I draw now me around,
And raise a war-cry that shall far resound.
And thou wilt have to go before them all,
For I must go: thou the new General."
Pari and panther, tiger to his fold
He drew, and tearing wolf and lion bold,
The king's commands by all were to be heard,
Of beasts an army, and of flock and bird.
Of *Paris*, wild beasts and of birds a host.
Led by a general who could valour boast,
Then Kayumúrs behind to move began,
His grandson marching forward in the van.
The black Dív came on with a trembling cry,
Whilst a thick dust obscured the very sky.
And as the beasts came, roaring for the fight,
The *Dív* grew fainter in the monarch's sight.

As to each other the two hosts drew near,
At the wild beasts the *Dívs* drew back in fear.
As lion fierce, Húshang stretched out his hand;
The world grew small for those brave Dívs to stand.
From head to foot the general him flayed,
And severed from his form his monstrous head.
Beneath his feet he cast him down and spurned,
The skin of the vile wretch he flaying turned.
When thus he had exacted vengeance meet,
The days of Kayumúrs became complete.
He went, the earth remaining of him bare.
Behold, in fame with him who could compare?
This world is briefly but a fleeting tale,
And bad and good alike with all must fail.
The world collected all in its deceit:
Traversed gain's road, its fruit he did not eat.

The reign of Hushang was for forty years—His ascension of the throne and bringing iron out of stone.

Húshang, of right, and with good counsel's grace,
Assumed the crown in his grand-parent's place.
For forty years the sphere turned in his reign,
Of justice full his heart, of sense his brain.
In his high place when he sat down alone,
These words he uttered from the royal throne:
"O'er all sev'n climates is my kingly sway;
As ruler me they everywhere obey.
Of God but by command the conqueror's will,
To do right shall my loins be girded still.
The whole world blessed with all prosperity,
The earth's face shall be filled with equity."
Bright with the skill that his own hand possessed,
Iron from stone his wisdom first expressed.
Out of the hard rock iron, when he drew,
Its essence water-like to form he knew.

This known, the blacksmith's art his own he made,
And fashioned axes and the saw and spade.
Water to use a plan did he devise
Drawn from the streams, the plain to fertilise
Rivers to join to streams he access gave,
To the king's glory labour thus to save.
For with this knowledge when mankind were filled,
Spreading the seed, they harvested, they tilled :
Thus all preparing for themselves their bread,
Each knew and for himself provision made.
Ere this was done, the people's wants to meet,
Nothing but fruit alone they had to eat.
This was not all men had with leaves to do,
They made them useful for their clothing, too.
Above all, God he'd worship and adore,
As was his grandsire's custom heretofore.
That there was fire in stone he also found,
And thence light kindled in the world around.

The Institution of the Saddah Festival.

One day went forth the monarch of the land
Towards the hills, with followers at hand.
Fleeing before him from afar he knew
A long and dark thing of a blackened hue.
Fountains of blood, two eyes were in its head,—
Darkness o'er all the land its mouth's smoke spread.
Húshang intelligently saw the sight,
And seized upon a stone, prepared for fight.
As he stretched forth his hand in kingly pride,
A world-consuming snake passed by his side.
The slight stone struck upon a heavy rock,
And thereon fell in pieces with the shock.
Out of both stones there sprang a flame of light,
And the rock's heart itself was rendered bright.
Unslain the dragon, yet with brilliant ray

The fire sprang forth its secret to display.
Whoever struck with iron on the stone,
A brilliant light at once appeared and shone.
To the Creator as he made his prayer,
Blessing invoked on Him the monarch there,
That such rare gift He should on him bestow,
And fire his place of worship vowed to know.
Exclaimed the monarch : "This is God's own light,
Which ye should worship if your mind be right."
As night came on, a fire as mountain high
That king lit round him with his company.
With wine, that night he made a feast withal,
And *Saddah* named that happy festival.
Húshang of *Saddah* memory will retain,
And may there many monarchs like him reign
As earth prosperity through him had gained,
That pleasing memory it e'er retained.
With pious dignity and kingly pride
Game, ass and wild beast all he set aside.
He set apart the bull, the ass, the sheep,
In useful ways their part to take and keep.
Thus in his wisdom did Húshang declare:
"Asunder keep ye them and pair by pair.
Make use of them, nor hesitate to eat,
And be prepared to pay the tribute meet."
Of running things whose hair is smoothly laid
At times he slaughtered and their skins were flayed,
Such as soft fox, and beaver, ermine, too,
And sable with fur warm and fine to view,
The skin of running creatures in this way
He clothing made upon mankind to lay.
He spread, he ate, in giving he was kind,
He died, and left but honoured name behind.
Exalted love of justice he retained,
And forty years a happy ruler reigned.

With many griefs that time to end he brought,
Enchantments many, many an anxious thought.
And when there came for him a better day,
The throne of greatness void before him lay.
As destiny no longer would delay,
King Húshang, wise and prudent, passed away.
Constant to thee the world will not incline,
Nor openly its face upon thee shine.

The reign of Tehmúras, the Dív-binder, was for thirty years. The ascension of the throne by Tehmúras, and his invention of the method of spinning, and the taming of animals.

One only son he dying left behind,
Worthy Tehmúras, who the Dívs confined.
He came and sat upon his father's throne,
And as a king his waist-belt girded on ;
The army Mobeds summoned at his call :
In words of mildness he addressed them all :
He said : "This throne befits me and this place,
This crown and this tiara and this mace.
By counsel ill from earth I'll wash away,
And on hills build a place my throne to stay.
From ev'ry place the Div's power will I sweep,
And will the world myself as monarch keep.
All useful things that in the world may be
I'll loose and make them of their bondage free."
From backs of sheep and lambs the wool and hair
He cut : to spin they sat down to prepare.
Clothing to make for them as well he strove,
And by his guidance carpets, too, they wove.
To fair-faced beasts that ran upon their feet
Hay, green-stuff, barley, he would give to eat.
There were wild beasts that fled, and out of those
The wily panther and the lynx he chose :
By tricks these from the plain and hill he caught.

And to captivity were divers brought.
Of birds all that to profit could be led.
The hawk, the falcon of the lofty head,
He brought together and their lesson taught.
And the whole world to wonder at him brought.
He bade with favour these to cherish all,
And only in soft accents them to call.
And cocks and hens, too, he collected by,
That at the hour of drum-beat they might cry.
Gathered together such as suited seemed,
Secret he chose what he of profit deemed.
He said to them: "Your voice in blessing raise;
The world's Creator, too, for ever praise,
For He has brought all beasts beneath my sway;
Praise unto Him who showeth us the way!"
A Vazir pure and perfect, too, had he,
Whose mind from evil thoughts was far and free.
In ev'ry place Shídasp was of renown,
And nowhere but for good his foot set down.
Against all food his lip he closing tight,
Stood before God in prayer the live-long night.
This friendship won him closely ev'ry heart,
In nightly prayer, in fast he chose his part.
He was the source of fortune to the king,
And his foes' souls would into bondage bring.
He showed the monarch nought but what was true,
And ranks' road only in his virtue knew,
Thus from all ill the king was purified,
And God's great glory, too, was dignified.
With a Vazir of knowledge so possessed,
The monarch you may know was greatly blessed.
In bonds of magic *Akriman* he tied,
And as a courser swift on him would ride;
From time to time on him a saddle bound,
He drove him *wildly the whole world* around.

The Binding of the Dívs by Tehmuras, and his Death.

The king's proceeding when the demons knew,
High at his words their haughty necks they drew;
And all assembling there in numbers great
Would rob him of his golden crown of State.
When Tehmúras of their tricks became aware,
Enraged, he closed their little market there.
Girding his loins up in his kingly grace,
He on his shoulder laid his heavy mace.
Magician demons there, a mighty force,
Came sweeping onwards in their magic course.
Came on the black Dív, too, the host before,
As to the heavens they raised their thundering roar.
The earth was darkened and grew black the sky,
And dimmed became to him the monarch's eye.
On came Tehmúras then in his lordly might,
His loins girt for vengeance in the fight.
On one side demons' smoke, as fire, there roared,
On that side warriors round the world its lord.
With the Dívs suddenly the battle raged,
But not for long was either side engaged.
Two parts of them with magic spells he bound,
His heavy mace cast others to the ground.
Some wounded he contemptuously tied;
Others to save their lives for quarter cried.
And said: "Slay not; from us that thou may'st learn
A novel art thou may'st to profit turn."
The *Kai* them quarter gave on their appeal,
That what was hidden they might clear reveal.
When from his chain their heads are free they feel
Helpless, to him for pledges they appeal.
The monarch they instruct then how to write,
And in this knowledge make his heart more bright.
Not one, but thirty writings then he knew,

Arabic, Rúmi, and the Persian, too.
The language, too, of China and Hindí,
You'd hear them everywhere, and Pehlavi.
And after this for thirty years and more,
The king of ev'ry art acquired a store.
He passed away. Time was for him complete:
His labours succour him in memory sweet.
O world! from nourishing the crop refrain:
As thou dost reap, what profit dost thou gain?
Aloft thou raiseth one to heaven high,
Obscure in dust to lay him by and bye.

The Reign of Jamshíd was 700 Years. His Ascension, Inventing Warlike Weapons, and Teaching Man other Arts.

When passed away this monarch of renown,
His son assumed his father's place and crown.
Worthy, his son Jamshíd embraced the part,
Loin-girt, full of his father's words his heart,
He sat upon his father's glorious throne,
Gold-crowned, he took the Kai's ways for his own.
Loins girt, in kingly splendour all arrayed,
The whole world to himself a slave he made.
Time rested 'neath his rule; obeyed his word
The *Paris* and the *Dív*, and e'en the bird.
The world in him fresh reputation gained,
And glorious with him the throne remained.
"I am the glory of the Lord," he cried,
"I am the king and I am priest beside.
The bad man from all ill I hold away,
And tow'rds the light I show the soul the way."
To warlike weapons he first turned his mind,
That warriors through them renown should find.
Of iron soft to make his glory knew,
Cuirass and coat of mail and helmet, too.

Armour, the coat of mail, the girth,
To all of those his intellect gave birth.
When in this manner fifty years had passed
He, by his labour, treasure great amassed.
On garments he reflected fifty more,
How they should dress for honour, how for war.
Of cotton, woven silk and spun, he made,
Of beaver fur, of linen and brocade.
He taught them how to spin and how to weave,
And how the woof within the warp to reeve.
Woven, he taught them how to wash and sew,
And all men took to task such things to know.
When this was done some other thing he tried.
He glad in time, time looked on him with pride.
Then workers of all trades assembling round,
For fifty more years he employment found.
There was a band Katuzis whom they name,
With those who worship these you'd call the same.
Apart from others these retaining still,
He made their place of worship on a hill.
With these another band he set aside.
Nisaris, such the name to them applied.
These were the mighty lions of the fight,
The army and the land who rendered bright.
These the supporters of the royal throne,
Who claimed all manly virtues for their own.
Of the third class *Nasudis* you may know,
Their praise on others who will ne'er bestow.
They plough, they cultivate, they reap the grain,
And no one hear who of their food complain.
Though clothed in rags, still no one they obey,
Scorn censure's voice and turn their ears away.
Rulers despising and their converts, too,
Of healthy body, they the earth renew.
Now the fourth tribe they *Ahnukhushi* call,

They ply all trades, but arrogant are all.
Though they at all trades and professions wrought,
Their very souls were ever full of thought.
And in this manner fifty years went by.
He ate and many things gave plenteously.
For ev'ry one position fit he made,
And to attain thereto the road he laid,
That his own measure ev'ry one might see,
And more or less know of his own degree.
Then after all this had been made complete,
The king, with purpose and with knowledge meet,
Ordered the impure Dívs in earnest toil
With ready water to mix up the soil,
And all that from the mud came when they knew,
This into moulds for forming bricks they threw.
Plans were by architects made at their call,
Of stone and lime the Dívs then made each wall.
Warm baths were built and many a palace high,
Halls where for refuge any man might fly.
Out of the hard rock he sought jewels bright,
Out of the brilliant gems he sought for light.
Jewels he had of ev'ry sort and name,
And ruby, amber, gold and silver came.
These from the hard rock he with magic drew,
With beauty even slaves' keys to renew.
Sweet smelling perfumes next did he acquire,
That for their scent would every man desire.
Balsam and camphor, musk, too, to allure,
Aloes and amber and rosewater pure.
Medicaments and remedies for pain,
The way all ills to stay, and health to gain.
These he revealed and every secret thing;
The world knew never such enquiring king.
Vessels on water then he took in hand,
E'er passing on in speed from land to land.

In this as well years fifty passed away,
And from his wisdom naught concealed there lay.
And then, as soon as all these things were done.
He saw himself as in the world alone.
When now these works of his had come to pass,
All bounds of greatness would his foot surpass.
Of pomp imperial a throne he made:
What store of jewels was there not inlaid!
This the Dívs lifted up at his desire,
And from the plain flew they the heavens higher,
And in the air just like the shining sun
This would the mighty monarch sit upon.
The world assembled then around his throne,
And fortune's glory high above him shone.
On Jamshíd as the people jewels streamed,
They cried, upon him that the New Year beamed.
On *Farvadin's Hormuz in this bright New Year,
Bodies were free from pain, all hearts from fear.
New year, new king, the world thus rendered bright,
He sat resplendent on the throne in light.
Before him all the nobles were arrayed:
They called for wine, as minstrels sang and played
Henceforth the memory of that banquet grand
As a memento of the king will stand.
Three hundred years proceeded in this way;
On death they did not reckon in that day.
In those days idle could no man remain,
Nor were they sick nor any suffered pain.
From trouble and all ill were they preserved,
And them the Dívs with girded loins served.
A throne magnificent beneath his feet,
The king sat for the world as lord to greet.
Jamshíd as Kai would on his throne recline,
Within his hand a royal bowl of wine:

*The first day of the month of Parvadin.

And many Divs would this great throne upbear,
And lift it to the clouds in middle air.
Generals about the throne in order due,
Birds in their serried ranks arose and flew.
While men with both ears to his will were bound,
The earth was full of joy and cheerful sound.
And in this manner as the years rolled on,
The king's magnificence still brightly shone;
The happy world was e'er at rest in peace,
And messages from God would never cease.

The turning back of Jamshid from the Commands of God, and the turning back of Fortune from Him.

For many days thus time passed on its wing,
And nought but goodness saw men in the king.
The world became a slave unto his will,
And on his throne he sat in glory still.
Sudden he looked upon his mighty throne,
And saw himself on earth the only one.
From faith in God then changing in his mood,
He from his God turned in ingratitude.
Out of the army he called worthy men.
What converse with them did he then maintain
To those great men of many years he cried:
" None in the world I know myself beside.
Only through me the world has virtue known:
Like me has none possessed the royal throne.
The world in beauty I alone arrayed,
All trouble on the face of earth allayed.
Food, sleep, and ease you find alone through me,
And clothing: all your hope in me must be.
Mine greatness, diadem and kingly sway:
Beside me who is king will any sa ?
The world will with my medicine firm remain:
Who death subdue, and of disea the pain;

Though many kings on earth bear lordly sway,
A mortal's death 'tis I alone can stay.
You have intelligence and life through me,
And Ahriman alone will not agree.
And this that I have done as ye know all,
Ye should me now the world's Creator call."
Then hung down all their heads the Mobeds there,
Why did to speak or question no one dare?
God's light forsook him when these words were said,
And varied rumours in the world were spread.
For twenty-three years from the palace gate
Themselves did the whole army separate.
From the Creator when he turned in pride
He found defeat, and fortune left his side.
What said that prudent orator in fear?
"Thou art a king: in service be thou near,
He who from God ungrateful stands apart,
Trouble from every side assails his heart."
For Jamshíd grew thus very dark the day,
And all his earthly glory passed away.
When the pure God on him His anger laid,
The king was conscious of it and afraid.
Were the pure God with him enraged to be,
They saw for such an ill no remedy.
Jamshid rained blood-red tears into his breast,
And prayer for pardon to his God addressed,
The glory of his God from him had gone.
And on himself the dread of ill brought on.

The *Story* of Mardás, the Arab, the Father of Zuhak.

There was a man once in those days of old,
From desert of spear-bearing horsemen bold,
A worthy king and a good man was he,
Who feared his Maker with humility.

Literally "with a cold sigh"

His name Mardás, and worthy of all praise,
Given to generosity his ways,
That gave him milk of each four-footed beast,
He had a thousand of all kinds, at least,
As many goats and camels and of sheep,
Pious, to milkers he had given to keep.
Equal milch cattle were at his command,
With Arab horses of appearance grand.
And of the milk as much as they required,
With lordly hand he gave those who desired.
This pious man an only son possessed,
Who of affection with no share was blessed.
His name, *Zuhák*, and most ambitious he,
Light-headed, brave and fearless as could be.
In Pehlavi was Bílvarasp his name;
Ten thousand Arab horses he could claim,
With golden bridles; thus the name had he—
Bílvarasp ten thousand is in Pehlavi.
And he two parts of ev'ry day would ride.
And not for vengeance sake, but in pure pride,
Now it so happened Iblís on a day,
Came him to visit in a friendly way,
The Chief's heart from the right path led astray,
The youth his ears bent to his words that day.
Of all his evil doings unaware,
He was well pleased his sweet discourse to share.
Conscience and heart to yield him he was led,
And thus was dust poured on the youth's own head.
And as his heart surrendered Iblís knew
At his own tales the more well pleased he grew.
Enticing, soft speech did he not restrain;
There was no knowledge in the young man's brain.
"Full many words have I to tell," said he,
"Which no man ever knows except through me."
The young man answered: "Speak! Do not delay

To teach me this good counsel as you may."
He said: "If thou wilt pledge thyself to me,
The word of truth will I reveal to thee."
The simple youth, to his command a slave,
Swore to the oath himself that Iblís gave,
And said: "Whatever I from thee may hear
Shall never pass on to another's ear."
He said: "O noted lord, excepting thee,
Why should a master in the palace be?
With such son, of a father what the need?
Do thou to this advice I give thee heed.
This ancient sire of yours for long will be,
And thou must linger in obscurity.
Up, then, and seize upon his palace now,
His place of dignity none suits as thou!
If on this word of mine thou wilt rely,
The whole world shalt thou govern by and bye."
When *Z*uhák of his father's murder heard,
His heart was full of sorrow at the word.
"This is unfitting," he to Iblís said,
"I cannot do it: say aught else instead."
Iblís replied: "If thou dost not agree,
Thou wilt then break thy pledge and oath to me.
The oath will bind thy shoulders as a chain,
Thy father noble, thou despised remain."
Ensnared the Arab's head in Iblís's hand,
Himself he yielded up to his command.
He urged on him: "Quick now thy plan produce,
Tell me the way. No farther make excuse."
"I have a plan," was Iblís's reply,
"By which to raise thy head up to the sky.
It is enough that thou should'st silent be,
Aid from no other is required by me.
I will do all according to my word,
Loose not from out its sheath of speech thy sword."

A garden fair within the palace round,
And heart-entrancing has the monarch found;
Thither at nightfall does the king repair,
The place for his own worship to prepare.
He bathes there secretly at dead of night;
No servant ever bears with him a light."
To his inverted counsel true to keep,
Did on the road the Dív a well dig deep,
Iblís the strayed one at that deep well's head
Closed up the wall and hid with rubbish spread.
When that ambitious king of Arab race
Toward the garden turned at night his face,
When to that well profound the king drew nigh,
Reversed, his fortune backwards seemed to fly.
Broken, he fell into the well that day.
The good, God-fearing man thus passed away.
Through good and ill report, upon his child
That noble-hearted king had ever smiled.
He brought him up in luxury with pain,
And giving treasure aye would glad remain.
And such an evil dispositioned son,
At first he through affection would have won.
When in his father's murder he concurred—
This story from a wise man I have heard—
That wicked son, a tiger had he been,
To shed his father's blood had not been keen.
But in the hidden world 'tis otherwise:
Search, and the secret with the mother lies.
The son who would his father's customs shun,
Call him a stranger: call him not a son.
The vile Zuhak, of justice with no trace,
By this means seized upon his father's place.
The son assumed the Arab's crown to wear,
And profit with them both and loss would share.
When Iblis at this object had arrived,

He soon another artifice contrived.
He said to him: "As thou hast turned to me,
All earthly hopes at thy desire shall be.
If thou art thus obedient to my will,
And thou to my command shalt pledge thee still,
The whole world now shall pass beneath thy sway,
Beast, man, bird, fish, all thy command obey."
This said, another plan did he unfold,
Another scheme, one wondrous to be told.
He made himself into a comely youth,
Clever, of facile tongue, and pure, forsooth.
Whenever to Zuhak he turned his face,
All else to praise upon his tongue gave place.
"On me would now the king with favour look,"
He said to him: "I am a famous cook."
This heard Zuhák, and praised him in his mood,
And made for him a fit place for his food.
The king then gave to him full liberty,
And brought him of the cooking-house the key.
There was not food then of a varied kind,
And little fit to eat could people find.
But Ahriman at heart was ill-disposed
And to kill living beasts for food proposed.
The yoke of egg he gave him first to eat,
And for a while he flourished on that meat.
Of flesh of ev'ry beast and ev'ry bird
He brought him one by one as he preferred,
And like a lion nourished him with blood,
So as to make the king bold on such food.
Ev'ry command he gave him he obeyed,
And of his heart a pledge to do it made.
The ill-fared chieftain gave him ev'ry praise
For food that he enjoyed in varied ways.
This constantly was the Enchanter's song:
"May God the monarch's life for aye prolong!

To-morrow I prepare another meat,
His honoured nourishment to make complete."
And Iblís was all night absorbed in thought
What wondrous dish to-morrow should be brought.
The next day when the emerald dome arose,
In heaven its yellow sapphire to disclose,
Partridge, white pheasant, mixed, a dish he made—
Before the king with hopeful heart he laid.
The Arab monarch as he sat to eat,
His unwise head gave up in love complete.
A dish of fowl and lamb on that third day
Mixed up in varied style did he array,
And on the fourth when he arranged the tray,
Before him a young ox's back there lay,
Mixed with rose-water and with saffron, too,
Nor did he old wine and pure musk eschew.
And when *Zuhák* this food to eat began
He was in wonder at that skilful man,
And said : "Good man, whatever thy desire,
Demand of me and at my hand require."
"O monarch great!" to him the cook replied,
"Happy and ruling may'st thou aye abide!
O king, my heart is filled with love for thee,
And my soul's nourishment thy face shall be.
But one thing of the king do I desire,
(Would that my claim to merit it were high'r!)
That he should bid me on his shoulders place
My lips, and kiss, and with my eye embrace."
Now when *Zuhák* from him this speech had heard,
In no way what his trick was he inferred,
But answered him : "I grant thee thy desire ;
Now may thy name to greater heights aspire!"
The Dív as to his wife the king did grant
A kiss upon his shoulders leave to plant.
Kissing, from earth he disappeared to view :

None in the world such marvel ever knew.
Two black snakes from his shoulders there arise,
And, grieved, he seeks on all sides remedies.
He cut them from his shoulders at the last:
At this thy wonder may for ever last.
Like branching tree again the black snakes spring
From the two shoulders of the harassed king.
Physicians eminent there gather round,
In varied tales who one by one abound.
Enchantments they essay of every kind,
And yet no sort of remedy they find.
As a physician Iblís then appeared,
And with intelligence the monarch neared.
"What was to be has been," the king he told.
"Cut them not down: what is to be behold,
Now let them rest, and give them food to eat:
No other remedy the case will meet.
Save brains of men naught give ye them to eat
And they themselves will perish with this meat.
As men's brains are the only remedy:
These to provide should be as grief to thee.
Two men for ev'ry day thou'lt need to slay,
Out of their brains this burden to defray."
What was it in his quest that sought the Dív,
And in this converse what did he conceive?
What but a hidden artifice to find,
To sweep from off the world all human kind?

The End of Jamshíd's Fortune at the Hand of Zuhák.

There rose on this from all Irán a shout,
On all sides war and tumult raged about,
The white and brilliant day to darkness turned,
And men of Jamshíd the connection spurned.
The glory of his God from him estranged,
All soon to crookedness and folly changed.

From ev'ry quarter then a king appeared,
Ambitious men themselves on all sides reared.
Armies collected; all prepared for war,
The love of Jamshid from all hearts afar.
In Irán suddenly arose a force,
Directing tow'rds the Arabs' land its course,
For they had heard there was a chieftain there,
Full of all dread, a dragon's form that bare.
And Iran's horsemen, searching for a king,
Towards *Z*uhak their face together bring.
With blessings him their monarch they proclaimed,
And of the Persian land the ruler named.
Then like the wind the dragon monarch sped,
The crown of Iran's land placed on his head.
Arabs and Persians, thus a host they found:
Heroes from ev'ry land there gathered round,
Towards the throne of Jamshid turned their face,
Just like a ring they would the world embrace.
And when from Jamshid fortune turned away,
Him did the new king quickly bring to bay.
He gave up to him treasure, crown, and throne,
Greatness, host, diadem, and then was gone.
He hid himself: the earth was growing dim,
As throne and crown he handed up to him.
None sees him on the earth a hundred years
And from the eye of man he disappears.
A hundred years, too, in the sea of Chín
That king of faith impure and creed is seen.
And when at last *Z*uhak him brought to bay,
He granted him to live no long delay,
But with a saw divided him in two:
No more the earth of him its terror knew.
Awhile he hid him from the dragon's breath,
But in the end did not escape from death.
That royal throne and power passed away,

And fate removed him just as withered hay.
He who had sat upon the throne before,
What profit gained he for the pains he bore?
Sev'n hundred years there passed above his head;
Both into good and evil he was led.
Of such long life what need, then, should'st thou feel?
The earth its secret never will reveal.
It feeds thee e'er with honey and with sweet,
And nought but softest sounds thy ear may meet.
When suddenly thou say'st: "Its love is mine:
Its face tow'rds evil never will incline."
Thou may'st be happy and in it be glad,
All secrets of thy heart it may have had—
A gentle game it with thy senses plays,
And blood into thy heart with pain conveys.
Such, then, is fortune, which can never last,
In it but seed of good thou shouldest cast.
Weary my heart of this world that must cease,
From this pain quickly, God give me release!

The reign of Zuhák was one day less than 1,000 Years. His Ascension of the Throne and Laying the Foundation of Injustice.

WHEN *Z*uhák sat upon the throne as king,
A thousand years for him were on the wing.
Fortune to him displayed an evil face,
But yet he lived a very lengthy space.
The customs of the good were then concealed,
And of the mad ones ev'ry hope revealed.
Virtue was scorned and magic had its way,
Hidden was truth, ill practised in the day.
The Dívs stretched out their hands tow'rds ill alone;
Men spoke of good but in a lowered tone.
From Jamshíd's house two girls they brought away
And led them out: as willows trembled they.
The two of Jamshíd both the sisters were,
The crown of all the women that were there.
One of the veiled ones was Shehr-i-naz:
The other moon-faced one was Arnaváz.
These fair ones, to *Z*uhák's own palace brought,
All kinds of magic and deceit he taught.
On such the vile *Z*uhák his will had laid,
And like a bead of wax the world had made.
Save ill *Z*uhák could set them naught to learn,
To plunder and to slaughter and to burn.
Two youths each night, it came to happen so—
A *Pehlaván*, it might be one more low—

The cook would to the monarch's palace bring,
So to provide the medicine for the king.
These he would kill, and drawing out their brain,
Would for that dragon make a dish again.
There were two pure men of the royal race,
Two men of worth and of a pious grace:
Pious Asmáil one of them was named,
Karmail, the other, was for foresight famed.
They chanced to be together on a day,
And talked of this and that in ev'ry way.
The king's injustice and the army's, too,
And of that evil food of which they knew.
One said: "As cooks the monarch let us serve,
And of the two the life of one preserve."
They went and, as cooks serving every day,
Prepared the dishes in the usual way.
The two alert ones therefore took in hand
The cooking-house of that lord of the land.
And when to shed blood there arrived the day,
From men's sweet souls their lives to take away.
From murderous keepers two young men they drew,
And, promptly seizing, on their faces threw.
These cooks were full of pain, their hearts of woe,
Whilst from their two eyes tears of blood would flow.
At the injustice of the king amazed,
Into each other's eyes the two men gazed.
One of the two they finished, one set free:
For any other plan they could not see.
To one they gave his life and said beside:
"Beware in secret place thy head to hide.
Beware in peopled cities not to dwell;
Deserts there are on earth and hills as well."
In his head's place a worthless head they slew,
And for the dragon food they gave this new.
In thirty days thus thirty youths obtained,

Through their assistance their sweet lives retained.
And in a manner such that no one knew,
When those assembled to two hundred grew;
As food they gave them all both goats and sheep,
And bade them in the desert far to keep.
In these their origin the Kurds now find,
For peopled places who have not a mind.
Their huts are made of tamarisk alone,
And in their hearts no fear of God is known.
Zuhák's ways were to such perversion led,
That should desire once penetrate his head,
Had he a daughter fair within the veil,
And good and pure, yet no talk would avail,
But he must have her as his slave, for he
Had not Kais' ways, faith or integrity.

The Seeing of Faridun in a Dream by Zuhak.

When forty years of life to him remained,
Now see upon his head what God ordained!
In the king's hall, immersed in slumber deep,
One night he was with Arnavaz asleep.
From the king's palace suddenly that night
He saw three warriors that came in sight.
Two older men, and one, a youth was there,
Tall as a cypress and with kingly air.
With loins all girded and of royal grace,
He carried in his hand a bull-head mace.
Zuhak he fierce attacked, to battle led,
And struck with ox-head mace upon his head.
Sudden the hero, fewer years who knew,
From head to foot on him a lasso threw.
On his two hands the string was interlaced,
And round his neck a halter had been placed.
He drew him to Damavand's hill along,

And drove him from behind all through the throng.
Writhing, that unjust one, *Zuhák*, was borne:
Thou would'st have said his very heart was torn.
And as the monarch shouted as he dreamed,
To shake the hundred pillared palace seemed.
The sunny-faced ones from their couches spring
At such disturbance from the famous king.
And Arnaváz began to him to say:
"What is it, king? In secret speak, I pray.
In thy own house in peaceful slumber laid,
Of thy own life why art thou thus afraid?
The sev'n climes of the world are in thy hand,
Beasts, Divs and men to guard thee here all stand.
The universal world to rule is thine,
The full moon waning down to its decline."
To those fair-faced ones then the ruler cried:
"Such strange occurrence it were well to hide.
If now this tale of wonder you should hear,
You for my life at heart would quake with fear."
Said Arnaváz then to the weighty king:
"Twere better to reveal to us the thing.
We might suggest some cure for thee still:
There is a medicine for every ill."
The ruler told them then that thing concealed,
From first to last the dream to them revealed.
The famous fair one to the king replied:
"Pass not this by: a remedy provide.
The signet-ring of time is this thy throne;
And in thy fortune shines this world alone.
Thou holdeth all the world beneath thy ring,
Beast, man, bird, *Pari*, bird and everything.
The wise men round from every country call,
The Mobeds, those who know the stars, and all.
Then to the Mobeds tell the tale entire,
Search into all, and for the truth enquire.

In whose hand is thy life, enqnire and find,
Of Divs, of *Paris*, or yet of mankind.
This remedy thou knowest of; then use it still,
And fear no harm from those who wish thee ill.'
The evil-minded king approved the word
He from that cypress in her answer heard.
When from the dark shade of the crow-winged night
The world had raised up on the hill its light,
Upon the azure dawn, thou would'st have said,
The sun its yellow topaz full had spread.
Where'er a learned Mobed could be found,
Fluent in speech and in all wisdom sound,
Him the king summoning called to him near,
That dream which rent his heart from him to hear.
Together summoning, he called them round,
To see what cure could for his pain be found.
"Quickly inform me," then to them he said,
"So that my soul may tow'rds the light be led."
In secret counsel of them he required,
And of time's revolutions, too, enquired.
"When will my fated time come to an end?
To whom this girdle, crown and throne descend?
For ev'ry secret full I fain would know,
Although my head despised ye may lay low."
The Mobeds' lips were parched, their cheeks were wet,
Their tongues tow'rds converse with each other set.
"What is to be should we now let him hear,
Worthless our lives, and at our throats the spear.
What is to be, should he not understand,
We presently of life may wash our hand."
After this manner the days passed away,
And none dared openly a word to say.
On the fourth day the king in anger cried
To all those Mobeds whom he sought as guide:
"Alive must I impale you on the stake,

Or known to me must ye the future make."
The Mobeds all their heads in sorrow bent:
Their eyes were filled with blood, their hearts were rent.
Of all these famous men of wisdom bright,
Clear-hearted ever, one strove tow'rds the right;
Zírak by name, of wisdom having store,
All other Mobeds he thus passed before.
Anxious at heart, yet fearless all among,
Speaking to *Zuhák*, he unloosed his tongue.
He said to him: "All wind drive from thy head;
For death alone are all from mothers bred.
Before thee many rulers have been seen,
Of thrones of greatness worthy who have been.
Full many joys they had and griefs beside,
And when their long life had been spent they died.
If on an iron base thou restedst here,
Thou art not firm, would wear thee down the sphere.
Possessor of thy throne there one shall be
To cast in dust thy fortune after thee.
To him the name of Faridún is given,
Propitious to the world shall he make heav'n.
He from his mother's womb has not appeared,
Nor has the time come when he shall be feared.
Of virtuous mother when he born shall be,
He shall grow up and be a fruitful tree.
Grown up, his head up to the moon shall rise;
He shall seek girdle, throne, crown for his prize.
Like cypress tall shall he be in its grace,
And on his neck shall bear of steel a mace.
Bull-headed mace shall he strike on thy head;
Chained, from this hall to street shalt thou be led."
Zuhák, of faith impure, to him replied:
"What spite has he that I should thus be tied?"
The brave man said: "In wisdom he who's right
Without excuse does no man a despite.

When his own father at thy hand will die,
This for his hatred will the cause supply.
And there shall be a cow of high degree,
To the young hero who a nurse shall be.
As she as well will at thy hand lie low,
Vengeance the bull-head mace will not forego."
Op'ning his ear, this *Zuhak* heard him say,
And falling from his throne there senseless lay.
And from the lofty throne the worthy man
For fear of further ill to turn began.
And when the king's heart once again did flow,
To mount the royal throne he was not slow.
Secret and open the whole world around
He sought where Faridun's traces might be found.
Eating no food, nor sleep nor ease he knew;
Bright day assumed for him a mourning hue.

Discourse on the Birth of Faridún.

When on their course had journeyed many days,
That dragon form was found in many ways;
When Faridun his mother brought to birth,
Another temper came upon the earth,
And like a tall straight cypress as he grew,
His royal splendour greater brilliance knew.
The hero all of Jamshid's might possessed,
And with the splendour of the sun was blessed,
To the earth necessary as the rain,
And to the soul as knowledge is in gain.
The circling sphere around his being rolled
By Faridún's great love and faith controlled.
A cow, Purmayah named, there used to be,
Beyond all other cows of high degree.
When she was born, she was of peacock hue,
And ev'ry hair a varied colour knew.
A crowd assembled of wise men around,

Astrologers and priests among them found.
On earth such cow by none was ever seen,
Or heard of by old men had ever been.
Zuhak the world filled of his quest with sound,
In his search roaming ever round and round.
Father to Faridun was Abtin known,
The world for Abtın had too narrow grown.
Of himself weary, Abtın fled away,
And in the lion's snare all sudden lay.
Some watchmen of impure birth and name,
On Abtín in his refuge sudden came.
They seized upon him, as a panther bound,
And into Zuhák's palace bore him round.
When Faridun's wise mother this had heard,
That to her husband harm had thus occurred –
A woman was she who adorned the day,
A tree in whose fruit royal splendour lay.
Her name Faranak : gracious was she, too—
Of Faridun's love her heart then fuller grew.
Wounded by fate, her heart all broken lay,
Then running, to the mead she found her way
To where the cow Purmayah was confined,
On which rare marks of beauty you could find.
The keeper of the mead she hastened near,
And rained into her breast the blood-red tear.
" With pitying care," she weeping to him cried :
" Oh ! for this sucking child awhile provide !
Him, father-like, take from his mother now,
And feed him with the milk of that pure cow.
Reward desirest thou, my life is thine ;
My soul I pledge to thee in this design."
Then he who was of that pure cow the slave,
Reply to that one of pure spirit gave.
" I of thy son myself the slave will make,
And him receiving, will thy counsel take."

Farának thus delivered him her son,
Ending the counsel that she had begun.
For three years, father-like, the milk he shared,
And for the child intelligently cared.
Zuhák with searching never grew content;
Through all the world, then, that cow's fame was sent.
In haste the mother to the meadow ran,
And to his keeper thus to say began:
"Through that intelligence God gives to me
My heart is filled with all anxiety.
Now must I carry out what should be done,
For my sweet child and my own soul are one.
Now from this land of magic I must flee,
And bear him off to Hindustán with me.
No longer with this crowd here must I stay,
But to Alburz its hill must bear away."
Thus saying, she with that fair-faced one went,
Her bleeding heart with many sorrows rent.
Swift as a courier she bore off her child,
As savage creature to the mountains wild.
A very pious man was dwelling there,
Who for the world's affairs had no more care.
"O pure of faith!" to him Farának said:
"In sorrow from Iran's land have I fled.
Know thou that this dear, precious child of mine
Should as the head of the assembly shine.
He should take off the crown from Zuhák's head
And in the dust his royal girdle tread.
Thou must his guardian and protector be:
Trembling, his life as mine I yield to thee."
The good man willingly received him there;
Thenceforward blew on him no chilly air.
News came to Zuhák of the evil deed,
Of cow Purmayah and that pleasant mead.
Like furious elephant enraged he flew,

And angrily the cow Púrmayah slew.
And all four-footed beasts he saw that day
Out of the place he swiftly cleared away.
To Faridún's house he quickly turned his face.
Much there he searched, but found of him no trace.
And casting sparks of fire his hall around,
His lofty palace burnt down to the ground.

The Enquiry by Faridún from His Mother Concerning His Lineage.

When sixteen years o'er Faridún's head had passed:
He came from Alburz to the plain at last.
Enquiring of his mother then said he:
" In secret what is hidden show to me.
Who am I, mother? Who my father? Say,
And sprung from whose seed have I seen the day:
Who shall I say I am, when people meet?
Some reasonable tale to me repeat."
" Ambitious youth!" Farának 'gan to say,
" I shall now tell thee what thou wilt this day.
Know thou that from the land of Persia came
A certain worthy man, Abtín by name.
He was of royal race and wisdom knew.
Alert was he, a harmless hero, too.
From Tehmuras his royal pedigree,
Father to son his ancestors knew he.
Thy father he, to me a husband dear;
With him alone my days were bright and clear.
A reader of the stars thus told Zuhák, the king,
His days that Faridun to end should bring.
Zuhák, the sorcerer it came about,
To slay thee from Irán his hand stretched out.
Concealed I kept thee from him many a day,
And that time passed in wretchedness away.

Thy worthy father in his precious youth,
His own life sacrificed for thee in truth.
Zuhak two snakes upon his shoulder bore,
And vexed Iran with ruin more and more.
Out of thy father's head the brain removed
Was for that dragon form the food approved.
I at the last had to a wood to flee,
Where there would be for none anxiety.
Out of thy father's head he took the brain—
Food for those fearful dragons to obtain.
Like pleasant spring a cow came to my view;
From head to foot adorned in varied hue.
Her keeper like a king in posture meet,
Sat there, beneath his robe withdrawn his feet.
To him wast thou entrusted long by me,
And in his breast he kindly nurtured thee;
The breasts of that cow, peacock hued, the while
Reared thee with milk a valiant crocodile.
Sudden of that cow and that mead of spring
At last they took the tidings to the king.
Thee from that wood I suddenly one day
From home and from Iran then bore away.
He came and cruelly that dear one slew,
That nurse was speechless yet benignant, too.
Up to the sun from our hall raised the dust,
And deep down to the pit, though lofty, thrust."
In great amaze, his mother's words to hear,
In anger opened Faridun his ear.
With grief his head, with rage his heart bowed down
His eyebrows knit with anger to a frown.
As to his mother thus he answer gave.
"But after trial is a lion brave.
As the magician now his will has wrought,
My hand as well must to the sword be brought.

*Literally: "Brought up steam from Irán."

And now pure God's command obey I must,
From Zuhak's palace must I raise the dust."
His mother said: "This counsel is not wise;
'Gainst a whole world thy foot unequal lies.
Zuhak's a king with dignity and crown,
To whom his army bows, loins girded, down.
If he desires, from ev'ry land afar
A hundred thousand there will come to war.
Him to despoil the way is otherwise,
The world regard not with a young man's eyes.
He who of youth the heating wine may taste,
Sees himself only in his worldly haste.
His head he casts in madness to the wind:
May future be to thee for ever kind!
My son, the counsel of thy mother hear:
All else be but as wind unto thy ear!"

The Demand by Zuhak of a Declaration from the Chiefs, and the Tearing of it up by Kavah, the Blacksmith.

Zuhak, it thus occurred, would night and day,
Take Faridun's name on his lip to say.
His heart of Faridun was full of dread,
Abased from that fear, too, his lofty head.
One day on ivory throne the king sat down,
And on his head was set his turquoise crown.
He sent for Mobeds out of ev'ry land,
Before his throne upright to take their stand.
Then the assembled Mobeds he addressed:
"Of skill and wisdom ye who are possessed,
Ye in your wisdom all must surely know
That I in secret have a certain foe.
In knowledge great, although in age he's young,
Yet in ancestral heroism strong.

"Although my enemy be small and low,
Yet as a foolish lad him none may know.
A larger army must I now maintain,
That demons, men and Paris shall contain.
To be of one accord we must not fail.
For I am out of patience with this tale.
Prepare a writing that it may be known.
Except good seed your leader naught has sown:
He never says a word that is not true,
And justice he would never fail to do."
In this affair, though upright, in their need
With their Chief's fear they all of them agreed.
To this, before the dragon impotent,
Both young and old their testimony lent.
Just at that moment through the palace high
Calling for justice rose a sudden cry.
Him who had seen oppression thus they call,
And seat among the great ones in the hall.
An elder asks him with a visage stern:
"Who has oppressed thee? Let us quickly learn."
He crying to the king, struck his own head:
"O king, I, Kávah, justice claim," then said.
"Now justice do: running I come to thee,
In my soul's anguish I complain of thee.
If to do justice is affair of thine,
By so much higher shall thy honour shine.
From thee for justice though I came before,
Thy lancet strikes my heart still more and more.
Oppression tow'ards my right should'st thou now doubt,
Why on me wretched is thy hand stretched out?
O pardon and in pity look on me,
For constantly my heart must grieving be.
What have I done, O king? Now to me speak,
If I am guiltless, no occasion seek.
Ill fate has giv'n me such a crooked back,

My heart is hopeful, though no pain I lack,
No young man is there left ; I have no son,
On earth there is as child connection none.
Oppression has a centre and a bound,
And for oppression pretext should be found.
The pretext that thou hast against me state,
Thou thinkest for me every ill of fate.
I am a blacksmith, and can be but dumb,
And the king's fire must on my head then come.
Thou art a king, although of dragon form,
And in this way to rule thou should'st conform.
Over seven countries as thou holdest sway,
On us why dost thou all this hardship lay ?
Thy reckoning with me should at once be told,
So that the world in wonder may behold.
Why of my son thou needest give the brain,
That these thy servants should a banquet gain."
To what he said the chief then gave his ear,
And was astonished such grave words to hear.
They gave him up his only son again,
And hoped by goodness thus his love to gain.
To Kávah then the monarch gave reply,
That he should to that writing testify.
As soon as Kávah the petition read,
To the realm's ancient men he turned his head ;
And said to them : " O ye by devils hired,
By terror of an earthly king inspired,
Your faces have ye now all turned tow'rds hell,
And to its words given up your hearts as well.
I'll not bear witness to the writing here,
Nor of this monarch have I any fear."
Trembling, he tore that writing then in two,
And shouting, it beneath his feet he threw.
Raging, his worthy son before him walked,
As from the hall into the street he stalked.

The nobles then the king with blessings crowned,
And said: "O monarch of the world renowned,
Upon thy head down from the heavenly bow
In day of fight may cold wind never blow!
Crude speaking Kavah, with his face aglow,
Why didst thou, as thine equal here, allow?
The writing, thy sole pledge beneath our hand,
He tears, and turns away from thy command.
Raging in heart and head, he turned and went.
Thou'dst said a pledge to Faridun was meant.
Worse act than this all we have never seen;
And in a manner stupefied have been."
Then quickly answered them the famous king:
"Hear ye the strange things I before you bring."
To the ancients of the land then did he say:
"I fear to darkness turns the shining day.
When Kavah came in at the palace gate,
And my two ears heard what he had to state,
Straight in the lofty hall between us two,
A seeming hill of iron came to view.
Up to his head his two hands when he threw,
My heart seemed wondrously to break in two.
Nor do I know henceforth what may appear,
For no one knows the secrets of the sphere."
When Kávah left the palace of the king,
The people flocked around him in a ring.
He cried aloud and shouted in his might,
And the world summoned to do what was right.
The leather with which blacksmiths clothe their feet,
What time the anvil and the iron meet,
Kavah at once upon a spear-head thrust.
In the bazar there arose a mighty dust.
Shouting, he forward marched with spear in hand,
And said: "In God's trust ye who take your stand,
He partisan with Faridun who now would be,

And from Zuhak's bonds now his head would free,
At once towards Faridun now let us hie,
Beneath his glory's shade asleep to lie.
Run! Ahriman this ruler ye should know,
Who of the Creator is at heart the foe.
And in this worthless leather ye may see
A friend calls to you or an enemy."
Forward he moved with the heroic band,
And no small army round him took its stand.
Knowing himself where Faridun would be,
With head bent towards him he went speedily.
Near the new general's palace as they drew,
From far they saw him and shouts raised anew.
When on the spear the Kai the skin could see,
He saw a star of happy augury.
From Rum brocade he fine upon it wound,
With jewelled figures on a golden ground.
As the moon's sphere this about his head he drew,
And thus the king of happy omen knew.
With hues of yellow, red, and violet
Mingled, they call it Kavah's standard yet.
Thenceforward every one of royal race,
Who on his head the kingly crown would place.
To blacksmith's leather, though of value none,
Jewels aye fresh and fair have added on.
Of painted silk both and of fine brocade,
That star of Kávah is so brilliant made,
In darkest night it shines as does the sun,
And in the world for all hearts hope has won.
After this manner some time passed away,
Yet what there was to be still hidden lay.
When Faridun thus saw the inverted world,
Zuhak had downwards into ruin hurled,
With girt loins to his mother he came near,
The royal crown upon his head shone clear,

And said: "To battle must I now proceed;
To thee for ought but prayer there is no need.
Higher than earth does the Creator stand;
To him in ev'ry need stretch out thy hand."
Then from her eyelash did the tear down fall,
As she with bleeding heart on God would call.
To the world's Lord then constantly she cried:
"I have my faith in Thee, and none beside.
Ill from bad men, oh! from his life turn back!
Clear from the world all such as wisdom lack!"
Lightly then Faridún went on his way,
These words from all he hidden kept away.
He had two brothers, both his noble peers,
These Chiefs were older than himself in years.
The one of them was Kayanúsh by name,
And one, Purmáyah, was of happy fame.
To these two Faridún unloosed his tongue:
"O brave ones, happy may ye live and long;
Except for good the spheres do not revolve;
The crown of greatness will on me devolve.
Bring me some cunning blacksmiths to this place,
That they may make for me a heavy mace."
Both of them rose as he to speak began,
And to the blacksmiths' quarter quickly ran.
Those of that craft, then, who were seeking fame,
With faces turned to Faridún there came.
The hero took a compass in his hand;
The figure of a mace with this he planned,
And in the dust that lay beneath their feet,
Designed the great head of a bull complete.
To fashion this the blacksmiths set their face,
As soon as had been made the heavy mace.
Its form resplendent as the sun they made,
And laid before the hero there the blade.
The labour of the smiths approving then,

Gold, silver, clothing, too, he gave the men.
As hope of further honour he bestowed,
Their hearts with thoughts of future gladness glowed
" That dragon when beneath the earth I thrust,
I'll wash off from your head the clinging dust,
And when towards justice I the world shall bring,
The name remember of the bounteous king."

The Going of Faridún to War with Zuhak.

Raised Faridún his head towards the light,
His father to avenge, loins girded tight.
With good and prosperous omens in Khurdád*
Under propitious star he went abroad.
His host assembled there his palace nigh ;
His dignity ascended to the sky.
Proud elephants and bullocks went before,
And for the army their provisions bore.
Purmâyah, Kayunúsh were there at hand,
As elder brothers in goodwill to stand.
He, like the tempest, passed from stage to stage,
His heart with justice filled, his head with rage.
They reached, on Arab horses as they rode,
A place where worshippers of God abode.
At that place of the good, as he alit,
He sent to them a salutation fit.
Upon that place as soon as darkness fell,
There came a man who seemed to wish him well.
Down to its rootlets dripped with musk his hair,
As heavenly *Húris*, too, his face was fair.
He was a messenger from Paradise,
Of evil and of good to give advice.
He like a *Pari* to the chief approached,
And of enchantments all the secrets broached ;

*Name of a Persian month, corresponding with May. The word is pronounced Khoordawa.

That of all bonds he thus might hold the key,
And all things secret thus revealed might be.
That he was heavenly Faridun they understood,
He was no demon and his deeds were good.
His face with joy grew purple in its hue,
His body young and fortune fresh he knew.
For dishes suitable his cook thus cared,
And for the chief a table fresh prepared.
The food consumed, when thus in haste he dined,
With heavy head to sleep he felt inclined.
That deity had gone his brothers knew,
And that his fortune was of rosy hue;
Quickly they rose, and then the two began
To ruin him to make another plan.
A rock upon a high hill stood near by;
His brothers went up to it on the sly.
Below the hill the king was sleeping fast;
Some portion of the night had long since passed.
Those two unjust ones went up to the hill,
And that they went from all was hidden still.
From that hard rock a stone they separate,
The ill deed seemed to them of little weight.
They hewed the stone out of its rocky bed,
To crush without delay their brother's head.
They rolled it headlong down from off the hill,
In hope their brother there asleep to kill.
By God's command as it to roll began,
Its crashing sound awoke the sleeping man.
In its own place His magic made it hold,
And kept it there till it no longer rolled.
Girding his lions, then Faridun withdrew,
Whilst he told no one of the thing he knew.
On pushed the host, whilst Kavah went before,
At King Zuhak his heart with anger sore,
And Kavah's standard was exalted high,

Conspicuous standard of prosperity.
His face toward the Arvand river turned,
For diadem as one who constant burned.
(If thou know not the tongue of Pehlavi,
As Dajlah be the Arvand known to thee).
At the third stage that king of noble rank
Founded Baghdád upon the Dajlah's bank.
As to the Arvand river near he went,
On to its guardians he a message sent :
" Send here canoes and boats without delay,
Across the river to this side convey.
Take me and all my army to that side,
So none of us on this bank may abide."
The guardian brought no boats, but said : " To me
The world-king gave his orders secretly ;
Till with my seal a permit thou receive,
To cross here in a boat give no one leave."
When Faridún heard this, his anger glowed,
And no fear of that river deep he showed.
Girding his royal loins, with eager speed
He mounted on his lion-hearted steed.
With anger in his heart and war in view,
He plunged in with his steed of rosy hue ;
And his companions, girding up their waist,
One after other came on in their haste.
On their four-footed chargers of renown,
To their wet saddles even they sank down.
The neighing of those fierce steeds in the stream
Awoke those proud ones' heads out of their dream.
Into the stream their bodies whole they threw,
Just as the sun the dark night rends in two.
And when the warriors on to dry land came,
*Beitul mukaddas** tow'ards was then their aim.

*The Arab name for Jerusalem. It is difficult to know here whether that or Mecca is meant.

In Pehlavi, if they spoke Pehlavi,
Gang-i-dizhukht its name they'd give to thee.
In Arabic this now the Holy House they call,
And in its midst was Zuhák's lofty hall.
As from the plain they went up to the town,
The people to behold them crowded down.
Whilst Faridún at distance of a mile
Saw the king's palace in the town the while.
The lofty hall than Saturn higher seemed,
To ravish down the stars, you would have deemed.
Like *Múshtari* it glittered in the sphere :
Love, gladness, peace, all seemed assembled there.
This was the dragon's palace well he knew,
For it was great, magnificent to view.
He to his comrades said : "Out of dark earth
From hell to such high place has given birth.
I fear the world with him some secret holds,
Concealing in his bosom that he folds.
And in this narrow place it seems to me
'Twere well that we should move on speedily."
His heavy mace grasped in his hand again,
To his swift charger then he gave the rein.
A very burning fire, thou would'st have deemed,
Before the keeper of the hall there gleamed.
From off his saddle his huge mace he drew ;
Thou would'st have said the earth was rolled anew.
None of the guardians to the door there came,
And Faridún his Maker called by name.
That youth with no experience to guide,
Into the palace did on horseback ride.
The Talisman that there Zuhák had placed,
With honour equal to the heavens had graced,
Its head with heavy mace he broke in two,
Struck every one that rashly near him drew,
Those things of magic that were in the hall,

And the abominable Dívs and all.
He cast them headlong with his heavy mace,
Seating himself in the magician's place.
Zuhák's throne 'neath his foot then treading down,
He took his place and sought and wore the crown.
He then brought forth from out their sleeping place,
Those black-eyed beauties of the sunny face.
At first their heads to wash commanded he,
That so their souls from darkness he might free,
And the pure judge's path become their guide,
And thus from all defilement purified.
For by idolaters they had been reared,
And like as drunkards reeling they appeared.
Next of King Jamshíd then these sisters two
Bathed from their face their cheeks of rosy hue.
To Faridún to speak thus they made bold:
"May'st thou be young whilst still the world grows old!
What star was thine, O thou of fortune rare?
What was the tree that such good fruit could bear?
That on the lion's pillow thou should'st lie,
And tow'rds the tyrant act so valiantly?
How has the world against us turned to ill,
Whilst he with senseless magic worked his will!
What kind of evil fortune did we lack
From this dread Ahriman of dragon back?
We never saw one who so bravely dared,
To reach this place the skill who ever shared."
Thus to them answered Faridun: "No one
Or fortune permanently held or throne.
Of worthy Abtín here the son I stand,
Whom once Zuhák seized in the Persian land.
He slew him cruelly. Revengeful, I
Towards the throne of Zuhák turn my eye.
The cow Parmáyah, whose milk nourished me,
Whose form was fair as beauty's mould could be.

Of such a speechless beast he shed the blood,
What was the counsel of his impure mood?
I needs must gird my loins, and look for war,
And angry turn my face from Irán far.
His head with this bull-headed mace I break,
I will not pardon, no, nor pity take."
These words of his when Arnaváz thus knew,
To her pure heart revealed the secret grew.
She said to him: "Thou, Faridún, art he
Who from all sorcery the earth shall free.
The life of Zuhák now is in thy hand,
And with thy loins' support the world shall stand
We two pure veiled ones of the kingly brood
Were through destruction's fear by him subdued.
With snakes to sleep and rise up with that pair,
Such agony, O king, how could we bear?"
An answer Faridun them gave again:
"If justice from the heavens I shall gain,
From earth will I cut off the dragon's feet,
And cleanse the world from what's not pure and meet.
But now must ye the truth to me reveal:
Himself where does that dragon form conceal?"
The fair ones then the secret told him all:
Perhaps the dragon to his knife might fall.
They said: "To Hindustán he's fled and gone,
To magic that the world be bound and won,
And he a thousand guiltless heads will shear,
Of evil fortune he's oppressed with fear,
Since some one said, the future who could see,
'From thee the world delivered shall be free.
For Faridún shall seize upon thy throne,
And thy good fortune withering be gone.'
From that bad augury his heart on fire,
Even for this life he has no desire.
The blood of beast, man, woman, in his wrath

He mixes all together in a bath,
In blood his head and body to immerse,
The astrologers' ill omens to reverse.
From those two snakes that on his back he wears
Strangely, long agony as well he bears.
From one land to another, still oppressed,
In pain from those black snakes he has no rest.
But now for his return has come the day;
In no place can he settle down and stay."
Thus did her tale the girl, heart-broken, tell,
That on the monarch's ear attention fell.

The flight of Kundras, Zuhák's envoy, from before Faridún, and his taking the news to Zuhák.

When of Zuhák the country had grown free,
There was a worthy man, a slave was he:
He had a palace, throne and treasure, too.
At his lord's sorrow he bewildered grew.
They called him Kundras, and his name was meet
Before the tyrant that he set his feet.
Into the palace running, as he flew,
He saw there in the hall a monarch new;
Sitting at ease and in the highest place,
Tall, cypress-like, the moon about his face.
On one hand the tall cypress Shehr-i-naz.
And on the other moon-faced Arnaváz.
The town was overflowing with his host,
Loin-girt, who at the gate had taken post.
Still unconfused, he asked no secret there,
But with his salutation offered prayer.
"O king," said he, and blessing stayed to give:
"As long as time lasts, may'st thou ever live!
Auspiciously with glory dost thou sit,
For thou art for the royal kingship fit.
The slaves the sev'n climes of the earth be led.

And higher than the rain-cloud be thy head!"
And Faridún then bade him forward go,
And told him all the secrets he would know.
Then gave command to him the warlike king:
"Things fitted for the royal throne, go, bring.
Summon the singers and bring here the wine,
Fill bowls, prepare a place for me to dine.
Him who in music's worthy to take part,
Who in the feast will open out my heart,
Bring here! Assemble all around my throne,
As suits the fortune that I call my own!"
As soon as Kundras, then, the order knew,
He did what the new monarch bade him do.
He brought the minstrels and the shining wine,
And jewelled chieftains fit with him to dine.
And Faridún then ate and took to song,
In fitting way the night-feast to prolong.
And Kundras then, when night to morning grew,
Came from the presence of the leader new.
At once he mounted his impatient steed
And took his way towards Zuhák with speed.
And, as he came his ancient leader near,
He told him all he had to see and hear.
He said: "O thou of proud ones who art king,
To thee the signs of fortune lost I bring.
Three men, who from another country hail,
With hosts, their heads to raise who do not fail,
Have come: of these one taller to be seen,
As cypress high, he has a royal mien.
Just like a piece of hill he holds a mace,
And in the crowd all brightly glows his face.
On horseback to the king's hall does he ride,
Two others, who are grand men, at his side.
He comes and sits upon the royal throne,
And thy enchantments he has all cast down.

Whoever there remained within thy hall
The manly warriors and thy Dívs and all,
These from their steeds o'erthrowing as they stood,
Their brains has he commingled with their blood."
"But," said *Zuhák*; "they may be guests to me,
And we at such guests only glad should be."
But to him thus his Minister replied:
"Never would guests a bull-head mace provide
To come to thee. Of him be thou aware;
He is no guest; of thy own head take care.
At ease to sit down in thy place he came;
From throne and belt has he removed thy name.
In his own way he shows ingratitude.
If him a guest thou deemest, well and good!"
Zuhák to him replied: "Thus do not wail.
As a good omen we a guest should hail."
Kundras *Zuhák* gave answer in his ear:
"This have I heard from thee. My answer hear.
This hero if thou reckon as thy guest,
What business has he in thy place of rest?
There with the sisters of Jamshíd the king
Sitting to counsel take in everything?
He has in one hand cheek of Shehr-i-náz,
And in the other lip of Arnaváz.
But worse than this, as soon as day is dead,
Of musk he lays a pillow 'neath his head.
In thy two moons' locks does he that musk find,
Till now whose love was to thyself confined."
Enraged as wolf, *Zuhák* with passion fired,
To these words listened and but death desired.
With vile abuse and with stern voice he cried.
Amazed that such ill-luck should him betide.
He said to him: "Here in this house with me
Never shalt thou hereafter guardian be."
At him did then the eunuch answer fling:

"It seems to me, from now, O mighty king,
To thee no profit will from fate betide:
How, then, employment wilt thou me provide?
From high place come, as out of yeast a hair,
Thyself some remedy, O Chief, prepare.
Thine enemy has come, sits in thy place,
And in his hand is a bull-headed mace.
Of thy enchantments he has left no trace,
Thy charmer seized upon, usurped thy place.
For thy own matters why dost thou not care,
For never came to thee such like affair?"
Zuhák, when all this talk had taken place,
Came to his senses, and sharp set his face.
To saddle horses then an order sent,
And, closely searching, on that road he went.
Raging he came, with all his mighty host,
All cruel demons who of war could boast,
By palace roof and gate he headlong came,
Along byeways, his heart with rage aflame.

The Fight of Zuhák with Faridún, and his Confinement on the Hill of Damavand by Faridún.

Of this when Faridún's host was aware,
Upon that road they all assembled there.
Toward that by-way they all set their face,
Off their war horses in that narrow space.
On roof and gate came people of the town,
And all who cared to gain in war renown.
Of Faridún in favour all were led,
From Zuhák's violence those who had bled.
Stones from the roof and bricks down from the wall,
Swords in the lanes, on all sides arrows fall.
Down from the darkening cloud like hail they rained,
To stand on earth for none a place remained.
Out of the city all those who were young,

With those who knew war the old men among;
Once joined to Faridún his company,
Of all *Zuhák's* enchantments they were tree.
With heroes' voice resounded now the hill,
With hoofs the beasts the very earth did fill.
Above the army's heads a cloud of dust,
In the rock's heart the spurs were wounding thrust.
From the fire-temple there arose a cry:
"Should a beast sit upon the throne as hign,
All, young and old, would his command obey,
Nor sudden from his order turn away.
Zuhák upon the throne we'll not endure,
That dragon-formed one with the back impure."
Then all the citizens and all the troops,
Came there like hills together in their groups.
A cloud above the town of black dust flew,
So that the sun assumed a purple hue.
Zuhák himself a remedy bethought,
To palace as from camp his way he sought.
In iron clad throughout from top to toe,
That none in the assembly him should know.
He went up on the palace with a thong,
Held in his hand, full sixty fathoms long.
He saw where Shehr-i-naz, with her black eye,
Of magic full, then Faridún sat by,
As night her locks and as the day her cheek,
Of *Zuhák* but with curses could she speak.
He saw the matter was of God ordained,
And that the evil hand was not restrained.
Fire in his brain lit up at envy's call,
He threw his noose straight out upon the wall.
No thought of life, and with no thought of throne,
Off from the high roof he descended prone.
Held in his hand of tempered steel a knife,
He thirsted of those *Paris* for the life.

With unsheathed dagger in his hand he came;
His secret told he not, and named no name.
As soon as lit his feet upon the ground,
Swooped Faridún upon him with a bound.
His bull-head mace he struck upon his head,
And thus his helmet into pieces shred.
An angel cried with his auspicious breath:
"Strike not; not yet has come his time for death.
Now as a stone he lies; him firmly tie,
And bear him where two hills together lie.
Within the mountain bind him with a chain,
That so his friends no access to him gain."
This hearing, Faridún no more delayed,
But of a lion's skin a lasso made.
And bound his loins and both hands with a noose,
Such as no raging elephant could loose.
He sat upon his golden throne then down,
And all his ill designs were overthrown.
He ordered proclamation at the gate:
"All ye whose minds are active in their state,
Weapons of warfare ye should now prepare,
For glory by such means do ye not care.
Soldiers with artisans should never vie,
Or tow'rds the same trade ever turn their eye.
One has to labour, one to hold the mace,
Suited to each is work in its own place.
If one man looks towards another's toil,
The world will clash together in turmoil.
Now he who was impure in bonds is he,
One from whose fear the earth was never free.
May all of you be happy and live long!
Now each back to his work with joyous song!"
Their wealth they carried off with joyful sound,
Their hearts to his obedience firmly bound.
Good Faridún then patronized with grace,

And gave in wisdom's way to each his place.
He gave advice, and praise bestowed on all,
And bade them on the world's Creator call.
Then he proclaimed to them: "This throne is mine;
By the stars' augury your fortunes shine.
From crowds the pure God chose me by His will,
And summoned me to come from Albnez hill,
That from the dragon the world might be free,
And in my glory your delivery.
If of His bounty God should favour give,
Us it behoves in goodness' ways to live.
As of the whole world I must master be,
To live in one place now becomes not me.
Here otherwise I'd calm and gladly stay,
And would be with you here for many a day."
The nobles kissed the ground before his feet,
Rose from the Court the sound of drums that beat!
The city turned their eyes towards the Court,
And shouts arose 'gainst him whose time was short.
They cried the dragon he should bring them round,
And with a noose he should be duly bound.
The army now the city quickly left,
(Of fortune long that city was bereft).
They brought Zuhák, contempt who did not lack,
And bound him firmly on a camel's back.
And to Shirkhan they drove him in this wise,
When this thou hear'st, how old's the world, surmise.
How many days upon this hill and plain
Have passed away and yet will pass again!
With wakeful fortune thus Zuhák he bound,
And to Shirkhan him quickly carried round.
Again did then God's messenger appear,
And good words softly whisper in his ear;
And said: "Him bound to Damávand convey,
And with him Arabs many as you may.

Take only those who will not thee forsake,
And who in danger to their breast will take "—
Swift as a courier he went on still,
And bound *Zuhák* on Damávand its hill
As with another chain him did he bind,
Nought of *Zuhák*'s ill-luck was left behind.
Vile as the dust through him was *Zuhák*'s name,
Rid of his vileness the whole world became.
Far from his friends and relatives, he still
Remained for ever chained up on the hill.
Thereon saw Faridún a place profound,
To which no bottom man had ever found.
The heaviest of nails he brought again,
And drove in so as not to touch his brain.
He fastened down his two hands to the hill,
So that long agony should pain him still.
After this manner was he hung up bound,
Until his heart's blood dropped upon the ground.
The world as evil let us not resign,
But be good whilst to good we still incline.
Nor good nor bad for ever will remain;
Let us in memory the good retain.
The gold and palaces at thy command
Will never have a profit in thy hand.
Thy words remain in memory of thee,
And weighty words despised should never be.
Not Faridún was of angelic mind,
Of musk and amber to the sort confined.
An angel Faridún could not be said,
Nor was he but of musk and amber made.
Through justice only he attained that grace:
Be just: of Faridún take thou the place.
Now Faridún through many a godly deed
This world from evil was the first who freed.
The first was this, in that *Zuhák* he bound,

Who was unjust and thus impure was found:
The next that for his sire he vengeance sought,
And thus the world round to his favour brought.
In the third place, of foolish men the land
He purified and took it from their hand.
O world, what evil is in thy alloy
That thou thyself should'st nourish and destroy!
Behold in Faridún what valour lay,
Who rent from old Zuhák the realm away!
The king five hundred years did here abide:
These were completed and his place was void.
Dying, the world to others he gave o'er
And nought but sorrow from the earth he bore.
Thus great and small shall we the fashion keep,
Whether we shepherds be or whether sheep.

After this Faridún is said to have reigned 500 years. He is said to have been a just king, and to have gone about the world doing good and planting cypresses and roses. After fifty years there were born to him three sons, two by Shehr-i-náz and one by Arnavaz. They were married, when they grew up, to the daughters of the King of Zaman in Arabia, and subsequently had the whole realm apportioned to them by their father. Before this, however, he tested their several qualities by appearing to them in the form of a dragon of terrible form. The eldest one remarked that a prudent man did not war with dragons, and ran away. The second strung his bow and defied the dragon, while the third threatened him with the vengeance of the three sons of Faridún. The dragon then disappeared, and Faridún, acknowledging the trick he had played, gave them all names, calling the eldest Salam, the safe one, because he had at once run away, and sought safety in flight, the second Túr, the courageous lion that a raging elephant would not overthrow, and the third Iraj, because he had shown mildness at first, but bravery in the hour of danger. In distributing his kingdom he gave to Salam Rúm and Khávar, or the Western region, the limits of which it is difficult to specify, to Túr Turan, or Scythia, and to Iraj Irán or Persia. The last being the finest part of the inheritance, Salam grew jealous of his youngest brother, and conspired against him with Túr, both their portions being comparative rude and unprofitable. Iraj, on the advice of his father, who desired peace between the brothers, agreed to give up his share to them, and went to Túr's country, Turkistan, for the purpose, but was himself murdered by Túr, and his head cut off, the head being sent to Faridún, who, with all his people, were overcome with grief, even their horses being stained blue in token of mourning. Faridún lay on the earth, making the dust his couch, and wept so continuously that grass grew on his breast. It was soon discovered that a slave girl, of the name of Irán-áfrid, had been left *enceinte* by Iraj, and from her was born Manúchehr, the future King of Persia. This event gave occasion for great rejoicings at the Court of Faridún, and is said to have been signalised by the sudden restoration of his sight to the king on his prayer to God, in order that he might see the royal infant. The child was brought up with the utmost care and in great splendour. A magnificent feast was held on the occasion of the birth, and as one of the celebrities present at it there appeared Sám, the son of Narimán, the celebrated Persian athlete and hero. Túr and Salam repented of their misdeeds, and sent an embassy to Faridún asking for pardon and offering their service to Manúchehr. Faridún, considering their past misconduct, did not believe in their sincerity, and, rejecting their advances, informed them, through their envoy, that the prince would be sent with an army and the hero Sám in order to punish them. The description of Faridún's Court given to Túr and Salam by the envoy is worth quoting:

He said: "He who has never seen the spring
Would see it when he looked upon the king.
A spring of Paradise 'twas to behold,
Its dust of amber and its bricks of gold.
Upon his palace heav'n found resting place,
With Paradise e'er smiling on its face.
In height no mountain came up to its plain;
No earthly garden could its breadth attain.
That lofty vestibule when I came near,
Its head held converse with the heav'nly sphere.
Here elephants, on that side lions stand,
And the world's fortune was at his command.
With throne of gold upon each elephant's back,
Jewelled gold chains its lions did not lack.
Men beating drums before them proudly stride,
With trumpets blaring upon ev'ry side.
The plain seemed e'en to boil up with the cry,
And earth the sound re-echoed to the sky.
That gracious monarch when I came more near,
I saw a lofty turquoise throne appear.
A moon-like monarch sat upon the throne,
Of brilliant ruby on his head a crown.

The two princes prepared and Manúchehr advanced with his army, headed by Káran, the son of the blacksmith Kávah. In the fierce battle that ensued Túr was killed by Manúchehr's own hand and his head sent to Faridún. The fort of the Alans, in which Salam took refuge after the defeat of his army by Manúchehr, was captured by Káran and burnt; but Salam appears to have escaped and to have been also killed by Manúchehr after an attack by Kákú, a grandson of Zuhák, had been defeated, and the leader slain by the prince. After this Faridún died, overcome by the misfortunes that had befallen his three sons, and was succeeded on the throne by his grandson Manúchehr. With Manúchehr's succession may be said to close the legendary and semi-mythical history of Persia, and its tolerably authenticated period to commence.

Manúchehr, whose rule is a tolerably well authenticated historical fact, is said to have reigned 120 years. On his accession he is congratulated by the Pehlaván Sám, the son of Narimán, who devotes himself to his service. The first great event narrated in Manúchehr's reign is the birth of a son to this hero, with the remarkable circumstance that the child's hair was entirely white, although otherwise he was of rare beauty. Considering this a cruel misfortune, Sám ordered him to be exposed, on the mountain of Alburz, where, after being suckled for a day and a night by a lioness that had lost its cub, he is discovered by the Simurgh,* the fabulous bird that figures so largely in Persian story, and tenderly brought up by the creature together with its own young ones. Growing up and becoming famous in the neighbourhood, he is dreamt of by his father, who, on being reproached by the Mobeds for neglecting his offspring simply on the ground of his having white hair like an old man, proceeded to the Alburz hills to search for his son. He sees the Simurgh who informs the young man whose son he is and gives him the name of Dastán. Sám, after blessing the bird, carries off his son, whom he finds to be worthy of a throne and crown, and whom he also names Zál-i-zar Zál is taken before Manúchehr, is received by him with great favour, and the Mobeds† are bidden to cast his

* The Simurgh was the same as the *Luka*, the over-shadowing of whose wings was a sign of royalty.

† The Mobeds are the priests of the Parsees.

horoscope, which proves favourable, and the father and son are dismissed with all honour, and with the gift of the sovereignty of Zabulistan. This included at all events Kabul and the intervening countries beyond Bust as far as the Indus, although the names of Dambar and Mai are now unrecognizable. The king having ordered Sam to proceed against Mazanderan, he handed over charge of his own territories to Zal and embarked on the undertaking with a numerous army. We now come to the episode of Zal falling in love with Rudabah, daughter of Mehrab, the tributary Chief of Kábul itself. This is related in a third Book.

The Dealings of Zál with Mehráb of Kábul and his becoming enamoured of Rudábah, Mehráb's Daughter.

MEHRAB by name, there was a king who reigned,
A tyrant, rich, with wishes unrestrained.
In height resembling a tall cypress tree;
In face like spring, a pheasant's gait had he.
With heart and brain to wisdom both inclined,
A hero's shoulders and a Mobed's mind,
Zúhák, the Arab, gave his race its birth,
In Kábul he was owner of the earth.
Each year he gave to Sám the tribute due:
He could not strive with him in war, he knew.
Of Dastán, son of Sám, he heard them say,
He came from Kábul early in the day,
With treasure, horse prepared, all he could find,
With slaves and property of ev'ry kind;
Rubies, *dinars*, and musk and amber, too,
Gold cloth, brocade and spun silk fair to view;
A royal crown, adorned with jewels bright,
A golden collar decked with chrysolite.
Then all the Captains of the Kábul host,
He brought upon the road to take their post.
Zál praised him when he met him on the way,
Providing fitting place for him to stay.
Then tow'rds the turquoise throne they backward turned,
With opened hearts as for the feast they yearned.
Fit for a Pehlaván a tray they laid,

Round which the nobles sat, in pomp arrayed ;
A cup-bearer brought bowl and wine, thereby.
On Sám's son when Mehráb had cast his eye.
He looked upon his face and found it fair :
More active grew his heart in his affair.
Such wisdom and such knowledge had his look,
Mehráb his senses and his heart forsook.
When from Zál's table Mehráb rose and went,
Zál on his form and shoulders gazed intent,
And to the Chiefs about him said: "Than he
None could a girdle wear more gracefully,
In face and height none can with him compare,
Or ball from him in sport away may bear."
One of the great ones there, a noted man,
"O athlete of the world," then thus began :
"He has a daughter there, behind the screen,
Than the sun's disk more bright was never seen.
From head to foot she is like ivory,
Spring-like her face, in height a plantain tree—
Two musky locks on her fair neck depend ;
Her head is of a fetter as the bend.
Pomegranate blooms her cheeks, lips cherry hue,
And on her silver breast pomegranates two.
Her two eyes like the mead's narcissus glow,
Their lashes darker than the black-winged crow.
Eyebrows resembling an embroidered bow,
Fringed with the purest musk the *túz** below.
Moon if thou seekest, it is in her face,
Or musk, this still in her thou mayest trace.
Armour of musk in her dark locks you find,
The ball together in thin knots that bind.
Like silver writing-pens her fingers ten,
Traces a hundred lines that civet pen.

* An ornament of thin bark, wrapped round the forehead by way of smoothing it down.

As Paradise from end to end arrayed,
With ornament and song 'tis perfect made.
O Pehlavan renowned, she's fit for thee,
For like the moon in heav'n she seems to be."
And when these words from him Zal eager heard,
His chords of love were violently stirred;
His throbbing heart to boiling point arose:
His sense forsook him, he found no repose.
Still in deep thought when night came on the scene,
For her he sorrowed whom he'd never seen.
His sword the sun above the hill-top drew,
And earth's white face became of camphor hue.
Dastan Sam opened then his audience hall:
With their gold scabbards came the warriors all.
The athlete's gate adorning, they stood round,
Until the places for the great they found.
Outside, Mehráb, the lord of Kabul, went
To where the lord of Zabul had his tent,
And when he came to the pavilion near,
Arose an outcry loud: "The road make clear!"
Like a tree laden with the freshest fruit,
Towards the Pehlavan he advanced his foot.
With heart rejoiced Zal glorified him then,
And raised his head above that crowd of men.
He asked him: "Say what now is thy demand,
Throne, seal, or sword, or king's crown at my hand."
"O mighty king," Mehrab to him replied,
"Of rank exalted, ruling in thy pride,
I have one wish that I just now require,
And thou canst easily grant my desire,
At my abode that thou wilt now alight,
And make my soul as with the sun's ray bright."
He answered him then: "Right it were not so;
Thy house no place to which I ought to go.
For Sam in this would surely not agree,

And neither when he heard rejoiced would be
With wine if we ourselves intoxicate
Of an idolater within the gate,
But this to what thou say'st will I reply,
That seeing thee myself will satisfy."
This heard, Mehráb gave Zal praise to his face,
But in his heart deemed his religion base.
Yet from his throne, as gracefully he went,
On his good fortune praises still would vent.
As yet upon him no one's eyes had dwelt,
Or tow'rds him other than to stranger felt.
And knowing his religion and his ways,
Their tongue would not enunciate his praise.
But as before Dastan he passed in view,
He greatly praised him, as became his due.
The clear-souled Pehlavan, with praises meet,
When warmly they him saw in converse greet,
The great ones in his eulogy grew keen,
As if he'd hidden him behind a screen.
For height, appearance and his modest ways,
For aptitude and manners they gave praise.
Sudden the heart of Zal more maddened grew;
As reason left him, warmer love he knew.
An Arab leader, chief among the wise,
A word conformable to this supplies.
"Aye, whilst I live my wife is my white steed:
No shelter but the circling heav'n I need.
I want no bride, lest tender I should grow,
And in dishonour wise men we may know."
To these thoughts Zal his wounded heart addressed,
Still in the matter was his heart oppressed.
And conversation lost its zest for him,
For fear his brilliant fame was growing dim.
Some time elapsed. The sphere yet turned above;
The heart of Zál was still absorbed with love.

Rudábah's becoming infatuated with Zál, and holding counsel with her female slaves.

Mehráb, it happened early on a day,
Out of his palace took his morning way.
To Zál himself he gave unbounded praise,
Of his form, bravery and generous ways.
And as he passed on to his sleeping place,
He saw two girls there, sun-like in their grace.
One was Rudábah, of fair face to view;
Síndúkht the other, loving, prudent, too.
Like gardens in the spring they both were fair,
Of colour full, of scent, of beauty rare.
Struck with Rudábah's grace, he stood and gazed
God's blessing calling on her, all amazed.
Above a cypress tall the moon was round,
And with a cap of amber she was crowned.
With jewels decked and clad in gold brocade,
Full as of wealth, of Paradise a glade.
Of Mehráb then Síndúkht enquiry made,
Her sweet lip opening its pearls displayed.
" Where goest thou and whence dost thou come here?
Before thee may all evil disappear!
Who, now, of Sám is this white-headed son?
And thinks he of the nest or of the throne?
Does he comport himself as heroes do?
Does he the footsteps of brave men pursue?
How of the Símurgh does this good Zál speak?
What is his face like and what like his cheek?"
Mehráb her answered and these words expressed:
" O fair-faced cypress of the silver breast,
On the broad earth no Pehlaván thou'lt find
To follow on Zál's footsteps from behind.
In painted hall such hand no rein may bind,
On saddle seated no such man thou'lt find.

The elephant's strength has he, the lion's soul,
His two hands firm as where Nile's waters roll.
He scatters gold, on his throne seated high,
And in the battle causes heads to fly.
His cheeks are as the Arghaván* to view:
Alert, young as his years his fortune, too.
Although in colour white may be his hair,
Brave, he the crocodile in two will tear
In anger like the crocodile of ill,
On saddle he's the sharp-clawed dragon still.
In anger whilst the dust with blood he lays,
With the well-tempered dagger still he slays.
Although his hair is white as that of deer,
Detractors' blame no other need he fear.
So well becomes him white hair on his head,
That he enchants all hearts, it may be said."
And all these matters when Rudábah knew,
Her face lit up to a pomegranate hue.
With fire of Zál's love full then grew her heart,
In patience, food or ease she had no part
To place of reason when desire presumed,
Her methods all a different phase assumed.
How well did that one of wise counsel sing,
"Heroes to women's memory ever bring!
A woman's heart's the dwelling place of Dívs,
And from their talk her counsel she receives."
Five Turkí female slaves did with her dwell,
Who while they served her loved her also well.
She made to those wise women her appeal:
"To you a secret do I now reveal.
For ye are they my secrets who possess,
And who dispel my sorrow none the less.
And now know all ye five, attention pay;

* The Syringa Persica.

May fortune e'er be with you on life's way!
I am in love just as the sea-waves rise
And toss their raging billows to the skies.
Filled with *Zál*'s love is now my tender heart,
His thought e'en in my dreams must bear a part.
In my soul ever has his love its place,
And night and day I think upon his face.
None knows of this my secret thought but you,
Who are both virtuous and kindly, too.
Is there a remedy that you can see,
And what security give ye to me?
For now some remedy must ye present,
My heart and soul's sore trouble to prevent."
The slaves were all bewildered with the thing
That from a Princess such ill deed should spring.
Anxious they rose up from their place at once,
As they prepared to give her fit response.
"Of all earth's women thou the crown of state,
And most exalted daughter of the great,
From Hindustán to China all men sing
Thy praises, thou of the *harím* brightest ring.
Of the mead's cypress thine the height alone,
With thy cheeks' brightness Pleiad never shone.
Sends from Kanouj the king thy portrait fair
To the West's king and all the regions there.
Hast thou no modesty in thine own eyes,
And thy sire's sorrow dost thou now despise;
That him whom thy own father casts away
On thy own bosom even thou would'st lay?
A bird has brought him up upon the hill,
And he among men is a beacon still.
Old man like him no mother ever bore,
Nor such will one conceive for evermore.
With musk-like locks and such a brilliant cheek
'Twere strange if thou an ancient husband seek.

Full of affection for thee mortals all,
Thy face is painted upon ev'ry hall.
With such a face, such stature and such hair,
From the fourth sphere the sun might be thy pair."
But when Rudabah heard such words as those,
Fire as with wind within her heart arose.
She burst out at them with an angry cry,
Bright blazed her cheek, and closed became her eye.
With a stern face and eye with passion lit,
With a hard frown her eyebrow stern was knit.
She said : "Now all in vain will you resist.
Unfit your words that I to them should list.
As with a star itself I far have strayed,
How with the moon could I be happy made ?
He who mud eats the rose will not admire,
Though to the rose than mud the name is high'r.
He for whose heart's pain vinegar's a cure,
Far greater pain from honey will endure.
Kaiser nor China's Faghfur I desire,
Nor of Iran those who to the cross aspire :
Zal, son of Sam, is equal full in height,
With lion's arm and back and breast of might,
And you may call him young or call him old,
My soul and body's place yet will he hold.
Bring no one else in memory to me,
For he alone shall in my heart e'er be.
From sight alone I have not him preferred,
But choose him only for what I have heard.
Me tow'rds him nor his face nor hair will move,
For valour only do I seek his love."
Thus heard the slave girls of her secret choice,
And broken-hearted listened to her voice ;
And as they loved the kind girl from their heart,
They all with one consent then took her part.
"We are thy slaves," with one accord they cried,

"And serving thee all love thee well beside.
See what command to give now thou wilt deign:
For from thy orders can come nought but gain."
One of them said to her: "O cypress rare,
See that thou tell to no one this affair.
Ten thousand be thy sacrifice like me!
May earth's intelligence all be with thee!
Ever be modesty in thy black eyes,
And blush of shame aye to thy cheek arise.
Now if enchantments thou would'st have us know,
And thus with magic arts men's eyes to sew,
Like birds of magic we aloft will fly,
Or run like deer to bring a remedy.
So to our moon that we may lead the king,
And to thee greater dignity may bring."
Rudábah's red lip smiling answer gave;
She turned her cheek of saffron to the slave.
"By thy devices should'st thou now succeed,
A lofty, fruitful tree thou'lt plant indeed,
That will produce fresh rubies ev'ry day
For wisdom in its breast to bear away."

The Going of the Slave-girls to Zál, and Their Return from him with gifts and a Message.

The girls before her rose up from their place
An turned to seek to beautify the face.
They all adorned themselves in Greek brocade;
Among their flowing locks they roses laid.
Down to the riverside all five they went,
Like pleasant spring, in colour and in scent;
In Favardeen's month, first of the year,
The camp of Zál was to the river near.
The girls on that side of the river walked,

And of Dastán in varied manner talked.
Of river flowers they themselves possessed:
They rosebuds were, with roses in their breast.
Still flowers gathering, they wandered round,
And soon themselves outside Zál's camp-screen found.
Then Zál beheld them from his lofty chair,
And asked them who those flower lovers were.
"Why do ye from my rosebud flowers take,
And thus light of my royal orders make?"
One spoke and to the Pehlaván replied:
"In clever Mehrab's palace we abide.
The moon of Kábulistán, with intent,
Her slaves to thy rose-garden has thus sent."
Dastán heard this, nor could his heart restrain:
From love he could not in his place remain.
He went on with a slave without delay,
From that side of the stream he made his way.
Upon the further side he saw them stand,
And for his bow stretched to his slave his hand.
He was on foot, and looking out for prey
Saw in the stream a Khashishár* that lay.
The red-cheeked Turk laid on the bow a string,
And placed it in the hand of that world-king.
A shout from off the stream to make it rise,
And at the bird an arrow quickly flies.
Bringing it down before full flight was gained,
Of ruddy hue was thus the water stained.
"Go thou across," he to the Turk then cried,
"And bring the broken-winged bird to this side."
A boat the Turk took, on his errand bent,
As gracefully towards the slaves he went.
One of the girls the Athlete's slave addressed,
And sweet tongue loosening, these words expressed:

*Name unknown and therefore kept in the original.

"This lion-arm, an elephant to see,
Whom rules he, and what kind of man is he?
He who an arrow shoots thus from his bow,
Before him of what weight is any foe?
His bow and arrow wielding in his might,
No fairer horseman e'er came to my sight."
Quickly his lip bit with his teeth the slave,
And "speak not of the king thus," answer gave.
"Sam's son is he, of realm of midday lord,
To whom the name of Dastán kings accord.
Never such horsemen whirl the spheres around,
Nor such renowned one in all time is found."
Smiled at the fair-faced boy the servant maid,
As "Do not say so," thus to him she said.
"A moon from Mehrab's palace I can bring,
Who by a head is taller than thy king.
Tall as a teak tree, ivory her hue,
With a divine crown of musk upon her, too.
Stern are her eyes, but eyebrows like a bow,
As silver pen the pillar of her brow.
Narrow her mouth as those who hearts lament
And like a fetter's ring her locks are bent.
Languid her eyes and full of splendour, too,
Musky her hair, her cheeks of tulip's hue.
No place upon her lip for breath to stir,
There is no moon upon the earth like her.
We come from Kabul here with graceful gait,
Upon Zabulistan its king to wait.
Now would it be but right and very sweet,
Zál and Rudabah should each other greet."
One after other all the slave girls there
Spoke of the beauty of the charming fair,
And that her ruby lip, 'twas their design,
In union should with Sam's son's lip combine
Then to the fair-faced slaves the boy replied:

"The bright sun with the moon should e'er abide.
And when the world tow'rds union turns its mind,
For love in ev'ry heart a place 'twill find.
No need to speak such bonds to separate;
It severs lightly partner from its mate.
The brave man looks for virtue in his wife,
And keeps her secretly apart from strife.
And that his daughter may not evil grow
Provides that vile talk she may never know.
Thus did a male hawk to his mate once sing,
That sat upon her eggs and spread her wing:
'If from these eggs a female should not lack,
We may take eggs out of their father's back.'" *
The smiling slave from near them then retired,
And Sam's son of renown of him inquired:
"Who is this, secrets that to thee has told?
To me those secrets must thou now unfold.
That thou should'st smile, to thee what did she say,
With opened lips thy silver teeth display?"
What he had heard the Pehlavan he told.
His heart in gladness became young and bold.
And to that fair youth he began to say:
"To those slave-girls take thou at once thy way.
Bid them awhile stay in the garden there,
That with their roses jewels they may bear.
Their way they must not tow'rds the palace wend;
I have a secret message there to send."
For gold and treasured gems demand he made,
As well as garments five of fine brocade.
Of royal gems a casket, too, he sought,
And from his ear a costly ear-ring brought.
Two rings that Manuchehr the king had giv'n,
He then selected for that moon of heav'n,

*Unintelligible. Translated by Mohl, "Si tu fais sortir une femelle de cet œuf, tu ôteras au père l'envie d'avoir des petits."

"These jewels take to them," thus did he say,
"But tell none; secretly to her convey."
To the five moon-cheeked serving girls they went,
With speeches warm and treasure that he sent.
To give them gold and jewels thus they came,
Of the world's Pehlaván, *Zálzar*, in the name.
The moon-faced serving girls to him replied:
"A secret 'tis impossible to hide,
Unless its keepers but two people are;
Three keep it not; four are too many far.
Tell him, wise man who of pure counsel art,
That he his secret should to me impart."
And now of *Zál's* condition when they knew,
That in his love he thus impatient grew,
One to another the five slave girls said:
"Into our snare the lion has been led.
Fulfilled Rudábah's and *Zálzar's* desire,
A happy omen we from fate acquire."
The black-eyed treas'rer to the king came near
Who in this matter had been his Vazir;
Of what that charmer said he told the tale,
And secretly to whisper did not fail.
To the rose garden passed the monarch on,
In hope the sun of Kábul he had won.
The rose-cheeked idols of Taraz came there,
Humbly themselves presenting with their prayer.
The monarch questioned them of what they knew,
Of that fair cypress' looks and stature, too.
Of speech, of looks, of wisdom, and of mind,
Of how they would agree that he might find.
"Now speak to me," he said, "of every thing;
Nor crookedness into your story bring.
If in your words there truth alone shall be,
The more shall ye gain dignity with me.
If in your words I crookedness shall find

'Neath foot of elephant you will I grind."
The hue of *Sandarús* the slaves' cheeks bore,
As they the ground kissed the king's feet before.
One of the girls was younger than the rest,
And for *Zál* sympathy had in her breast.
"Among the mothers of the world," she said,
"Will no one of the great be brought to bed
With one of Sám's appearance or his height,
Of his pure heart and of his judgment right.
For none, O athlete bold, comes up to thee,
In stature, form or lion's bravery.
Wine, as it were, doth trickle from thy face
Hair, as of ambergris, lends thee its grace.
Again, Rudábah, with her moon-like mien,
In hue and scent as silver cypress seen,
Has rose and jessamine around her spread,
With Naman's star above her cypress head.
And from that silver dome upon the ground,
An ambuscade of roses trails her round.
With musk and amber woven round her head,
Rubies and emeralds o'er her body spread.
In China no such idols may be seen,
Praised by both moon and Pleiades, I ween."
Warm speech then to that slave the king addressed,
And in soft accents thus his words expressed:
"For me what remedy there is, now say,
That to approach her I may find a way;
For full of love for her my heart and soul,
Desire to see her is beyond control."
The girl "Command!" then gave to him reply,
"And we'll to that cypress palace hie.
With the world-athlete's fine intelligence,
His speech, appearance, and exalted sense,
Will we enchant her, what thou art will say,
Nought unpropitious is there in thy way.

We'll bring her head, musk-scented, to our net,
And on the lip of Sam's son hers will set.
Close to her dome the athlete now should go,
His noose aloft upon it there to throw;
Upon the battlement its folds to lay,
Rejoice the lion with the lamb his prey.
Thou shalt then find how happy thou can'st be,
And how my words shall joy increase for thee."
Their counsels thus together laid with art,
Relieved of sorrow was the athlete's heart.
Then Zal turned back; those fair ones went their way,
That long night seemed to him a year's delay.
Hard by the palace dome they took their stand,
Of roses double branches in each hand.
The porter saw them and prepared for fight;
His tongue grown impudent, his heart made tight.
"At a time importune ye leave the hall,
And I am wond'ring what may you befall."
The fair ones answered him with cunning art,
And rose up from their place with anxious heart.
They said: "This differs not from ev'ry day,
Nor more perverse the mead's Div in his way.
We gather roses in the spring anew,
And from the ground we pick the spikenard, too,
By order of Rudábah, fair of face,
And out of love for her for flowers chase.
What is thy purpose in this kind of speech?
We but pluck flow'rs from thorns within our reach."
The porter answered them: "In many ways
Ye must not reckon as on other days.
For Zal, the General, is in Kabul,
Of soldiers and of tents the land is full.
Do ye not see, from Kabul's palace dome,
On horseback seated he at night will come;
The whole day long to come here he intends,

For they are with each other earnest friends.
If he should see those roses in your hand,
Soon will he throw you down upon the strand.
Outside the *harím* must ye now not walk;
Lest there of more or less be any talk."
Entered those idols of Taráz the hall;
Seated, they to that moon recounted all.
"We never saw a being of such light,
His cheek a rose, although his hair is white."
Rudábah's heart with love was burning bright,
Of his face in the hope to see the light.
They showed the *dinars* and the jewel store,
Rudábah asking questions less or more.
"With Sám's son," she enquired, "what did ye do?
Is his name greater than he is to view?"
Of speed those *Pari*-faced ones found the way,
And hastening, told her what they had to say.
"No horseman on the earth may ever ride,
Equal to Zal in manner and in pride.
He is a hero like a cypress tall,
With beauty and with kingly pomp and all;
With colour, perfume, bright and branches blessed,
A rider thin of loin and ample chest.
His eyes narcissus of a heav'nly blue,
Pistachio lips, his cheeks a blood-red hue.
Like lion's claw and forearm are his hands,
With Mobed's heart, in royal grace he stands.
Upon his head although the hair is white,
As is a deer's, there's no shame in the sight.
On *Arghavan* flow'r that athlete of the world
Like silver breast-plate has his ringlets curled.
Thou would'st have said: It should be ever so,
Or otherwise his love would never grow.
Good news of seeing thee did we convey,
And with heart full of hope he went away.

Some plan devise for him to be thy guest,
For us to go to him as may seem best."
That cypress to the servant girls replies:
"Your counsel was but lately otherwise,
That very Zal who by a bird was reared,
So ancient too, and withered who appeared.
Now like a rose blooms, *Arghavan* of hue,
Of cypress stature, and an athlete, too
My cheek before him beautiful ye've named,
Ye spoke, and your reward ye now have claimed."
This with a smile upon her lip she said,
Blushing her cheeks as a pomegranate red.
That lady of the ladies further cried
To that slave girl: "No longer here abide,
Hasten with this good news to him away,
And tell it him: hear what he has to say:
'Thou hast thy wish: make preparation due,
And come the fair face of thy moon to view.'"
The good news to impart went off the slave
And to that cypress of Taraz the tidings gave.
And to her lady of the moon face cried:
"Come now, some new device must we provide.
For all thy wishes God has granted thee.
May the affair at last propitious be!"
Quickly Rudábah ev'ry thing prepared,
And from her friends to hide it duly cared.
A house she'd joyous as the spring and new,
Adorned with great men's portraits through and through.
This all they decked out with Chinese brocade,
And ample golden caskets there were laid.
Cornelians, emeralds, they scattered round,
Amber, musk, wine, together mixed were found.
Here rose, narcissus, *Arghavan* were set,
On that side jessamine and violet.
And bowls were there of ruby and of gold,

Rosewater pure and clear to drink to hold.
From that house of the girl of sunny face
To the sun rising, perfume you could trace.

The Going of Zal to Rudábah and his giving her a Pledge of Marriage.

And when the shining sun men ceased to see,
They closed the door and then was lost the key.
To Dastán, Sám's son, took a slave her way,
"Arrangement has been made, proceed!" to say.
The king his face toward the palace turned,
Just as a man to gain a wife who burned.
Up to the roof that black-eyed beauty sped,
As cypress, with the moon upon her head.
When Dastán, Sam's son, saw her far away,
That famous girl appeared without delay.
Op'ning her lips, her voice was loud and clear:
"O happy hero, thou art welcome here!
Now may God's blessing ever be on thee
And on her who has brought forth one like thee.
And may my happy slave to joy be led,
For such art thou as she to me has said.
The dark night through thy face has turned to day
And through thy scent the whole world's heart is gay
On foot thou com'st me from thy camp to greet,
And thus are paining thee thy royal feet."
As from that tow'r the monarch heard the sound,
He looked and there the sunny-faced one found.
The roof appeared to him a jewel bright,
The earth a ruby through her cheek of light.
"O moon-faced one," to her he made reply:
"Greeting from me, and blessing from the sky!
On the *Samak** how many nights I gazed,

*The two stars, Spica virginis and Arcturus.

As to pure God my voice aloud I raised.
To the world's Lord went up the cry from me,
That I thy fair face secretly might see
Already now I glory in thy voice,
In luxury at thy sweet tones rejoice.
Seek from thy tow'r a way from me to thee:
Whilst in the street how canst thou ask of me?"
The king heard what the Pari-faced one said,
As she pomegranate locks loosed from her head:
A curl undoing from her cypress tall,
Of musk thou could'st not weave such noose at all.
Snake upon snake, and curl a curl within,
Ring upon ring upon her double chin,
Her ringlets from the rampart she unwound,
So that at once they trailed upon the ground.
Then from the battlement Rudábah cried:
"O athlete, sprung from warrior in his pride,
Quickly thy loins extend and upright stand,
Stretch forth thy lion form, thy royal hand.
Now hold fast of my ringlets by the end:
'Twere meet that I my locks to thee should lend.
It is for this that I my hair have grown,
That sometimes friends should its assistance own."
Zal on the face of that moon-faced one gazed,
And at that hair and features stood amazed.
A soft kiss to those musk locks he applied,
And the sound reached above his waiting bride.
Thus answer gave he then: "This were not right!
On that day may the sun not give his light,
To take my own life when I wield a dart,
Or pierce with arrow this my wounded heart."
Knotting a noose in his slave's hand that lay;
He threw it up above without delay.
The lasso to the battlements made fast,
From bottom to the top he climbing passed.

And on the tower top as he sat there,
That fairy-face came and preferred her prayer.
As in each other's hands their hands they placed,
Upon the tow'r as if intoxicate they paced.
As to the lofty palace they came down,
She held his royal hand within her own.
Into the gold-decked house they downward came,
Down to the meeting-house of royal fame;
It was a Paradise all full of light,
Slave maidens stood there fronting *Huris* bright.
And Sám's son, *Zalzar*, stood bewildered there,
And saw that stature and that glorious hair,
With bracelet, collar, in her ear the ring,
Jewelled, brocaded like a mead in spring.
Mead tulips were her two cheeks to behold
With clustering ringlets falling fold on fold.
And *Zál*, as well, in all his kingly grace,
By that resplendent moon there took his place.
A jewelled dagger in his belt he bore,
Whilst on his head a ruby crown he wore.
Rudábah, seeing him in unrest burned,
Then stealthily her eye towards him turned.
That form she saw with royal splendour girt,
That mace that treated the hard rock as dirt,
That brilliant cheek that lit of life the store,
And as she longer looked she burnt the more.
With wine to drink, with kiss and with embrace,
Will not the lion, then, the wild ass chase?
The king with that moon-face his talk renewed:
"O thou of musk-scent, cypress silver-hued,
When Manúchehr shall come to hear the tale,
To flout the matter he will never fail:
Sám, son of Nairam, too, will raise a cry,
Will spit at me, his anger raging high.
My body and my soul I do not prize:

Willing, I'd wear a shroud and these despise.
And with the just Creator I agree
That I will never break my pledge with thee.
Going to God, will I His praises sing,
As those who worship supplication bring,
That the king's heart and Sám's he'll wash aright,
Cleanse them of anger and all strife and spite.
May the Creator to any words agree,
That openly my bride thou mayest be!"
Rudábah said to him: "I, too, believe
Faith and religion both from Him receive.
Of my word the Creator witness be,
Never shall there be monarch over me
But Sam Zalzar, of this world the Athlete,
For throne and grandeur who alone is meet."
Loving each other, they together drew,
Reason departing as their longing grew.
And this went on until the dawn had come,
And in the camp awoke the kettle-drum.
Farewell to that moon-faced one Zal then bade,
His form the web and her the woof he made.
On their eyelashes hot tears formed a cloud,
And to the sun these words they cried aloud:
"O glory of the earth, awhile delay:
Come not too quickly now to plague the day."
Perchance of love these who endured the pain,
By sight might from their hearts remove the chain.
Zal from above the lasso casting loose,
Came down from off the palace by the noose.
The shining sun appeared above the hill,
The warriors assembled, trooping still.
They saw the Pehlavan early in the day,
And from the place went quickly on their way.
The king then sent a messenger to call
Those who were wise, to there assemble all.

The next section contains an account of a letter sent by Zal to Sam, and its receipt by the latter. Having received and read it, Sam falls asleep with the idea that God will instruct him as to what he should do, and there follows the Section translated below:

The Consultation of the Mobeds in the Matter of Zál and the Letter, and Sending him an Answer.

When he arose from sleep, of Mobeds then
He held a meeting with the wisest men.
He opened speech with one the stars who knew,
"What would the end be," asked he, "in thy view?
Water and fire gems too together bring
Would at the bottom be a cruel thing.
Just as hereafter on the Judgment Day,
Zuhak and Faridun would have their fray.
Consult the stars and give me your reply:
Point with the end to happy augury."
For a long time the astrologers retired,
And of the secret from the heav'ns enquired.
They come to him and with a smile disclose,
From his own fortune there have come two foes.*
"Of Zal and Mehrab's daughter news we bear;
For they together are a happy pair.
A raging elephant the two shall have,
Who'll gird his loins, and who shall grow up brave,
With sword the world beneath his feet will bring,
And on the clouds set up his throne as king.
From earth of wicked men he'll hew the feet,
No cave left on the earth for their retreat.
Sagsar, Mázandaran, shall be no more:
With heavy mace he'll sweep of earth the floor.

*This is a literal translation, but the passage is unintelligible.

Turan through him much evil will betide,
But for Iran's great benefits provide.
Of ailing ones the head will he give sleep,
The door closed 'gainst pain and mischief keep:
Iranîs all in hope on him will sing,
And to the Pehlavan good news he'll bring.
To fight his war-steed will course on with grace,
On him the fighting panther rub its face.
All fighting elephants and lions fierce,
That Pehlavan's unwieldy mace shall pierce.
Happy shall be the kingdom while he reigns,
And on its record, time his name retains."
Of the astrologers the words he heard,
The praise accepting that they then preferred.
He gave them silver without stint and gold,
In time of terror who had made him bold.
The envoy sent by Zal then summoning,
Converse he held with him on many a thing.
He said: "Go, tell him in a pleasant way,
That this mad wish of his will never pay.*
But as I have already pledged my word,
Plea for injustice now cannot be heard.
Be at thy ease, the matter closely hide,
So at this time that none may know beside.
And I, behold, this night will I proceed,
And tow'rds Irán's land will my army lead.
There shall I know what order gives the king,
And to what end the matter God will bring."
Dirams he to the envoy gave away
And said: "Arise, thy road take nor delay."
Dismissing him, he stood upon the way,
The king and army happy were and gay.
A thousand of the *Karagsars* they bind,
And lead on foot, despised the force behind.

*A slang phrase, but exactly suited to the occasion.

Of the dark night two-thirds came to a close,
As from the plain the horseman's shout arose.
The beat of drums and wailing of the horn
From the camp's guardroom to the ear were borne.
The leader towards Iran his forces drew,
And Dehistan the army coming knew.
Blessed by good fortune and with omens good,
Proceeding, near to Zal his envoy stood:
Coming, he gave Sam's message that he had,
And Zal rejoicing heard it and was glad.
To God thanksgiving did then Zal accord
That he such gifts and fortune should afford.
Alms he distributed among the poor;
Gave favour to his people more and more.
And called for Sám all blessings down from heav'n
For the glad message that he thus had giv'n.
He had no rest by day, no sleep at night,
He drank no wine, indulged in no delight;
Of wife desirous as his heart became,
He spoke of nothing but Rudabah's name.

Síndukht becomes aware of the infatuation of Rudabah and Zal, and her delight at it. (This woman appears to have been the mother of Rudábah).

A woman bringing Zal's presents comes to her and is assaulted by her in ignorance of her errand. Rudábah, however, sets matters to rights, and Sindukht dismisses the go-between kindly. This Section is not translated. the next is headed:

Mehráb becomes aware of the infatuation of Zal and Rudábah. He is enraged at it, but is brought round by Síndukht.

Mehrab rejoicing from the Court came back,
For Zal in speaking of him did not lack.
The worthy Sindukht there asleep he found,

Pale-cheeked, her heart disturbed with rage profound.
He questioned her and said: "What ails thee, say—
Why do thy rosy cheeks thus fade away?"
Him answering, thus Sindukht gave reply:
"My heart endures a lengthened agony.
This wealth and treasure that we here have laid,
These Arab horses in their pride arrayed,
This peopled palace and this garden's round,
Our happy friends with whom our hearts are bound:
These slaves who all before the king lie down,
This royal residence and kingly crown;
These features, and this cypress-gait erect,
This knowledge, reputation, intellect:
With all this splendour and this truthful way,
From time to time that undergoes decay,
All this must we surrender to our foe,
And but as wind our labour learn to know.
A narrow box will but for us remain,
A tree whose medicine is but our bane.
We planted and we watered it with care,
Hung crown and treasure on its branches there.
It shot up soon, and boughs around it thrust,
Its broad head then was levelled with the dust.
This will our ending be and such our gain;
I know not where repose we shall obtain."
To Sindukht thus Mehráb his answer told:
"Thou bringest forth as new what is but old.
For of this fleeting world this is the way:
One is depised, at ease one in his day.
One comes within, another passes by:
Whom hast thou seen that fate did not destroy?
Grief from the heart will mourning never drive,
And with the Just One we can never strive."
Sindukht replied to him: "The words I say
The true exhibit in another way.

Such secrets how can one conceal from thee,
And matters weighty as can ever be?
A Mobed wise, whom wisdom did not fail,
Once to his son told of a tree the tale.
I tell the tale so that in wisdom's way
The king may to my words attention pay."
Low'ring her head, she bent that cypress high
And moisture poured out from that rose-red eye.
"Around us does not now revolve the sphere
As we would have it, thou of wisdom clear.
Know that in secret ev'ry kind of net
This son of Sám has for Rudábah set;
Her pure heart from the road has turned aside.
Thou should'st for us some remedy provide.
I gave her counsel, but without avail;
Her heart is darkened and her cheeks are pale.
Of sorrow full her heart and pain I see,
Her lip is dry and she sighs heavily."
When Mehráb heard this to his feet he leapt,
His hand upon his sword-hilt tightly kept.
His body trembled and his cheek grew blue,
Heart full of blood, his cold lips sighs indrew.
He cried aloud: "Now for Rudábah's sake
The very earth a stream of blood I'll make."
This Síndukht saw and leapt upon her feet,
Around his waist she made her two hands meet.
She said aloud to him: "Thy servant hear,
Give to my words awhile attentive ear.
Act then just as thy wisdom may decide,
Let reason now and judgment be thy guide."
He turned and threw her with his hand aside.
Like raging elephant aloud he cried:
"As soon to me as was a daughter born,
Her head I from her body should have shorn.
I slew her not in my ancestors' way,

And now on me this sharp trick did she play.
The son who may his father's modes forsake,
Not as his father's son the brave will take.
Akin to this a panther once declared,
His sharp claw for the conflict full prepared:
He said: 'I am with hope of battle fired;
And my forefathers, too, this way inspired.
A father's signs should in the son be still,
Nor should there be in him a lesser skill.
There may be fear for life, of honour lack:
Why from the conflict dost thou hold me back?
Should hero Sam, or Manuchehr, should he,
Prevailing, now obtain the victory,
From Kábul smoke shall rise up to the sun,
It shall be waste, no harvest shall be won."
Thus to the Governor did Sindukht say:
"Let not thy tongue loose in this evil way,
For Sam, the horseman, is of this aware.
At heart be not thou anxious or have care.
Sám back from Kargasar is on his way,
Secret no more, 'tis open to the day."
To her of moon-like face Mehráb replied:
"No word of crookedness be on thy side.
The Kai himself must this accord and say:
'The dust must of the wind confess the sway.
Security from ill if thou obtain,
Myself I shall not trouble at this pain.
In this both small and great will all agree,
Than Sam, no son-in-law could better be.
With Sam alliance should we now acquire,
From Kandahar to Ahoaz none were high'r.'"
Sindukht replied: "O thou of high degree,
For crookedness there's no necessity.
'Tis clear that ill to thee must give me pain,
And if thy heart's distressed 'twill be my chain.

Twas this that ever in my heart I nursed.
And such was my suspicion from the first.
Thus sleeping hast thou seen me in my grief,
No gladness in my heart to give relief.
If this should happen, strange it would not be,
Nor should it bring such evil thoughts to thee.
In Yaman's Sarv did Faridun rejoice;
Seeking a world thus Sam, too, made his choice.
When fire and water, wind and earth unite,
Then turns the dark face of the world to light."
Síndukht from Mehráb's ear attention claimed,
Though full of hate his heart, his head inflamed.
Bringing the latter's answer then, she said:
"Happy, thy wishes to completion led.
When relative a stranger thou shalt find,
Dark of thy enemy shall grow the mind."
Then Síndukht ordered he of high degree:
"Go, bring Rudábah quickly here to me."
But Síndukht, of that savage man afraid,
Lest in the dust Rudábah should be laid.
And of that Paradise-resembling mead
The face of Kábul should be void indeed,
Said to him: "First by oath thyself be bound
That thou wilt give her to me safe and sound."
From him exacting thus an oath severe,
She made his heart from trace of passion clear.
To Síndukht then he gave his word anew,
That to Rudábah no harm he would do.
"The monarch of the land, behold!" he said,
"Will, full of anger, turn from us his head.
She'll be bereft of parents, land and all,
Low will Rudábah and the stream both fall."*
When Síndukht heard this, she bent low her head,
And in the dust her face before him laid.

* There is a pun here on the words Rudábah and Rúdah.

Then to her daughter coming, smiling light,
Open her cheeks as day beneath the night.
"The warlike panther," this the news conveyed,
"From the wild ass his claw aside has laid.
Mehrab to God who is for evermore,
An oath of great severity now swore.
His rage should not disturb a single hair,
Upon the body of that moon-faced fair.
Prepare thy ornaments and quickly go,
And utter to thy father all thy woe."
Rudábah said: "What jewels dost thou call?
What is a worthless thing to capital?
On Sám's son as my spouse my mind is bent,
And why conceal that which is evident?"
She to her sire went like the Eastern sun,
In gold and rubies drowned that she had on.
Of paradise a beauty fair to see,
In pleasant spring as the bright sun was she.
Her father at her beauty stood amazed,
And called upon his Maker as he praised.
He said: "O thou whose brain of reason's free,
How will the excellent in this agree;
That Pari should to Ahriman be mate,
And neither crown nor ring should thee await?
And a snake-charmer of Kahtani's plain,
With arrow should, a *Magh** become, be slain."
And when Rudábah heard her sire's reply,
Burnt up with shame became her cheek and eye.
Upon her tearful eye then she let fall
Her eyelash black, and hardly breathed at all.
The sire's heart full of rage, his head of war,
As savage panther he began to roar.
The daughter went away, herself beside,
Her cheeks of saffron hue with blood were dyed.
Above the sole asylum to their view,
In God both mother and the daughter knew.

* A Magian or priest.

The becoming aware by Manuchehr of the Alliance of Zal and Rudábah, his sorrow thereat, and his sending Naozar to bring Sam.

To the supreme king then the news there came,
Of Mehrab and of Dastan Sam of fame,
Of Zal's love and Mehrab's alliance fair,
And of that noble and unrivalled pair.
Between that monarch of exalted race
And Mobeds talk of all sorts there took place.
The monarch said then to those who were wise:
"Fortune seems hard and bitter to my eyes.
From lions' and from panthers' claws Iran,*
We have by prudence and by war withdrawn.
The world of Zuhák Faridun has cleared,
Of whose seed Mehráb of Kábul was reared.
And through the love of Zal it were not well
A plant so beaten down should now excel.
From Mehráb's daughter and of Sám the son,
Out of its sheath were now a sharp sword won.
From us on one side he would not descend,
And with his medicine would poison blend.
And if he leant towards his mother's side,
But evil words would in his head abide;
On Iran's land would he cast woe and pain,
That crown and wealth might come to him again.
Now tell me by your counsel what to do,
That so the matter I may carry through.

* Pronounced Irawn.

And make ye no delay, that I may see
Within my noose that proud one speedily.
Now to these words what answer do ye give?
Strive that good counsel I may now receive."
The Mobeds of him now the praises sing,
And call him of religion pure the king.
They said: "More learned art thou, far, than we,
More capable in all that now should be.
In ev'rything with wisdom do thy part,
For wisdom will destroy the dragon's heart."
Now when the worthy king had heard their say,
To settle the affair he sought a way.
Thither he ordered Naozar to repair,
With his near friends and with his nobles there,
"Now tow'rds the horseman Sam proceed," he said,
"And ask him in the war how he has sped;
Then seeing, tell him that he here must come,
And from us he may go on to his home."
That king, enlightened, rose without delay,
And with his friends proceeded on the way.
Tow'rds Nariman's son Sam their faces turned,
With raging elephants for war that burned.
When of the matter Sam became aware,
That king's son to receive he bade prepare
Then to receive him all the nobles come,
With raging elephant and sounding drum.
To Sam, the horseman, all of them then came,
The great ones all, with Naozar, too, of fame.
Each other to consult they all began,
The valiant noble and the prudent man.
They sat down after this upon the mead,
And spoke to ev'ry one that had the need.
Then Naozar gave the royal word he had;
The hero seeing him at heart was glad.
Answer he gave: "The order I obey,

And seeing him my heart will then make gay."
As guests of Sám they all that day remained,
And at the sight of him all pleasure gained.
They laid the food trays, and the bowls they seized,
And called the name of Manúchehr, well pleased.
Of Naozar, Sám and Chiefs on ev'ry hand,
They asked for good news out of ev'ry land.
With merriment the night came to a close;
Revealing secrets, the bright sun arose.
The sound of drums awoke the gate outside,
And camels forward came of rapid stride.
Tow'rds Manúchehr's palace then without delay,
They took by his command their forward way.
When Manúchehr of this became aware,
His Royal diadem did he prepare.
From Sári and from Amul rose a cry,
As of the ocean with waves running high.
Those armed with javelins then all advance,
Clothed in their breastplates, and with heavy lance.
From one hill to the next the army spread,
Shields interlaced, the yellow and the red.
With brazen cymbal, and the drum and reed,
The treasure elephant, the Arab steed.
On this wise came the great ones him to meet,
Their banners flying as the drums they beat.

The Coming of Sam to Manúchehr, his relation of the events of the War in Mázandarán, and the Despatch by Manúchehr of Sám to War with Mehrab.

When to the palace he came now more near,
The king, dismounting, made the road more clear.
When of the world the monarch showed his face,
The king the ground before him kissed with grace.
Rose Manúchehr from off his ivory throne,

Of brilliant rubies, on his head a crown.
Sam tow'rds the crown as near himself he drew
The praise he gave him that was justly due.
Then of Mazandaran and Kargasir,
And of the Divs who were inured to war,
He asked him much and with all care enquired,
The General told him all that he desired.
"O king, may'st thou this life for ever know!
Far from thy life be evil from thy foe!
I to the city of those demons went:
Divs are they? Lions fierce on conflict bent!
Than Arab horses are they far more fleet,
Than warriors of Iran more brave to meet.
The soldiers whom the people call Sagsár,
Them panthers reckon they more fierce in war.
Of my arrival when the news they heard,
When by my rumour all their brains were stirred,
Within the town they raised a wailing shout,
And afterwards passed from the city out.
A mighty force, from hill to hill so wide
As with its dust the shining day to hide.
Towards me all they came, prepared for fight,
And ran together bravely in their might.
Trembled the earth and darkened was the day,
A hill behind, a cave before them lay.
Fear on this army fell, nor could I see
For this how to provide a remedy.
On me had fallen what there was to do:
I shouted at the army of the foe.
I lifted of three hundred *mans** my mace,
And urged my iron steed on to the chase.
Forward I went and battered out their brain,
And through my terror void became their brain.†

*A Persian weight equal to an Indian maund.

†A poor line, but exactly with the original.

Casting a hundred down with ev'ry thrust,
My mace crushed at each blow a Dív to dust.
Just as a fawn before a lion male.
All fled before my bull-head, turning pale.
The grandson of king Salam of great name
Fierce as a raging wolf before me came.
This youth ambitious they Karkúi call,
Of fair face he, and as a cypress tall.
He by his mother was of Zuhak's seed,
And proud men's heads he, too, as dirt could knead.
His troops as ants and locusts in their flight,
Desert and mountain disappeared from sight.
Above their army as the thick dust flew,
The faces of our warriors paler grew,
And when on high I raised my one-blow mace,
I left the army lying in the place.
I from my saddle raised a cry so shrill,
That the earth seemed to them a grinding-mill.
My army then again plucked up their heart,
And in the battle strove to do their part.
Karkúi heard then of my voice the sound,
My mace that beat down heads upon the ground;
As raging elephant he came to me.
For fight a long noose in his hand held he;
To seize me with his lasso with intent.
This seen, from mischief's road aside I bent,
And seizing in my hand my royal bow,
My arrows with their spears of steel to throw,
I urged against him my swift eagle steed,
And at him shot like fire the arrow's reed.
I thought that I the anvil of his head
Had to his helmet sewn as if with thread.
Like a mad elephant through dust I pored,
And found him coming with an Indian sword.
The thought, O king, into my fancy came

That ev'n the hill from him would quarter claim.
Onward he rushed in haste. and I the while
Waited within my grasp him to beguile.
From horseback stretching out my hand in haste
I seized the valiant warrior by the waist,
Threw him like raging elephant to dust,
The Indian sword into his middle thrust.
And as thus to the ground despised he fell,
His army from the battle turned as well.
To hill and desert, high both and below
In crowds together fled away the foe.
And there were reckoned, fallen as they lay,
Twice thirty thousand horse and foot that day.
Of soldiers, citizens and warlike horse,
Three hundred thousand men were in that force.
And out of these war captives there became
Twelve thousand officers of mark and name.
Those who wish evil to thy fortune's day,
Against its worshippers what do they weigh?"
And when the king heard what the General said,
He raised up to the moon his crownèd head.
His ear fear passed from as does day from night,
And disappeared behind the hill of light.
Of wine the feast prepared and jollity,
From mischief of his foes the world grew free.
With entertainment they make short the night,
And in the General's praises all unite.
The tent-screen raised as night was turned to day,
The king near to approach they made a way.
Thus Sám, the General of warlike fame
To Manúchehr, the monarch, forward came.
Peerless, the king to praise he did not fail,
And of Mehráb and Zál began the tale.
But interrupting, him the king addressed
And words of sternness upon him impressed.

Thus said to Sám, then, of the world the king:
"Out of the great ones warriors chosen bring.
Tow'rds Hindustán thy face with fire now turn.
Of Mehráb of Kábul the palace burn.
That he doth not escape thee, be thou ware,
For of the dragon's seed alone he's there.
Cries in the world he's ever raising still,
And will the earth with war and tumult fill;
And ev'ry one that is with him allied,
Or to Zuhák, the sorcerer, is tied.
His body from his head must severed be,
Of him and of his friends the earth washed free."
To him when thus the king displayed his rage,
No more in talk with him durst he engage.
To him, he answered: "I will do my part,
Of rage that may be cleared the monarch's heart."
He kissed thereon the great throne of the king;
His cheek rubbed on his seal and on his ring,
And with his steeds that beat the wind in pace,
Turned with his army towards home his face.

The becoming aware by Zál of Sám's Coming to War with Mehráb and his restraining him from it.

To Mehráb and Dastán the news arrived,
Of plans by General and the king contrived.
In Kabul's town excitement rising high,
Of anguish came from Zuhák's hall a cry.
Síndukht, Mehráb, Rudábah, from each one
All hope of life and property was gone.
Shouting came out, then, Zál from Kábul's town,
His arm stretched out and his lip hanging down.
Aloud he cried: "Should dragon, fierce and stern
With fiery breath, come here the world to burn,
Before the land of Kábul they obtain,

My very head must they first cut in twain,"
With bleeding heart he tow'rds his father went,
On speech his head, on thought his heart intent.
Of this the news when Sám the mighty knew,
That his lion's whelp himself towards him drew,
All of his army rose up from their place,
And fluttered Faridun's flag in its grace.
Sounded the drums in salutation meet,
Sám and the army marching him to greet,
The backs of elephants in colours set
Of red and yellow and of violet.
To Sam afar as Dastán came in view,
His golden bridle he toward him drew,
Until Zalzar, the brave, approached him near,
Then in his face, his height, he found good cheer.
And when Sam's Dastan saw his father's face,
He quickened, 'lighting from his horse, his pace.
The nobles in two rows, too, 'lighted down,
The generals both, and those who served the crown:
Zál kissed the ground in salutation due.
Into long converse Sam his son then drew.
His Arab steed remounted Zal, the bold,
That like a hill seemed shining as with gold.
His nobles all then came before him there,
To talk and tell him of their anxious care:
"With thee thy father now has angry grown;
Be not thou proud, but for thy fault atone."
"I have no fear," to them he answer gave,
"For man at last there's nothing but the grave.
Good sense should now my father call to aid.
And vain words on each other not be laid,
Ere words of passion from his tongue arise,
Ashamed, he'll pour the hot tears from his eyes."
Thus it went on till to Sam's palace gate,
With open hearts and minds they came elate.

The horseman Sám then from his steed descends,
And for his son at once in audience sends.
When Zalzar came before his sire the king,
He kissed upon the ground and stretched his wing,*
The great and glorious hero Sám he praised,
And from his cheek with tears the rose† erased.
" May thy alert heart joy for ever see !
Thy soul of justice e'er the servant be.
The diamond from thy sword be ever bright,
And the earth weep when thou art in the fight!
Where thy steed in the battle proudly rears,
Active the army only then appears.
Thy whistling mace when sees the anxious sphere,
'Twill in the sky not let the stars appear.
The world entire is through thy justice green,
On wisdom based is thy foundation seen.
Rejoicing in thy justice all mankind,
Both earth and time in thee their justice find.
Though I to thee by kinship am allied,
To me alone thy justice is denied.
A bird that eats the dust has nourished me,
None with me in the world at strife can be.
No single fault I in myself perceive,
That any one should give me cause to grieve.
Save this, that Sám, the hero, is my sire,
My rank through my descent is no way high'r.
When I was born thou castedst me away,
And didst me helpless on the mountain lay.
When born thou broughtest on me trouble dire
And as I grew didst cast me on the fire.
I knew no cradle and of milk no breast,
And of no loving friend was I possessed.
To the hill carried I was thrown apart,

*As a bird does when it is at ease.

†The rose colour of his cheeks.

Ease, luxury, were rooted from my heart.
With the Creator thou wast e'er at war,
As to whence white and whence black colours are?
But now the world's Creator nourished me,
And with His own eye God deigns me to see.
I've virtue, manliness, a hero's sword;
The Kabul chief me friendship doth accord.
Throne has he, treasure, and a heavy mace,
Wit, zeal, and men whose lofty heads crowns grace.
By thy command as I at Kabul dwell,
Thy counsel and thy oath I keep as well.
Thou said'st that thou would'st never injure me,
Would'st bring to fruit as thou didst plant my tree.
Gifts from Mázandarán did'st thou present,
And com'st from Kargasír with this intent.
The home to ruin where I now abide,
Such is the justice thou dost me provide.
Lo, then! Before thee here I helpless stand;
My living body's in thy angry hand.
Into two pieces cut me with a sword,
But as to Kabul say not thou a word.
Though Mehrab and Kabul are neath thy sway,
Thou canst not with thy promise do away.
What has he done, and what fault dost thou trace,
That thou tow'rds him dost turn an angry face?
As I might wish, didst thou again declare,
That thou would'st make me famous ev'rywhere.
Do what thou wilt, for in thy hand 'twill be;
What ill to Kabul's done is done to me!"
The monarch heard all that he had to hear,
Lowered his arm and leant to Zál his ear.
He said to him: "It is so, it is true,
And to its truth thy tongue bears witness, too,
My doings tow'rds thee all injustice show,
The heart rejoicing thus of every foe.

What thou hast wished of me didst thou demand,
And with an anxious heart hast left thy land."
Thus with soft words the valiant Sám replied.
"But now, O lion's whelp, in ease abide.
Be not too keen, till remedy I see,
Thy market soon will I make brisk for thee.
Now will I write a letter to the king,
And by thy skilful hand to him will bring.
Perchance the king to the right road again
Will come, and at this tale his hate restrain.
And when he sees thy face and virtue too,
He will not wish thee injury to do.
All needful things will we bring to his mind;
His heart towards justice now shall be inclined.
And if assistance from our God is won,
According to thy wish shall all be done.
The lion ever strives with all his strength,
And gains in ev'ry place his prey at length.
Would it might happen just as thou hast said,
And all accomplished be from base to head!"

Mehráb's Anger at Síndukht, and her Going to Sám, with Regard to the Marriage of Zál and Rudábah.

(A Section is here omitted relating to the sending of Sám's letter to Manúchehr by the hand of Zál).

The rumour of these things in Kábul spread,
And filled with anger was the warden's* head.
With fury raging, for Síndukht he sent,
Rage at Rudábah upon her to vent.
He said to her: "There is no other way;
(Against the world's king I can never stay)
To take thee with that girl of impure faith,
And in the Council put you both to death.

*Mehrab.

The king may thus his anger turn aside,
And on the land repose and peace abide.
In Kábul who with Sám can e'er contend,
Or who before his heavy mace not bend?"
This hearing, Síndukht pondering sat there,
And sought some remedy with anxious care.
Out of her heart a remedy she brought,
For quick of sight was she and keen of thought;
Then crossing on her breast her arms she ran,
And to the sunlike king to speak began.
She said: "Now listen to one word from me,
And then do that which fittest thou may'st see.
Money thou hast; if thou desire to live,
The night is frequent with events—five, five?
Although the night be long, thou may'st be sure,
That darkness will for ever not endure.
When the sun rises, 'twill be day again;
Like Badakshan once more will be the plain."
Mehrab replied to her: "These tales of old,
Of warriors in the midst, should not be told.
Say what thou know'st: to strike for life prepare,
A bloody shirt if thou would'st now not wear."
"O mighty king!" to him thus Sindukht said:
"It may not need that thou my blood should'st shed,
For I to Sám myself must needs proceed,
From sheath to draw this sword as I have need.
I must then tell him what is right to tell:
Wisdom will ripen my crude words as well.
Wealth on thy side and pain of soul to me:
Wealth must thou give me now abundantly."
"Here is the key, behold!" Mehrab then cried:
"By lack of cash and gems we are not tried.
Go, then: slaves, horses, throne and crown prepare,
These with thyself upon the road to bear.
For us to Kábul Sam will not set light:

Withered through us, it will again grow bright."
Thus said Síndukht then to the famous king:
"Compared with life think wealth a trifling thing.
And while myself I seek a remedy,
Too hard upon Rudábah do not be.
But for her life in this world I've no fear,
And thou this day art surety for it here.
This sorrow for myself I do not bear,
For her alone have I this grief and care."
She took an oath him stringently to bind,
Then bravely went a remedy to find.
Her body she adorned with gold brocade,
Whilst pearls and rubies on her head she laid.
Three hundred thousand *dinárs* then she found,
From Mehrab's treasury to strew the ground.
Ten valuable horses there,
Gold saddled, fifty slaves gold belts that wear.
With golden bits she thirty horses sought,
From Persia both and from Arabia brought.
With golden collars sixty slaves there stand,
Each one with golden goblet in his hand,
Full of musk, camphor, rubies and of gold,
One filled with wine, and sugar one to hold.
With forty lofty thrones of gold brocade,
With varied gems their fringes interlaid.
Two hundred swords of gold and silver made,
Fine-tempered, glittering each Indian blade.
A hundred female camels, red of hue,
And loads to bear a hundred roadsters, too.
A crown that many royal jewels deck,
An armlet, ear-ring, collar for the neck.
The sphere resembling, too, of gold a throne,
With many kinds of jewels woven on.
Its breadth of royal cubits was a score,
Than a tall horseman's, too, its height was more.

Of Indian elephants, too, there were four;
These creatures huge both clothes and carpets bore.
This all completed, she a horse bestrode,
Azar-gushasp* like, as a warrior rode.
Upon her head a Rúmi helmet placed,
Her steed beneath her as the swift wind paced.
Thus moving grandly to Sám's Court she came,
In silence riding, and she gave no name.
To those acquainted with the thing she told:
"Go quickly: say ye to that ruler bold,
An envoy now has come from Kábul here,
To Zábul's hero to a message bear,
From valiant Mehráb here a word to bring,
To the world-conquering Sám, the hero king."
The curtain-keeper to the hero went,
And for an audience with her brought consent.
And Síndukht then alighting from her horse,
Betook herself to Sám in graceful course.
She kissed the ground and praise began to sing
Of that world Pehlaván and mighty king.
Slaves, horses, offerings, elephants of state,
Extended for two miles outside the gate.
She brought them there to Sám, and as he gazed,
The Pehlaván was at the sight amazed.
With head hung low and arms crossed on his chest,
He sat as one drunk, with his thoughts oppressed.
He thought: "When such great wealth there seems to be,
Why should they send a woman here to me?"
His head was lowered and he breathed no more;
To think on great or small things he forbore.
"If all this wealth from her I should receive,
I shall the monarch of the people grieve.
If from before Zál I send back the thing,
As the Símúrgh will he stretch out his wing.

* The mythological Persian guardian of fire.

He will be troubled and annoyed with me;
What in the Council can my answer be?"
When through Sám's mind thus many thoughts had passed,
To this conclusion came he at the last.
His head uplifting: "All this wealth," he cried,
"These slaves, these elephants arrayed in pride,
Go ye, and in the name of Kábul's moon
Convey them to Zal's treasuries full soon."
Before Sám, Síndukht of the Pari face
Was glad at heart, and her tongue found its place.
Accepted all those presents, she might say
The good had come and evil passed away.
There were three idol-faced ones with her there,
Of cypress stature and as jasmine fair;
A cup they held in ev'ry hand at rest,
Filled with red rubies, pearls from oysters pressed
And these, all mixed together on the floor,
Before the Pehlaván they 'gan to pour.
This saw the Pehlaván, in wisdom bright,
And praise began to give her, as 'twas right.
When with him matters thus they brought to end
Out of the house did they all strangers send.
And to the Pehlaván then Síndukht said:
"Young through thy counsel grows the aged head.
In thee the great ones wisdom gain aright,
And give through thee the gloomy earth its light.
Thy justice e'er the bad man's hand restrains,
Open the road of God thy mace maintains.
'Tis with Mehráb, if any fault there lies,
With hearts' blood wet the lashes of his eyes.
Of Kábul's innocents what did the chief,
That thou must bring him to the dust in grief?
The very dust they worship of thy feet;
And live but in thy service to compete.

Fear Him who has created mind and force,
Through Whom Sun, Nahid shine along their course.
Though on thy part his deeds are not approved,
Gird not thy loins; to shed blood be not moved.
Of us and thee the Lord there is but one;
Against our God no contest can be won.
Outside our worship there but idols are,
In Kabul, Hindustán or China far.
The bright fire thou in all thy worship seek,
Thou know'st in this that I no falsehood speak.
In serving both an evil road ye trod,
But as for us our hope is but in God.
Thou know'st to shed blood's not the rightful way,
Nor with the lives of innocents to play."
Then did to her the hero Sam command:
"Make no excuse, but answer my demand?
Art Mehráb's slave or art thou e'en as he?
His daughter in what place did *Zalzar* see?
To me her face, her hair, her temper tell;
For whom, too, she is fitted say as well.
Her looks, her stature, and her dignity,
As thou hast seen them, one by one tell me."
"O Pehlavan!" to him Sindukht replied:
Thou chief of Athletes, and of heroes pride:
I ask a stringent oath first at thy hand,
At which may tremble both the sea and land,
That thou wilt do my life no injury,
Nor harm to anyone who's dear to me.
Both palace and a peopled hall have I
Treasure and friends, on whom I can rely.
When I am safe, say what thou hast in mind,
And telling thee in this my honour find.
All Kabul's treasure that e'er hidden lay
To *Zábul* I'll endeavour to convey.
And, this beside, whate'er may fitting be

That Chieftain wise, too, shall obtain from me."
Both of her hands within his own Sam laid,
And gave the pledge that with an oath he made.
Now when Síndukht his solemn pledge had heard,
His truthful speech with oath that he preferred,
She kissed the ground and rose up on her feet,
And what was secret told him, as was meet.
"I, Athlete, to Zuhak am kin," said she:
"Mehráb, of brilliant soul, is wed to me.
Rudábah, of the moon-face, too, I bore,
Whom Zál would offer up his life before.
Before pure God my family and kin,
Till on the gloomy night bright day breaks in,
Engage themselves all night thy praise to sing,
As well as the world's lords, the mighty king.
Here am I come thine own desire to know,
In Kábul who thy friend is, who thy foe.
If we are criminals of evil race
And are not fitted for this royal place,
Behold me here, most wretched to be found ;
Thy victims kill, and bind those to be bound.
Hearts innocent in Kabul do not burn,
That out of darkness day to light may turn."
And when these words had reached the Athlete's ear,
He found the woman of a reason clear,
Of spring-like face, and like a cypress straight:
A reed-like waist, and with a pheasant's gait.
Thus he replied to her : "My pledge to thee
Is firm and true, though my life forfeit be.
So all in Kábul, ev'ryone thy friend,
May healthful be and joyous to the end,
And Zal, your wishes I reciprocate,
May in Rudabah find an equal mate.
And though ye may be of another race
This crown and glory ye will not disgrace.

Such is the world, and no shame in the end:
With the Creator one can not contend.
All He creates according to His will,
And we are ever in amazement still.
One is exalted, one is lying low;
Increase may one, another decrease know.
The one with increase may his heart adorn
Whilst tow'rds decrease another's may be borne.
And in the end dust is of all the place,
From ev'ry race that's gone there's sprung this race.
O lady of good counsel, list to me:
Reflect not nor with sorrow burdened be.
With thy affair myself I occupy,
With thy desire and thy distressful cry.
Thy wish and pain before him now to bring
I write a letter to the lofty king.
To Manúchehr *Zál-i-zar* now has gone,
Thou mightest say that he on wings has flown.
He sits as though no saddle he had found:
His charger's shoes seem not to touch the ground.
To *Zálzar* will the king now give reply,
And, if propitious, good advice supply.
For, by a bird brought up, sad heart he bears
His foot in mud that's moistened by his tears.
And should his bride's love be to his akin,
They both of them might leap out from their skin.*
That dragon-child's face once to me now show,
That I may see it and its value know.
Perhaps her hair and features when I see,
Her dignity may be approved by me."
An answer to the Pehlaván Síndukht thus gave:
" If thou wilt honour and rejoice thy slave,
Come to my palace, mounted on thy steed;
My head thus raise above the clouds indeed.

*A literal translation.

A king like thee to Kabul if we bring,
The lives of all will be thy offering."
Then Sam's lips full of smiles thus Sindukht saw,
And from his heart all sign of wrath withdraw.
As with a smile the brave Sám to her said:
"Fill not thy heart with ev'ry sort of dread.
As thou desirest, soon the thing will be."
This hearing, Sindukht made apology.
The place she left then with a happy mind,
Her cheek with joy to ruby red inclined.
With the wind's speed a courier took his way,
This happy news to Mehrab to convey.
"Thy dire forebodings think of now no more,
With glad heart lay in for a guest a store;
Behind the letter I am on my way,
And on the road for ought will not delay."
The second day the fountain of the sun
Out of its dream awoke its course to run,
The worthy Síndukht turned her smiling face
To the king's palace who was crowned with grace
And at Sam's palace gate appearing soon
(The people of all ladies called her moon)
She Sam approached and made to him her prayer,
And for some time held conversation there,
To go back home permission to obtain,
And glad to Kábul's king to go again;
To Mehráb then to show her promise new,
And for a new guest to make ready, too.
The hero Sam said to her: "Turn and go,
And all that thou hast seen to Mehráb show."
Out of his treasures bringing what was rare,
A fitting dress of honour they prepare,
This both on Mehrab's and on Sindukht's part,
And for Rudábah, charmer of the heart.
And at Kabul all else that Sám possessed,

Palace and garden, field with harvest blessed.
Four-footed beasts that to be milked are led,
For clothing cloth and carpets to be spread;
To Sindukht all he gave, her hand he drew,
And gave himself a pledge to her anew.
The girl, accepted, as she suited seemed;
For Zal's wife he Rudabah fitting deemed.
Two hundred men and warriors beside
He gave and told her: "Here no more abide.
Happy to live there, now to Kabul go,
And henceforth fear no evil from a foe."
That withered moon-face once again then bloomed,
And, by good fortune led, her way resumed.
As Zal tow'rds Manuchehr went on his way,
Of fortune that befell him hear the lay.

The coming of Zál to Manuchehr and giving him the letter from Sám.

Then to the king the tidings there came on
That Zal had come, of horseman Sam the son.
There went to meet him all the proud ones then,
All in the kingdom who were noted men.
As he approaching came the palace near,
They hastened tow'rds the king the road to clear.
When near the royal throne himself he found,
He uttered praises as he kissed the ground.
Awhile he laid upon the ground his face;
Then gave him all his heart the king in grace.
They brushed the dry dust from his face away,
And musk proceeded on his cheeks to lay.
The throne he mounted of the gracious king,
Who questioned him of this and many a thing.
"Upon this weary road of dust and wind
Thy way, O Pehlavan, how couldst thou find?"
"To thy good fortune all," he said, "belongs,

And all our pain is turned to joyful songs."
The Pehlavan's letter taking in the while,
From joy his soul betrayed a genial smile.
He read the letter, and to him replied:
"The sorrow of my heart is multiplied.
But in this letter grateful to the soul,
Writes Sám, the old man, of his heart the dole.
And though from this I am in woe and pain,
Of less or more, I will not think again.
The whole of thy desire will I fulfil,
For right thine aim is and for good thy will."
A golden dinner-tray the cooks then brought,
Where sitting-room the king with Zalzar sought.
He ordered all those famous in the day
To with the king be seated round the tray.
And on the viands there when they had fed
The wine upon another bench was spread.
And when Sám's son of wine had no more need,
He mounted on his golden-bridled steed.
Going, the long night to an end he brought,
With speech his lip full and his heart of thought.
With girded loins he started off at night
Tow'rds Manuchehr, victorious in fight.
Blessings on him invoked the king anew,
And praised him, when he went, in secret, too
He bade the Mobeds, who the stars could tell,
The wise ones, those who learning had as well,
To the king's throne they should themselves betake,
There of the sphere to due enquiry make.
They went away and struggled long in pain
To try their secret from the stars to gain.
To solve the matter three whole days they sought
Then Rumi tables* in their hand they brought.
Loos'ning their tongue, they to the monarch said:

* Astronomical tables.

"With rolling sphere we've calculation made.
From the stars' omens doth it now appear,
That the bright water will be running clear.
From Mehrab's daughter and Sam's son," they said,
"A noted and great hero shall be bred.
A hero powerful will come to birth;
With none beneath the sky like him on earth.
His life shall, be assured, be very long,
Bright, moderate shall he be, and also strong.
In arm and brain he capable shall be,
In war and feast none may his equal see;
And where his steed shall even wet his hide,
His heart who strives with him will soon be dried
Eagles above his helmet will not mount,
The heroes of the world as nought he'll count.
Of lofty stature shall he be and bold,
And lions in his lasso's noose shall hold.
A wild ass roasting on the fire he'll keep,
And with his sword the air shall cause to weep.
Servant of kings, loin-girded shall he be;
In him their refuge Iran's horsemen see.
His love shall ever be towards Iran,
And he will e'er wage war against Turán.
And of Irán's king's heart to be possessed,
With Rúm and China will he take no rest."
At these words Manuchehr rejoiced again:
His heart was freed then from its former pain.
And in reply to them thus said the king:
"Whatever you have said, conceal the thing."
Zál's presence near him then the king required,
And many other things of him enquired.
That other matters might be clearly seen,
Matters as yet concealed behind a screen,
Mobeds of intellect together came
With Zal and many prudent men of fame.

A translation of the next four Sections is omitted. They contain an account of Zal's being tested by the Mobeds as to his ability by having certain riddles put to him and his answering them satisfactorily, and a further Section in which he shows his prowess before Manuchehr in an encounter with some of the latter's warriors. The next Section contains

The Return of Zal with Manuchehr's Answer, and Sam's Giving Information to Mehrab.

The king an answer to the letter wrote
In happy terms and wonderful to quote:
"O valiant Pehlavan, of great renown.
Lion who all with victory dost crown,
No one like thee beholds the rolling sphere,
At fight, at feast, in love and counsel clear.
Now has thy son Zal, of auspicious rein,
Whose memory the world will long retain,
Come here. I know now all of his desire,
And what his counsel and his peace require.
The Pehlavan's letter has come to me here,
As I have heard it with a spirit clear.
I now have granted thee thy whole desire,
To Zal such mind's peace as he may require;
His hopes bestowing on him none the less,
Have counted to him years of happiness.
To lion who has panthers for his prey
What can be born but lion fierce in fray?
I have dismissed him happy in his mind,
May evil from his foe him never find!"
Thus Zal-i-zar came out with joy and glee,
And high above his heroes towered he.
Forward a message did to Sam they bring:
"With heart rejoiced I come back from the king

With royal dress of honour and a crown,
With bracelet, collar and an ivory throne."
These words the Pehlavan rejoiced in truth
So that his aged head renewed its youth.
To Kábul he a messenger sent fast
To tell Mehrab of all that there had passed.
"As soon as Zal-i-zar shall come to me,
As it becomes us, we will come to thee."
The envoy took to Kábul quick his way:
The king heard from him what he had to say.
Rejoiced the monarch of Kabulistán,
At that alliance with Zabulistan,
As if his soul a dead man should regain,
Or an old man become a youth again.
To give their souls, thou'd'st said, all men prepare,
From each place as they summoned minstrels there.
Mehrab, rejoicing thus, his soul was clear,
With smiling lip his heart was of good cheer.
Worthy Sindukht to him then calling near,
Many soft words he whispered in her ear.
He said to her: "O wife of happy thought,
Thy counsel to this dark place light has brought.
Thou hast thy hand extended to a branch,
To which earth's kings shall in their praise be staunch.
Thou from the first thyself to this did lend,
And should'st now seek for it a perfect end.
Ready before thee all my treasures lie,
My throne, my crown, and all my property."
Síndukht went back when she had heard this thing,
Before her daughter to this secret sing.
She gave the good news that she Zal would see,
And gain a mate who would her equal be.
To men and women all, of lofty mind,
'Tis right that they no more reproach should find.
"As thou hast hastened towards thy heart's desire,

And hast attained to what thou didst require,"
Rudábah said: "O wife of royal ways,
In all assemblies thou dost merit praise.
On thy foot's dust as pillow will I lie,
And thy command as my Faith dignify.
Thy life may not the eye of demons blight!
Thy heart and soul be the abode of light!"
To Sindukht's ear when these words had been borne,
She set her face the palace to adorn.
As Paradise each hall she would prepare,
Wine, musk and amber she would mingle there.
A figured carpet on the floor she threw,
With emeralds interwoven through and through.
All of its figures were with pearls arranged,
Each grain as if of limpid water made.
And in that hall a golden throne she placed,
With ornaments in Chinese fashion graced.
Each figure was with jewels made complete,
Adorned with pictures to the pattern meet.
The throne's foundation was on rubies laid,
A royal throne magnificently made.
Rudabah like to Paradise was decked,
Or as a sun with talismans beflecked:
In a fair golden house they made her sit,
To audience with her no one would admit.
Kábulistan was decorated, too,
With wealth and perfume and in varied hue.
The backs of elephants they decorate
With fine brocade of Rum in fitting state.
Musicians on the elephants reclined,
With crowns upon their heads of gold refined.
To meet him then, bedecked, all forward drew,
And sent for female slaves from Kabul too.
Amber and musk on ev'ry side they shed:
Carpets of silk and spun silk there were spread.

Both gold and musk upon her head they laid,
And with rose water wet the dust was made.
Then Zal, with his companions, side by side,
Tow'rds Zabul all their faces turning, ride.
With ev'ry haste Dastan then forward drew.
Like ships on water or as birds they flew;
And all who of his coming were aware
With pomp and state went out to meet him there.
Out of the palace there arose a cry
That Zal upon his road was drawing nigh.
With glad heart Sam to meet him forward pressed,
And clasped him for a while upon his breast.
Released, Zal kissed the dust beneath his feet,
And what he'd seen and heard would then repeat.

The going of Sam with Zal to Mehráb of Kábul, and the taking by Zal of Rudábah to wife.

Then worthy Sam sat on his throne apart,
With Zal well-pleased and of a gladsome heart,
And a soft smile endeavouring to conceal,
Síndukht's own words began then to reveal.
" From Kabul," thus he said, " a message came,
Brought by a woman, and Sindukht her name.
I gave at once the pledge that she required
With spite against her not to be inspired;
With the requests she gently made of me,
With words in truth sincere could I agree.
This first, that Zabul's monarch be allied
With the fair moon of Kábul as his bride.
The next was this, that I should be her guest,
A medicine pure for all ills in her breast.
A messenger from her a message brought,
Ready was he who the alliance sought.
How to the message shall we give reply?
What tell Mehráb of lofty dignity?'

These words into Zal's heart such freshness put
That he grew ruby-hued from head to foot.
"O mighty Pehlavan," he gave reply;
"If thou agreest in thy counsel high,
Urge on the retinue. We come behind,
So as to seek and fitting answer find."
On Dastan looked the happy Sam, his sire,
To know in this what was his son's desire.
Alone of Mehráb's daughter would he speak,
And in the dark night Zal no sleep would seek.
Such is the measure of affection's way,
When it its face shows wisdom goes astray.
Indian and Abyssinian drums to sound
He ordered, and the tents struck from the ground.
The hero sent a beast without delay,
Tow'rds lion Mehrab so to make his way.
The king was on the road, he was to say,
With Zal, and elephants in their array.
To Mehrab came the messenger with speed,
And what he'd seen and heard to tell gave heed.
When Mehráb heard it he with gladness beamed,
His cheek of *Arghvan* as the flower seemed.
Tied on the drums, the brazen trumpets blared,
Like a cock's eye the army was prepared.
Raged elephants; with minstrels side by side,
A Paradise became earth in its pride.
All kinds of banners fluttered o'er their head,
Of violet, of yellow, green, and red.
Sounded the soft flutes, with of harps the sound,
The sound of horns and drums went booming round.
Thou would'st have said 'twas the Last Day at least,
Or Resurrection day or hour of feast.
After this manner he tow'rds Sam progressed;
Alighting from his horse, he forward pressed.
Him to his heart the Pehlavan then strained,

And of revolving time the news, too, gained.
The king of Kabul then his blessing gave
To Sam both and to Zal-i-zar the brave.
Upon his swift-paced steed he mounted soon
Over the hills as mounted the new moon.*
Upon the head of Zál-i-zar the bold
He placed with jewels decked a crown of gold.
Smiling, to Kabul they went on their way,
And called to mind tales of a former day.
With Indian drum the town was no more mute,
With twanging lute and with the harp and flute.
The gates, thou wouldst have said, with minstrels swarm,
And fate itself assumes an altered form.
To horses' crests and manes from side to side,
Saffron and musk anointing they applied.
On backs of elephants drums, flutes complain,
With noise and song resounded vale and plain.
With all her serving men Sindukht came out ;
Three hundred female slaves stood round about,
These, each of them, with golden bowl there stand,
With musk and jewels filled in each one's hand.
To Sam their blessings all of them repeat,
And scatter jewels round about his feet.
Then all who sat down to the feast, indeed,
Of other property could have no need,
Beneath the foot of elephant and horse,
Shone gems as stars upon the heaven's course.
With jewels and *dinars* of a value great,
There but as nothing one might *dirams* rate.
Then Sám to Síndukht laughingly replied :
" How long Rudabah fair wilt thou, then, hide ? "
Síndukht the Pehlavan told in her place,
" Give me my fee that I may show her face."
And to Sindukht thereon gave Sam reply :

*Not quite correct. The new moon sets behind the hills.

"Ask all thou wishest of me by and by,
City and treasure, and my crown and throne,
All I possess here, reckon them thine own."
On to the house they went with gold that gleamed,
And all within a cheerful spring there seemed.
And Sam, when he on that moon-faced one gazed,
Stood at her beauty suddenly amazed.
He did not know enough how her to praise,
Or to look on her how his eye to raise.
"O thou of fortune rare," to *Zál* he said:
"Thy God has given to thee wond'rous aid,
This sun so full of light when chose thy eye,
It chose the choicest one. Why should I lie?"
Then he commanded Mehráb to appear,
And compact made by Faith and custom clear.
Happy they seated them upon one throne;
Upon them agates, emeralds were thrown.
On the moon's head they placed a crown of gold,
On his one jewelled, royal to behold.
A list of all the gifts he had prepared,
And with the list of treasures there compared.
To him the list of all the gifts was read:
No ear could take them in, thou would'st have said.
When Sam had seen them all, he stood amazed,
And called upon the name of God and praised.
They to the sitting place together went,
And wine in hand a week together spent.
Thence to the palace went they from the hall,
And there a whole week spent in pleasure all.
The town excited grew beyond all bounds,
The General's house was full of joyful sounds.
Nor *Zal*, nor that moon of lip coral-bright,
Slept for a whole week either day or night,
One with the other there sweet converse made,
And of a royal pearl the seed was laid.

With bracelets decked, the army leaders all
Drew up their ranks before the palace tall.
They passed their time in jollity and song,
Music and wedding feast a whole week long.
A month had passed: Sam Nariman then went
To go towards Seistan his face was bent.
And after he had gone did Zal again
Another week in pleasure full remain.
Litters and lofty *howdahs* * they prepare,
A litter to convey that moon so fair.
Mehrab, Sindukht, and their relations, too,
Towards Seistan then took their road anew.
They went with happy heart and were content,
Lips full of praise for bounties to them sent.
Tow'rds Nimruz † thus in triumph as they went,
The world was brightened by their glad assent.
Ling'ring, Sindukht herself remained behind,
The road to Kabul with her troops to find.
When Zal, the worthy and of honoured name,
Sam saw in his heart he content became.
His kingdom he resigned at once to Zal, ‡
And with good omens marched his army all
Tow'rds Bákhtar and of Kargasan the land,
With the auspicious banner in their hand.
" I go," said he: " the kingdom's truly mine,
Though they tow'rds me their heart may not incline.
Its patent did me Manuchehr provide,
Bade me enjoy it and e'er there abide.
Mischief I fear from those of evil race,
Who to Mazandaran their hopes may trace.
To thee, O Zal, this place do I resign,
The kingdom and this throne and crown of mine."
Departed one-blowed Sam, Zal in his place
Prepared wine parties with becoming grace.

* Wooden seats on elephants backs. † On the South. ‡ Pronounced " Zawl."

After this is related the birth of Rustam, the great hero, to Zál and Rudabah. This is described in considerable detail, and is remarkable in several ways as showing a knowledge of obstetrics which one would not have looked for in Persia in those early days. The mother is drugged with wine in order to produce insensibility to pain, and some surgical operation performed by a male accoucheur (a thing unknown in the East) by means of which the child is born alive. The name Rustam is given to the child in consequence of his mother having uttered the word, which means in Persia, "I am saved," on learning of the event after she had recovered from her state of unconsciousness. A curious part in this narrative is that played by the Simurgh, which arrives immediately. Zal burns the feather the bird had given him when he left the Alburz mountains with Sam, as a method of summoning it to his assistance if he ever happened to be in any great difficulty. It is on the bird's instructions that the accoucheur acted. Whilst in the milk-drinking stage Rustam is said to have been fed by five wet nurses, and when he grew older his food consisted of bread and meat sufficient for five men. The next Section describes a visit paid to his grandson by Sam, who is much pleased. During this visit, at a banquet, Mehráb, who is one of the guests, becomes intoxicated, but is only laughed at, and finally Sam returns home after giving good advice to Zal and Rustam. The next Section contains the descriptions of the killing of a white elephant by Rustam, and his being sent off by Zal to the hill of Sipand, to avenge the death of Nariman, the father of Sam, during which expedition he is recommended to disguise himself as a camel driver in charge of a troop of camels loaded with salt. By this artifice Rustam gains access to the castle on the hill of Sipand. which contains those who killed his great-grandfather, and takes possession of it after performing prodigies of valour with his mace. The next two Sections describe the reception of the news by Zal and Sám, and that following the appointment of Naozar to succeed him by Manuchehr, after giving him a long exhortation of which the following is a translation.

The royal crown's deceit and empty air;
Thy heart should never place reliance there.
Twenty beyond a hundred years my life,
My loins girt up for grievous pain and strife,
With majesty of Faridun girt round,
In his good counsels have I profit found.
Whene'er his word I hastened to obey,
Much joy and comfort found I on my way.
From Salam and from Tur, the proud of thought,
For Iraj my grandsire I vengeance sought.
From many miseries I've freed the earth,
To many a town and fortress given birth.
"He never saw the world," well might'st thou say;
Its count in secret has all passed away.
Those trees whose fruit and leaves but poison give,
Their death were better than that they should live.
After much pain and trouble borne by me,
Treasure and royal throne I gave to thee.
Just as from Faridun 'twas handed down,
Have I bestowed on thee this king-tried crown:
Enjoyed by thee and passed on, thou should'st know
Thou to a happier time thyself must go.
The trace of thee that may remain behind
When many days have passed will men still find
To praise it. This should not be otherwise,
For from good birth pure Faith should ever rise.
Beware from God's faith not to turn aside,
For a pure conscience God's faith will provide,

There must a new rule in the world be near,
A Moses as a Prophet must appear.
He from the Western land his way will wend:
Beware in no way that ye him offend.
Believe in him: it is a faith from heav'n;
And see what pledges from the first were giv'n.
Upon the road of God proceed thou still:
Of Him good cometh, but there may come ill.
Of Turkomans should there a host arrive,
They might Iran's throne of the crown deprive.
A time shall come to thee of woe and rout:
This in its course the sun will bring about.
Many hard matters there will come to thee,
At times a wolf, at times a sheep thou'lt be.
To thee from Pushang's son will mischief flow,
And harm from Turan thou shalt also know.
Behold, my son, if trouble on thee fall,
Seek thou the aid of Sam and that of Zal,
And of this tree of Zal that from the root
Has just now sprung, and sends forth branch and shoot.
Through him the strength of Turan's land shall fail,
And him as thy avenger thou shalt hail.

Naozar, who succeeded Manuchehr, reigned only seven years. He soon forsook the ways of Manuchehr, and the people contemplated a rising against him, but owing to the good advice of Sám he repented and conducted himself properly. When Pushang, the Chief of the Turkomans in Turan, heard of Manuchehr's death, he determined to wage war against Iran, and assembled for the purpose his great warriors, among whom was his son Afrasiab, well known in Persian history as the opponent of Rustam. Afrasiab becomes excited with the idea of exacting vengeance for the deaths of Salam and Tur, and collects his army to march against Naozar. Aghriras, Pushang's second son and Afrasiab's brother, remonstrates, but finally consents to go with the latter. Naozar prepares his army in Dehistan to meet them. When they approached the Jaihun, they received news of the death of Sam, and hearing that Zal was engaged in performing his obsequies, Afrasiab dispatched a separate force of 30,000 men under Shamasas and Khuzravan to Zabulistan to take vengeance on him, and himself drew towards Dehistan to meet Naozar. When the two armies approached each other the latter is challenged by Barman on the part of Afrásiáb, and the challenge is accepted by Kobad, son of Kavah, the black-smith, and brother of Karan, notwithstanding his advanced age and the remonstrances of the latter. The combat takes place and Kobád is killed. The two armies then encounter each other, withdrawing at night. On the next day the fight is renewed, and Naozar and the Persians are defeated and retire for the night. Meanwhile he sends away secretly his sons Tus and Gustaham, instructing them to take the ladies of the family to the Alhurz hills. A third conflict takes place the next day. Naozar is again defeated and escapes to the fortress of Dehistan. Afrasiab sends a force towards Fars with the intention of capturing the families, and Karan at night indignantly informs Naozar, and starts with an army to meet this force, and encounters it at the Diz-i-safid, or White fort, of which Gazdahum was in command. In this fight Karan singles out for vengeance Barman, who had killed his brother Kobad, and slays him. Hearing of the march of Karan, Naozar follows him and is taken prisoner. Meanwhile Afrasiab informs Visah, the general of the Turkomans, of the death of Barman, who was his son, and Visah attacks Karan to avenge his death. The fight is indecisive, and Visah returns to Afrasiab, grieving for his son. Next follows an account of the separate expedition of Shamasas and Khuzravan to Zabulistan. They advance as far as the

Kirmand and are met by an envoy from Mehráb, who pretends that he is disaffected towards *Zál*, and proposes to hand over *Zá*bulistán to the Turkomán army. Meanwhile he dispatches a messenger to *Zá*l, begging him to come to his assistance, and *Zá*l at once obeys the summons. Arriving near the town, he shoots three arrows into the enemy's camp, and Shamásás recognizing them as *Zá*l's, but nothing daunted, encourages Khuzráván and prepares to fight In the single combat that ensues between Khuzráván and *Zá*l the former in the first instance breaks *Zá*l's breastplate with a blow of his mace, but *Zá*l, having put on a coat of mail, kills him and tramples him under foot. Shamásás will not answer *Zá*l's challenge, and, after *Zá*l has killed Kalbád with an arrow, takes to flight. He is met by Káran, and the remainder of his force annihilated, although he himself escapes again. Afrásiáb becomes aware of the deaths of Khuzráván and Kalbád, and in retaliation sends for Naozar and cuts off his head. He then ascends the throne of Irán. *Zá*l and Rústam, having heard of Naozar's death, assemble an army to go against him (Afrásiab). On hearing this, the chiefs who are in confinement at Sári appeal to Aghríras to get Afrásiáb to release them, for fear of what he might be led to do when he heard of the preparations of *Zá*l and Rústam. Aghríras was afraid to interfere for fear of provoking the anger of his brother, but promised to find some other means for succouring them. On this the Chiefs at Sári sent a message to *Zá*l that Aghríras had become their friend, and if *Zá*l would come forward and offer him battle he would withdraw his army to Raí. On receiving this message *Zá*l asks who will go, and Kishvád accepts the enterprise. He starts with an army for Amil, *en route* to Sári, and Aghríras retires, leaving the prisoners at that place. These are released by Kishvád, who then returns to *Zá*bulistán. Afrásiáb, on hearing of the escape from

Sári of the prisoners, whom he had intended to execute, reproaches Aghríras and puts him to death. *Zál* puts his army in motion against Afrásiáb, and there ensues a great battle in which many on both sides are killed, the encounter ceasing then for a fortnight in consequence of the fatigue of the combatants. The next Section relates the selection as king of *Záo*, the son of Tehmásp, of the race of Faridún, apparently because he was the most kingly person they could find. His reign only lasted five years, as he was an old man of eighty years of age, but he was a good king and did not allow his army to oppress the people; the people enjoyed peace, but a great famine unfortunately occurred, and the people acknowledging that it was in consequence of their own misdeeds, appear to have agreed to a delimitation of territory. All beyond the Jaihún as far as the frontier of Rúm and in the direction of Khatan and China was to be included in Túrán, and presumably Irán was to reach only to the Jaihún.* *Zál* then retired to his own country of *Zábúlistán*, and the country flourished during the remainder of the life of *Záo*, who died at the age of eighty-six. *Záo* was succeeded on the throne by his son Garshásp, who, according to the Macan edition, reigned for nine years. Hearing of *Záo*'s death, Afrásiáb advanced again as far as Rai, but was not received by Pushang, who was angry on account of the murder of Aghrírás. Whilst communications on this subject were proceeding Garshásp appears to have died, and Pushang to have sent a message to Afrásiáb not to delay but to cross the Jaihún at once. This he did with an army to advance into Persia and seize the throne. *Zál* becomes aware of this through the entreaties of the Iránis that he would come to their assistance, and replies that he is too old, but will send his son Rústam, and gives him accordingly the great mace of his grandfather Sám.

* These circumstances are not alluded to in Macan's edition.

Rústam agrees to go, and choosing the celebrated Rakhsh for his charger, advances. When the two armies are at a short distance from each other, *Zál* exhorts his chiefs to have a king placed over them in order to give unity to their counsels, and accordingly sends Rústam to Mount Albuz to bring Kai-kobád. This is done and Kai-kobád is seated on the throne, his reign lasting 100 years. Just after this Afrásiáb, the ruler of Turán, invades Irán, and a detailed account is given of the fight between the armies of the two countries. At the first encounter Káran overthrows Shamásás, and then Rústam attacks Afrásiáb himself, who is pointed out by *Zál*. After a short struggle Rústam seizes him by his belt with the intention of carrying him off bodily to Kaikobád, but the belt breaks with his weight, and Afrásiáb falls to the ground and is surrounded by his warriors. His crown is snatched off his head by Rústam, but he again mounts, and, leaving his army, flies by the way of the desert. The Turkomán army is now attacked, and Rústam is reported to the king as having slain 160,000 of them. They retreat to Dámghán, and thence to the Jaihún, and Rústam and the Iránis return laden with spoil to the king, who receives the father and son with great honour. The next Section contains the account of his fight with Rústam given by Afrásiáb to his father, Pushang; in this he acknowledges that he cannot withstand Rústam, and recommends the latter to sue for peace, and that the Jaihún should be the boundary between the two countries. An envoy is accordingly sent with presents to Kai-kobád, who accepts the boundary proposed and leads his army back across the river. Kai-kobad, after bestowing rewards on Rústam and other warriors, and conferring all the country from *Zábúlistán* to Sind on *Zál* and Rústam, retires to Istakhar, in Fárs, where he establishes his capital. He is said to have ruled with justice, and to have employed himself for ten years whilst he travelled through the world building cities, like the ten towns he established round Rai. He had four sons, Káûs, Arish, Pashín, and Armín. He died after exhorting his son Kai-Káus, who succeeded him, to rule with rectitude, for which he would have his reward in the next world.

Kai-Káus is said to have reigned 150 years. He is excited by a Dív, who disguises himself as a singer and sings to him of the enchantments of Mázandarán, to invade that country. His warriors disapprove of the expedition and go to *Zál* to try to dissuade him. *Zál* comes to him for the purpose, but fails in his endeavour, and goes home to Sástín. The invading army then starts, and the warrior Giv is sent forward with 2,000 men to destroy everything on the way to Mázandarán itself. He found a fine town full of treasures and beautiful women, and the king advanced towards it. Meanwhile the king of Mázandarán had applied to the White Demon, the *Dív-i-safíd*, for assistance against the invaders. The army of Irán is overtaken by a storm and most of it destroyed, the king himself and the remnant being taken prisoners by the White Demon and escorted to the town of Mázandarán, whence he managed to send a message to *Zál* of the wretched condition of himself and his chief warriors, who had been almost blinded. *Zál* received the message, and agreed to send Rústam to his assistance. Rústam on his road encountered seven perils, the account of which will now be translated in full.

The sending of a message by King Káus to Zál-i-zar, and the going of Rustam to Mázandarán by the road of the seven stages.

And after this, with broken heart, the king
A warrior sent like bird upon the wing.

At that time far from king and host he lay,
But to the king came raging on his way.
As smoke flies swiftly up in its ascent,
Him fast to Dastán in *Zábúl* he sent,
"What lot has fate decreed to me," he said:
"That throne and crown should in the dust be laid?
Gold, treasure, and that army of renown,
Adorned like flowers that the young spring crown:
A blast has come, and the revolving heav'n,
Thou would'st have said, to demons had been givin.
My eye is dim, and darkened is my fate,
And all inverted are my crown and state.
Wounded, I lie in Ahriman's control,
Who from my body will drive out my soul.
When in my memory thy good counsels rest,
A chilly sigh there rises from my breast.
Through what thou said'st I became not wise,
But through my folly mischief on me lies.
If thou thy loins now gird not for my aid,
No profit can on capital be paid."
An envoy to Mázarandán then went,
Like flying bird or smoke in its ascent.
And when the runner came to Dastán bold,
What he had seen and heard and knew he told.
With sorrow then his skin did Dastán rend,
But told it neither to a foe nor friend.
With a clear mind he saw the mischief all
That through ill fortune on the king would fall.
Dastán Sám said to Rústam then this word:
"Within its sheath has now grown short the sword.
Henceforward should we neither graze or drink,
Nor fitted for the crown ourselves should think.
In dragon's jaw the monarch of the world,
What evils on Iránis have there now been hurled!
The saddle now's the hour on Rakhsh to bind.

Vengeance with world-bestowing sword to find.
It is indeed just for this very hour
That aye has brought thee up the Lord of pow'r
It is for such deeds that art fitted thou.
More than two hundred years I reckon now.
And from such deeds great fame will come to thee,
For thou the king shalt from all mischief free.
'Twould not become the demon strife this day,
That thou should'st seek thy ease or e'en delay.
Thy form should'st thou in panther vest enfold
And from thy head both sleep and thought withhold.
For ev'ry one thy spear that henceforth sees,
How should he say his soul is still at ease?
Bloody the sea where thou dost strife maintain,
And at thy voice the hill becomes a plain.
Nor Arzang nor the Demon White in strife
Should look on thee with any hope of life.
Break of Mázandarán the monarch's head;
With heavy mace his joints in pieces shred.
And if in this life thou acquirest fame,
Men's hope is dissipated through thy name.
When thou hast gone thy fame shalt thou retain.
Go to Mázandarán, nor here remain,
That Sám the Great's name magnified may be,
For in the world none fame has gained as he.
Obedient to thee thou the world shalt make,
And at thy name the very Dívs shall shake."
Then Rústam said: "The road is long to take,
And on it how shall I my vengeance slake?"
And more he said: "Six months thou shouldest know
The king took to Mázandarán to go.
And if I go, what offspring will there be
Of Kai-Kobád as delicate as he?"
Thus Zál him answered: "From this kingdom here
There are two roads, both full of pain and fear,

The one the longer, by which Káus went,
The other, on which two weeks may be spent,
Of lions full and *Dívs* and darkness, too,
On which amazing things will meet thy view.
Take thou the short one and those wonders see·
May the Creator thy companion be!
The foot of Rakhsh, although its pain may burn.
Will pass along it and the road will spurn.
All the dark night until the day grows clear
To the pure God I'll cffer up my prayer.
And oh! that I may see thy arm, thy face,
Thy head, thy armlet, and thy heavy mace!
If through the Universal Lord's command
Thy life should pass into the demon's nand,
Can any one the matter here restrain?
Just as one comes, one must pass on again.
Now may his place for ever here retain;
Him will they summon though he long remain.
He in the world that has a name that's high,
Need fear no evil when he passes by."
Then to his happy sire did Rústam say:
" My loins are girt, thy orders to obey.
But on their own feet to go straight to hell
The great of former days did not think well,
And none who is not weary of his life
Would face a raging lion in the strife.
And now my loins are girt. Behold me gone:
I ask assistance but from God alone.
Soul, body, the king's offering I make;
Magicians' talismans, these all I'll break.
Iránis, those who still alive remain,
I'll bring and will their loins gird up again.
Not *Arjang* will I spare, nor *Dív Safíd*,
Not *Sanjah*, *Ghandi's* son *Pulád*, or *Bíd*.
In our God, the Creator's name, O say

That Rústam will from Rakhsh not turn away,
Till Arjang's hand I bind as with a stone,
And on his neck my halter I have thrown,
Till of Pulád I trample on the brain,
And Rakhsh's hoofs replace the soil again."
From the crow's back the sun raised up his head,
The earth was mead-like as the New Year spread
He stretched his arm as he put on his mail,
And *Zál* to praise him greatly did not fail.
" O'er all the earth thy footsteps find their way,
Nor thy foes' bodies now to melt delay!
In ev'ry place thy name be noted high,
And thy Rakhsh plant his foot upon the sky!
May'st ever thou from God's assistance know,
And may the head reversed be of thy foe!"
To mount on Rakhsh when Rústam forward came,
With a firm heart and ruddy cheeks aflame,
Rudábah came, and full of tears her eye,
And seeing her Dastán wept bitterly.
Rudábah, moon-faced, thus to Rústam cried:
" Setting thy face wilt thou now forward ride?
If in my grief thou now wilt leave me here,
What from God hop'st thou in thy day of fear?"
To her: " O my good mother," Rústam said:
" By my own wish to this am I not led.
This happens to me but by Fate's decree.
My soul and body do thou guard for me!"
Forward they came, then, him to bid farewell,
For would they meet again could no one tell.
It is in this way that time fleeting flies,
Nor counts upon it ever he who's vise.
Know, from those days that over thee have passed
The world has gained prosperity at last!
The hero of Nímrúz then went away
From his great father who illumed the day.

After this manner traversed Rakhsh the track
In brilliant day both and in darkness black.
His body, wanting food, to cry began ;
He saw a place where there wild asses ran.
He with his thigh pressed Rakhsh upon the track,
And the wild ass's course to his grew slack.
From Rústam on his steed and lasso, too,
No running wild beast ever quarter knew,
His royal noose the valiant hero threw,
As in its folds the bold wild ass it drew.
He drew, and thus the wild ass in its fold
Upon the ground like raging lion rolled.
A fire then with an arrow's point he lit,
With firewood, thorns, and rubbish nourished it ;
And motionless without life as it lay,
He placed upon the fire to roast his prey.
He ate it and the bones he threw away ;
It served him both as cauldron and as tray.
The bridle from his horse's head he drew,
And loosened him to graze the meadows through.
A cane-brake as a sleeping couch he prized,
The gate of fear a safe place recognised.
And though beneath his head a sword he kept,
Still like a lion at his ease he slept.

The killing of a lion by Rakhsh.

Now in that cane-brake was a lion's lair :
No elephant to cut those canes would dare.
An hour of night had passed. The lion then
Returned back to his own accustomed den.
An elephantine form he saw there lie,
A steed infuriated standing by.
" First," then he said, " I must the courser kill,
The rider's in my hand just as I will."

Roaring with rage, at Rakhsh the lion came,
And Rakhsh like raging fire stood all aflame.
He struck the lion's head with both his feet,
And in his back his sharp teeth made he meet.
Struck to the earth he him in pieces tore;
The helpless beast found remedy no more.
From sharp-clawed Rústam when his sleep had flown
Dark to the lion had the world then grown.
"O unwise Rakhsh!" reproachfully he said:
"To fight a lion who put in thy head?
If at the lion's hand thou hadst been slain,
How to Mázandarán could I have ta'en
This panther-corslet, helm of warlike use,
This sword and heavy mace and bow and noose?
Nowhere a swift-paced courser like to thee,
So fierce, so sharp, so tender do I see.
Why with a cry didst thou not come me near?
For, if thy voice had once come to my ear,
If this to me had in my dreams been known,
Thy lion combat would but short have grown."
Thus said the warrior renowned and strong,
And went to rest and slept at ease for long.
From the dark hill the sun his head had raised,
When Tuhamtan from sweet sleep rose, half dazed.
Then did he upon Rakhsh his saddle bind,
And called God's generosity to mind.
On Rakhsh's back he took his brilliant place,
And tow'rds his second stage then turned his face.

Stage Second. The sinking of Rústam from thirst, and arriving at a spring of water by the guidance of a sheep.

There was a road there through a dreary waste:
He had to traverse it with ev'ry haste.
The desert waterless, so hot as well,

Birds' bodies in it into pieces fell.
So hot the desert and the plain became,
Thou would't have said that it was scorched by flame
The horseman's tongue and Rakhsh's body, too,
Through heat and thirst together useless grew.
With spear in hand, dismounted from his horse,
He like a drunken man held on his course.
To find a road he saw no remedy,
And turned his face then upward to the sky.
Thus then he cried: "O ruler, who art just,
Thou pain and hardship all on me hast thrust.
If pleasure in my pain here Thou hast found,
In the next wo ld my treasure should abound.
I hasten that perchance the mighty Lord
To king Káüs his kind aid may afford.
And whether God (this now I haste to see)
From demon's claw those of Irán will free.
We are Thy worshippers, Thy servants all,
And as Thy criminals before Thee fall.
Now at my hand may they redemption know;
On them my soul and body I bestow.
Thou said'st that I a ruler just had been,
Had aided those who had oppression seen;
If in my actions thou dost justice see,
Make not my market all too hard for me.
In this heroic thing take thou my part,
And of the old man *Zál* burn not the heart.
Bring with Thy wind this army not to pain:
Me and my country bid rejoice again.
Himself his admonition Piltan gave,
When he remembered his own shroud and grave.
If this were with an army to be done,
I like a lion to the war had gone:
I in one onslaught them had overthrown;
At once the breath should from their souls have flown,

And if the hill of Gang came in the way,
To cast it down there had been no delay.
With heavy mace I would have laid it low,
And through my valour it defeat should know.
And if the river Jaihún it had been,
In which no boat salvation could have seen,
Of the eternal pure God by the power,
With earth would I have filled it in that hour.
But of no profit manliness you find
When fate conspires the eye to render blind.
In arid waste what plan now can I try?
What magic is 'gainst death a remedy?"
When this was said, his elephantine form,
Limp through his thirst, fell on the desert warm.
Rústam fell on the earth, for he was spent,
And in his throat his tongue in pieces rent.
Just at this time a sheep with buttocks fat
Passed Tuhamtan before in goodly state.
Seeing the sheep, the thought rose in his mind:
"Where does this beast its source of water find?
Of the great God it must the bounty be,
That at this very time has come to me."
He moved on with his sword in his right hand:
God gave him strength upon his feet to stand.
With sword in hand the sheep still he pursues,
And in his other hand his rope and noose.
The sheep and hero onward took their way,
And this he reckoned as a happy day.
Upon the road a fountain there appeared,
And this the sheep of lofty head soon neared.
To heaven turned then Tuhamtan his eye,
And said: "Thou speakest truth, O God on high.
Here at this spring no sheep's marks do I see,
Nor is the deer a relative to me.
In any place where thee thy speech may fail

Thyself of refuge in thy God avail.
Whoever from the one God turns aside,
In its own place his sense does not abide."
He uttered loud upon that sheep his praise:
"The rolling sphere no evil to thee raise!
In deserts green grass play for thee its part,—
No thought of thee be in the panther's heart!
He who with bow and arrow seeks thy track,
His bow be broken and his soul grow black!
For Piltan's body owes its life to thee,
Else of his shroud his thoughts now full would be.
Had he not gone into the dragon's breast,
He in a wolf's claws would have found his rest.
His garments all to pieces had been shred,
To Rústam's foes a trace been left instead."
The end of all his praises thus he found,
The saddle from his steed he then unbound.
Washing his body in that limpid stream,
It shone as does the sun with brilliant gleam.
His thirst appeased, he turned his thoughts to prey,
His quiver arrow-filled, he took his way.
As raging elephant the ass o'erthrew,
From this the legs, the skin, the loins he drew.
Just like the sun a brilliant fire he lit,
And, from the water bringing, roasted it.
With this accomplished he began to eat,
And with his hands stripped from the bones the meat.
To the pure fountain then he came to drink,
And satisfied began of sleep to think.
Then to the ardent Rakhsh said Tuhamtan,
"Fight no one, and associate with none.
If a fox comes, run thou to me in flight,
With Dívs and lions do thou never fight.
To strive in war the great God gave me birth;
Thee has He made for saddle and for girth."

Rústam, lips closed, to rest and slumber laid,
Till midnight Rakhsh around him grazed and played.

Third Stage. The killing of a dragon by Rústam

And in that desert there a dragon lived;
Ought could escape him, thou hadst not believed.
How shall I sing this dragon in my song?
From head to tail *gaz** eighty he was long.
That dragon's place for taking rest was here,
No Div passed by the spot of him through fear.
No elephant or Dív or lion there
To go along that road would ever dare.
He came and saw where the great hero slept,
Whilst watch around him a fierce charger kept.
What had occurred, of this with thought oppressed,
Who in this place had dared to take his rest?
At first on Rakhsh then as his eye he bent,
The charger running towards the monarch went.
His brazen hoofs he struck upon the ground,
He spread his tail and moved like thunder round.
Rústam, from sleep awoke, become aware,
Wisely began for combat to prepare.
As round the desert then his eye he threw,
That furious dragon disappeared from view.
Reproaches then on Rakhsh did Rústam heap,
That he had wakened him out of his sleep.
When once again he sank down to his rest,
The demon in the darkness stood confessed.
To Rústam's pillow Rakhsh again then ran,
The ground to beat on with his hoofs began.
Out of his sleep the angry hero rose,
His flushing cheek put on the hue of rose.
Again upon the desert looking round,

* A cubit.

Nothing but deepest darkness could be found.
Awake, to kindly Rakhsh again he cried:
"The darkness of the night thou canst not hide.
Out of my dream my head why dost thou take?
Why dost thou hasten to keep me awake?
Such resurrection if thou cause again,
From cutting off thy head I'll not refrain.
Then to Mázandarán on foot I'd go,
And take my helm, sword, mace of heavy blow.
I told thee, if a lion came to fight,
I'd seize him for thee with my hand of might.
Towards me haste I did not bid thee make,
Be still, then, so that I may not awake."
For the third time he laid his head to rest,
His panther corslet laid upon his chest.
Then once again the fearful dragon roared,
Flames with his breath, thou wouldst have said, he
poured.
Rakhsh for the moment left his grazing place,
He did not dare the Pehlaván to face.
His heart at that strange wonder broke in two,
Frightened at Rústam and the beast he grew.
From love for Rústam not at ease his mind,
Neighing, he ran towards him as the wind.
He roared with anger and tore up the ground,
And with his hoofs kicked up the earth around.
Then Rustam from his pleasant slumber woke,
Enraged his steed should him again provoke.
But now the world's Creator would provide
That no more should the earth the dragon hide.
That dragon form obscurely came to view,
And from its sheath his sword quick Rústam drew.
As in the spring the thunder claps resound,
He made the plain full with the conflict's sound.
He roared, as clouds in spring give thunder birth,

And with the fire of war filled full the earth.
"Tell me thy name!" he to the dragon said,
"Earth to thy wish henceforth shall not be led
Without a name it were not meet and fit,
Thy soul should now thy darksome body quit.'
The evil dragon thus an answer gave:
"Out of my claws a man can no one save.
As in this waste for centuries I dwell,
The air of its high heav'n I breathe as well.
Above no eagle dare pass in his flight,
And the stars see it not in dreams by night."
The dragon added: "What may thy name be,
For she who bore thee must now weep for thee."
"Of Dastán Sám and Nairam offspring I,
Myself am Rústam," thus he gave reply.
"In seeking vengeance a whole host am I,
And over earth on valiant Rakhsh I fly.
The conqueror in the battle shalt thou see,
And to the dust I'll bring thy head for thee."
The dragon, though he pulled and held him tight,
Did not escape from Rustám in the fight.
So closely then did he to Píltan hold,
Thoud'st said he had become of him a fold.
And when the mighty dragon Rakhsh beheld,
That to the Crown-giver in such wise held,
He pricked his ears and ran, and, strange to say,
Bit with his teeth his shoulders as he lay.
He tore his skin just as a lion would,
And the brave Pehlaván astonished stood.
With his sword striking he cast down his head,
And like a river flowed the blood he shed.
Itself a fountain of pure blood upreared:
In this the ground beneath him disappeared.
When Rústam on that fiery dragon looked,
Upon that beak and on those talons hooked,

And when he looked upon that form of dread,
The sight with sheer amazement filled his head.
He saw the desert 'neath him empty lie,
And warm blood from the dark earth trickle by.
At all this Tuhamtan then stood appalled;
And on the name of God the hero called;
With water washed his body and his head,
To seek the world but in his God was led:
"O just one!" to his Maker then he cried:
"Knowledge thou gavest me and strength and pride.
An elephant, a Dív, I nothing deem.
A desert waterless or Nile's swift stream!
Be my foes many, or yet be they few,
Grown angry, all but as one man I view."
Thus when His praises he had made complete,
Rakhsh he caparisoned in fashion meet.

Fourth Stage. The Killing by Rústam of a Female Magician.

Sitting on Rakhsh, he took his forward way
To where the land of the magicians lay.
Urging his steed that long-drawn road upon
When from above declined the shining sun,
He saw a tree, some grass, a flowing stream
Fit place for a young hero that would seem.
Like pheasant's eye he saw a fountain shine,
On which a golden cup lay, full of wine.
A roasted sheep and bread above he found,
With salt and sweet confections ranged around.
When Rústam now beheld such fitting place,
He rendered thanks to God for all His grace.
It was magicians' food. When Rústam neared,
The Dív had heard his voice and disappeared
Saddle removed, he 'lighted on the ground,

And thus roast sheep and bread, astonished, found.
He sat well pleased upon the fountain's brink,
In hand a cup of ruby wine to drink.
Close by the wine a sweet lute did he see;
The home of feast how could such desert be?
The lute raised Tuhamtan up to his breast,
And struck a chord and thus these words addressed:
"Rústam an evil fate to exile drives:
From happy days small profit he derives.
All places are to him a field of war,
His flower gardens hills and deserts are.
With Dívs and dragons must he ever strive;
Escape from deserts he can ne'er contrive.
Wine-cup or mead or flow'rs of fragrant scent
To me did not propitious fate present.
With crocodiles for ever I'm at strife;
In war with panthers, too, I spend my life."
To an enchantress' ears these sweet sounds flow,
With Rústam's couplets the soft-striking bow.
After spring's fashion she adorned her face,
Although such charms by no means gave her grace.
Perfumed she came and decked in varied hue;
To sit and question him then nearer drew.
His orison to God then Rústam raised,
Whilst he the world's creator duly praised,
That of Mázandarán within the waste
He found wine, youth and song all to his taste.
'Twas an enchantress' guile he did not know,
Nor *Ahriman* concealed that hue below.
Upon her hand he placed a cup of wine,
And sang the praises of the Grace divine.
Of the great God as thus the name he took,
Th' enchantress' face put on another look.
Her soul had never any thought of praise,
Nor could her tongue of prayer the accents raise.

Hearing God's name, her features blackened grew,
And this when Tuhamtan perceived and knew.
Sudden the noose he of his lasso cast,
And held the head of the enchantress fast:
Then spoke and said: "Tell me what thing is this,
And show me now thy face just as it is."
Then in the noose a hideous hag appeared,
Of wrinkles full and magic to be feared.
He with his dagger cut her loins in two,
Magicians frightened he with terrors new.

Fifth Stage. The Tearing out by Rústam of both Ears of the Field Keeper and his Complaining of him before Aolád.

And thence towards the road he set his face.
Just as a traveller his way would trace.
He went on hastening towards a place,
Where the world's light by darkness was effaced.
The night was dark as face of *Zangi** black.
No moon shone out; there was of stars a lack.
Thou would'st have said in fetters was the sun,
And that the stars into a noose had run.
He gave the rein to Rakhsh and set his face;
In darkness height or stream he could not trace.
And thence towards the light did he proceed;
The land was silk-like or a well sown mead.
The old world turned to young could there be seen,
And there were running streams and all was green.
In garments as of water he was dressed,
And he had need of slumber and of rest.
His panther corslet he removed; 'twas wet;
His helmet seemed as if 'twere drowned in sweat.
These both he laid out in the sun to dry,

*An inhabitant of Zanzibar.

And hastened on for rest in sleep to lie.
From off his horse's head he loosed the rein,
And let him run free in the field again.
Helmet and corslet he put on when dry,
Prepared like lion on the grass to lie.
Under his head his shield, his sword he laid
In front, his hand upon its hilt and blade.
And when he saw the horse upon the green,
Running, the keeper shouting loud was seen.
Tow'rds Rakhsh and Rústam as he raging ran
On Rakhsh's legs he a stick to strike began.
As Píltan, roused up from his sleep, awoke,
The keeper: "O thou *Ahriman*!" thus spoke,
"Why in the field dost thou thy horse let loose
Of what thou hast not toiled at making use?"
The hero, angry at such words as these,
Leaping, delayed not both his ears to seize;
Both ears he rooted then from out his cheek,
But neither good nor bad word did he speak.
Quickly the keeper his two ears regained,
And roaring loudly still amazed remained.
Aolád, of that land Pehlaván was he,
A youth who was well known for bravery.
To him the keeper then went with a shout,
Bloody his hands and with his ears torn out.
"Like a black Dív a man," to him he said:
"With panther breast-plate, iron on his head;
All full of demons is the desert by,
Or dragons in cuirass that sleeping lie.*
Out of the field I went the horse to scare,
But neither horse nor land would he leave there.
He saw me, leapt, and spoke no word in vain,
But tore out both my ears and slept again."
When Aolád heard the words the keeper spoke,

*There is no end to this sentence in the original.

He leapt, and from his burnt heart issued smoke.
He came what kind of man he was to see,
And why to him he'd done this injury.
Straight to the road Aolád thus made his way
With famous warriors who with daggers play.
Thus with those haughty ones he turned his rein
When there were signs of Rústam on the plain.
As he approached within a narrow space,
Towards Rakhsh Tuhamtan then turned his face
He sat upon the saddle, drew his sword,
And like a thundercloud advancing roared.
Near to each other then approaching bold,
Each to the other thus his secret told.
"What is thy name?" Aolád to Rústam said.
"Who art thou? Who the king above thy head?
Thou canst not be allowed to pass this way.
Or to encounter demons in the fray.
The keeper's ears why tear out by the root,
And turn thy horse into the fields to boot?
To thee now will I render dark the world;
That crown of thine shall in the dust be hurled."
"I am a cloud," Rústam to him replied:
"And if a cloud, a lion in my pride.
Both spears and swords will it bear as its fruit,
And from their bodies great men's heads will root.
If e'en my name should pass across thy ear,
Thy soul and thy heart's blood would freeze with fear.
In ev'ry company dost thou not know
Of Piltan's moon both and of Piltan's bow?
A son like thee whatever mother bears,
We call her mourner who a shroud prepares
With such a force against me if thou come,
It were to scatter walnuts on a dome."
Misfortune's dragon from its sheath he drew,
Before his saddle his raw noose he threw

Of that fine-watered iron with one blow,
He cut two warriors' bodies through and through.
As lion in amongst the flock he flew,
And all that came before him there he slew.
Their heads he to his feet brought with his blows.
And with his noose laid many another low.
The plain itself was full of valiant horse
That tow'rds the mountains took their headlong course
Furious as elephant rode Rústam bold,
Around his arm his lasso sixty-fold.
Aolád towards as Rakhsh thus nearer drew,
The day, like night, put on a darker hue.
As Rústam to full length his lasso threw,
The haughty man's head in its noose he drew.
Off from his horse thrown, his two hands are bound,
And Rústam mounts as he falls on the ground.
He said to him: "If thee I truthful find,
And thy words hide no crookedness behind,
Of the White Demon if thou show the place,
Of Pulád, Ghandi's son, and Bíd the trace,
And where is bound king Káüs let me know
And him who did this evil to me show;
If what is true thou wilt reveal me here,
With what is justice wilt not interfere,
This throne, this diadem, this heavy mace,
I'll make Mázandarán's king here replace.
To use if thou no crookedness shall bring,
Then shalt thou be of all this land the king.
If in thy speech thou crookedness shalt show,
Of blood a river from thy eye shall flow."
Aolád said: "If from rage thy brain thou free,
And open wide thine eye for once to see,
My body from my soul to part refrain,
Then what thou mayest ask thou shalt obtain.
The place where they the monarch Káüs bind,

The town and road through me thou mayest find.
Bíd's and the White Dív's dwellings, too, I'll show,
For cheerful tidings thou hast let me know.
Warriors approach me and, down-hearted, know
From essence God my earth created so.
Thou of blest foot, to where Káûs is seen
At least a hundred *farsangs* intervene.
Towards the Dív a hundred *farsangs* more;
The hard and bad road there wilt thou deplore.
Between two hills there is a place of dread:
No *Húmá* * ever flies above its head.
It lies among two hundred other wells,
Its wondrous depth by measure no one tells.
Twelve thousand demons all prepared for fight,
Stand on the hills around on guard by night.
Like Púlád, Ghandi's son, their general,
Like Bíd, like Sanjah, guardian over all,
The head of all the Dívs, the Demon White!
The hills, like willows, tremble at his sight,
His body like a mountain thou wilt find;
His shoulders round ten cords would hardly wind.
With bulk and hands and reins thou showest here,
With wielded sword and heavy mace and spear,
With thy great height and deeds thou hast to tell,
To combat with a Dív it were not well.
Beyond this passed, a desert will appear,
Upon whose stones can hardly pass the deer.
And this beyond a river wilt thou see;
More than two *farsangs* wide its breadth will be.
The Dív *Kunárang* there as guardian stands,
Of Dívs the whole obeying his commands.
Beyond, of Bazzúsh and Narmpais the land,
Three hundred farsangs long the castles stand.
From Bazzúsh to Mázandarán its town

*The fabled Persian phœnix.

A road of hardships one might write it down.
And all about that royal country side,
Thousands of horsemen scatter far and wide.
Of this armed host, of *dirams* with their store,
Not one of them thou'lt see who's sad and poor.
War elephants twelve hundred stand around,
For whom room in the town is hardly found.
Of iron though, yet one alone the while,
Canst thou saw up a demon with a file?"
A smile then Rústam turned at him, and said:
"If on the road I may by thee be led:
What one brave elephant can do thou'lt see
Of horses even to a company.
Through the great pow'r of God, victorious still,
With arrow, sword, and destiny, and skill,
The power of my arm what time I show,
Thou shalt in war behold my mace's blow:
Their skin will split from fear of that dread blow:
Their stirrups from their reins they will not know.
Inform me now where Kai-Káüs may be:
Lift up thy feet and show the road to me."
With gladdened heart he sat on Rakhsh once more,
And like the wind Aolád ran on before.
He rested not by night or open day,
But took tow'ards Aspráz hill his onward way,
To that place where Káus his army led,
And Dív's and magic's ill fell on his head.
Of the dark night when half had passed away,
Shouts came and drums beat in the desert way.
Mázandarán's land then to render bright,
In ev'ry place did they a fire ignite.
"What places these both to the left and right,"
He asked Aolád, "where all these fires they light?
"Mázandarán," he said, "doth vigil keep,
And in the dark night two-thirds do not sleep,

Arjang, the dív, *Púlád*, the general,
To the White Dív obedient athletes all.
There is a tree that reaches to the sky,
To stars as with a rope to hang it by.
And in that place *Árjang*, the Dív, must be,
From time to time a loud shout raises he."
Rústam, the warrior, then went off to sleep,
But when the shining sun began to peep,
He tied Aolád up firmly with his noose,
That from the tree his bonds he might not l

Sixth Stage. The Killing of Arjang Dív by Rústam.

Above the dark when raised its head the sun,
The world fresh brilliancy and glory won.
Awoke from sleep then he who crowns bestowed,
And thence tow'rds Rakhsh he took his onward road.
His grandsire's mace upon his saddle hung,
Of craft his heart full as he forward swung.
Upon his head a royal helm he wore;
A sweated panther-skin his body bore.
Towards their General he turned his face,
When he arrived near to his camping place.
Up from amongst the crowd there rose a roar,
Its hill and river thou hadst said it tore.
And when that sound there fell upon his ear,
Out of his tent leapt *Arjang* and drew near.
When Rústam saw him he urged on his steed,
Like Azargúshasp then advanced with speed.
Boid seizing on his ear and arm as prey,
He like a lion tore his head away.
The torn head of the Dív besmeared with blood,
He on the ground threw where the army stood.
And when his heavy mace the demons saw,
Their hearts were torn with terror of his claw.

For land or country then they no more cared,
To turn their sons aside their sires prepared.
His sword of vengeance Tuhamtan then drew,
And cleared the demons out of all that crew.
When the world-lighting sun went down at last,
Tow'rds Asprúz he rode on, raging, fast.
His lasso's noose from Aolád letting go,
They sat down there on lofty tree below.
Then of Aolád asked Tuhamtan the road,
To that town where the king Káüs abode.
When this he heard he firmly turned his face,
Running before him fast the road to trace.
And when his voice had heard king Káüs too,
From first up to the last all things he knew.
To the Iránis then did Káüs say:
"The days of evil from me pass away.
For Rakhsh's neighing falls upon my ear,
And to my doleful heart the sound brings cheer.
In the same way for Kobád the king he neighed,
When onslaught on the Turkománs he made."
The army said: "The chains that he has worn
To Káüs' soul have now distraction borne.
Both dignity and sense to leave him seem,
And one might say he speaks as in a dream.
We have no remedy in this sad strait.
Now is our fortune surely desperate."
The Pehlaván had girded up his waist,
While the Iránis spoke these words in haste.
And then the hero, breathing fire, appeared,
And, anxious for the fight, the monarch neared.
To Káüs came the elephantine form.
The haughty leaders then began to swarm,
Gudúrz and Giv the brave, and valiant Tus,
Behrám the lion, Gústaham, Shaidús.
Loud he lamented and preferred his prayer

Asked of long troubles he had suffered there.
Káüs then took him in his arms again,
Asked him of *Zál* and of the road the pain.
"Out of the demon's sight," to him he cried,
"Great care must we now take our Rakhsh to hide,
When the White Dív of this becomes aware.
Of *Arjang's* face the earth must be made bare."
To king Káüs then Piltan drew more near,
"All the brave demons are assembling here.
When all the Dívs assemble here again,
Then all thy labours will have been in vain.
Take now the road the Dív's abode toward,
And labour with thy body, arrow, sword.
If now shall aid thee God in whom I trust,
Enchanters all shalt thou lay in the dust.
O'er snowy mountains thou wilt have to pass,
Where ev'rywhere are demons, mass on mass.
Before thee thou shalt find a gruesome cave,
I hear 'tis full of fear and terrors grave.
The passage to it warlike Dívs will bar,
All fierce as tigers, and prepared for war.
Within that cave the Safid Dív resides,
Its fears and hopes in whom his army hides.
Thou may'st be able to destroy them all,
For he is their support and general.
Blind through his grief his host's eyes thou may'st mark,
And my eye, too, is through this dimness dark.
Physicians who have seen me hope for cure,
The White Dív's heart and brain if I procure.
To me an excellent physician said:
"If like a tear his heart's blood can be shed,
And then three drops of this fall in thy eye,
The darkness with the blood will then pass by.
I on God's generosity rely,
This warlike Dív that thou wilt soon destroy."

The hero Piltan then prepared for fight,
Forward to go he set his face aright.
The wakeful hero the Iranis told:
"I go to war with that White Demon bold.
Than warlike elephants more tricky found,
An army numerous stands him around.
If he should manage now my back to bend,
Long time will ye despised and mourning spend.
Come to my aid the monarch of the sun,
And through propitious stars great strength he won.
All of this land and country ye'll obtain,
The royal tree shall come to fruit again."
The nobles all his praises chanted back,
"May horse and saddle, mace, thee never lack!"
With firmly girded waist he forward rode,
War and deep rage still in his heart abode.
Whilst with himself he bade Aolád proceed,
He urged Rakhsh forward like the wind in speed.
The well-intentioned hero took no rest,
To show the road Aolád he forward pressed.
When to the Seven Mountains Rakhsh comes near,
Troops upon troops of demons then appear.
"In what of thee, I on the road enquired,
Thou answeredst," Aolád he told, "by truth inspired.
Before me lies a very heavy task:
Thou of good omen, tell me what I ask.
To enter when the due time shall appear,
Reveal the secret and the road make clear."
Aolad replied: "When the hot sun mounts higher,
The demons to their slumber will retire.
Thou in the end shalt conquer in the fray
But now 'twere better for a while delay.
None of the demons seated shalt thou see;
A few magicians on the watch there'll be.
If the Victorious One thy aid shall be,

Then only shalt thou win the victory."
Rústam determined then awhile to wait,
Until the sun was hot as day grew late.
Firmly both Aolád's head and feet he bound,
And sat upon his lasso on the ground.
Out of its sheath his fighting sword then came,
As thunder growling he gave out his name.
Like dust among the host on ev'ry side
His dagger scattered heads both far and wide.
Their very lives in peril by his sword,
His power from themselves they could not ward.
No master combatting against him fought,
Against him name and glory no one sought.

Seventh Stage. The Killing by Rústam of the White Demon, his Releasing of Káus and the Iranis from their Bonds

To the White Div he went on to the fight,
He came on as a brilliant shining light.
He saw a cavern like a very hell;
In darkness demons' forms he could not tell.
Awhile he stood, his sword in hand held tight.
There was no place to see, no room for flight.
He washed his eye and rubbed his eyelash, too,
Seeking what in the cave might come to view.
And in the darkness there he saw a hill,
That seemed in hiding the whole cave to fill.
Of night-like hue and with a lion's mane,
Its length and breadth a world would scarce contain,
Within the cave to sleep himself he'd laid.
But Rústam no haste in his slaughter made.
He roared just like a tiger in his might,
And when he was awake came on to fight.
A millstone then he snatched up in his hand,

Like smoke to Rústam came and took his stand.
At him then Piltan's heart was full of dread,
He feared into the hole he would be led.
Enraged he like an angry lion flew,
And aimed his sword to cut his loins in two.
With all the force of his commanding height,
One foot and hand he cut off in the fight.
He caught and clung to him, though maimed in limb,
Like a huge elephant or lion grim.
On one foot with the hero thus he fought,
And great confusion in the cave was wrought.
Seized on his arm and neck the hero bold,
Perchance his form he might beneath him hold,
The hero Rústam in an onslaught warm
Came on and firmly seized him by the arm;
Each from the other tearing off the skin,
Did earth with blood to turn to mud begin.
"If I survive," said Rústam in his heart,
"In life eternal shall I bear my part."
The White Dív said, too: "Of all hope bereft,
Of life no prospect to me here is left.
If from this dragon I escape in peace,
With feet and skin cut I shall gain release.
Neither the great nor small of lofty race
Shall in Mázanderán behold my face."
Against each other thus the fighters set,
Their bodies ran down with their blood and sweat.
Then Tuhamtan, whom God gave strength, again
Strove on and on with mingled rage and pain.
The famous hero, who with anger burned,
Upon himself at last in battle turned;
The Dív the lion seizing in his hand,
He lifted up, and cast him on the strand.
Like lion cast him down, beyond control
So that his body parted from his soul.

He drew his dagger and cut out his heart,
From his dark form the liver tore apart.
A body slain the whole cave seemed to be,
The earth appeared just like a bloody sea.
And when the demons saw what he had done,
To flight betook themselves then ev'ry one,
And in that place not one of them remained.
Rústam came out ; from vengeful war refrained.
To loose the royal belt he did not fail;
He took his *khaftan** off and coat of mail.
He washed his head and body both for prayer,
Seeking for worship for a fit place there.
He lifted then from off the ground his head,
And "O Thou just and gracious Ruler!" said.
"Thy servant's refuge Thou in ev'ry ill,
Valour Thou givest me and power still,
My manliness, my glory, my resolve,
All my desire as sun and moon revolve.
These are Thy gifts : yet see I come more base,
Oh wretched man ! of earth upon the face.
Anxiety, grief, sorrow, care and all,
Both good and evil that to man may fall,
Decrease and increase and a happy fate,
Highness and lowness and the pride of State,
All from Thy justice comes to me, I own ;
No other hand is in it, Thine alone.
For through Thy grace becomes a sun each mote,
And in Thy glory spheres are of no note."
When with this praise the hero proud had done,
All his accoutrements he fastened on.
He came and from Aolád his chain unwound,
His royal lasso to his stirrup bound.
To Aolád then he gave that liver torn.
As towards Káüs he went, there to be borne.

*A garment worn under armour.

Aolád said to him: "Valiant lion, thou
Beneath thy sword the world art bringing now
There in Mázandarán is none alive,
With thee heroic who would dare to strive.
In ev'ry matter fortune is thine own,
And thou art worthy of the crown and throne.
'Twere well if my affair thou'dst keep in view,
For all that I have told thee has been true.
My body of thy bonds still bears the sign,
Under thy lasso's fold I still repine.
In all thou gavest to my heart good news;
Hope for the future now itself renews.
To break thy pledge in thee would not be right.
Though raging lion, thou'rt a monarch bright."
"Mázandarán," Rústam to him replied,
"To thee I give up all, from side to side.
A hard thing lies before me, lengthened woe,
Both that which is above and that below;
Now from his place Mázandarán its king
Must I cast up and in the well must fling.
A thousand thousand demons from their crown
With my sharp dagger must I now cast down;
And after that must lay them in the dust;
If not, with thee I'd not fulfil my trust.
Hereafter shalt thou be without a want:
Mázandarán in dignity I grant."
On that side nobles all expectant wait:
"Why is the hero then in coming late?"
When from their bodies he has cut the head,
From demons' battle he's victorious led.
He comes rejoicing and the heroes cry:
"Behold, the leader comes in dignity!"
Giving him blessings, on they ran before,
Bestowing praises on him more and more.
The Pehlaván, lion of auspicious feet,

Came forward then Káüs, the king, to meet.
He said: "O king, who wisdom hast ordained,
Be glad that thou thy foe's death hast obtained.
The White Dív's liver have I torn away,
The king has no more hope on him to stay;
I drew the liver out with mine own hand.
And what will now the conquering king command?"
Blessings on him king Káüs showered back:
"May army and the crown thee never lack!
The mother who has borne a son like thee
Without due benediction should not be.
A happier lot than both me fortune gave;
The lion-slaying elephant's my slave.
The blood must thou bring hither for my eye,
And for the eyes of all this company,
That we may see the better in the end,
And may the world's Creator be thy friend!"
Brought forward Rústam then the demon's heart
And of the blood dropped in his eye a part.
Into the eye then as the blood they threw,
His darkened eye became a sun to view.
Rústam at once, of perfect skill possessed,
Of liver blood a portion, too, expressed.
Upon their eyes at once a light was spread,
And the world seemed to them a flower-bed.
Below him there the ivory thrown they spread,
And placed an ivory crown upon his head.
Then Mázandarán's throne he occupied,
With Rústam and the nobles by his side,
Such as Gudúrz, Kíshvád, Giv, and Ruham,
As Tús and Gúrgin, and the brave Berham.
And thus did Káüs for a week at least
With wine and singing deck the joyous feast.
On the eighth day their horses mounted they,
The haughty heroes and their company.

Each one of them drew out his heavy mace,
Throughout Mázandarán his way to trace,
And all came out by order of the king,
As from a cane-brake a hot fire might spring.
They lit the flames up with their swords of ire,
And ev'ry city they burnt up with fire.
Of the magicians too such hosts were killed,
The running river with their blood was filled.
When came upon them there the dark'ning night
All of the warriors rested from the fight.
And to the army king Káus then cried:
"Vengeance for all crimes now is satisfied.
All have been punished as became the day.
And any more ye should refrain to slay."
To Rústam king Káüs to say began:
"Oh! of propitious feet thou worthy man,
We need a man of intellect and weight,
Upon Mázandarán its chief to wait.
One who great haste knows from undue delay,
His brain to weigh down though his heart is gay."
Agreeing equally, the nobles all,
Consented to be king the son of Zál.

King Káüs now writes a letter to the king of Mázandarán, telling him to submit and appear at his Court as a vassal and pay tribute. This letter is dispatched by the hand of Farhád, one of his courtiers. The king receives him, and is much affected by the news of Rústam's victories over the Dívs, but refuses to submit, and announces his intention of proceeding with an army against Irán. On receipt of this reply Káüs despatches Rústam to Mázandarán, and he on the road gives proof of the strength of his hand by squeezing those of some of the heroes of Mázandarán till their nails fall out. The king, however, still refuses to yield to Irán, and Rústam returns, and Káüs prepares for war against him.

The armies meet each other, and Rústam kills Júga, one of the heroes of Mázandarán, who opposes him. A general action between the two armies thus ensues, which lasts seven days. On the eighth day Káüs prays to God for help, and leads on his army, and Rústam attacks the king of Mázandarán, who, however, just as Rústram advances to make an end of him, transforms himself by enchantment into a rock. Rústam, after others had failed to move it, lifted up the stone and carried it to the king's tent at the foot of the Seven Mountains. There, on his threatening to break it in pieces, the king appeared like a thick cloud with a steel helmet on his head and clothed in mail, and was cut to pieces by Rústam by Káüs's order. The king remains in prayer, thanking God, for seven days; on the eighth his treasures were opened, and liberal gifts presented to the army for another seven before he returned to Irán and, according to Rústam's promise, conferred the throne of Mázandarán on Aolád. Rústam has magnificent gifts conferred on him, and is invested with the realm of Nímirúz, which appears to be synonymous with Zábulistán. At the same time Tús is given the command of the Persian army and Gudúrz the próvince of Isfahán. After this Káus made a tour in China (Chinese Tartary), Túrán (Scythia) and Mekrán, and engaged in war with Barbaristán. What this country was cannot be made out from the text; its opposition, however, seems to have been easily overcome, and the king proceeded to Zábúlistán, where he enjoyed the hospitality of Rústam. Just at this time the Arabs are said to have revolted, and Káüs conducted an expedition against them by sea. On his left hand was Misr (Egypt) and on his right the country of Barbar, and in the middle the cities of Hamávarán: this description does not render the position at all clearer. The king of Hamávarán made his submission and agreed to pay tribute. After this Káüs demanded the hand of the daughter of the king of Hamávarán in marriage, sending an embassy for the purpose ; this request was, with great reluctance on the part of the king, granted, after the consent of Sudábah, the daughter, had been obtained, and she was sent in great state, and on her arrival married to Káüs. The king of Hamávarán then formed the design of seizing the person of Káüs, whom he accordingly invited to a banquet for the purpose in the city of Shahah. The invitation was accepted, in spite of the remonstrances of Sudábah, and Káüs and his chief officers were seized and confined in a hill fortress, where they were followed by Sudábah, who was loyal to her husband and waited upon him.

Finding the throne of Irán thus unexpectedly vacant, Afrásiáb determined again to attack it, and overran the country. The people, however, at once resorted to Rústam to implore his assistance, which he was ready to give, and sent a threatening message to Hamávarán. This was unavailing, and Rústam at once prepared to attack Barbaristán or Hamávarán. The two are not synonymous, for the king, on hearing of Rústam's approach, sends to the kings of Barbar and Egypt for assistance. Rústam meets the armies of the three kings, and defeats them, himself unhorsing the king of Egypt, or of the West, as he is called, and making him prisoner with sixty of his nobles. The king of Barbaristán, having also been made prisoner with forty of his warriors, the king of Hamávarán sends to Rústam and asks for quarter, promising to release Káüs. Rústam acquired great booty from this conquest, and Sudábah is said to have been sent off on a palfrey (Hákuence in Mohl's translation), where is not specified. This first battle appears not to have been decisive, for there is an account of a second fight, in consequence of which king Káüs is released. The account of the affair is rather confused, but the three armies are at all events broken up. The next two Sections relate the sending of letters to the Kaisar of Rúm and Afrásiáb by the king of Irán, to the former for the assistance of the Greek army and to the latter calling on him to retire from Irán. The latter replied that he claimed the domain of Irán as his own for two reasons, viz., that Túr, the son of Faridún, was his grandfather, and he had himself destroyed the army of the Tázis, by which must be meant the Persians, and not the Arabs, as translated by Mohl. Both sides prepare for war, and in the battle that ensues Rústam breaks their centre, and Afrásiáb calls upon his troops to make a great effort to make a prisoner of Rústam, offering the kingdom of Irán and the hand of his daughter in marriage to whoever accomplishes the undertaking. The Turkománs, however, rally in vain, and Afrásiáb takes to flight and retreats to Turán. Káüs also returns to the province of Fars, re-establishes the splendour of his throne, and sends Pehlaváns to Marv, Nishapúr, Balkh, and Herát to establish order. All men practised justice; the wolf left the sheep; and such were the king's riches and dignity that *Paris* and Dívs, as well as men, became his slaves. Rústam is proclaimed Pehlaván of the world, and the king makes the Dívs construct a magnificent palace for him on Mount Alburz. In consequence of the labours imposed on them the Dívs take counsel together to turn Káüs away from the service of God, and a cunning Dív is accordingly dispatched to tempt him into the idea of his own omnipotence. He conceives the idea of flying to heaven, and sends out men to collect from their nests young eagles, which should be well brought up until they were strong enough to raise a throne he had made for the purpose, with long lances projecting from it, to which were hung pieces of lambs' flesh. Seated on the throne, he attached four strong eagles to it, and these making for the meat, were to lift and carry it through the air. The throne with the king on it was carried up to the clouds, but the birds finally got tired and came down again, landing him in a forest near the town of Amul, where in his miserable condition he prays to God for pardon. He is now discovered by Rústam and the other Pehlaváns, who heap reproaches upon him for his folly. After repenting with tears of blood for forty days he receives pardon from God, his army gathers round him again, and matters are restored to their former prosperous condition. The next Section contains the account of a hunting expedition of Rústam with other Pehlaváns in the hunting grounds of Afrásiáb. He entertains at a grand feast Tús, Gudúrz, and other Persian heroes at a place called Narand, where the fire of Barzin, apparently a generic name for all fire-temples, burnt. Gív proposes that they should make an expedition into Túrán and Afrásiáb's own hunting grounds. The expedition is organized and goes on for seven days, when Afrasiab hears of it and assembles an army to attack it. Gurázah informs them of this, and Rústam laughs the matter to scorn. The army of Turán, however, advances, and Pirán, son of Visah, is sent forward by Afrásiáb to meet Rústam, and Pilsam, Pirán's brother, also comes forward to attack the Iránis. A general melée then takes place, which ends by Pilsam taking to flight when Rústam comes up. Alkús, another Turanian hero, is now sent forward by Afrásiáb, and has an encounter with Zúarah, Rústam's brother, and having unhorsed him is about to finish him when Rústam appears and in his charge lifts him out of the saddle on his lance and throws him to the ground. The seven heroes all join in the fight and the Turanians, and with them Afrásiáb himself, forsake the battle field and run away. Afrásiáb narrowly escapes being caught in Rústam's lasso. He had asked the world, as it is said, for honey and received only poison. After having thus conquered the Turanians, Rústam and his companions return with their spoils to the hunting ground, where they remain a fortnight in the enjoyment of the chase, first writing to the king to report their achievements, and then go back to Iran.

After this commences the history of Suhráb, Rústam's son. It begins by the recital of Rústam's adventures at the town of Samangán, when he went there to hunt, and where his horse Rakhsh is stolen from him whilst he is asleep. On following Rakhsh's tracks into the town he is hospitably entertained by the king of the place. When retiring for the night, he is visited by the king's daughter Tahmínah, who avows her love for him, and whom he then and there marries with the consent of her father. The next Section relates the birth to Tahmínah and Rústam of Suhráb. Suhráb is said to have been at the age of a month like a boy of a year, at the age of three to have practised arms, and at that of five to have had the heart of a lion. At the age of ten no one in the country was able to contend with him. He now discovers the name of his father from his mother, and in the next Section selects a horse for himself, and subsequently collects an army to fight against Káus and the Iránis. Afrásiab, hearing of Suhráb, sends Bármán and Homán to him to excite him to war, in hope that the father and son may meet and the latter kill his own father. With the troops that accompany Homán and Bármán, Suhráb marches to the White Castle (Dúj-i-Safid), belonging to Irán, the Commander of which was Hajír. Hajír goes out to attack him, but is unhorsed, and is about to be killed when he asks for quarter, and receives it, and is sent off bound to Homán. Meanwhile Gúrd-áfrid, daughter of Gajdahúm, one of the old Iranian warriors, who appears to have owned the Castle, hears of the affair of Hajír, and arming herself like a man, goes out and encounters Suhráb. He, however, catches her in the noose of his lasso and discovers her sex, and she takes him into the castle. Gajdahúm writes a letter to Káüs, informing him of the arrival of the Turanian army with the young hero Suhráb, who had not yet attained the age of fourteen years. He describes his prowess and the result of his fight with Hajir, and announces his own intention of joining him. This he apparently does, for Suhráb, on preparing to attack the Castle the next day, finds Gajdahúm and Gúrd-áfrid and the garrison gone. Káüs receives Gajdahúm's letter, and writes to summon Rústam from Zábulistán, sending the letter by the hand of Gív. Rústam, instead of starting at once, as directed in the letter, enjoys a debauch of wine for three days and only leaves on the fourth. The next Section gives an account of the king's quarrel on this account and their final reconciliation through the intervention of Kishvád and others. After an entertainment, at which they were all intoxicated together, Káüs and Rústam start off on the campaign. Rústam now assumes the disguise of a Turkomán, and goes to the camp of Afrásiáb, where sitting at the banquet he sees Suhráb, Homân, and Barmán. Meanwhile Zindah-razm, brother of Tahmínah, and uncle of Suhráb, who had been told by Tahmínah to look after Suhráb, meets Rústam outside the banquet, and on enquiring who he is, is killed by a blow of his fist on the head, and the entertainment breaks up in confusion. Suhráb vows vengeance for the death of Zindah-razm, whose dead body has been discovered.

Rústam returns to the Persian army, meeting on the road Gív, who is patrolling round the camp. The next Section relates how Suhráb takes Hajír with him and, pointing out different banners and tents in the Persian camp, enquires to whom they belong; he, however fails, to discover Rústam, towards finding whom his enquiries are specially directed. Suhráb now attacks the Persian army, and Rústam, urged on by Tús and others who had witnessed Suhráb's prowess, arms himself and goes out against him. Rústam sees him, and, knowing that he has a formidable opponent, begs him to draw aside, and to join the Iránis. Suhráb, suspecting it is Rústam, questions him, and is answered as follows :—

" Not Rústam I," then he in answer said,
" Nor of the seed of Sam of Naram bred.
For he's a Pehlaván ; no weight have I.
No throne, no crown, nor any dignity."
Suhráb from hope to sheer despair fell back,
The face of brilliant day to him grew black.

The Combat of Rústam with Suhráb.

Grasping his spear, he to the combat led,
In great amaze at what his mother said.
Into a narrow space they now descend,
While with short spears in combat they contend.
Nor long on spear and lance do they rely,
Turning to left they pass each other by.
Their Hindi sabres then at once they drew,
And from the iron sparks of fire there flew,
Till with the heavy blows their weapons broke.
What fight was this the Judgment Day that woke !
Then after this each seized his heavy mace,
Struck this on that and that on this apace.
Proud steeds and fiery warriors, as they went,
From mace and arrows turned aside and bent.
Their saddle-cloths from off their saddles fell,
And from the heroes' loins their coats of mail.
Both horse and warrior from the battle stayed,
They had no hands nor strength themselves to aid.
Their bodies full of sweat, of dust their mouth,

Their very tongues were split up with the drouth.
Asunder from each other stood the twain,
The father full of aches, the son of pain.
"O world inscrutable, this is thy way,
Thou mendest up what thou hast spoilt to-day!"
Now love moved neither of them from his place,
Wisdom had failed: nor friendship showed its face.
All living creatures know their young again,
Fish in the sea and wild ass in the plain.
Yet nor from pain nor love the mortal knows,
His very offspring from one of his foes.
"No crocodile," then Rústam musing thought,
"That I have seen in this wise ever fought.
The White Dív's fight a trifle seemed to me,
Now from a man I in despair must be,
At his hand who the world has never known,
No hero, one who has not gained renown,
And I have but fulfilled my destiny,
That witness to this fight two hosts should be.'
Of hero and of horse the conflict ceased.
From battle's pain and battle's shame released.
Each of the two his bow then promptly strung,
One in his years advanced, the other young.
With panther-skin, cuirass and coat of mail,
The spear could do no harm or arrow hail.
Both shot their cloud of arrows thick and fast;
Thou would't have said a tree its leaves had cast.
Each with the other was at heart distraught,
And by his waist-belt each the other caught.
If Tuhamtan should seize upon a rock,
He could uproot it in the battle's shock.
A mountain from the earth he could have raised,
And the hard rock as so much wax appraised.
He now sought Suhráb's belt this wise to use,
Him from his saddle in the fight to loose.

Not knowing how the young man's waist to hold,
The hand of Rustam failed its skill of old.
His hand unable now the belt to clasp,
He wondering released him from his grasp.
The lions had enough fight for the day,
As sore and wounded they both sought delay.
With hard-pressed thigh Suhráb again his mace
Drew out before his saddle from its place.
Struck with the mace, his shoulder wrung with pain,
Insensibility must Rústam feign.
Laughing, then Suhráb said: "O horseman bold,
'Gainst brave men's blows thyself thou canst not hold.
Thy Rakhsh beneath thee thou an ass may'st deem,
For both its rider's hands now useless seem.
My heart upon thee truly pity takes,
That of the mud a paste thy blood now makes.
'The cypress tree is tall,' although thou say:
'Old men are senseless, youth is strong and gay.'"
To these words Tuhamtan made no reply,
And with pain writhing gave way helplessly.
Down this on that and that on this they threw,
The earth for these brave men so narrow grew,
That from each other both then turned away,
And to anxiety their souls were prey.
Rústam tow'rds Turán's host now in the fight
Turned as a panther with his prey in sight.
Suhráb tow'rds Irán's host then charged again,
And to his swift-paced courser gave the rein.
Thus when on Irán's host himself he threw,
Full many a man renowned his hand then slew,
Wolf-like, among the army did he ride.
Small, great, were killed and scattered far and wide.
But Rústam to Turán's host drawing nigh,
Was grieved and from his heart gave out a sigh,
Mournful in heart and thought, for he could tell

The certain ill to Káūs that befell
From that young Turk, in skill who did not fail,
With arms adorned and in his coat of mail.
Swiftly towards his own encampment turned,
With dread for him his heart in such wise burned.
He saw Suhráb as tow'rds the host he sped,
The ground who had with pure blood stainéd red.
Bloody cuirass upon his breast there lay,
Yet furious he like lion with his prey.
Savage grew Rústam as he spied him out,
And raised, like lion fierce, a mighty shout.
And said: "O Turk, keen in devouring blood,
Who among Irán's host has thee withstood?
Why dost thou now from me thy hand withhold,
And enterest like a wolf among the fold?"
Suhráb replied: "Turán's host in this war
Are innocent and from the fight afar.
'Twas thou who on them onslaught mad'st at first,
None in his rage for fight with thee would thirst."
"The day is growing dark," then Rústam said,
"When it shall raise its world-illuming blade,
Let us two wrestle at to-morrow's dawn,
And see for whom the host's tears shall be drawn.
Pulpit and stake both on this place are found,
But now bright earth beneath the cloud* is bound.
If now thine arm these arrows and this sword,
Knows well, thou canst to perish not afford."†
They went, and as the heaven's face grew black,
Dark fate on Suhráb also turned its back.
Thou would'st have said him Heav'n tow'rds fight had
pressed,

* The word in the text is "tigh," a sword, but is probably a misprint for "migh," a cloud.

† In the original, "do not thou ever die," but the meaning is very doubtful.

And that from charging he would never rest.
Once more upon his iron horse he came,
Wondrous in spirit and of brass his frame.
Homán he told : " When the sun rose to-day,
It filled the earth with noise as of a fray.
By that bold horseman's head to thee I swear,
He'd hero's arms, claws such as lions bear.
Why did he come ? What did he do or say,
For he was quite my equal in the fray ?
What did he with the army when he came ?
None know I on the earth of equal name.
He is a lion, though a man of years,
Content with fighting never he appears.
If of his deeds I told you all I knew,
It would be such you would not deem it true.
His arms are huge as is a great beast's thigh ;
The Nile's waves boil up at his strident cry.
I know not that world-hero who may be,
In war who girds his loins up as can he."
Homán replied : " The order of the king
Was not beyond this place the host to bring.
All that I now have done was strictly right."
When movement was beginning tow'rds the fight.
A valiant man of war, for combat keen,
Coming towards this mighty host was seen.
Thou would'st have said that he was mad with pride,
When one man simply a whole host defied.
He turned away and backward pulled his rein,
As he returned tow'rds Irán's host again.
" Out of this army," thus Suhráb went on,
" Of these brave heroes he has not killed one,
Whilst of Irán now I have many slain,
The ground with mud of bloody hue to stain.
But if a lion came across him, know,
He would not have escaped that mace's blow.

But when to look on silently you stood
And no one came, what gain from that accrued?
For panthers or for lions what care I,
Who with my spear bring fire out from the sky?
When heroes very stern my face shall see,
Torn into pieces shall their breast-plates be.
To-morrow comes, a most important day;
Let him come forward, valourous who may.
In that God's name who gave the world its birth,
None of their heroes will I leave on earth.
But now must we the feast and wine prepare,
And drive out from our heart all thought of care.'
Rústam the other side his host beheld,
As he with Gív this conversation held.
"Suhráb in war experienced, this day
How then did he comport him in the fray?"
Then warrior Gív to Rústam thus replies:
"We never saw one brave upon this wise.
Tow'rds the host's centre first he raged in might,
And from the host tow'rds Tús, who longed for fight.
He was on horseback; in his hand his spear.
Then Gurgín mounted and approached him near.
When with spear coming he him gazed upon,
Like a fierce lion he went raging on.
With force he struck with his bent mace a blow
Upon his form; his helmet fell below.
He could not bear this and turned round his face,
And many brave men came there to the place.
None of the warriors had the needful grit;
To fight with him was only Píltan fit.
Strictly I acted on the ancient use,
And on him did not let the army loose.
Alone no warrior would to meet him dare;
For him we left the field of battle bare.
No single horseman to attack him strong,

From centre to right wing he rushed along,
With fury raging rushed on ev'ry side,
His horse careering 'neath him, too, in pride."
Grieved Rústam at the news that thus he learned;
Towards king Káüs then his face he turned.
When Káus Kai beheld the athlete brave,
Near to himself at once a place he gave.
Of Suhráb and of his commanding height.
In words did Rústam then the tale recite.
"No one has ever seen, in very truth.
A lion-man in such an unformed youth.
In height he rubs the planets with his head;
The earth can hardly bear his footstep's tread.
His thigh than that of wild beast's is not less,
And greater thickness ev'n his arms possess.
With arrow, sword, mace, lasso, ev'ry way,
Him to the test have I brought here this day
With this result. Before this now I own,
I from their saddles many men have thrown,
Of him the waist-belt, too, to-day I seized,
And though his very joints with force were squeezed
In vain I tried to lift him from his seat,
And throw him down, like others, 'neath my feet.
That hero sat upon his saddle still,
Unmoved as when the wind blows on a hill.
I turned back from him, for the day was gone;
The night was very dark and no moon shone.
So that to-morrow we again may meet,
And wrestling with each other may compete.
To-morrow when he comes upon the plain,
By means of wrestling must I strive again.
I know not who in strife may victor be;
What counsel God may offer must we see.
Of Him comes victory, of Him comes aid,
For He alone the sun and moon has made.

"God who is pure," then Káüs to him said:
"Thy foeman's form will now in pieces shred.
On earth to Him who did the world create
Will I the night long humbly supplicate.
That He may quickly hasten to thine aid
Against this Turk, who from the path has strayed,
The hope in thee that withered is and gone
Revive, and bear thy name up to the sun."
Rústam replied: "The glory of the king
His friend's desire will to a good end bring."
These words when he had spoken, Píltan, then
Left, stern become, this company of men,
Towards his own encampment as he turned,
Heart-thoughtful, whilst his head with anger burned.
Pricked to the soul, Zuárah came to ask:
"How fared the athlete this day in his task?"
"Something to eat," was Rústam's first request,
As from all care he set his heart at rest.
At the same time Suhráb the hero's state,
As it occurred, did he in full relate.
"Two *Farsangs* lay between the armies two,
And none dared there his waist-belt to undo."
These words he to his brother 'gan to speak:
"Do nothing rash, nor let thy heart be weak;
To battle when I shall advance at night,
To meet that Turk who's eager for the fight,
The army with my banner lead on bold;
Bring up my throne and slippers, those of gold.
As from his place the bright sun shall appear,
Before my tent enclosure be thou here.
If I am victor in the fight to-day,
Long on the battle-field I'll not delay.
But if events should turn out otherwise,
Do not lament nor utter mournful cries;
Toward the battle-field no man proceed,

The way there not to seek take thou good heed
But to Zábulistán go, nor delay,
And to Dastán at once take ye your way.
To him at once the grevious news present,
That Rústam's day has from its base been rent.
Such of almighty God was the decree,
That by a young man he destroyed should be.
Be to my mother's heart this solace giv'n,
That on my head this fate was fixed from heav'n.
Tell her upon me not her heart to bind,
Nor for my life for ever vex her mind.
None in the world for ever has remained,
And no excuse for me has Fate ordained.
Lion and panther, crocodile and sprite,
My hand has worsted in the day of fight.
Many a tow'r and fort have I laid low,
And none my hand could ever overthrow.
Say: He who death's gate would on horse assail
Of his own self assuredly will fail.
More than a thousand years should there have passed.
This method and this way will ever last.
Consider Jamshíd, king of lofty pride,
As well as Tehmurs, who the demons tied:
Like these into the world no prince there came,
But to his God went ev'ry one the same.
In valour than Gurshásp was none more high,
Whose head was fretted 'gainst the lofty sky,
And Sám and Narimán, those men of worth,
There was no path but death's for them on earth.
For these earth did not wait, but passed them by,
Upon the same road, then, must travel I.
All we are bound for death, both young and old,
No one by earth can permanently hold.
When she is soothed, then thus to Dastán say:
Turn from the world's king not thy face away.

If he should make war, be thyself not slack.—
Go: in this counsel he will never lack,"
Their talk of Suhráb half the night transgressed:
The other half was given to sleep and rest.

The Wrestling of Rústam and Suhráb, and Rústam's Escaping by a Trick.

When came the sun forth in his feathered glow,
The head was lowered of the black-winged crow.
His panther-mail then Tuhamtan put on,
And on his raging dragon-steed sat down.
Down to the plain and battle-field he sped,
And placed an iron crown upon his head.
On that side Suhráb and his company
Were drinking wine to strains of minstrelsy.
He said to Homán: "A heroic man
Is he the combat who with me began.
His height is not inferior to mine,
And in fight never does his heart repine.
His shoulders and his neck are just like mine,
As if an expert measured them with twine.
His foot and stirrip my regard excite,
And with the blush of shame my visage light.
The signs my mother showed I fain would find,
And for a while revolve them in my mind.
I have a fancy this may Rústam be,
For in the world no warrior is as he.
For with my hero father 'twere not right
That I should meet him face to face in fight.
I should before my God be much abased,
And have from this dark world to flee shame-faced.
No hope, then, of the next world would there be,
If with my sire I fought for victory.
Before earth's kings should I be blackened then,
Nor of Irán nor of Turán, the men

Ought that was good of me would ever say,
And in both worlds my hope were dashed away.
I should be, aye, bewildered in the fight;
From shedding blood would not flow ought that's right."
Homán said to him then: "With me as foe
Did Rústam often to the battle go.
What in Mázandaran with mace of fear
He did in war didst thou, then, never hear?
That steed of his, too, Rákhsh himself might be,
But legs and tread he has not such as he."
When but one watch of night there had passed by,
There from the forward pickets rose a cry.
The hero Suhráb, full of war his breast,
From the feast table had retired to rest.
When at the dawn the sun displayed his beam,
The heroes' heads awoke up from their dream.
Suhráb put on his battle panoply,
Head full of war, at heart still feasted he.
Shouting he came upon the battle-field,
A bull head mace was in hand to wield.
He asked of Rústam with a smile serene—
All night together, thou had'st said, they'd been—
"How hast thou risen? From what kind of night?
And how hast thou prepared thy heart for fight?
Cast sword and arrows from thy hand away:
Hand of injustice on the ground now lay.
Let us together on the ground recline,
Our countenances stern light up with wine.
Before the world's God let us pledges take;
Our hearts of thought of war repentant make.
Before another comes thy foe to be,
Adorn the feast; be reconciled to me.
Thee with affection would my heart embrace,
And bring the tear of shame upon my face.
As thou art sprung from heroes of renown,

Thy noble origin to me make known.
Thy name I made all effort to unfold:
Now tell thy name which no one else has told.
As thou a battle now with me hast tried,
Thy name from me thou should'st in no way hide.
Canst thou, Dastán, the son of hero Sám, then be?
Rústam, of Zábul monarch known, art he?"
Rústam replied: "Thou who for fame dost seek,
On such a subject never did we speak.
Of wrestling yesterday was all the talk:
Try not that gate: thy trick me shall not baulk.
Though thou art young, no more a child am I.
A wrestling bout I gird my loins to try.
Now let us strive. The end of this affair
With counsel the world's ruler shall declare.
Moreover, in the things of fame and war,
Never will heroes make excuse too far.
In many places wand'ring low and high,
No man of hypocritic speech am I."
"O man of age," Suhráb to him replied:
"If by my counsel thou wilt not abide,
I had a hope, when laid upon thy bed,
Thy life from thee whilst in full sense had fled.
He whom thou leav'st here should thy tomb prepare,
Thy form in bonds, thy soul should fly in air.
But if thy senses lie beneath my hand,
Will I now bring them out by God's command."
Off from their war-steeds did they then alight,
Arrayed in conscious pride, with helmets bright.
Each fastened up his charger to a rock,
And pained at heart both rushed on to the shock.
Like lions fierce in wrestling as they met,
From both their bodies poured out blood and sweat.
Like raging elephant, Suhráb his hand
Struck, lion fierce, as he leapt up to stand.

He pulled at Rústam's waist-belt with a strain,
Thou would'st have said the earth he rent in twain.
Like a wild elephant he to Rústam clung,
And, lifting him, upon the plain he flung.
Of rage and spite he uttered loud a sound,
And threw the lion Rústam on the ground.
Sitting, he took on Piltan's chest his place,
His hand was full of dust, his mouth and face.
Just as a lion a male ass that slays,
He strikes, and with his life the wild ass pays.
A tempered dagger from his belt he drew,
And would his head from off his body hew.
This Rústam saw as with his voice he said,
"Thy hidden secret now must bare be laid."
He cried to Suhráb: "Lion-slayer thou,
Sword and mace wielder, lasso who dost throw,
Our custom here is of a different kind,
In other ways adorned our faith thou'lt find.
In wrestling combat he who may have fought,
And to the dust a Chieftain's head have brought,
When first upon the earth he lays his head,
He will not cut it off, by anger led.
If for the second time he throws him down,
As a brave lion he acquires renown.
The head if from the body then he smite,
It were allowed him in our ancient rite."
Out of the dragon's claw with which he fought
He by this stratagem release thus sought.
The brave youth listened to the old man's word,
Justice and battle would it room afford,
First fate and next had pluck this brought about,
And third, youth's bravery without a doubt.
Released his captive, he then went below,
Down to the plain, where deer passed to and fro.
He had his hunting and then thought no more

Of him with whom he'd striven just before.
Some time elapsed. Homan came up to ask
How he had prospered in his battle task.
He told Homán the place where he had gone,
And all the talk with Rústam carried on.
Homán to him replied: "Young man, alas!
Thy life to its completion now must pass.
Woe for this body and this stature tall,
These stirrups long, heroic feet and all!
The lion to the snare that thou hadst brought
Thou hast released and all hast brought to nought.
See, from this foolish act that thou hast done,
What conflict in the plain will this bring on.
A king once told a story in this wise:
'Never a foe, though he be small, despise.'"
Speaking, from hope of life his heart he raised,
And mourning full of sorrow stood amazed.
Towards his own camp then his face he turned,
Astonished, though his heart with sorrow burned.
Then to Homán thus did Suhráb say:
"Drive from thy heart anxiety away.
In fight to-morrow should with me he cope,
Thou shalt behold around his neck my rope."
Out of his grasp when Rústam was released,
Like to a hill of steel his force increased.
Proudly he went towards a running stream:
Him dead and brought to life one well might deem.
Water he drank, his body washed and face,
The world's Creator nearing first for grace.
To Him who needs no prayer he whispered low,
And prayed to Him who remedy would know.
Of sun and of moon's bounty unaware,
For victory and aid he made his prayer,
That as the sphere itself had passed him o'er,
The crown upon his head, twould place no more.

When the affair began, thus have I heard,
On Rústam God such mighty strength conferred,
That if upon a stone he down would sit,
Both of his feet at once would sink in it.
From that day of that strength he e'er complained,
And his heart distant from his hope remained.
He prayed that He his strength would take away
That he might walk upon the rightful way.
As of pure God he asked this day by day,
The strength of that hill-form would waste away.
And when the matter this complexion bore,
Fear of Suhráb his heart in pieces tore.
"Almighty!" then to God did he bewail:
"Let not Thy guardianship Thy servant fail.
As from the first, for the same strength this day,
From Thee, Almighty, purest God, I pray."
All that was now desired God gave him back,
And gave him increase in what he might lack.
The place of battle from the stream he sought,
Pallid his face, his heart full filled with thought.
Suhráb, wild elephant, too, sought the field,
His arm the lasso, hand the bow to wield.
Growling, he like a lion roared again,
His steed went leaping, tearing up the plain.
When Rústam saw him coming on this wise,
He turned and looked on him with wond'ring eyes.
Though sorrowing, he saw him with amaze,
And reckoned in the conflict on his ways.
And when Suhráb beheld him coming nigh,
With wind of youth his heart was beating high.
He saw him as he near approached at length,
And looked upon his dignity and strength.
He cried: "Thou who the lion's claw didst flee,
Why hast thou boldly come again to me?
Why comest thou again before me, say,

And of thy safety seekest not the way?
Art thou already wearied of thy life,
That boldly thou dost brave the lion's strife?
Twice did I give thee quarter in the war,
O famous one, of old age on the score!"
And Piltan to him then the answer gave:
"O army-breaker, O thou hero brave,
Men speak not thus who heroes are allowed,
But thy raw youth has made thee far too proud.
And from this brave old man thou now shalt see,
O thou male lion, what will come to thee,
For ev'rywhere in evil fortune's tracks,
The hardest rock becomes to me as wax."

The Slaughter of *Suhráb* at the hand of Rústam

Once more, then, to the rocks their steeds they bound,
Above their heads whilst ill fate hovered round.
Themselves to strive in wrestling they addressed,
And each of them the other's waist-belt pressed.
Mighty of hand, Suhráb the general,
High heav'n, thou would'st have said, had made him fall.
Rústam, though sorrowful, his hand then clasped,
The neck and arm of that fierce panther grasped.
The back of that brave youth he downwards bent,
His strength had vanished, his full time was spent.
The lion struck him on the ground a blow;
He knew that he would not remain below.
Quick from its sheath a sharpened sword he drew,
His son of wretched heart he thus pierced through.
Then Suhráb flinched and heaved a mournful sigh:
All thoughts of good or bad had passed him by.
He said: "This from myself has come to me;
And fate has giv'n into thy hand my key.
That crook-backed one (in this thou'rt blameless still)
Has dragged me here and made all haste to kill.

And my companions in their sport will say:
A hero now has passed to dust away.
My mother gave me tokens of my sire;
In love of him my soul must now expire.
That I might see his face I sought him long,
And for this yield my life, in hope still strong.
Alas of pain that I should not be free,
And of my sire the face I should not see.
Now, though as fish in water thou remain,
Or of the night the darkness thou should'st gain;
If thou up in the spheres a star should'st prove,
And from earth's face all pure love should'st remove,
If he upon a brick my pillow see,
My father will avenge me yet on thee.
And of these far-famed heroes of the day,
This token one to Rústam shall convey
That slain Suhráb was left contemptuously.
A full requital he will claim from thee."
Dark, then, grew Rústam's heart when this he heard,
And to his sight earth's face itself was blurred.
Bereft of power, he lost all his strength,
And fell unconscious on the ground at length.
He came back to his senses by and bye,
And thus addressed him with a wailing cry:
"Of Rústam say what tokens thou hast held,
From lofty ones that his name be expelled.
I Rústam am. May that name pass away,
And may the son of Sám sit on my clay!"
He uttered wailing cries; with boiling blood
He tore his hair, and made lament aloud.
And when Suhráb in this state Rústam knew,
He fell and from his head the senses flew.
He said to him: "If thou should'st Rústam be,
Thou'st strangely slain me in malignity.
To thee a guide in ev'ry way I proved,

And yet in thee of love no atom moved
The knot of my cuirass do thou undo,
And see my body in its naked glow.
See now thy talisman my arm upon;
Behold what to his son my sire has done.
When at my gate rang out of drums the din,
With bleeding cheeks my mother came within.
Her soul struck of my going with the wound,
Upon my arm the talisman she bound.
She said: 'This is a token of thy sire;
Keep it, till thou thyself its aid require.'
Now has it come to use; the fight is done,
And lying low the father sees the son."
Opened the coat of mail, there came to view
The talisman. His robe he rent in two.
He cried: "Alas! thou hast been slain by me,
O brave one, praised in ev'ry company."
Tearing his hair, his blood he freely shed;
His face was full of tears, of dust his head.
Suhráb said to him: "This is worse than all.
Let not the blinding tears from both eyes fall.
What in self-slaughter do we profit see,
For that has happened which was doomed to be?"
When down the bright sun passed from off the sphere,
Did Tuhamtan not from the plain appear.
There from the camp came twenty clever men
What had occurred in fight to ascertain.
They saw two horses that were standing there,
For Rústam full of dust then stood elsewhere.
The hero Piltan on his saddle set
The warriors on the war-plain saw not yet.
They sadly fancied thus that he was killed.
The nobles' thoughts were with confusion filled.
To Kai Káus they with the tidings hied,
"The throne of greatness was of Rústam void."

Out of the camp arose a shout on high,
The host in agitation raised a cry.
Káüs then bade the drums and trumpets play,
And Tús, the General, hastened on his way.
The king then gave his orders to the host
That to the battle field a beast should post
How it had fared with Suhráb there to see,
If Irán's land prepared to weep should be,
With valiant Rústam slain that they might know
Who in Irán to him would dare to go.
Fleeing like Jamshíd, then must they decide
In hills and deserts all their heads to hide.
In crowds the wounded men must then be slain,
And none upon the battle field remain.
From the assembly as the uproar spread,
To Píltan there the dying Suhráb said:
"Now that my dwindling hours of life are few,
The Turks' affairs assume another hue.
Oh! mercifully act, that so the king
Against Turán may not his army bring.
For they but for my longing for the fight
Tow'rds Irán's land had never turned their sight.
Let them incur no pain upon the road,
And look but on them with an eye for good.
I gave myself good news for many days,
And entertained a hope in many ways.
I said: 'If I but see my sire in life,
No king on earth will I leave in the strife.'
O hero of renown, how could I see
That in my father's hand my life would be?
There is in this fort now a warrior bold,
Who was made captive in my lasso's fold.
Of him I asked thy tokens ev'ry day,
For ever in my eye thy image lay.
As from his talk no better hope I knew,

No wonder that my bright day darker grew.
Now of Iránis he who there may be
See that he may not come to injury.
The sign my mother gave me I received,
But seeing it, my eye had not believed.
My evil star had written on my brow,
My father's hand should slaughter me and now.
I came like lightning, wind-like now pass by.
Oh! may I see thee happy 'neath the sky!"
Rústam held hard his breath to still his cries,
His heart was full of fire, of tears his eyes.
Rústam like dust on Rakhsh his steed now rode,
Full of cold sighs his lip, his heart with blood.
Shouting, he came back to the host with speed,
With heart of anguish full at his own deed.
And when the men of Irán saw his face,
In dust did they their faces humbly place,
Nor did they tow'rds God in their praises lack,
That from the conflict he came living back.
When thus they saw his head upon the ground,
All torn his robes, his body all one wound,
They took to asking him of this affair:
"For whom is now thy heart so full of care?"
He told the strange deed he himself had wrought,
And how that dear one he to pain had brought.
All with him there his mournful shout maintained,
And in the leader's self no sense remained.
He said to those about of station high:
"To-day nor hero's heart nor form have I.
Join no one with the Turks in battle fray;
Suffice the evil I have done to-day!"
Zuárah hastening to Píltan went,
His body wounded and his garment rent.
His brother's state when Rústam looked upon,
He told what said to him his murdered son.

"Of my own deed have I repented now,
And to take more than common vengeance vow.
The heart's place of my youthful son is rent,
And this the very spheres will age lament.
In my old age I've killed my only son;
That hero's stem and root have I undone."
Then to Homán he sent at once this word:
"Sheathed must remain of vengeance now the sword.
Thou art the guardian of that mighty host:
Now guard them well and sleep not at thy post.
With thee to combat is not now my day;
Beyond this have I nothing more to say."
The Pehlaván to his brother said in turn:
"O hero of enlightened soul return.
Now with him to the river do thou go,
But hastiness from thee let no one know."
In his due time *Zuárah* forward went,
And gave Homán the word the athlete sent.
Homán the hero to him gave reply:
"Hajír, the mischievous, of evil eye,
With fraud o'er Suhráb an advantage gained,
For the chief's myst'ry secret he retained.
His father's tokens he refused to tell,
And into ignorance his soul thus fell.
His wickedness has us to mischief led,
And rightly now should we cut off his head."
Zuárah Píltan coming back to seek,
Of Homán and his band ceased not to speak.
In Hajír's matter he began to doubt
If this Suhráb's end had not brought about.
Those words heard *Tuhamtan* in great surprise,
And darkened grew the world before his eyes.
Near to Hajír he from the war plain drew;
His collar seized, him on the ground he threw.
He drew a tempered dagger from his waist,

His head to sever then prepared in haste.
The nobles then came up to intercede,
And Hajír from the gate of death was freed.
The Pehlaván turned him from the place away,
And came to where his young son wounded lay.
Together with him there the nobles came,
Gudúrz and Tús and Gustaham of fame :
And all the army to that noble man,
Loos'ning their tongues, to give advice began.
" The remedy for this will God prepare,
And make these sorrows light for thee to bear."
Then Rústam seized a dagger that was near,
From off his body his own head to shear.
To cling to him the nobles instant sped,
Though from their eyes great drops of blood they shed.
Gudúrz said: " What to thee will be the gain
If thou should'st raise up smoke upon earth's plain ?
Give thou thyself a hundred wounds like these,
And to thy darling thou wilt not bring ease.
If any time for him on earth is spared,
To live with him as well be thou prepared.
But if from this world he must passing be,
Behold, who lives here to eternity ?
We all are prey for death to hunt us down,
Those who may wear a helmet or a crown.
When one's time fully comes they bid one go,
And what they more may do we do not know.
Death's way is long, though it may narrow be,
We are all lost, should he accompany.
Who is, O Chief, of death without the pain ?
Yes ; each *of us must for himself* complain."

The demanding by Rústam of an elixir for Suhráb, and Káus not giving it to him.

And to Gudúrz replied the athlete then :
" Hero of brilliant soul, well known 'mong men,

A message to Káüs from me convey,
And tell him what has come to me to-day.
My brave son's heart have I with dagger rent.
(May Rústam in the earth not long be pent!)
With favour my brave deeds if thou dost see,
Now take some trouble in regard for me.
Of that elixir in thy treasure stored,
By which the wounded may be fully cured,
To us here with a cup of wine convey,
And it must reach me with the least delay.
If by thy fortune's aid he may be cured,
Like me, for thy throne is a slave secured."
With the wind's speed the General then went,
These words at once to Káüs to present.
"Than Píltan's self," Káüs to him replied:
"Who in more honour with me could abide?
That harm come to him I would not desire,
None greater honour with me can acquire.
But should I now my sweet elixir give,
And thus the elephantine hero live,
Rústam with force might overpower thee,
And then no doubt would work his will on me.
Hast thou not heard he said: 'Who is Káüs?
And if he is the king, who, then, is Tús?'
If ever he should do me a despite,
Only him with evil could I then requite
And this Suhráb, though fortunate no more,
By his own throne and by his crown he swore,
And said: 'With this spear I thy life will take
And I will fix thy head upon the stake.'
How could the world contain this man of pride,
With all his pomp and all his strength beside?
To stand beneath my throne would he consent,
Or be beneath the Húmá's pomp content?
Though he throne-giver or a warrior be,

I can not view him with complacency.
He for a period did me defame,
And with the army took away my name.
If his son living should before me stand,
He yet would be mere dirt within my hand.
Suhráb's words, too, have they not told to thee,
Man of experience though thou may'st not be?
'A thousand men of Irán's heads I'll shear,
And Káüs living on the stake hang here?'
If he upon the earth alive should be,
Both small and great men will before him flee.
He who the enemies of himself may love
His own name evil in the world will prove."
When Gudúrz heard the words that Káüs spoke,
To Rústam he returned with speed of smoke.
He said: "The king's bad temper, it appears,
Is colocynth that bitter fruitage bears.
In rashness no man can with him compare,
And no man's sorrow will he ever share.
Now it behoves myself to go to him,
And lighten up his soul that is so dim."
Rústam his chamberlain at once then bade,
A figured robe to bring him of brocade.
Upon that gold-embroidered robe he laid
The youth, as to the king his way he made.
And thus the hero Píltan took his way;
One quickly went before, these words to say:
"Suhráb has left this wide earth for his doom,
He asks no palace of thee, but a tomb,"

The lamenting of Rústam over Suhráb and carrying his body to Zábulistán to Sám and Rudábah.

Rústam heard this, his cheek scored in despair,
He struck upon his breast and tore his hair.
As forth he leaped he heaved a bitter sigh,

Bewailed, and closed the eyelash of his eye.
Lit from his horse, as wind then Rústam sped,
And in his crown's place poured dust on his head.
The army Chiefs together with him went,
Wailing and weeping, raising their lament.
Bitter he cried: " O warlike thou and young,
Of lofty head, from seed of athletes sprung.
Like thee none may the sun or moon behold,
Cuirass or helm or throne or crown of gold.
To whom e'er came what came to me to-day,
That I my son in my old age should slay?
Grandson of Sám, the rider of the steed,
And from thy mother of illustrious breed.
To cut off my two hands were right and meet,
May nothing but the black dust be my seat!
My son Suhráb I've given to the wind,
A hero like him one may never find.
Than Narimán's Sám, than Gursháسp of Giv,
Than heroes brave more generous to give.
Among world-heroes there is none like me,
I was his child in generosity.
What shall I say when this his mother hears,
How shall I send a message to her ears?
The guiltless, why I killed, what shall I say,
And why to darkness I have turned her day?
What father such a deed has ever done?
Worthy am I cold words to heap upon.
Who in the world his son has ever killed,
Youthful and brave and with all wisdom filled?
Her sire, most honoured warrior of the day,
What can he to his youthful daughter say?
That Rústam in his spite him overbore,
And his breast open with his dagger tore.
Upon the seed of Sám they'll vent a curse,
As void of love and faith my name rehearse.

And this belovèd child, who could have known,
Would in these years a cypress tall have grown?
A host he would array, be wise in fight,
And thus my bright day he would turn to night?"
He ordered and a piece of royal brocade
They brought, and on his young son's face they laid.
City and dignity were his desire,
And but a narrow grave would he acquire.
When from the battle plain his bier was brought,
In his own tent then Rústâm shelter sought.
Into the tent enclosures fire they thrust;
The army on their own heads poured out dust.
Brocaded tents of ev'ry hue and shade.
Gold beds, rich thrones, upon the fire were laid.
Then with the fire arose a wailing cry,
The hero's voice in lamentation high.
"Horsemen like thee the world will never see,
Hero and famed for generosity.
Woe for that manliness and counsel bright!
Woe for that beauty and commanding height!
Woe for that pain, that grief that frets the heart,
With father sad, from mother far apart!
How much will Zálzar, son of Sám, me blame!
And how reproach Rudábah, fair of fame!
What will the lofty-headed heroes say
When they to them of this the signs convey?
And when the news of this to them convey,
The cypress from the mead I tore away?
In this affair what pretext can be found,
To side with me by speech to bring them round?"
Rooting up dust, upon it blood to pour,
Upon his form his regal robe he tore.
Of king Káüs the Pehlaváns around
Sat with him in the road upon the ground.
The nobles' tongues were full of counsel wise,

And Tuhamtan's heart bound with painful ties.
Such is the way by destiny laid down,
A noose in one hand, and in one a crown.
When any with his crown sits down well pleased,
In his own noose perhaps he may be seized.
Why have affection for the world below,
When with one's comrades one must surely go ?
Nor king nor slave stern Fate will recognize ;
Nor fool it knows nor one who may be wise.
The world will pass from ev'ry one away,
In such a fashion antics does it play.
Care when it comes, endure it long we must;
For we must all return towards the dust.
If knowledge of this has our destiny,
It is as if its brain of this were free.
Know, of this revolution it is not aware,
There is no road to why and wherefore there.
We must not sorrow if we have to go,
What is the matter's end we cannot know.
When of Suhráb the news the king they brought,
The hero brave he with his army sought,
These words to Rústam then said Káüs Kai,
" From the reed's leaf to Alburz' mountain high,
The spheres will bear us onwards as they glide.
Our love towards this earth must not abide.
One does it quickly, one more tardily,
The end of all must by death's passage be.
Thy heart and soul tow'rds going make content,
And let thy ear to wisdom e'er be leant.
If thou the heavens down to earth should'st cast,
Or if the whole earth thou with fire shouldst blast.
Of him that's gone thou could'st not find a trace,
But in that world is of his soul the place.
I from afar saw both his form and face,
His figure of such lofty height, his mace.

'He can not dwell among the Turks,' I said,
'But of some noble lineage must be bred.'
Him with his army Fortune here has brought,
That by thy hand he should be brought to naught.
What wilt thou do? What measure wilt thou keep?
For him who is departed how long weep?"
Rústam thus answered: "He has passed away;
On this broad desert Homán still will stay.
The Chiefs of Turán, those from Chín remain,
Anger against them do not thou retain.
Now let Zúarah guide them to their land,
In God's own strength and by the king's command."
"Fame-seeking hero," answered him the king,
"This fight of thine to thee must sorrow bring.
Although they did some injury to me,
And smoke from Irán have raised grievously,
Yet as to war thou art not now inclined,
To fighting, too, I will not turn my mind.
With thy grief now my heart is full of pain,
Yet rancour tow'rds them will I not retain."
Brave Hajír came up from the road to say:
"Before us all that host has gone away."
The king his army there no more delayed,
But took on to Irán, whilst Rústam stayed
Until Zuárah came at break of day,
When Rústam took his host at once away.
The tail of ev'ry lofty steed was shorn,
The hide of ev'ry brazen drum was torn.
The army in the coffin's front was led,
Whilst nobles scattered dust upon their head.
He took his way towards Zábulistán,
When news of this at length had reached Dastán.
The whole of Sistán there before him came,
In pain and grief and with their hearts aflame.
Dastán, the son of Sám, the bier beheld,

Leapt off his horse, by golden bridle held,
Whilst Tuhamtan on foot before it went,
His garment and his heart in sorrow rent.
The heroes ev'ry one his waist ungirt,
All by the bier their heads laid in the dirt;
Their faces blue, their robes in pieces torn,
Dust scattered on their heads with sorrow worn.
The heroes then the coffin brought down low.
Oh! woe for such a famous hero, woe!
Wailing, came Tuhamtan his father near,
And lifted head from off the gold-sewn bier.
He cried to him in mournful tones: "Behold!
How on this narrow bier lies Sám, the bold!"
Dastán from both his eyes the blood-tears rained,
And to his God, his guide upon the road, complained.
And Tuhamtan said: "Hero of great name,
Thou'rt gone, and I remain here in my shame."
"To thee it seemed strange," *Zál* to him replied,
"That Suhráb with a heavy mace should ride.
Among the great yet has this sign been giv'n,
No mother bears one like him under heav'n."
He spoke. His eyelashes with water poured,
And but of Suhráb could he speak no word.
To his own hall when Tuhamtan came near,
He cried aloud. They placed in front the bier.
Rudábah on the bier saw Suhráb lie,
And with the tears of blood o'erflowed her eye.
The youth upon his narrow bier was laid:
"O royal Pehláván!" she wailing said.
Again her lamentation to renew,
A cold sigh from her grieving heart she drew,
And cried: "Young lion of an athlete's birth,
Than thee none braver ever bore the earth."
She wailed: "O hero of the lofty crest,
Lift up thy visage from thy narrow chest.

The secret wilt not to thy mother tell,
What in thy hour of gladness thee befell?
Whilst still a youth thou comest to this jail,
To this abode of wretched ones who wail.
Of what thy father did wilt not say more,
And why thy heart he from thy body tore?"
Her cry up from the hall to Saturn leapt,
At ev'ry word she heard she wailed and wept.
Mourning, within the screen she took her place.
Her heart was full of pain, of dust her face.
When Rústam saw this, he again wept sore,
And in his breast rained blood-tears more and more.
Thou would'st have said: "Has come the Judgment Day,
That from all hearts the joy has fled away?"
And once again of brave Suhráb the bier
He brought before the nobles who were near.
The father of the boards the lid unclosed,
Drew off the shroud and Suhráb's head exposed.
He showed the body to those heroes high:
Thou would'st have said that smoke rose from the sky.
For ev'ry one, both young and old, who came,
Women and men, all void of strength became.
The great ones of the world their garments rent,
And clouds of dust up to the sky there went.
And the whole palace there were head to head
Upon the coffin of that lion laid.
Twas as if Sám, with arm and chest exposed,
All wearied with the conflict, there reposed.
And when the people looked upon the shroud,
Each one of them raised poignant cries aloud.
He covered him again with gold brocade,
And fastened firmly down the coffin's head.
He said: "*A dukmah** if I make of gold,

* The Persian tower of silence, where the dead are placed to be eaten by vultures, &c.

In dark-hued musk I will his corpse enfold.
When I am gone, it may no longer be;
If not, no counsel is there left for me;
Worthy of him to be, what can I do,
On earth that there may live his scent and hue?"
As horse's hoof a *dukmah* made he round,
The earth was troubled with men's mournful sound.
Raw aloes cut his coffin to prepare,
They fasten'd it with golden horse-nails there.
The earth from end to end was full of care,
And every one that heard was in despair.
Though many days for Rústam thus passed by,
There came into his heart no gleam of joy.
At last to patience he himself resigned,
For no resource but this was there to find.
Many of this sort in the world there are,
On whose hearts has been laid of grief the scar.
He who in this world wisdom has and sense
Is not deceived by time and its pretence.
The men of Irán, when this news they learnt,
Were all with fire of affliction burnt.
Thence Homán to Turán's land went as well,
Afrásiáb what he had seen to tell.
The measure of the matter understood,
Turán's king at it in amazement stood.
Then did the cities of Turán complain,
That on the battlefield Suhráb was slain.
To Samangán's king when the news they bore,
He tore in fragments all the robes he wore.

The hearing by his mother of Suhráb's Death.

And soon the grievous news his mother knew,
His father's sword Suhráb the hero slew.
Loudly lamenting, as her robes she tore,
For that youth immature she wept right sore.

With her own hand her boay-vest she rent,
Her form shone forth like ruby ornament.
With shouts and groans lamenting to the day,
From time to time her senses passed away.
Her eyeballs from their sockets then she drew,
Lifting them, high into the flames she threw.
Her ringlets, twisted like a noose, she clenched,
And from their roots with her own hand she wrenched.
The streams of blood, as rivers when they swell,
Flowed down her cheeks: at times she prostrate fell.
Black dust she strewed upon her head afresh,
And with her teeth tore off her arms the flesh.
Then fire upon her head she cast and lit,
And all her musk-like locks were burnt with it.
" Besmeared with blood, with dust upon thy head,
Soul of thy mother, where art thou ? " she said.
A stranger, prisoner, withered up and thin,
Thy hero's body lies the dust within.
Fixed on the road, mine eyes were waiting here,
Of Rústam and Suhráb some news to hear.
Such was my fancy, and I spoke the thought,
Round the earth wandering must thou be sought.
Now has he sought his father, now has found,
Now hither to return is hastening round.
My son, could I this news have ever guessed
That Rústam's dagger now had torn thy breast ?
Did pity not o'ercome him at thy sight,
At form and strength of thine and at thy height ?
And at that navel did not pity flow
That Rústam's cutting blade has severed now ?
His tender body reared I with delight,
By brilliant day and by long weary night.
But now thy body in thy blood is drowned,
A shroud as bleeding rags about thee wound
Who is there now in my embrace to lay,

And who will now my sorrow drive away?
Whom can I tell my sorrow and my care?
For whom instead of thee a place prepare?
Woe for my body, soul, my lamp, my eye,
From gardens torn thou in the dust dost lie.
O army's succour, thou'st thy father sought,
And in his stead a grave to thee is brought.
Of hope despairing, thou wast full of woe,
And liest in the dust, despised and low.
Out of its sheath ere he his dagger drew,
To rend thy silver bosom through and through,
The token that thy mother gave to thee,
By thee remembered, why did he not see?
Thy mother's sign to know thy father by
Why upon this, then, didst thou not rely?
Without thee is thy mother captive made,
Bewildered, low with care and sorrow laid.
Why did I not with thee the journey trace
Among world-heroes where thou hadst thy place?
Rústam afar would me have recognized,
And thee, his son, with me had surely prized.
That lofty one his sword had thrown away,
Nor opened wide thy heart's place to the day."
Wounded, she spoke, and wildly tore her hair
And with her hand struck on her features fair.
Again she cried: "Thy mother is forlorn;
That dagger has thy breast to tatters torn."
From ev'ry side the people gathered round
And drowned with tears of blood her there they found.
And as she wept and uttered wailing cries,
Were filled with scalding tears the people's eyes.
And in this way she senseless lay and low,
And all the people's hearts were wrung with woe.
When like a corpse she fell upon the ground,
Her blood, thou would'st have said, was frozen found.

Restored to consciousness she 'gan to wail,
And of that slain son told again the tale.
Now with his blood she made the river red,
And Suhráb's steed in front of her was led.
His horse's head upon her breast she raised,
And at the sight the world looked on amazed.
At times she kissed its face, at times its head,
Beneath its hoof of blood a river shed,
With blood from eyelash made earth red in hue,
And on its nails and hoof her face rubbed, too.
Upon it then a royal robe she placed
And as a son in her own arms embraced.
Cuirass and coat of mail and bow she brought,
His heavy mace, his spear and sword she sought;
Remembering that form's imposing height,
That mace upon her own head did she smite.
His coat of mail and helmet as she brought,
She cried: "O lion who the battle sought!"
Saddle and shield she brought and took the bit,
And her own head essayed to strike with it.
She brought his lasso seventy fathoms long,
And threw it out before her firm and strong.
Out of its sheath Suhráb's sword then she drew,
Docked his steed's mane and cut his tail in two.
These goods were all bestowed upon the poor,
Horses accoutred, gold and silver store.
The palace door she closed, tore up his throne,
And from its height then threw it headlong down,
The place where feasts were held in ruin rent,
The banquet hall whence to the war he went.
She made the house doors all of sable hue,
Palace and audience hall in dust o'erthrew.
She put on garments of the hue of Nile,
And these, too, with his blood did she defile.
By night and day she mourned and shed the tear,

And after Suhráb's death lived but a year.
And in her grief for him she died at last,
To go to Suhráb as her spirit passed.

After this interlude the history goes on with Siávash. Tús, Gív, Gudúrz, and other heroes go to hunt in the forest of Daghín, and there find a beautiful woman, who informs them that she has run away from her father because he has beaten her in a drunken fit, and that she is of the family of Garsívaz, and descended from Farídun. Gív and Tús's first discovery is received with acclamation and of joy. The king places a crown on his head and would have executed Súdábah but for Siávásh's pleading for her. After this, however, he becomes reconciled to Súdábah, and is as fond of her as ever.

Kai Káüs now learns that Afrásiáb is about to attack him; he designates Siávash for the command of an army to confront him with the assistance of Rústam. The army assembles, and it is remarkable that among them are numbered men from Kúch (by which Kachh is probably meant) and Balúchis, with five Mobeds to carry the standard of Kavah. Káüs goes with them for one march, and leaves Siávash with the impression that they will never meet again. The army after remaining in Zabulistan for a month marches towards Balkh by way of Herát, Talikán and Marv. Garsívaz, Bármán and Sipahrám, who are with the Turanian army, meet them at the gates of Balkh, and after a three days' battle Siávash takes possession of the town, and Sipahrám flees across the Jaihún. On announcing his victory, he is directed by Káüs to cross the Jaihún. This is reported to Afrásiáb by Garsívaz, who is driven out of his presence by the former in a rage for talking of repose and slumber under such circumstances. Afrásiáb has a dream, in which he sees the plain covered with snakes, the earth full of dust, and the sky of eagles: his standard is thrown down by a high wind, and streams of blood, flowing about, throw down his tents. A vast number of his warriors lay about in the dust with their heads cut off, and an army of Iránís were coming on like a tempest, some carrying lances with a head on each, with another in their arms. A hundred thousand Iránís clothed in black threw themselves on his throne, from which they cast him down, and having bound him, carried him before king Káüs, who was about to cut him in two when he cried aloud and awoke. The Mobeds are consulted as to the interpretation of this dream, and disaster at the hands of Síávash is prophesied. Afrásiáb consults his nobles, who are all in favour of coming to an accommodation with the Iránis by dividing the world as it was in the time of Faridún, and Garsívaz is sent to Siávash on the errand with valuable presents. After consultation with Rústam terms are come to by which a hundred hostages are delivered to Irán, and Garsívaz is allowed to return to Afrásiáb. Siávash now sends Rústam to announce these events to Káüs, who, considering all the evils inflicted on him, gives an unwilling consent, saying that Rústam has over-persuaded Siávash in the matter in order to gain repose for himself without considering the glory of the throne. He sends him back to Seistán, telling him he will send Tús to take his place with Siávash, and that he will no longer call him his friend. Thereupon Rústam leaves him in anger. Káus writes an angry letter in reply to that of Siávash, ordering him when Tús arrives to place the hostages, heavily chained, on asses, and send them to his Court and follow up his invasion; or, if he objects, to return, giving up command of the army to Tús. Displeased at this proposed breach of faith, Siávash consults Behrám and Zangah, son of Shávarán, and notwithstanding their remonstrances decides for sending back the hostages to Afrásiáb with Zangah, rather than violate his pledges, and asks for an asylum in his country. Zangah goes with the hostages and all the presents Afrásiáb has sent, and is received by Afrásiáb graciously. Afrásiáb consults Pirán, his commander-in-chief, who advises him to receive Siávash, in hope that through him peace between the two countries may be brought about. Afrásiáb accordingly writes to Siávash to ask him to come, and saying that he would receive him as a father would his own son. Siávash writes to his father informing him of what he is about to do, and hands over charge of his army to Behrám pending the arrival of Tús. Starting towards Turán, he finds great preparations made for him at Tarmaz, Cháj, and Káchárbáshi, where he halts for some time. Meanwhile Tús arrives at Balkh, and in great sorrow at what has occurred, leads back the army to Irán. Pirán meets Siávash on the road and they ride in company to Káchárbáshi and thence on to Ganz, the residence of Afrásiáb. Afrásiáb welcomes him when they meet, and assigns him a palace to live in. Siávash shows him his skill at polo, and they go together to hunt; after which Pirán gives his daughter Gúlshehr to Siávash in marriage, and solicits for him the hand of Farangís, Afrásiáb's own daughter. The marriage is celebrated, and seven days afterwards Afrásiáb hands over to his son-in-law the whole country between Ganz and the sea of Chín (China). After a tour through all his territory Siávash determines on building the town of Ganzdiz, a glowing description of the beauties of which are given. He consults the astrologers as to the results of this enterprise, but receives an unfavourable prophecy. (This, by the way, appears to be omitted in Macan's version). Pirán, seeing his sadness on this account, questions him, and is informed that he does not hope to enjoy his good fortune very long, and Afrásiáb will soon sit in his place. On Pirán assuring him of Afrásiáb's good-will towards him, he prophesies that the latter will soon become suspicious of him and kill him, that Irán and Turán will be upset and the whole earth filled with misery. Then a great army will come from Irán to revenge him, and the king of Irán will repent too late, and his blood will bring about trouble among men. Shortly after this orders reach Pirán to go into all countries as far as India and China and collect tribute. Afrásiáb also writes to Siávash to go about his country and fix upon a place in which to build a palace for his own residence: he finds this in Behar,* and builds Siávashgadh (the fort of Siávash) there, and it is visited by Pirán on his return from India and China. A feast for seven days is held in his honour, on the eighth he presents gifts brought for Siávash and Farangís, and then returns to Afrásiáb with the tribute money that he has collected, and gives a description of the beauties of Siávashgadh. After this, Afrásiáb dispatches Garsívaz again to Siávash with gifts for him and Farangís. He is cordially received by Siávash, and during his stay there the birth of a son to Siávash, to whom the name of Farúd is given, is announced to him: its mother's name was Jasírah, but no further description of her is given. Siávash now shows his skill at polo, &c., before Garsívaz, and overthrows two Turks' warriors, Gari Zarah and Damúr, who venture to encounter him. On the eighth day Garsívaz and his party return to Afrásiáb with a friendly letter from Siávash, but not before Siávash has entertained suspicions with regard to him. On seeing Afrásiáb pleased with the letter, Garsívaz

*This cannot be the Behar in Bengal.

retires full of hatred and grief, and the next morning begins to insinuate to Afrásiáb with regard to Siávash, saying that he has secretly received envoys from Káûs and from Rúm and China. Afrásiáb takes three days to consider the matter, but finally sends Garsívaz to induce Siávash and Farangís to come and visit him. Garsívaz goes, and when he arrives near the new town sends one of his own men to Siávash to persuade him not to rise from his throne to meet him, on the pretence that his position is now too high to admit of his stooping to such humility. Siávash is, however, not taken in by this plausible persuasion, and meets Garsívaz as usual. He also proposes to return to Afrásiáb with Garsívaz, but the latter, apprehensive of the effect his coming will have on Afrásiáb, endeavours to dissuade him from the journey by telling him that Afrásiáb has turned against him, and warning him of the fate of Aghríras, whom Afrásiáb had killed, notwithstanding that he was his own brother. He finally over-persuades Siávash not to trust himself to Afrásiáb, and to write him a letter for Garsívaz to take. In this letter he makes the excuse that Farangís is ill and he cannot leave her. Garsívaz hastens to Afrásiáb with the letter, and tells him that Siávash had refused to meet him as usual, and given him the lowest place near his throne, that armies were ready to march from Rúm and from China, and if any delay occurred Siávash would commence war against him. On this, Afrásiáb at once determines to march against Siávash. Siávash now sees Farangís and, to allay her fears, explains to her that Garsívaz was already on the way to her father with a friendly letter, and he put his trust in God. Siávash now has a dream, which, on her urgent entreaty, he tells his wife. He had seen a rushing river in front of him and on the other side a mountain of fire. The border of the river was lined with horsemen armed with lances. The hill of fire was consuming Siávashgadh, and in front of him was Afrásiáb mounted on an elephant. Afrásiáb, on seeing him, looked fierce, and rushed to the fire, which Garsívaz had lighted and which burnt him (Siávash). Farangís endeavours to console him, and he assembles his army before his palace. Meanwhile, towards morning, a vidette comes in with the news that he has seen Afrásiáb advancing. Another messenger arrives from Garsívaz to beg him to save his own life by flight, and Siávash believes in his sincerity: in this he is backed up by the entreaties of Farangís to save himself. He now explains his last wishes to her, being convinced that his life will soon come to an end, foretelling that she, who has been five months pregnant, will bear a son who will become illustrious, who will be called Kai Khusru, and that he himself will lose his head and his body, will have neither bier nor shroud nor tomb, but that Pirán will beg her life for her and it will be under his roof that her son will be born. He also foretells the future greatness of Kai Khusru, and takes leave of Farangís. He lets loose his horse Bahzád, and burning his valuables before the palace mounts another horse and prepares to flee. His Iránis soon meet the army of Turán, and Siávash stands unarmed before the latter, hoping so to overcome the calumnies that have been uttered against him, and appeals to Afrásiáb. Garsívaz, however, intervenes, and Afrásiáb listens to him and orders an attack. The Iránis are all exterminated and Siávash falls from his horse wounded. Girúi Zarah ties his hands, but notwithstanding the remonstrances of his own army and Pílsam, a brother of Pirán, and the entreaties of Farangís, Afrásiáb listens to Garsívaz and allows Girúi Zarah to drag Siávash away and finally to kill him with a dagger. His head is cut off over a bowl, into which his blood is allowed to flow, and the blood is poured out in a place pointed out bv Afrásiáb. Some editions say that there sprang from this blood the plant called the blood of Siávash, which Mohl translates by the words "dragon's blood." Afrásiáb hears the outcry raised by Farangís on hearing of the death of her husband, and ruthlessly orders that she should be beaten until she is delivered of the child she is about to bear to Siávash, in order that no offspring of Siávash should remain alive. The people curse him, and Pirán, hearing what is about to take place, begs her life and carries her off. He now has a dream, in which he sees a light coming from the sun, in which Siávash is visible with a sword in his hand. He bids him awake, and be alert, for Kai Khusru is about to be born. He awakes Gúlshehr and bids her go to Farangís, and on her doing so she finds the event has just taken place. He informs Afrásiáb, who bids him send away the child, to be brought up among shepherds, so that he might know nothing of the circumstances of his birth when he grows up. Pirán accordingly hands him over to the shepherds in the mountain of Kalú. When he arrives at the age of seven, he already shows his great qualities by making a bow for himself and combating wild beasts. He refuses any longer to obey his foster parent, who goes and informs Pirán. Pirán goes to see the boy, and clothes him in royal apparel and gives him a horse, and conceives a great affection for him. He is sent for by Afrásiáb, who is troubled by the remembrance of what he has done, and pretends to him that the child having been brought up among shepherds is wanting in intelligence, but brings him, on his swearing a solemn oath that he will do him no injury. Before bringing him, he instructs the boy to answer any questions the king might put to him as if he were only half-witted. Afrásiáb is thus persuaded that he has nothing to fear from his vengeance, and permits Pirán to take him away to his mother at Siávashgadh.

The first volume of Macan's edition of the Shah-námah ends here with a lamentation from Fardúsi at his advanced age of 60, and a promise to relate what Rústam did in Turán to avenge Siávash.

The second volume opens with an account of Káûs hearing of the death of Siávash and of his grief, and of Rústam's going to him and reproaching him for having listened to Súdábah and vowing to sacrifice his heart and head to avenge Siávash. Rústam proceeds to drag Súdábah out of her palace by her hair and kill her, Káûs not interfering. He assembles his army with Gudúrz, Tús and other heroes, and invades Turán in their hatred of Afrásiáb and his deeds. On the road the army comes across an advanced post commanded by the king of *Sapanjáb*, called Varázád, who is killed and his country ravaged by Farámúrz, son of Rústam, who commands the advance guard of the Iránis. On hearing of this, Afrásiáb dispatches an army under his son Súrkhah to meet that of Rústam. Farámúrz encounters Súrkhah, and takes him to Rústam as prisoner, and Rústam orders him to be put to death in the same manner as Siávash had been, but Tús, who was ordered to carry out the sentence, takes compassion on him, and Zuárah, Rustam's brother, finally carries it out. Afrásiáb now puts the army of Turán in motion to avenge his son. When the two armies arrive near each other Pílsam offers to fight Rústam, and is allowed to do so by Afrásiáb, notwithstanding Pirán's remonstrances. He first encounters Gív and Farámúrz, but Rústam finally fells him with a blow of his mace and throws his body into the midst of the army of Turán. Afrásiáb, seeing the state of affairs, himself advances and attacks the right wing under Tús, who is put to flight. Rústam then comes up and engages Afrásiáb, whose horse he kills. Humán, who is by Afrásiáb's side, strikes Rústam on the shoulder with his mace and gives Afrásiáb the opportunity of mounting another horse and escaping. Humán also escapes by the aid of his friends, and Afrásiáb leads his defeated army to the sea of China, probably the Caspian sea. He now consults Pirán as to the disposal of Kai Khusru, for fear he should be taken to Irán and made a king. On the advice of Pirán he does not kill him, but allows him to be sent away to Khatan, by which may probably be understood Chinese Tartary, so as to be out of hearing of Irán. Rústam now sits on the throne of Turán. He at last agrees to return to Irán, knowing that Káüs is alone and may want assistance in case Afrásiáb should attack Irán again, and Afrásiáb, hearing of his retirement with Tús, Gudúrz, and others, comes back to Turán to find it desolated, and proceeds to harry Irán by constant attacks. Added to this, it had the misfortune to suffer from want of rain for seven years. About this time Gudúrz dreams a dream, in which the *Surúsh* tells him that Gív, his son, must find Kai Khusru and bring him back to Irán in order to avenge Siávash. Gív is accordingly dispatched, and goes alone for fear of his search for Kai Khusru being interfered with. When he meets anyone on the road who on enquiry with regard to the object of his search denies any knowledge of him, he kills him and passes on. Wandering thus throughout Turán for seven years in his search, he fed on grass, and drank bad water and lived on wild asses. Pirán had in the meantime sent for Kai Khusru by order of Afrásiáb and handed him over to his mother, and Gív, one day passing through a forest and lamenting his bad luck comes upon Kai Khusru and recognizes him by his likeness to Siávash, and is further convinced by Khusru's showing him on his arm the black mark that all the scions of the race bore there hereditarily from the time of Kai Kubád. They go away together, Kai Khusru mounted on Gív's horse. They consult Farangís, who proposes that they should go off without delay, for fear Afrásiáb should prevent them, and bids them take a saddle and bridle to a certain meadow, where they would find Behzád, the horse of Siávash. This they do, and the horse, recognising the saddle and bridle, allows himself to be mounted without difficulty. Finally the three start off, but are overtaken on the road by Gulbád and Nastihan, whom Pirán, hearing of their flight, had sent after them. Kai Khusru and Farangís, tired with their journey, were sleeping, but Gív was awake and on guard and, mounting his horse, soon put them to flight. The travellers pursue their journey by unfrequented roads, and Pirán, after reproaching Gulbád bitterly for being overcome by a single warrior, pursues them. Farangís, who is watching while Khusru and Gív sleep, rouses them, and a fight takes place between the latter and Pirán. Gív pretends to run away, but when he is at a distance from Pirán's men, turns round upon him and in turn makes him run and catches him with his lasso. Making him precede him on foot for some distance, he then throws him down, binds him, and, taking his banner, advances towards the Turcománs and drives them back. Then returning to Pirán, he makes him walk ignominiously behind him to Kai Khusru. Pirán begs for his own life, pointing out what he had done for Farangís and her son, and finally is allowed to go on the entreaty of Farangís, after he has has had his ears pierced by Gív in order that the latter may not break his oath as to shedding Pirán's blood. Afrásiáb meets Pirán on his way back, and is informed by him of the discomforture of himself and his army by Gív, and the escape of Farangís and Kai Khusru; and accordingly declares he will kill Farangís when he catches her. The fugitives go on to the ferry over the river where toll is collected. The toll-collector will not carry them across without one of four things, viz., Gív's coat of mail, his black horse, the female slave (Farangís), or the gold crown that Kai Khusru is wearing, but instead of yielding to his extortionate demands, they swim the river and get safely across. Afrásiáb, with the army of Turán, arrives at the river and desires to cross, but is dissuaded by Humán, and the Turcomán army goes home again. Kai Khusru now returns to Irán viâ Isfahán, and is joyfully welcomed by Káüs and all the people, and Gív is suitably rewarded for all the hardships he has endured in his search for the prince. The only exception to the rejoicing is in the case of Tús, who, on the pretext that he is the guardian of the standard of Kávah and has a right to beat drums before him and wear golden shoes and is not allowed to exercise the right, refuses to go to the palace of Kishvád, where Gudúrz was to have a grand meeting of all the nobles to receive Kai Khusru. Gív is sent by Gudúrz to remonstrate with him, but he remains obdurate, and Gudúrz leads a force against him. Tús and Gudúrz are both summoned before Káüs, and argue the matter out, Tús, apparently, claiming the throne for Faribúrz. Káüs decides the question by sending both of them to Ardabíl to attack the castle of Bahman, saying that he will give his throne and treasure to whichever of the two gains possession of it, and does away with the evil wrought there by Ahriman in preventing the resort of Mobeds and the worship of God. They agree, and Tús, taking Faribúrz with him, makes an unsuccessful survey of the place with a view to attacking it, and they return without attaining their object. Gudúrz and Gív then take up the matter with Kai Khusru, who writes a letter in Pehlavi threatening to destroy the place, and places it on the head of a spear for Gív to deliver. Gív affixes the letter to the wall of the castle, which thereupon, by order of God, cracks and falls down. Khusru orders a flight of arrows to be sent into the castle, numbers of Dívs are killed, and the rest take their departure. A great temple is built there, and the fire from Azargushasp placed in it. After a year Kai Khusru returns victorious, and Tús lays the standard of Kávah at his feet by way of submission. Káüs then welcomes him, and offering him valuable gifts such as Kávah's standard and golden slippers, descends from the throne and places Kai Khusru upon it.

Zál, Rústam, and the other grandees of the kingdom, render homage to the new king, who, accompanied by them, makes a royal progress through the country, hunting and enjoying himself, and after worshipping at the fire-temple of Adargushasp returns to Káüs, to whom he swears on the fire to avenge him on Afrásiáb. The oath is recorded in Pehlavi on a royal scroll, which, after being attested by Rústam and other chiefs, is handed over to the care of Rústam. They have a feast for seven days at Káüs' palace, and on the eighth Kai Khusru assembles all his warriors, and, supported by them, gives out his intention of punishing Afrásiáb, the author of all the evils that have befallen the country. Kai Khusru now reviews the Pehlaváns and their forces, and confers valuable gifts on them, offering others for the head of Paláshán, whom Afrásiáb has placed at the head of his army, and the capture of Tajád and his crown. Bezar, son of Gív, undertakes this. Ten gold tables covered with money, musk and precious stones, two beautiful female slaves, 200 pieces of silk and brocade, a royal crown, and ten waist belts are also offered to him who shall go to the Kásah river and salute the soul of Siávash: he would see there a hill of firewood gathered by Afrásiáb in order to block the road between the two countries of Irán and Túran, which he was to burn up: this task is undertaken by Gív. Another valuable present is offered to him who will take a message to Afrásiáb, and this offer is accepted by Gurgín, son of Milád. Fárámúrz is dispatched to Hindústán, which the king hands over to him from Kanúj to the border of Zábúlistán, inclusive of Kashmír and Sind, and he goes off, full of good advice from the king and Rústam. Tús is now sent against Túrán and Afrásiáb, a grand review of the army takes place, and the names of the different chiefs who pass before the king are enumerated. As Tús takes his departure Kai Khusru warns him and his officers to fight only with those who oppose them, and to leave alone all artisans and cultivaters of the soil and not to pass by Kelát, where his mother Jarirah lives with his brother Firúd, born to Siávash by the daughter of Pirán, but by way of the desert. Tús agrees to take whichever road is pointed out to him. On arriving at the point where the two roads separate, however, he determines to take the road by Kelát and Jarm in consequence of the want of water on the desert route. Firúd hears of the approach of the Iránian army, and has all his cattle driven in from the country and the hills and taken to Anbúh by way of the hill of Sipad. He consults his mother, who advises him to meet the army and associate himself with Kai Khusru in exacting vengeance for their father's death. He accordingly goes out with Takhvár, who his mother says will point out to him who the different Iránian Chiefs are. This Takhvár does, and Tús, seeing them at a distance on a hill, sends Behrám to ascertain who they are. Firúd satisfies him as to his relationship to Siávash by showing the mark on his arm, and Behrám reports to Tús, who, notwithstanding, orders him to be attacked. Rívníz proceeds to do so in spite of Behrám's remonstrances, and is killed by an arrow from Firúd's bow. Zarasp, son of Tús, goes to avenge him by order of Tús and meets with the same fate. Tús then goes up himself and Takhvár advises Firúd not to face Tús, but retreat into his castle. Firúd, however, shoots the horse of Tús dead, so that Tús retires to his camp covered with dust, pursued by Firúd's taunts. Gív now takes up the quarrel, but is forced to retire with his horse wounded. On this his son Bezan twits him with having been worsted by a Turk, and Gív hits him over the head with his whip. Bezan thereupon vows to avenge Zarasp or be killed himself. Gústahum at his request supplies him with a horse, and he goes to the encounter. Firúd shoots this horse, too, and Bezan comes on on foot, and wounds his horse, but Firúd runs away from him and gets into the castle. Tús now attacks the castle, outside which a fight takes place, and Firúd retreats inside only to die, to the great distress of his mother, who, with her female slaves, kills herself in grief, after Jarírah has set fire to and burnt all her treasures. The Iránis gain an entrance, and finding Firúd dead, all, including Tús, who regrets his hastiness, are overcome with sorrow at the death of such a noble young prince. Tús erects a royal mausoleum for him on the summit of the mountain, where he is interred with Zarasp and Rívníz in graves near him.

Staying there only three days, Tús leads his army towards the Kásah river, killing every Turánián that he meets, and devastating the country. They soon come in contact with the Turkomán army, and Gív kills its leader Pálashán, and cuts off his head and carries off his armour. After this a violent snowstorm occurs, and buries the whole Iráni force, so that for seven days none could see the ground, and they had to kill their horses and eat them for want of other food. On the eighth day the sun appears and converts the whole place into a sea. They however, reach the Kásah river, and Tús burns the hill of firewood, as he engaged with Káüs to do. In the fourth week, after the fire was extinguished and the river had gone down, the army began to cross the river, advancing with every precaution. Kabúdah, one of Afrásiáb's shepherds, is sent to examine them as they advance, but is caught and has his head cut off by Behrám. Tajáo, who has the fort of Girogadh on the road, encounters the Iránian army, but the Turánians are worsted, and Tajáo fleeing from them is pursued by Bezan up to the gate of his fort, where Isnapúi, his female slave, meets him and reproaches him for running away. He takes her up behind him and both flee together till his horse is exhausted. Isnapúi dismounts in order to let Tajáo escape, and Bezan takes her up and carries her into the camp, whilst Tajáo makes off to Afrásiáb. The Iránis occupy the fort and plunder it, and then go off to collect Firúd's cattle. On learning of the arrival of the Iránian army, Afrásiáb reproaches Pirán for not having assembled an army. Pirán immediately does so, resigning the command of the right wing to Barmán and Tajáo, and of the left to Nastíhan, the whole amounting to 100,000 men. A spy brings word that Tús is careless and engaged in feasting, and Pirán attacks the camp at night, taking it by surprise, after seizing the Iránis' flocks and killing the shepherds. Gudúrz was the only one sober. The rout was complete, and many lost the whole of their tents and baggage, fleeing away to the Kásah river, followed by the Turkománs, and thence to the hills, where the latter, tired of slaughter, turned back. Two-thirds of the Iránis had been killed. Word is sent to Khusru, who writes a letter to Faribúrz full of the doleful news, and showing how Tús had disobeyed his orders and brought about this calamity. Faribúrz recalls Tús, who hands over to him the royal standard, the golden slippers, and other insignia of rank, and goes to the king, who after reproaching him bitterly sends him into confinement. Faribúrz now sends Rehám to Pirán with a proposal for an armistice, which Faribúrz agrees to for a month in order to let the Iránis retreat out of Turán and return home. At the end of this time, however, the armies again encounter each other, and the Iránis are heavily defeated for the second time, notwithstanding prodigies of valour performed by their chief heroes, stimulated by the sight of the banner of Kávah which Bezan takes away from Faribúrz, who is unwilling to give it up, by cutting through its pole with his sword.

In the course of the night Behrám, notwithstanding the remonstrance of his father Gúdurz and Gív, goes to the battle-field from the camp to look for his whip, which he has dropped, as it was one that Farangís had given him. He goes on to the field, attending to his brother, who was wounded, by binding up his wounds, and is detained by his horse escaping from him and running after some mares; he follows it and catches it with great difficulty, and at last cuts off its head. Meanwhile the Turkománs are alarmed and run towards him, but he kills a number of them with arrows. His enemies disappear, and he stays to pick up arrows. In the meantime Pirán hears what has taken place. Ruín, who is present, listens to this, and Pirán orders him to go with as many men as he can get together and capture Behrám. Behrám, however, meets them with such a hail of arrows that Ruín retires with his men and goes back to Pirán, who himself approaches Behrám and offers to eat bread and salt with him by way of making an alliance with him. Behrám refuses, but asks for a horse in order to enable him to rejoin his own friends. This Pirán agrees to, but on the road back he unfortunately meets Tajáo and tells him what he has been doing. Tajáo immediately returns to the battle-field with a troop of men, who attack Behrám, and though fighting bravely, he at last falls to a treacherous blow given by Tajáo himself. Finding that Behrám does not return, and seeing Tajáo on his rounds at nightfall, Gív attacks him and catches him with his lasso; he ties his arms, and remounting his horse after giving him 200 blows with his whip over the head, drags him to where Behrám, still alive, is lying. Behrám begs Gív not to kill him, but to let him live in order to keep his memory fresh in the world. Seeing his brother wounded, however, Gív seizes Tajáo's beard and cuts off his head. Behrám dies, and Gív raises a *dukhmah* over him, and places him in it with royal rites.

Faribúrz now retires with the Iránis, and Pirán conveys the intelligence of his victory to Afrásiáb. Soon after this he retires to Khatan, loaded with gifts by Afrásiáb, and warns him to be ever on the alert lest Rústam should suddenly pounce down upon him. Faribúrz, Tús, and the other warriors now return to Kai Khusru thoroughly crestfallen and afraid of his anger. He is naturally very angry, and mourns for his brother and the other victims of the war. Rústam goes to Kai Khusru and intercedes for the unfortunate men, and at last the king agrees to pardon them. Tús and the others also come and ask for forgiveness, and Tús offers to return to Turán and sacrifice his life rather than fail again. Kai Khusru spends the whole night with Rústam and other nobles in consultation as to what is best to be done. In the morning all offer to sacrifice their lives in order to retrieve the disaster, and Tús is again sent to fight the army of Turán. Pirán endeavours to avert war by sending a pacific message to Tús, but Tús, although he offers to get him rewards from Kai Khusru if he will come over to him, is evidently insincere, as he longs for revenge, and both sides prepare to renew the war.

Afrásiáb sends an army to Pirán in order to stop the Iranis who are reported to be again invading Turán, and the latter advances to the river Shahd, notwithstanding the treaty he has entered into. Tús also advances. The first event of the war is the killing by Tús of Arjang, the son of Zarah. Ḥumán advances in front of the Turánians and Tús from the Iránis, and after the usual defiant and boasting speeches they engage each other ineffectually, Humán being taken off the field by his companions. The armies engage again, and this time the Turánians try the effects of magic practised by Bázúr, one of their number, who is sent up to the top of a mountain by Pirán in order to hurl a violent snowstorm down upon his enemies. The Iránis in their frozen condition are attacked by the Turkománs and many of them slaughtered. The magician is pointed out to Rehám on the top of the hill, and he goes up to attack him, and cutting off his hand brings it down to his father, another tempest having now cleared the air. In the fight which ensues Tús and the chief warriors acquit themselves valiantly, but those in the rear giving way, they are obliged to return for fear of being surrounded, and fall back on Mount Hamávand. This the Turkománs surround. On the advice of Humán Pirán follows them up to the mountain, and has one of the usual combats of words with Tús, who, however, will not give in, and they plan a night attack to break through the army that has hemmed them in on the mountain. This is carried out, and the fight goes on all night, and in the morning both forces retire to rest themselves.

Kai Khusru now receives tidings of Pirán's victory over his army, and summons Rústam with his army. He sets before him the state of affairs, and the losses that have been suffered by Gudúrz and his family, and pointing out that his only hope lies in him, engages him to go to the succour of Tús's army. Faribúrz, at Kai Khusru's request, is given command of the advanced guard of Rústam's army, and Farangís, at Rústam's request, and with the consent of the king, agrees to take Faribúrz as her husband, although with great hesitation, as she is devoted to the memory of Siávash. Three days afterwards Rústam goes off to the seat of war, marching double stages by day and night. Just at this time Tús dreams, and sees a flame rise out of the water, with Siávash sitting on an ivory throne in the midst of the flame. Siávash tells him to hold on, as he will be victorious, and not to fret about the relations of Gudúrz, as they were sitting in a fair garden of roses, drinking wine. He informs Gudúrz of his dream, and the two armies are arrayed face to face, but neither seems disposed to fight the other. Humán urges Pirán, but the latter prefers to let the Iránis alone until they come to the end of their resources on the mountain.

Afrásiáb now sends the Khákán of China to reinforce Pirán, who announces his intention of dividing his army into three corps, one to go to Balkh, one to Zábúlistán, and the third with the army of Turán to Irán, and orders his army to avoid a conflict with Tús's army, but merely to keep a watch that the Iránis do not escape from the hill, whilst he himself goes to see the Khákán. The chiefs of the Iránis hold counsel together and Gív consoles Tús and Gudúrz, who seem disposed to despond. Gudúrz, however, goes to the crest of the mountain and there obtains from a sentinel the cheering news of the approach of Faribúrz and his army. Tús also sends up Bezan, son of Gív, who confirms the news of the arrival of an army, but seems to consider it is that of Túrán, but when the moon rises they are seen to be Iránians. The Khákán goes to reconnoitre the Iránis, and determines to attack them the next day, as there appeared to be only a few men among bare rocks.

The next day Faribúrz arrives and announces that Rústam is following behind him, and had given orders that they were not to fight until he arrived. On the appearance of the army of Faribúrz Pirán holds counsel with the Khákán, and Kámús offers to lead the attack, although some of the Turánian generals hesitate. Kámús, however; advances next day, and a combat takes place between him and Gív, in which he makes the latter lose his stirrups and attacks him with his sword, cutting his lance in two. Tús comes to Gív's assistance, and the fight goes on till they are parted by the darkness. Rústam now arrives, and is welcomed by Gudúrz and the rest. In the morning Humán announces to Pirán the arrival of reinforcements for the Iránis, and he, finding that Rústam has arrived, is in despair, fearing that neither Kámús nor the Khákán nor Shangul will remain alive before him. Kámús, however, declares that when Rústam sees his banner he will tumble to the bottom of the sea of China. The two armies then face each other, and Ashkbús comes forward to challenge the Iránis to combat. Rahám attacks him, but is obliged to retire to the hill, but Rústam now comes forward, and, despising Ashkbús's arrow, pierces his chest with an arrow, the sphere kissing his hand, Fate crying "Take it," and destiny "Give." Kámús now inquires who the hero is who can wield such a bow and shoot such an arrow, and Pirán assures him it is not Rústam. The two armies are again arrayed against each other, and are encouraged by the Khákán on one side and Rústam on the other. Kámús advances and kills Alvá, a man from Zabúl taught by Rústam. Rústam then comes forward and, catching Kámús, throws him to the ground, when the Iránian chiefs put an end to him. The Turánians and the Khákán, grieved at the event, endeavour to find out who Rústam is, and for this purpose Chingish offers himself, but feeling that Rústam's arrows will soon pierce him, turns to fly. Rústam follows, and catches hold of his horse's tail. He dismounts Chingish and cuts off his head. Humán now goes forward at the desire of the Khákán to ascertain who Rústam is, and Rústam offers that the war shall cease at once if Garsívaz, Zarah, and his sons and others who have taken part in the murder of Siávash are delivered up. He refuses to give his name, but asks to see Pirán, as the only man in Turán who had grieved at Siávásh's murder. Humán returns to the camp with the news that this is indeed Rústam. The Khákán is informed, and he desires Pirán to go to Rústam and ascertain if he is really desirous of peace. On his going Rústam listens to what he has to say and offers peace on two conditions, viz., that those concerned in the murder of Siávash, who are answerable for the war, shall be sent in chains to Kai Khusru, and that he shall come to him himself. Pirán goes away to lay the matter before the family of Vívah and the Khákán, and it is determined on the advice of Shangal, called the king of India, to continue the war, much to Pirán's sorrow, as he anticipates a fatal result. Rústam, on the other hand, exhorts his army, and the two armies are drawn up against each other. Shangal advances in front of the army of Turán according to his promise to Pirán, who tells Rústam the result of his consultation with the Turánians after he has told them the conditions of peace offered by Rústam. Rústam reproaches him for his deceit, and the battle commences. Shangal is unhorsed by Rústam, but is saved by the Turánians surrounding him and getting him off the field. The Khákán on being told by Shangal of the prowess of Rústam, orders Rústam to be surrounded, but he breaks through the ranks of his enemies and afterwards kills Saváh and Kahár Kaháni, and makes a prisoner of the Khákán with the noose of his lasso. He draws him off his elephant and hands him over to Tús. The army of Turán is thoroughly defeated, and flees away, and Rústam distributes the booty among the Iránis. He now writes a letter describing his victory, and sends it by the hand of Faribúrz to Kai Khusru, stating also that he is about to go on to Gang in the hope of catching Zarah and his sons and disposing of them. After thanking God for His mercy, Kai Khusru sends an answer to this letter praising Rústam, and sends him valuable gifts by Faribúrz. On Afrásiáb's hearing of the defeat of his army* he lays the matter before his nobles, who declare that if Rústam should dare to invade their country they will not leave a single Iráni alive. On this he opens his treasury doors and distributes money among them. Rústam in the meanwhile leads his army through Sugh (Soydiana) to a place called Bídád (the unjust) inhabited by a cannibal king who ate a beautiful slave every day. Rústam orders 3000 horsemen under Gústaham, Kazír, and Bezan to attack the castle held by him, whose name is Káfúr; he sallies out and becomes engaged with Gústaham. Gústaham sends off Bezan to Rústam to ask for assistance, and Rústam coming up makes an end of him. Advancing against the castle, the people in which resist him valiantly, he kills with arrows every one who shows his head above the wall, and undermines it until it falls down. The place, with numerous prisoners, is then captured, and Gív is sent with a force to the frontier of Khatan to intercept the fugitive Turkománs. This expedition is also successful, and Gív returns with a number of prisoners. A feast is then held, and they halt for three days. Afrásiáb on hearing of the advance of Rústam determines to

*Nothing is said of his release from the hands of Tús.

prosecute the war. He sends one Farghár to reconnoitre Rústam's army and consults his own son Shídah, who supports his view. He hears Farghár's report of Rústam and his army, and directs Pirán to advance against him, and also writes a letter to Puládvand for Shídah to take to the mountains of China, where he resides. Puládvand assembles Dívs and warriors, and goes to see Afrásiáb, and is told the state of affairs. Meeting the Iránis, he first of all overthrows Tús with his lasso and then catches Gív by the head, and when Rahám and Bezan ride at him they are also thrown to the ground and trampled under foot; he rushes at the standard of Kávah and cuts the staff in two, and Faribúrz and Gudúrz appeal to Rustam, who answers the appeal and goes forward to attack Puládvand. At this moment Tús and Gív, whom Gudúrz supposed to have been killed by Puládvand, appear on foot again. Rústam strikes Puládvand's head with his mace, but he declares he is not hurt, and attacks Rústam with a magic sword, but this has no effect, and the two wrestle together. Rústam finally lifts him up and dashes him to the ground, leaving him as it were dead, but Puládvand manages to raise himself and escapes on a horse to Afrásiáb. Rústam now leads forward his army again, and Afrásiáb takes flight towards Chín and Machín. Half of the Turánians ask for quarter, and the remainder make off like sheep without shepherds. Rústam puts a stop to further slaughter, and after collecting all the booty and devastating the country returns to the Court of Kai Khusru. He receives a warm welcome, and is feasted for a month before he returns to Seistán after receiving rich rewards, accompanied for two stages by the king himself. A report soon reaches Kai Khusru from one of his shepherds that a wild ass has appeared among his horses: he, however, discerns that it must be a Dív, and asks which of the heroes will encounter him. None seeming willing to do so, he dispatches Gurgín with a letter to summon Rústam, who comes and goes out with the herd to look for the Dív for three days. On the fourth he sees an animal of a brilliant gold colour that evades his lasso, and that he is sure is the Dív Akván. He follows him ineffectually for three whole days, and becoming wearied throws himself down to sleep by a spring. Here the Dív sees him and carries him up to the sky; he then offers him his choice of being thrown down upon the mountains or into the sea. In order to get himself thrown into water, and not on land, where all his bones would be broken, Rústam tells him he has heard that the souls of those who perish in the sea do not attain to Paradise, but wander miserably on earth, and he would therefore prefer being cast upon the mountains for tigers and lions to see how the hands of a brave man are made. The Dív throws him into the sea in order that the stomachs of the fish should provide his shroud, but Rústam draws his sword to defend himself against crocodiles, etc., and swims to shore with his left foot and hand. Finding his horse Rakhsh has disappeared, he picks up his saddle and bridles and follows the horses' tracks in a watered meadow, on all sides of which were woodcocks and turtle doves, to a wood in which the keeper of Afrásiáb's horses was lying asleep. Here he lassoes his horse and rides off, followed by the guardians of the horses. He announces who he is, and they turn back, but at this moment there appears on the scene Afrásiáb, who has come to see his horses, and the herd informs him of what has happened. Afrásiáb pursues him with four elephants and his escort, but Rústam puts them to flight with a hail of arrows, and they run away. He follows them for two farsangs and returns to the water, where the Dív Akván again threatens him, but he lassoes the Dív and breaks his skull with his mace, and giving thanks to God for his victory returns to Irán.* He is joyfully received, distributes the horses, sends the elephants to the king's stable, and is entertained for three weeks; he then returns home.

All now prospers with Irán. Kai Khusru is enjoying himself in festivities with his nobles when his chamberlain comes and announces that the people of Armán, on the boundary of Turán and Irán, have come to ask protection against wild boars that have taken possession of their forests and are injuring their flocks and their crops. When Kai Khusru *asks his warriors* who will volunteer to abate the nuisance, no one comes forward but Bezan, the son of Gív, whose services the king accepts. Bezan takes Gurgín with him as a companion, but when they are about to enter the forest the latter refuses to assist him further than to point out the road, as it is Bezan who has received all the presents the king has given. Notwithstanding this, Bezan proceeds and kills several boars, whilst Gurgín stays outside. He welcomes him back, and after they have eaten and drunk together entices him to go with him to a beautiful part of the country not far off, to which Maníjah, daughter of Afrásiáb, resorts for pleasure, and which abounds in all kinds of delight. Bezan determines to go and observe from a distance the entertainments the Turánians engage in, and see the lovely women Maníjah brings in her train. Manijah sees him from a distance, and sends a nurse to find out who he is. The nurse ascertains this from himself, and Bezan at once goes to Maníjah's tents, where he is rapturously welcomed and remains three days and nights. When he is about to go she orders something to render him insensible to be mixed with his drink,

*There is a noteworthy remark here that every bad man who does not worship God is a *Dív*.

and carries him off in that condition to her own palace by night. The matter gets to the ears of the chamberlain, who informs the king that his daughter has married an Iráni. Afrásiáb sends Garsívaz to bring Bezan; the latter gets ready a dagger to defend himself with, but is finally brought in chains before Afrásiáb, to whom he tells the true story of how he was entrapped. Afrásiáb will not believe him, although he offers to fight with any of his warriors, and orders him to be hanged on the spot. As the gallows is being put up Pirán appears on the scene, and having heard from Bezan what has happened, begs his life from Afrásiáb. Afrásiáb finally agrees to put him into close confinement in a ditch with a stone to close its mouth, and orders Garsívaz to destroy the palace of his daughter, tear off her veil and put her in the same ditch with Bezan. She, however, manages to procure some food which she passes in to Bezan through a hole she makes in his place of confinement, which she guards sorrowing.

Gurgín remains at the wood for a week and then returns to Irán. He makes up a story to Gív that Bezan had disappeared from his sight with a wild ass at which he had cast his lasso, but which in reality must have been the White Dív. Gív does not kill him, as he is tempted to do, but takes him to Kai Khusru and reports Gurgín's story. Kai Khusru encourages him with the hope that Bezan still lives, and promises him to march forthwith against the Turánians. When Gurgín comes before him he does not believe what he says, and orders him to be put into fetters. Gív is directed by Kai Khusru to make inquiries for his son in all directions, and he himself looks in the cup that reflects the world, and discovers Bezan in the ditch loaded with chains, and the young girl near it. He informs Gív of this, writes once more to summon Rústam, and gives the letter to Gív to take.

Rústam promises his assistance, and declares that he will not dismount from his horse till he takes the hand of Bezan. After feasting for three days they start to go to Kai Khusru. Rústam is duly met on the road and feasted. He agrees to go to the release of Bezan, but begs for pardon for Gurgín, whom the king hands over to him. Rústam desires to go with his train disguised as traders, and the king provides him with treasure for the purpose, designing to send with him as leaders Gurgín, Zangah, son of Shavarán, Gústaham, Guárah, Rahám, Farhád, and Ashkash. They take off their warlike apparel and put on woollen clothes, and thus approach the town of Khatan, where Pirán is residing. He offers Rústam a palace to live in, but Rústam prefers remaining with his caravan, to which Maníjah, not knowing who Rústam is, makes her way and describes Bezan's situation to him. Rústam pretends to be angry with her, and declares that he knows nothing of Khusru or his heroes, but gives her food, amongst which there is a cooked fowl, into which he manages to slip a ring. She takes the fowl to Bezan, who discovers the ring with the name of Rústam on it, and thus knows that the hero has come to release him. He sends her to Rústam to inquire if he is the master of Rakhsh, and he tells her who he is, and bids her bring from the forest a heap of wood to light it at night so that he may see the entrance to Bezan's ditch. Bezan is informed, and Rústam's plan is carried out, but Rústam will not pull Bezan out of his ditch until he has promised to forgive Gurgín for his sake. Rústam now tells him to go on with the caravan and Maníjah, while he himself attacks Afrásiáb and finishes him the same night, but Bezan insists on going with him. Rústam breaks open the door and enters the palace, after killing a number of Afrásiáb's men, but the latter escapes out of the house. Rústam presses forward his march in order to get out of the country as soon as possible, and in the morning the Turkománs start in pursuit. Rústam hastens off Maníjah and the convoy, and he and his warriors stay to meet the Turkomán army, which he now defeats and returns to Kai Khusru, who gives him a grand reception and entertainment. Rústam, after receiving valuable presents, returns towards Seistán. Presents are also bestowed on Maníjah.

Afrásiáb now determines to revenge himself on Irán, and assembles his army again, supported by the Mobeds and his warriors, and appoints his son Shídah to lead a force of 50,000 to Khárazm, whilst Pirán leads the same number into Irán. Kai Khusru also makes his preparations. He sends Rústam with 30,000 by way of Seistán and Ghazui towards the North, assigns the country of Alán and Gharchah to Lehrásp, Khárazm to Ashkash against Shídah, and Turán with a fourth army to Gudúrz, Gudúrz now sends Gív with a long message to Pirán. reminding him of what he has done in the past, and recommending him to apprehend those who were concerned in the murder of Siávash and send them to him in chains, like dogs, to send also offerings for the king and his own son, and his two brothers as hostages, and go himself to Kai Khusru, or otherwise to prepare for war. Gív takes this message to Pirán to *Tásahgudh*. Whilst negotiations are going on between Gív and Pirán, the latter sends word to Afrásiáb, who forwards 30,000 men to him, and on this Pirán plucks up courage and dismisses Gív and prepares to fight. Gív reports this to Gudúrz, who arrays his army with a mountain on his right and a river on his left. The disposition of the army and the leaders of various portions of it are given in detail, but it is unnecessary to do so here. The two armies stand facing each other for three whole days, Pirán watching to see if Gudúrz will not advance too hastily without securing his rear, in order, if possible, to attack him from behind, and on the fourth day Bezan begs his father to allow him to offer battle, but is refused permission. Similarly Humán asks Pirán for leave to attack, but is also refused for strategic reasons. Humán challenges Rehám, who will not accept it without the order of Gudúrz, and Humán proceeds to challenge Faribúrz, and is similarly refused. Gudúrz is also challenged and begged to send some hero to fight if he will not venture himself. Gudúrz refuses to do either, even when his own men urge it. Bezan, hearing of what has taken place, begs Gív again to allow him to go forward, but is refused, and proceeds to lay his case before Gudúrz, who at last gives him leave, and Gív provides him with the cuirass of Síávash for the purpose. He makes a final appeal to his son not to undertake the encounter, and the usual defiant talk takes place between the two combatants. A whole Section is taken up with the description of their struggles with maces and swords and in a personal wrestle. Bezan finally throws Humán down and cuts off his head. Bezan, afraid of being attacked by the Turkománs out of revenge, takes off Siávash's armour and puts on that of Humán, so as not to be recognized, and taking Humán's banner, rides off on his horse. The Turkománs are deceived, and Bezan reaches his own camp in safety. Nastíhan, Humán's brother, at Piráni's suggestion makes a night attack on the Iránis and is killed by Bezan. The two armies engage each other the whole of the next day, and at night retire to their respective camps. Gudúrz now writes a letter to the king, giving details of what has occurred and asking for reinforcements, by his own son Hazír. In answer to this Kai Khusru informs him of what has occurred with Rústam, Ashkash, and Lehrasp, and points out that if Afrásiáb were to cross the Jaihún he would be attacked in the rear, and he would be certain, accordingly, not to risk doing so; that he would accompany Tús with an army to reinforce him, and meanwhile he must not desist from opposing Pirán. Having dispatched this with Hazír, he orders the head of the family of Naozar to march against Dehistán and occupy all the plain of Khárazm, and himself makes his preparations for the campaign with 100,000 men. Hajír delivers the letter, and Gudúrz prepares for a battle. Meanwhile Pirán writes to Gudúrz suggesting that after all the slaughter that has taken place it would be advisable to make peace, promising that he will move Afrásiáb to give up all the country that Kai Khusru has taken, that he will return from Irán as far as the hills and the country of Gharchah and Bust, so as to include in Irán Tálikán as far as Fáriáb and Balkh as far as Andaráb, with the five towns of Bámián, the country of Gurgán, all from Balkh to Badakhshán, the plains of the Amí and Zam, with Gilán, Shanghán, Tarmuz, Visahgadakh, Bikhara, and Sugd; that he will give up to Rústam Nímrúz and all the countries as far as India, including Kashmír, Kábul, Kandahár, up to Sind, and on the side where Lehrasp was the country of Alán. He would also satisfy Kai Khusru's demands in the way of treasure and hostages and would cede the whole country as far as the hill of Káfó and all that Askash had occupied. He also offered to decide the matter by a personal combat with Gudúrz, or a fight between chosen warriors on each side if he would agree to a treaty engaging that neither should interfere with the retreat of the other's army on their return homewards. This letter Pirán sends by his son Ruín with an escort of two horsemen. Gudúrz entertains him for seven days and then sends an answer refusing all the terms offered. Ruín delivers the letter, and Pirán accordingly prepares for battle and sends to

Afrásiáb for help, describing the position of the Iránis at Raibad on a hill, and declaring that his army cannot resist the Iránis without assistance. Afrásiáb, in answer, announces his determination to cross the Jaihún and enter Irán, and sends him a reinforcement of 30,000 men On receipt of this answer Pirán encourages his troops, but in his own heart despairs of the results. The two armies being drawn up opposite each other, he sends Lahák and Farshídvard to the attack, the former on the side of the hill and the latter from that of the river. Gudúrz perceives this and sends Hajír to Gív to bid him send assistance to the troops who are holding the hill and the river, to choose a capable commander for the rearguard, and to come himself to Gudúrz. Gív entrusts this command to Farhád, sends off Zangah, son of Shavarán, to attack Farshídvard, and goes to his father. He, with Gurázah, Gústaham, Hajír, and Bezan, at Gudúrz's order, then attack the centre of the army of Turán. A personal combat now takes place between Gív and Pirán. Pirán showers arrows upon him, and Gív advances against him, covering his head with his shield, but his horse stops short and refuses to move on. Assistance arriving for Gív, Pirán turns back and Lahák and Farshídvard attack Gív. The former is unhorsed through a blow struck on his horse by Gív, and the latter cuts Gív's lance in two, but Gív retaliates by a blow with his mace. Others join in the fight, and the matter finishes for the day by darkness coming on. On assembling again the next morning, Gudúrz exhorts them, and all enter zealously into the matter, Gudúrz determining to enter into single combat with Pirán, notwithstanding the remonstrances of his Chiefs, as it had been predicted that Pirán would fall by his hand. On the other hand, Pirán informs his Chiefs that Gudúrz and he have come to an agreement that in place of the two armies contending with each other certain selected warriors shall fight. To this all agree, and Gudúrz and Pirán choose their respective champions. Gív was opposed to Girui, Kalbad, son of Visah, to Faribúrz, son of Káüs, Rahám to Barmán, Gurázah to Siámak, Gúrgin to Andarimán, Bezan to Ruín, Akhvàst to Zangah, Bartah to Kahram, Farúhil to Zangulah, Hajír to Sipahram, and finally Gudúrz himself to Pirán. The standards of the two leaders were erected on opposite hillocks from which the whole field was visible, and the combatants were directed to repair each to the hillock on his own side with his banner. From the commencement the Turánians appear to have been dispirited. The various combats resulted as follows. Faribúrz kills Kalbád with his sword. Gív had determined to take Girúi, son of Zarah, alive to Kai Khusru; after fighting for some time with their lances, Gív approaches his opponent, who drops his bow through fear, and draws his sword, but Giv strikes him on the head with his mace and knocks him off his horse, and then, tying his arms, carries him off in triumph to the hillock. Gurázah throws down Siámak so violently as to break his bones and kill him. Farúhil shoots both Zangulah and his horse with an arrow, and cuts off his head, which he takes to the hillock. Rahám pierces the thigh of Barmán with his lance and unhorses him. Barmán runs off, but is pierced in the back and through the liver by Rahám, who rubs his face with his blood, and is tied on his own horse and carried off. Bezan knocks Ruín's brains out with his mace, cuts off his head and ties it on to his saddle, and goes to the hillock with his standard. Sipahram is killed by a blow of Hazir's sword on the head, and his body is dragged there as well. Andarimán is killed by two arrows in his head shot by Gúrgin. His head is cut off and he is carried away bound to Gurgín's stirrup. Bartah and Kahram now fight, and the former cuts the latter down through the head to the chest with his sword ; his body is carried off to the hillock on Bartah's horse. In the fight between Zangah, son of Shavarán and Akhvást, they engage each other with their maces till they are exhausted and then separate in order to recover themselves. Zangah then unhorses his opponent with a spear thrust, drags him along the earth face downwards, and finally lifts him on to his horse and carries him off. Gudúrz shoots Pirán's horse, and it rolls over its rider in its fall and breaks his right arm. Pirán now tries to run away and manages to get to the top of the hill in hope that Gudúrz will not pursue him. Gudúrz offers to take him to Kai Khasru to beg for forgiveness. Pirán answers that he was but born to die, and Gudúrz then begins to mount the hill, when Pirán throws his dagger at him and wounds him on the hand. Gudúrz in turn throws a javelin at Pirán and pierces his liver, and finds him lying on the hill in this miserable state. He refrains from cutting off his head, and planting his standard on the hill mournfully leaves his enemy on the hill and regains his own people. Thence he sends Rahám to bring in Pirán's body. The dead are now taken to the camp, to which Girúi, son of Zarah, is made to run in front of the warriors. Lahák and Farshídvard make great lamentation at the death of Pirán, and finally, on the advice of their troops, determine to fight no more. The two Chiefs take the desert road back towards Turán, but find it beset by a party of Iránis. A fight takes place, and while seven of the latter are killed, the only ones of the Turkománs who escape are the two leaders ; but they are pursued by Gústaham with the consent of Gudúrz. The army that Afrásiáb is leading to the assistance of Pirán turns back on hearing of his death. Bezan, seeing Gústaham going off alone in pursuit of the two fugitives, desires to follow in order to assist Gústaham, and Gív, his father, remonstrates with him. Notwithstanding this he follows them up. Lahák, who has fallen asleep on the road with Farshídvard watching over him, is roused by the former, and the two come out of the wood where they have been. Gústaham comes up and kills Farshídvard. Lahák and Gústaham now engage each other, and Gústaham kills Lahák with his sword, but being himself severely wounded has to pass the night in torture. Bezan now comes up and finds Gústaham, and binds up his wounds. Then meeting some wandering Turkomán horsemen, he kills two of them and spares the life of another in order that he may assist him in carrying away the wounded man as well as the bodies of Lahák and Farshídvard.

Khusru now prepares a *dukhmah* for Pirán and the other Turánian Chiefs, and orders Girúi, the son of Zarah, to be put to death with torture and have his head cut off. The army of Turán now ask for pardon from Kai Khusru, and he forgives them after depriving them of their arms. Gústaham is brought in by Bezan and recovers from his wounds. The king remains a week at Raibad and distributes rewards, bidding his nobles to be prepared for a fresh war.

Then follows a Section in praise of Sultán Mahmúd and abuse of Fate, which it is unnecessary to notice further.

Kai Khusru now prepares his army for another campaign against Afrásiáb. It includes all the heroes who have distinguished themselves in the former war, and troops from Rúm and Barbaristán and all parts of the country. They start from Mount Káf. Afrásiáb, whose residence is given as Kúndúz, which was changed to Baigand, when he hears of the death of Pirán, laments the loss of Ruín, Lahák, Farshídvard and others, and declares that he has no more pleasure in life; that he will no longer wear a crown, but will make his cuirass his tunic, his horse his throne, and a helmet his crown. Hearing news of the march of Kai Khusru, he vows vengeance, and the nobles respond to his call. He places half his army under his son Karákhán, and orders him to Balkh to act as rearguard and constantly to send him fresh troops and provisions. He himself leaves Baigand and crosses the Jaihún, leaving Karákhán to collect boats and send down provisions by the river; and distributing commands to his sons Shídah (whose name was really Pushang) and Jahan and others, he makes all necessary dispositions. Khusru hears of Afrásiáb's march, and himself advances, and the two armies face each other for two days. On the fourth day Pushang appears before his father and declares that if he is allowed to go against them not an Iráni shall be left alive. His father deprecates haste, and prefers the plan of sending out single warriors to fight instead of making a general attack. Pushang burns to attack Kai Khusru himself, but is discouraged by his father, who sends a message to Kai Khusru by him, insisting that Siávash had deserved his fate, and if he would forget what had occurred, peace might be made, Pushang and Jahan would become his brothers, and the Turkománs should evacuate the territory he claimed. Otherwise, he should meet him in single combat, or they might let the matter be decided by warriors chosen from both sides. Shídah goes with the message and is met by Káran, sent by Kai Khusru, who hears the message. Kai Khusru and all his nobles, especially Rústam, disapprove of Afrásiáb's proposals, and Káran is sent back with a message to Shídah, accepting his challenge to single combat with Kai Khusru. Notwithstanding Afrásiáb's unwillingness, the fight takes place, and Kai Khusru kills Shídah. A general engagement now takes place between the two armies, and the combat ceases at night, although Afrásiáb still appears defiant. In the course of the night, however, Afrásiáb crosses the river in flight, and the whole Turánian army breaks up. The Iránis remain five days on the field of battle, and collect their dead in a *dukhmah* worthy of warriors. Kai Khusru reports his victory to Káüs. Afrásiáb sends to the Faghfúr of China to ask for assistance, and takes refuge in Gangdiz, making a halt at Bukhárá on the way, and for three days on the bank of the Gulzariún, where his scattered forces collect together and enjoy themselves. Kai Khusru crosses the Jaihún after Afrásiáb up to the borders of Sughd (Soghdiana ?), where he learns that Kákulah, a descendant of Túr, had joined the latter full of thoughts of hatred, and that a large army had collected in the desert to oppose Kai Khusru. Kai Khusru orders the army from Barda and Ardabíl under Gústaham, and that of Nímruz under Rústam, up to surprise the Turkománs by a forced march, and after remaining some time in Sughd, himself advances towards Turán, devastating the country, but dealing mercifully with all who did not resist. Afrásiáb issues from Gang, and the armies encounter each other again near the Gulzáriún. A great storm comes on, and the Turkománs suffer greatly from it, but Afrásiáb rallies his troops to renew the fight when news reaches Kai Khusru from Gústaham of a successful night attack he has made on Afrásiáb's army, and that only Karákhán and a few of his men were left alive from it, as well as another message from Rústam to say that the Turkománs in the desert had been scattered before him and he had entered Turán. This bad news also reaches Afrásiáb. Khusru sends word to Rustam that Afrásiáb is probably about to attack him, and that he should be on his guard. Afrásiáb is about to do sc when he finds Rústam on the alert, and instead of attacking him takes shelter with his army in Gangdij (or Gangbehist, as it is also called), whence he addresses a letter to the Faghfúr of China to send him assistance, and prepares himself in a depressed state of mind, for a siege in the fort. Kai Khusru arrives before the place and regularly invests it. Jahan now comes out of the fort with a message from Afrásiáb to Kai Khusru to say that he repents of the murder of Siávash, to which he was instigated by an impure Dív, and reminding him of the misery that has been brought about by the war, offers to cede to him Chín, Máchín, Khurásán and Mekrán and recognize him as king. Kai Khusru replies that he cannot believe his lies, and trusts only in God and his own sword. Khusru disposes his troops round the fort, and attacks it from all four sides. Rústam plants the flag of Irán on the ramparts, throws Jahan and Garsívaz from the walls, and the Iránis thoroughly sack the place, whilst Afrásiáb takes flight through a subterranean passage and disappears. Kai Khusru orders certain of his nobles whom he can trust to protect the family and palace of Afrásiáb, notwithstanding the desire of the Iránis to take summary vengeance on them all, and when the wives and female slaves appear before him in terror reinstates them in the palace. He also exhorts his army to treat the people with leniency, and pardons the Turkománs who are dispersed abroad. The whole country submits to him, and he writes a letter to Káüs to announce his conquest, sending also spies out to ascertain whither Afrásiáb has fled. Through these he finds that the Faghfúr has entered into an alliance with Afrásiáb, and that the whole country as far as the Gulzáriún was full of troops, who were joined by those of the old army of Turán whom he had just pardoned, in order to attack him and avenge themselves for their defeat. Kai Khusru accordingly recalls his army and advances from the fort. Before the armies meet, a message comes from Afrásiáb to Kai Khusru by three men of experience, offering to give up his throne, his army and the country of Turán if his life is spared, or otherwise to fight him single-handed. If he is conquered he asks for protection for his family. Khusru confers with Rústam, who advises him to let his army advance, and gives an answer to the message accordingly. A fight takes place between the two armies, and is put a stop to by darkness. Kai Khusru arranges his army under Rústam and Tús in such a way as to guard against a night attack by Afrásiáb. Afrásiáb makes this attack, which is so thoroughly defeated by Kai Khusru's arrangements that only ten out of every hundred escape. Amongst those who do so Kai Khusru searches in vain for Afrásiáb, who has again escaped, and receives the submission of the Turkománs who, seeing their standard no longer in the centre of the army, give themselves up. He thanks God for victory, and gives up the spoil to his army.

The Faghfúr and Khákán send a conciliatory message to Kai Khusru, who accepts it, and Afrásiáb is warned off their territories. Afrásiáb in his flight arrives at the water of Zarah, which he and his nobles cross, and arrive at Gangdíz. The nobles at first refuse to venture across the water in pursuit, but consent on the remonstrance of Rústam that all their labours should not be allowed to be in vain.

Kai Khusru now sends his prisoners and gifts to Káüs with a letter by the hand of Gív, who is feasted by the latter. The female prisoners are given an asylum in Káüs's own female apartments. Jahan is assigned a place to live in, and Garsívaz is confined in an underground place under the palace. Letters are also sent out into all the provinces announcing the victories, and Gív returns to Kai Khusru with a congratulatory answer from Káüs. Kai Khusru sends on an army under Gústaham towards China, and himself visits the town his father had founded (? Siávash-gadh), where he sees the place where his father's blood had been shed and vows to God to shed the blood of Afrásiáb in the same manner. Messages are now sent to the Faghfúr, the Khákán, and the king of Mekrán demanding their submission, and the two former agree, but the king of Mekrán defies him. The Faghfúr and Khákán meet him three stations from the frontier, bring presents and submit, and in the fourth month Kai Khusru marches for Mekrán, to the king of which he sends a message demanding provisions for his army. These are refused. A horseman of the country, who comes out at night to reconnoitre the army, is cut in two by Takhvár, the patrol from the camp. A battle ensues, and the king of Mekrán is killed by Tús, but Kai Khusru forbids his head being cut off. After slaughtering a great number of the enemy and devastating the country, Kai Khusru orders his army to retire. In Mekrán he himself remains for a year, and when he goes leaves Ashkash behind him to maintain his authority in the country. Arriving on the shore of the sea of Zarah, he employs the sailors of China and Mekrán in collecting supplies for a year on board ships, in which the army embark, and are buffeted about for six months until they reach a place called by the sailors the "lion's mouth." In this they see bulls and lions combating with each other, men whose hair was like lassos, and covered with wool like sheep, some with fishes' bodies and leopards' heads, others with wild asses' heads on crocodiles' bodies, others with buffaloes' heads and two hands behind and two feet in front, &c.; the sea was full of such creatures. In the seventh month when Kai Khusru reached the shore, he found towns like those of China, but the language of the people was like that of Mekrán. He sends out a man who knows all the languages to enquire for Gangdíz and Afrásiáb, and finds the place is only 100 farsangs distant, and that Afrásiáb was there. He arrives at Gangdíz only to find that Afrásiáb has escaped, but sends men in search of him while he remains enjoying himself for a whole year, until he is advised by his nobles to return, and goes back to the sea for that purpose, and crosses it without adventure in seven months. Disembarking his army, he is received with due state by Ashkash. On the borders of China he is received by Rústam and arrives at Siávash-gadh, where he sorrowfully inspects the place where his father had been murdered by Garsívaz and Gírúi, and asks God's assistance in carrying out his vengeance. Gústaham meets him and both go to Gang-i-behisht, where he rests from the fatigues of war for another year before returning to Irán for the remainder of his reign, the account of a part of which, together with that of the origin and rise of Zaroasterianism, is contained in the following translation.

The Returning of Kai Khusru towards Irán and his Going to Káus in Fárs.

As to great length his stay in Gang thus drew,
The need for seeing Káüs once more grew.
To Naozar's Gústaham he gave the land
Of China's sea from Kipchák to the strand.
A countless host to Gústaham he gave,
And said : " Thy glad heart be alert and brave,
To Chín and to Mekrán thy hand extend ;
Letters prepare to ev'ry one to send.
To seek Afrásiáb hast thou a mind,
Empty of him the world thou mayest find."
And thence whatever thing of worth might be,

Dinars and jewels and new property,
Of musk, and camphor, and of golden shoes,
Collar and horse and slave and throne to use,
Chinese brocade and carpets for the ground,
What in Mekrán there might be to be found,
Bulls forty thousand, chariots to haul,
The monarch to drive in determined all.
Each one declared that he had never seen
More wealth than this, nor could there e'er have been.
His army such that over plain and hill
By night and day it went on passing still.
When he who went in front passed out of sight,
Would others to the stage come and alight.
And in this manner he to Cháj passed on,
And hung his crown upon the ivory throne
More than a week at Saghd away he wore,
Whilst Talimán and Khúzán went before.
When thence again Bukhárá's town he neared,
The ground beneath his army disappeared.
He ate and for a whole week took his rest.
The next week in an unused garment dressed
He came, and of his past days in lament,
With shouts into the house of fire he went,
Founded by Túr, of Faridún the son,
Who many a lofty dome had built thereon.
With fervour then to the pure God he prayed,
On the dark earth as down his head he laid.
On *Mobeds* silver he bestowed and gold,
Nor did he jewels from the fire withhold.
The king, his heart's wish glad fulfilled to find,
Still further on to go made up his mind.
Tow'rds Balkh he crossed the Jaihún with no halt;
Of earth he both the bitter tasted and the salt.
In Balkh again the king a week abode,
Then at its end took on from Balkh his road.

And as he went some chieftain of renown
Was with an army there in ev'ry town;
With *Azin** decked highways and byeways too,
Where with his host the king was passing through
On ev'ry road as king and army went,
Banquets and royal feasts did they present.
To Marr-i-Rúd, and Pálikán he came:
Of song and wailing flute earth full became.
The cities ev'rywhere were gaily decked,
Nor minstrels' song and wine did they neglect.
Dirams and saffron spreading far and wide,
Musk and *dinars* they poured on him beside.
The road to Nishápúr the monarch sought,
And many elephants and horses brought.
He as a *Darvísh* who in town remained,
Or his own living by his labour gained,
To each of them some *dirams* did he give,
And thus expended purses fifty-five.
Dámghán towards he onward took the road,
And gold and *dirams* as he went bestowed;
For a week there himself with rest renewed,
Horse, elephants, and army were reviewed.
After a week to Rai he went along,
With wine upon the road and joy and song,
Two weeks in justice and in giving spent;
And in the third towards Baghdád he went.
And certain dromedaries on from Rai
Forward he sent to Fárs to Káüs Kai.
The king's heart was rejoiced when this he knew,
Thou would'st have said that he in stature grew.
Then thrones of gold he placed within each hall,
Houses with Chinese goods adorning all.
On road and town then *Azín* they erect;
Bazár and street and house were gaily decked.

*Processional decorations.

To welcome him among them chieftains went,
Champions and Irán's great with one consent.
Domes on the highways and the byeways, too,
The world was like brocade of golden hue.
Jewels and musk together mingling all,
On heads below they from the domes let fall.
Out of the city when king Káüs came,
With heroes of propitious feet and name,
Aside, the new king saw his grandsire stand,
And urged his steed till he was close at hand.
Leapt from his horse, in prayer he did not lack,
And Káüs many blessings gave him back.
They held each other's bodies in embrace,
With many kisses on the head and face.
And on each other they both sorely wept
That they without hope had so long been kept.
Then Kai Káüs gushed out in blessings meet
On that king fortunate of blessed feet,
"Of thee may ne'er the world be lacking," cried,
"Nor throne of greatness nor the crown of pride.
The sun has never seen a king like thee,
Nor horse, nor mail, nor crown of dignity.
From Jamshíd down to Faridún there came
Ne'er to this earth a king like thee of fame.
Should from the *Dukhmah* Siávash come back,
He of thy dignity would surely lack.
May all the world propitious be to thee
And thy foe's heart and soul uprooted be!"
The king replied: "Thy fortune was the root,
And of thy tree a branch has borne this fruit.
Like thee a grandsire he who has on earth,
For him the hard rock unto grass gives birth."
This said, he kissed his mouth, and lip again,
"Devoid of thee nor day nor night remain!"
Em'rald he brought and gold and ruby, too,

And on the king's head 'gan to pour anew.
Thus, till the gem-besprinkled throne he neared,
His feet beneath the offerings disappeared.
He bade them then the company to call,
And spread the feast out in another hall.
The nobles then, with him who wore the crown,
In the gold-spangled mead were seated down.
Then of those wonders said the king this word:
" Such strange things no one ever saw or heard."
River and Gangdiz then he brought to mind,
And filled the heroes' lips all full of wind,
Of city joys and of the plain and hill,
Of melon-grounds as bright lamps shining still.
Thus Káūs ever in amazement grew,
And of his mighty deeds the measure knew.
He said: " The bright words of a youthful king
Renew the day and to months freshness bring.
Never on earth did such a king appear,
Nor such tales ever fell upon the ear.
And now this new star let us all adore,
In wine remember Khusru more and more."
He had the gold-bespangled mead prepared,
Brought wine and ruby lips that in it shared.
Out of Káūs his hall for seven days
The cups of wine of waves a tempest raise.
Op'ning, the eighth, his treasure door again
He gave out due rewards for all their pain.
Those nobles who with him would ever go
In war and feasting, and in joy or woe,
He gave robes suited to each man's degree,
What was most valued in his treasury.
Each went away, with head on high to boast,
To his own country with a mighty host.
He made the matter for the army clear
In giving them their wages for a year.

The hero and his grandsire then withdrew,
To ask each other what was best to do.
Then Khusru, Káüs' son, began to speak:
"Except from God the road how shall we seek?
A year we traverse desert, sea, and hill,
Together from a scarred heart suffer still:
Yet in the desert and in hill and sea,
No record of Afrásiáb we see.
If he to Gang should ever find the way,
He'd bring from all sides hosts without delay.
Hardships the while and pain there will abide,
However much God may be on our side."
His grandson's words when the great king had heard,
As an old man he counsel wise preferred.
"At once on horses two," to him he cried:
"To Azargushasp's temple let us ride.
Our bodies let us wash, our feet and hands,
As he before God who to worship stands,
And to the world's Creator whispering there,
Make to him secretly our fervent prayer.
On foot before the fire let us abide—
Perchance the pure God may be now our guide.
And in the place where He for rest would stay,
Of Justice the Dispenser, show our way."
Both in these counsels then became as one,
Nor on this road to go did either shun.
They sat upon their steeds like wind of flame
To Azargushasp's temple till they came.
They entered there in garments all of white,
Both full of hope and yet at heart afright.
Bitter their weeping when they saw the fire,
As if themselves upon it might expire.
Both kings were weeping and bewailing sore
Before the Lord whom sun and moon adore.
They called upon the world's Creator there,

And on the Mobeds scattered jewels rare.
Washing his cheek, tears Khusru's eyelash poured;
With *dinárs* he the *Zandavast** adored.
A week before God they were standing there
(Think not, it was the fire they worshipped there!)
For fire was as the Mehráb† in that place,
And tearful of the worshipper the face.
Lengthy though thy reflections be indeed,
Of the pure God thou always wilt have need.
In Azar Abádghán a whole month then
Remained those kings with other noblemen.

The taking refuge by Afrásiáb in a cave of a hill, and his falling into the hand of Húm, of the race of Faridún.

Afrásiáb, it thus had come about,
Foodless and sleepless wandered in and out.
His life unsafe, his body not at rest,
Ever by fear of injury oppressed.
He sought a place on earth, and sought again
Both safety for his life and health to gain.
Near Barda on a hill a cave there lay;
The cave's head from the world was hid away.
Above it was no place where hawks could soar,
Below no feet of lion or of boar.
When far from men he found the cave indeed,
The king went up the hill there in his need.
In terror for his life some food he brought,
And in the cave a lofty place he wrought.
Within this cave he dwelt some time apart,
His deeds repenting, full of blood his heart.

* The recess in a mosque towards which worshippers turn when engaged in prayer.

† The book of Zaroaster, the religious book of the old Persian fire-worshippers.

When great men's hearts from blood can not refrain,
On royal throne they will not long remain.
When such a monarch, of the throne possessed,
With stars propitious and good fortune blessed,
Becomes bloodthirsty, there appears a foe.
Happy is he who kings' blood does not know!
A worthy man was living in that age,
Of seed of Faridún, a learned sage.
A worshipper of royal dignity,
Yet girded with the royal *zone* was he.
He made his place of worship on the hill,
Far from the crowd, from all joy further still.
Now of this well-known man was Húm the name,
For worship far, from distant lands, he came.
One day he went up on the hill-top there,
To Him, the Just One, to address his prayer.
Upon the hill he went in prayer to call
On the world's Ruler, Lord Supreme of all.
As, clothed in wool, he made to God his prayer,
Out of the cave a wailing reached his ear.
Hearing the wailing, he excited grew,
To the cave hast'ning, whence the sound he knew.
His ear he opened to that mournful cry,
Where now Afrásiáb's voice, uplifted high,
Was saying: " Higher than the Highest Thou,
Who of my heart the secret knowest now,
If in my day some dark deeds I have done,
And paining Thee, have Thy amazement won,
Though fully guilty, I am yet Thy slave,
And in my wretchedness Thy refuge crave.
My throne and crown oh! let me no more lack,
My treasure and my army give me back;
Else from my body part my soul for me;
I have no crown nor men nor treasury.
This life of pain I now no more desire

Land, crown and treasure do I not require.
Alas for all that country and that land,
That gold, that wealth, and all those gems in hand!
Alas for golden and for ivory throne,
For collar, bracelet, and that golden crown!
For heavy mace and sword alas, again,
And for those horsemen of the twisted rein!
Alas for brother, and alas for son!
What ills are these that I from Fate have won!"
Afrásiáb thus mourned with bitter a cry,
Whilst with the flowing tear was filled his eye.
"O wretched head, O Chieftain of renown,
O noble one, of nobles all the crown!
Turkey and China all beneath thy sway,
In ev'ry place thy treaties held their way.
Here of a cavern art thou now possessed.
Where are thy men of war with valour blessed?
Where are that treasure and that generous sense,
Thy bravery, valour and magnificence!
Where is that greatness, throne and crown to boast,
That teeming country and that mighty host?
Where are thine arm, thine arrow and thy bow.
That of them now so little thou dost know?
Where is the ruby of thy signet ring,
Beneath thy sway two parts of earth to bring?
Where is thy ravaging by day and night,
That army ready for the plundering fight?
Where are those great ones who stood thee before,
Who as thy guides thee ever forward bore?
Where are the edifices built so high,
A place for refuge that would thee supply?
Where are those Mobeds in their lengthy row,
With whom the wise ones their alliance know?
Where are those warriors and those men of might,
Who stood before thee in the day of fight.

That in this cavern thou art shut up tight,
Enclosed in this stone fort as if in flight ?"
In Túrkí when he heard this wailing there,
Húm went and for the time gave up his prayer.
" At sleeping time this mourning sound," said he
" Must of Afrásiáb the wailing be."
As this impression in his heart grew strong,
The door of that dark cave he sought for long.
He saw Afrásiáb was lurking there,
And had for rest and sleep prepared a lair.
Like a fierce lion came he on in haste,
The woollen girdle loosing from his waist,
The lasso in his zone's place thus he wore,
From the world's Lord that him protection bore.
Entering the cave, he held his lasso's pleat:
When he came near the king leapt on his feet.
For a long while the two together clung,
But on the ground at last Húm had him flung.
And when Húm threw him down upon the ground,
As he lay low his arms he tightly bound,
And dragging him along he pulled him on,
And fiercely shook as if his sense had gone.
That one at this should wonder, is but meet;
He in the world who holds a royal seat,
Should seek for nothing but a name to praise,
However much he drink or he may graze.*
Luxuriously he lived as he desired,
And army, power, and wealth and name acquired.
Of all the world he chose the cavern there,
Nor knew that it would be misfortune's snare.

The flight of Afrásiáb from the hand of Húm

When Húm bound of that king the arm that day,
He drew him from his hiding-place away.

* Difficult to understand.

He said to him : "O thou whom one must fear,
Who knowingly the pure God dost revere,
What would'st of me? Who in the world am I,
Who in this groundless cave sit secretly?
I but a trading merchant am forlorn.
My money gone, who but sit here and mourn.
With aching head and full of sorrow, too,
Who in this narrow cave but sit and mew."
Húm said to him : "'Tis not thy place of rest:
Thy name in all the world is thus known best :
Among earth's kings his brother who has slain,
And with the pure God still dost strife maintain.
Such as Aghríras, Naozar of renown,
Siávash, too, as Kais' heir handed down,
These hast thou killed. Dost thou bear this in mind?
Like thee a king unjust may no one find!
The blood of monarchs should'st thou never shed,
Nor to a gruesome cave have ever fled."
And when Afrásiáb his purport knew.
Sense from his head, thou would'st have said, all flew.
He said : "O hero, thou of dignity,
In the world faultless what man dost thou see?
Such on my head the lofty spheres' decree
That pain, grief, injury, were due to me.
But God's command can no one e'er transgress,
His foot though on the lion's neck he press.
My misery pity for me should have won,
Injustice though to some I may have done.
Grandson of Faridún in me behold,
And loosen off from me thy noose's hold.
Whither thus bound wilt carry me away?
Dost thou not fear God on the Judgment Day?"
"O man of evil thought," Húm said again :
"Not many days on earth for thee remain.
As is the rosebud, so thy words are sweet,

But fate at Khusru's hand must thou now meet."
From injury to him Húm's heart drew back,
He let the royal noose's knots be slack.
And when the king had for himself perceived
That good man's heart was at his wailing grieved,
Out of his hand he drew himself away,
Plunged in the river and was lost to day.
Just then Gudúrz, Kishvád's son, it was found,
With Gív and other nobles wandered round.
Then proudly as they course about the king,
Some on the river near their glances fling.
They saw Húm with his lasso wandering there,
On the stream's edge with miserable air.
The water, too, was darkened to their gaze,
The holy man's eyes looking in amaze.
"This man of abstinence," he said, "I think,
Is going fishing on the river brink.
Perhaps a crocodile has seized the bait;"
And gazed still more in a bewildered state.
Húm he addressed thus: "O thou holy man,
Now openly reveal to us thy plan.
What in the water dost thou hope to find?
To wash thy dark form in it hast a mind?"
"Look and behold me now," Húm to them cried,
"And what has happened to me, man of pride.
I have a place upon this sword-like hill,
A place to worship, far from man and still.
When night was dark before my God I lay,
The whole night long to worship and to pray.
As for the cocks to crow the hour drew near,
A mournful wailing struck upon my ear.
The thought to me my heart began to bear
That evil's root I from the earth might tear,
For at the hour of sleep such notes of wail
Should from Afrásiáb to rise not fail.

I sought and sought in ev'ry cave and scaur,
Till of that famed one's cave I found the door.
Within that fate-forsaken one there slept,
And bitter for his crown and fortune wept.
As I went in up from his place he leapt,
On the hard rock his feet firm footing kept.
Then with my zone his hands I tightly bound,
So that blood gushing from his nails was found.
Running, I brought him out upon the hill,
Wailing and crying like a woman still.
Of his loud cries and oaths on the excuse,
I let his fastened bonds a little loose.
Here in this place he leapt out from my hand;
To seek him now with wounded soul I stand.
Here in this Khanjast lake he lies concealed,
And the whole truth have I to thee revealed."
And when Gudúrz this narrative had heard,
An ancient saying there to him occurred.
Then the fire-temple seeking full of thought,
He hastened like a man with heart distraught.
Towards the fire then first a prayer he raised,
And then the world's Creator fervent praised.
This done, the secret that had been concealed
And what he saw he to the kings revealed.
The monarchs, on their steeds then seated all,
Of Azargúshasp left the lofty hall,
And the world-monarch, full of anxious thought,
Without delay of Húm the presence sought.

The Description by Húm to Káüs of what had occurred to Afrásiáb.

When of those kings Húm saw the head and crown
On all the monarchs he called blessings down,
And they of blessing also showed no lack,
But from the world's Creator gave them back.

And further then to Húm king Káüs said;
"Thank God, who is the refuge for our head,
That of a pious man I've seen the face,
So powerful and strong, with wisdom's grace!"
Then Húm, God's worshipper, to him replied:
"Long 'neath thy justice may the land abide!
Propitious may the New Year be to thee;
The heart of all thy foes uprooted be!
I worshipped God upon this mountain high
What time the king Gangdiz was passing by.
The world's Creator humbly I besought,
Earth's face through him to gladness might be brought.
When he returned back glad and smiling there,
I raised again to God my humble prayer.
Sudden a heav'nly messenger one night
Brought what was hidden from me into light.
From that unfathomed cave there came a sound
To which I turned my ear, attentive, round.
Some one wept sadly for his ivory throne,
His country, army, dignity and crown.
Into that cave I came down from the crest,
And in my hand my zone was firmly pressed.
There of Afrásiáb I saw the head
And ear, where he had made for rest his bed.
Stone-like, I bound him with my lasso strong,
And from that narrow cave dragged him along.
At those tight fastenings he wept right sore,
'Thou of good fortune,' wailing more and more.
'These bonds of mine, oh! slacken and undo,'
I did so, and he to the river flew.
He in the water here must hidden be;
Cutting his feet the world would I make free.
Him from his purpose would the spheres now move,
His blood stirs of Garsívaz with the love.
If so should order now the lofty king,

His brother bound in fetters they will bring.
Upon his neck a bull's hide let them sew,
Till no more strength or power he may know.
And when his voice Afrásiáb shall hear,
Out of the water he will soon appear."
He gave the warders at the gate command,
To go with sword and rounded shield in hand.
Thither the while Garsívaz then they brought,
Who for the land had all the evil wrought.
The executioner from off his face
Removed, when bid, the veil of his disgrace.
A bull's hide then upon his neck they bound,
And in his body no more strength was found.
His skin pulled off, he begged forgiveness sure,
Of the world's Maker pardon to implore.
His voice pierced of Afrásiáb the ear,
And from the water straight did he appear.
And with his hands and feet both swimming bold,
Came to a place there where his foot would hold.
On dry land when his brother's cries he heard,
He to that piteous sight death had preferred.
Garsívaz saw where in the stream he stood
With hast'ning heart and both eyes full of blood.
"O monarch of the world!" he wailed and said,
"Chief of renowned ones, of the great the head.
Where are the rites that should surround thy state,
Thy head, crown, army, and thy treasure great?
Thy ambush, bow, and noose where canst thou find,
Dívs and magicians all wherewith to bind?
Where are that horsemanship, that plain and ball,
And that *changan** which was the talk of all?
Where is that lion-like attack at night,
Subduing raging lions in thy might?
Where are thy wisdom and thy strength of hand,

* The Persian equivalent of a "polo mace."

Those nobles who the king to serve should stand?
Where are thy name and glory in the fight,
And in the feast desire of wine cup bright?
That of the river thou should'st now have need,
A star malignant shines on thee indeed!"

The capture of Afrásiáb and the slaying of him and Garsívaz at the hand of Kai Khusru.

Now weeps Afrásiáb when this he hears,
And sheds into the water blood-stained tears.
"Around the world," his answer thus gave he:
"I've wandered openly and secretly.
In hope this hard fate yet might pass away.
From bad to worse yet evil on me lay.
This life to me has now become a thorn,
In care for thee so has my soul been torn.
Grandson of Faridún, son of Pushang.
In snare of crocodile am I thus hung.'
The Chiefs in this talk occupation found,
Whilst in his search the hermit wandered round.
Round by an island there a man appeared,
He from a distance saw him as he neared.
He loosed the royal lasso from his waist,
And like a raging lion came in haste.
And as that twisted lasso he threw loose,
The head of that king came within the noose.
Him from the water with contempt he drew,
And as a worthless thing his life then knew.
He gave him to the kings and went away;
The wind was his companion, thou would'st say.
With his sharp sword-blade then the monarch came,
His head was full of rage, his heart aflame.
Afrásiáb said in a foolish way:
"'Twas this I thought of in a dream to-day
Above me have the heavens long revolved,

And now of secrets has the veil dissolved."
He cried: "O thou who vengeance seek'st to-day
Thy grandsire why dost thou desire to slay?"
He answered him: "O thou of evil heart,
Worthy of all reproaches thou who art,
First of thy brother's murder will I speak,
Evil to great men who would never seek.
And next of Naozar, celebrated king,
Iraj, whom all the world to memory bring.
Upon his neck thou'st struck thy sharpened blade,
Uproar of judgment in the world hast made.
And third, Siávash, valiant rider he,
And such as no one in the world may see—
Just as a sheep hast thou cut off his head,
And far beyond the sky thy rumour spread.
Thus with my sire why didst thou do away,
And did'st not think thee of this evil day?
In doing evil thou hast made all haste,
And evil in return dost thou now taste!"
He said: "What was to happen could not fail,
But thou awhile must listen to my tale.
Till I thy mother's cheeks see, now delay,
And then repeat what thou may'st have to say."
"My mother, thou would'st see," to him he said,
"Now see what ill thou hast brought on my head!
My sire was guiltless, I still hidden lay,
Yet in the world what mischief didst thou play!
Thou hast cut off a king's head whom his crown
Has deeply mourned for and his ivory throne.
If bonds from me without harm thou desire,
No man can quench an all devouring fire.
The herd on whom a raging wolf lays hold,
Though he may live, will not again be bold.
The man who in the wood's the lion's prey,
How long will he on earth survive and stay?

And if on him the lion pity show,
Will the same lion not him overthrow?
Now let it be! It is of God the might,
And evil to the ill will He requite."
Into his neck his Indian sword he thrust.
And cast his dark form down into the dust.
Red from the blood his white beard and his ear
His brother of the world was in despair.
Devoid of him the royal throne remained,
His days of happiness came to an end.
From evil deeds he reaped calamity,
"*Seek not, my son, of evil bonds the key!*"
What seek'st thou? For an evil deed, be sure.
Will at the last but evil end secure.
A General who God's glory may enjoy,
In rage both chains and prison may employ.
If he shed blood the injury still remains,
And from the lofty heav'ns he vengeance gains.
To hasty Behram once a Mobed said:
"Never the blood of guiltless ones be shed.
If thou desire thy crown to last for thee,
Calm and of pure mind thou should'st ever be."
Behold what to the head the crown once said:
"May wisdom to thy brain be ever wed!"
He to Garsívaz from his brother went,
Pale were his cheeks, his heart on fraud intent.
Him to the headsman with contempt they drew
In heavy chains, with evil fate in view.
With guards and people dragging him along,
He went as one who had done grievous wrong.
Him to Kai Khusru painfully they drew;
Tears raining on his cheek of livid hue.
His lips then opened of Irán the king,
That dish and dagger both to mind to bring.
The headsman then he bade to draw his sword,

And he came forward zealous at his word.
He cut the General in pieces two,
The army's hearts all full of terror grew.
Pieces they scattered wide from hill to hill,
Whilst round about the mob was standing still.
They clothe the body in Chinese brocade,
The shroud of silk and *malham** then is made.
A golden throne they in the *Dukhmah* place,
With amber-scented crown his head they grace.
They place it on a throne as if it slept,
And o'er the wretched man exceeding wept.
"Revenge complete," then Khusru said again,
"Within our heart we quench of fire the pain.
Ready should be my grandsire to forgive,
For me in ease and quietness to live.
New institutions must we now prepare,
And captives treat with kindness ev'rywhere.
I dealt with blood for my grandsire alone·
What matters it to me now he is gone?
Do no one wrong, the end can be but ill;
Thy name in this world lives as evil still.
This vast revolving sphere do thou behold;
It holds no secret, but is hot or cold.
Live ever in the world in dread and fear,
To the pure God in prayer be ever near.
Ill luck through Him, through Him we victory gain,
Hardships from Him arise, and health and pain."
When his desires from God the king had won,
To Azar from the stream he hastened on.
Upon the fire they scattered there much gold,
Whilst of God praises whispering they told.
One day and night on foot they there abide
Before the Ruler of the world, their guide.
When came Zarasp, the Treasurer of the king,

* A peculiar kind of cloth.

Treasure for Azargushasp did he bring.
On Mobeds robes of honour then he threw,
Dirams, dinars and many presents, too,
Treasure amongst all these thus scattered he,
A world lived on his generosity:
Then on the throne of Kais as he reposed,
Gave public audience and his lip kept closed.
To ev ry country letters wrote they round,
To Chiefs and noted men, wherever found;
Letters they wrote to West and to the East,
To ev'ry Chieftain, greatest or the least.
The face of earth, where dragons there might be,
War by Kai Khusru's sword all rendered free.
And by God's strength who victory bestows,
His loins nor he unbound nor sought repose,
Until the world from evil was released,
No fear remained or terror of the least.
To Siávash's soul fresh life he gave,
And the whole world throughout became his slave.
And after this the world's king gave command:
"O heroes happy, great ones of the land,
Women and children from the town take out,
With food and music in the plain about."
On *darvíshes* he ev'rything bestowed,
And his own people, those who worshipped God.
This done, they occupy themselves with song,
Heroes who to the royal house belong.
And all who of the seed were of *Zarasp*
Went to the temple of Azargushasp.
When all of these with Káüs Kai then went,
There forty days with wine and song were spent.
And when the young new moon arose and shone
As a gold crown the new king's head upon,
Tow'rds Fárs the nobles then their face addressed,
From this and that talk and from strife at rest.

At ev'ry town where on the road they went,
The crowds themselves would to the king present.
And his own purse the monarch opened wide,
For pious men wealth ample to provide.

The reign of Kai Khusru was for 60 years. The death of Kai Káüs and ascension of Kai Khusru.

When in security Káüs grown bold,
All his heart's secrets to his Maker told.
He said: "Than Fate O Thou who higher art,
And ev'ry good thing dost to us impart.
Glory and fortune through Thee I obtained,
Throne, diadem, and place of hero gained,
As to me profit hast Thou given none,
A lofty name with treasure and a throne.
Some hero, of Thee this did I demand,
Siávash to avenge should take in hand.
My grandson 'twas, through whom the world I see,
This vengeance as his own who wrought for me.
This hero grand, of wisdom full and tall,
The monarchs of the earth surpasses all.
Have passed above my head thrice fifty years,
My musk-hued hair as camphor white appears.
My tender cypress is as bended bow;
Time ended would not be a heavy blow."
Short time elapsed and thus to pass it came,
On earth there was left of him but the name.
Then came down from his place Khusru, the Kai,
And sat upon the dark earth by and by.
Of the Iránis those who sought for fame
On foot, unpainted and unscented came.
Blue or black robes by all of them were worn.

As for the king two weeks they came to mourn.
More than ten lassos high a lofty dome
They then erect to serve him for a tomb.
The servants of the monarch then there brought
Rúmi brocade on cloth of damask wrought.
Aloes and camphor and dry musk they bring
To pour on the dry body of the king.
They laid beneath him there an ivory throne,
And on his head a musk and camphor crown.
As Khusru turned him from the throne away,
They closed the door fast where in sleep he lav,
And no one saw Kai Káüs from that day,
From strife and combat where at rest he lay.
The way of this world fleeting is and vain :
Grieve not, for ever thou canst not remain.
The wise to meet death's claw may never fail,
Nor warriors who helmet wear and mail.
What though a king or though *Zárdusht** we be.
Our carpet earth, our couch a brick we see.
Sit down in cheerfulness, seek thy desire ;
If thou obtainest it, good name acquire.
And know thou that the world is e'er thy foe,
The grave thy vestment, earth thy couch below.
His grandsire mourned the king for forty days,
His crown avoided and all cheerful ways.
The forty-first upon his ivory throne
He sat and wore his heart-enlivening crown.
Around the palace gates the army came,
The wise, the gold-crowned noblemen of name.
With joy invoking blessings on his head,
Upon his crown they costly jewels shed.
And feasting on the whole earth was maintained,
That on the throne a conqueror there reigned.

*Zoroaster.

The release of Jahan by Kai Khusru and his giving the kingdom of Turán to him.

Jahan, son of Afrásiáb, the king,
Bade them with dignity before him bring.
Then those who had received the order went,
With Jahan to approach, their faces bent.
And Jahan when in fetters there they see,
They break the chains and do no injury.
And brought up to the monarch thence he came
To that palatial edifice of fame.
And when his sad eyes fell upon the king,
He kissed the ground just as a wretched thing.
And when that king of righteous men he neared,
Upon his eyelash waves of blood appeared.
He was still weeping as on foot he stood,
That well-known man of understanding good.
Thus pity on the man king Khusru knew,
Up from his heart as a cold sigh he drew,
Although upon his cheek the tear would swell,
The bold Afrásiáb rememb'ring well.
" His hand with blood if he had not imbrued,
His faith and due rites would he have renewed.
He had not dyed so red his whitening beard,
Nor of his country would he have despaired.
As son before him had I ever been,
Nor him as other than a king had seen.
Yet such his evil destiny at root,
His leaves were poison, and a snake his fruit."
When Jahan heard the king such words relate,
For his life safety he obtained from Fate.
And many words of praise to those he said,
Who from his place of hiding him had led.
" With crown and throne may'st thou long here abide,
In ev'ry place may victory thee betide!

The great ones of the world are slaves to thee,
And through thee raise their heads in dignity.
Now of the palace the bond-slave am I,
Where'er I am at thy good pleasure lie.
Only at thy word will I give the land,
And only yield its cube at thy command."
When this he heard the king rose to his feet,
And gave him on his own right hand a seat.
He asked him: "How does fate now deal with thee,
That counsel of the teacher thou dost see?"
Now take thy ease: the fruit of fortune know,
A throne and crown on thee will I bestow.
The land of Túr I give to thee by choice;
Of all Túr's seed in thee do I rejoice.
Thou'rt Pushang's grandson, Faridún's thy race;
From justice turn not thou away thy face.
For thee I've love, and there's of blood the tie:
Out of my bondage thou must never fly.
Ever should'st thou the world as nothing take;
Wisely the way of justice ne'er forsake.
From justice if thou ever turn thy head,
I'll shear it off, as was thy father's shred.
Thy father from all evil cleared the world,
But by the dragon's breath to hell was hurled.
When to the paths of ill the demons took,
They fell from God and their own faith forsook.
And when Siávash innocent was slain,
I seized him only by a trick again.
With courage in mine own especial way,
I followed up my vengeance day by day,
His head sheared as I would a partridge slay,
And shorn of all strength in the dust he lay.
With blood were stained his beard and grizzled hair,
And of the world he fell into despair,
In bitterness for him then no one wept,

In that to path and deed of ill he kept.
Now of *Zuhák* and Túr must I declare,
That both of them blood-thirsty tyrants were,
For in his rage *Zuhák* did Jamshíd slay,—
With Iraj of pure faith Túr did away.
When Faridún that hero's lasso threw,
It was in God's strength, and with courage, too.
Zuhák, the tyrant, with the lasso caught,
Towards the throne that vile one then he brought.
He bore him off and threw him in a well,
And heaped upon his head a hill as well.
Thus from his malice freed was all mankind,
Nor failed his war and strife their end to find.
See what to Manúchehr the just occurred
When Iraj to avenge he passed his word.
Irán he left and went to China far,
His heart was full of wind, his head of war.
Thus by God's pow'r, to victory Who led.
He of the tyrant Túr cut off the head.
Such is of God the order and the law,
He who beheads a man who has no flaw,
His head they sever, too, nor know dismay,—
And in the dust his heart impure will lay.
To be like such an one do thou beware,
For none to come to thee with aid will care."
Jahan, replying, gave his answer then:
"O thou who art a righteous king of men,
When thou shalt order will I gird my waist;
My head in dust before thee shall be placed.
Than all thy servants I myself am less,
Nor throne, nor crown nor diadem possess.
If to Turán thou send me, in that land
In prayer for thee before God will I stand.
Due tribute to thee ev'ry year I'll pay,
And from that garden food before thee lay.

I'll gird my loins for thee in ev'ry place,
And come myself to see my ruler's face.
And I will kiss the ground before thy throne,
Will bless that throne and thy good fortune own.
Musk, amber, aloes, offerings shall be found,
And I will drape with Chinese silk the ground.
But one desire I ask thee as thy slave ;
Of thy high majesty one mercy crave.
My son and those whose face is hid from view,
My sisters and my near connections, too,
My hope to gain if I should worthy be,
That to Turán to bear thou'lt grant to me."
When the desire the king learnt of his mind,
To grant his wish in answer he inclined.
They summoned there a scribe at his command,
With inkstand, musk and amber in his hand,
On silk a royal patent to indite,
After Kais' methods and with royal rite,
When of Turán gave Faridún the land,
" Hereafter seek thou not," was his command,
" From this vile earth thy profit to derive,
But for the poor oppressed for justice strive."
Commanded then his treasurer the king :
" Go, royal crown and robes of honour bring."
Then did the treasurer to bring proceed
The robe of honour and a noble's steed.
The crown he bade them on his head to lay,
Glad in the king, he passed from harm away.
His sisters and his relatives were brought,
All who in him a remedy had sought.
All these the ruler of the world then sent
To Jahan at the time with glad assent.
And with each one some present that would suit
With robe of honour and a crown to boot.
At the same time he bade the writer there

On silk a royal letter to prepare.
For Gustaham, the son of Naozar. He
Should to Irán come, full of dignity:
The whole land to Jahan he should give o'er,
Should use dispatch and should delay no more.
Next night at what time early the cock crows,
The sound of drums from Jahan's palace rose.
To go to Túr he sat upon his steed,
With feasts and merriment along to speed
When in Turán he to the city went,
And an auspicious envoy forward sent.
He said to him: "To Gustaham repair:
Relate to him in full all my affair."
What the king spoke, the envoy heard him say,
And with the speed of wind went on his way.
In friendly guise the envoy forward went,
And said: "Comes Jahan whom the king has sent."
When Gustaham of this became aware,
Upon the road he went to meet him there.
Adorned, Turán's town then there came in view,
Wine, song, they sent for, and the minstrels, too.
When Jahan came near his ancestral town,
With rites the olden kings had handed down,
Each place with costly fine brocade was hung,
Along the streets and fields they *dirams* flung.
With Gustaham for two weeks stayed the king:
He gave him robes and many another thing.
On this his treasure gates he opened wide,
For Gustaham his journey to provide.
All this he gave to Gustaham and cried.
"O hero who with wisdom art allied,
Now take these presents for the monarch's sake;
Tell him from God Whom men their refuge make:
'Thou art the king; thy servants all are we,
Adoring ev'rywhere and praising thee!'"

These Gustaham took as he bade farewell,
And said: 'In song and pleasure may'st thou dwell!'"
That night they lingered in enjoyment there,
And with them of Taráz the idols fair.
And when the white dawn's army came to view,
The night its sable-tinted skirt withdrew.
Sat in the saddle then King Naozar's son,
With royal rites, of luck good omen won.
From Turan tow'rds Irán he took his way,
The land in which the warrior king held sway.
When of his coming there the warriors knew,
Instant to meet him on the road they flew.
There Tús with all the Pehlaváns went down,
And when the warrior saw his head and crown,
Alighting then, he held Tús in embrace,
Pressed him upon his breast and kissed his face.
The other Pehlaváns, with necks unbent,
All at this signal zealous, forward went.
The warriors, mounted each upon his steed,
Like Azargushasp driving on with speed,
Into the town with those men great in name,
With Gustaham towards the palace came.
When on the monarch's face his eye then fell,
Within the porch he kissed the ground as well
When the king saw him glad and free of care,
He took him to his breast and held him there.
When on the royal seat he took his post,
He asked of Jahan, and Turán its host.
And Gustaham in answer said: "O king,
From Jahan greeting I, and off'rings, bring.
Void of thy memory never is his mind,
At thy command his loins he'll ever bind."
Then to the table-decker: "Youth!" he said,
"Fill up the goblet and the table spread."
From eating at the tray when rise up all,

For minstrels and for wine and song they call.
With flute and singing all the night they spend
And hearty greeting all to Khusru send.
Then did the sun his golden face display,
And blackness in his love thus washed away.
With the gifts forward Gustaham then went,
That Jahan there had giv'n him to present.
These to the monarch of the world they bring,
And when on them had cast his eye the king,
He gave them the Iránis eve'ry one,
And the world's king thus sat upon his throne.
And when thus sixty years had passed away,
Beneath the royal hand the whole earth lay.

The raising of his heart from the world by Kai Khusru and closing the door of the palace to people and supplicating God.

The rich soul of the king grew full of thought
At God's power and the deeds that He had wrought.
He said: "All of the peopled world around,
From Ind to Rúm and up to China's bound,
From farthest East up to the Western strand,
All hill and desert, sea and the dry land,—
All this from enemies have I made free;
Rule and the throne of greatness are with me.
To fear of enemies the world is dead,
But many years have passed above my head.
Yet though from God all my desires I gained,
My heart from vengeance have I not restrained.
My soul upon itself should not bring death,
It broods on ill, is Ahriman in faith,
For like Jam and Zuhák I evil do,
And am at one with Tús and Salam, too.
Although from Káüs here I may descend,

Tow'rds wind and vengeance in Turán I tend.
As vile Afrásiáb, like Káüs, too,
Who in their dreams but crookedness e'er knew,
Sudden to God shall I ungrateful grow,
And my bright soul thus endless horror know?
The glory of my God will me forsake,
If I to crookedness and folly take.
In dust should I my head and crown then lay,
And after this to darkness pass away.
On earth will rest of me but evil name,
Before God, too, the end will be the same.
This face and my cheeks' hue will fade away,
And in the dust my bones will all decay.
My virtue to ingratitude will turn:
In the next world my soul will darkly burn.
'Twould take away from me my throne and crown,
My fortune in the dust would trample down.
No name but evil would of me remain,
A thorn become my former rose of pain.
Now have I taken vengeance for my sire,
Nor beautiful the earth made to admire,
Have killed him who to execute was right,
As he was crooked in the pure God's sight.
Of desert or of city none remain
That title from my sword do not maintain.
The great ones of the world me lord confess,
Though some of them both crown and throne possess.
For dignity I give God praises meet,
For stars propitious and this form and feet.
Now were it better I on God should wait
For reputation in this happy state.
It may be for the beauty I possess,
He who the prosperous sends the earth to bless
My soul may to the righteous' place convey,
For this Kais' throne and crown must pass away.

None greater blessings can obtain than these,
Rank, beauty, cups of wine, and ease.
The secret of the world I've seen and known,
Its good and ill, what's hidden, what is shown.
Be he a husbandman, be he a king,
By the same path to go will death him bring,"
The king then ordered those on duty there:
"Should any to the Court to come prepare.
With words polite and sweet turn ye them back:
Do nothing rude, in courtesy nor lack."
As this he said, at once with loins unbound,
Shouting, he went within the garden's round.
He washed his head before he went to pray,
By reason's light he sought of God the way.
In a new robe of white himself he dressed,
With hopeful heart in prayer then forward pressed.
With graceful gait he reached the place of prayer,
And told his secrets to his Maker there.
He said: "O thou Who'rt higher than the soul,
And fire and wind and atoms all control,
Preserve, and wisdom into me instil,
And give me fitting thoughts of good and ill.
Whilst I may live Thee will I still adore,
And what good deeds I do will I do more.
On my past sins forgiveness now bestow,
And crookedness let not my wisdom know.
Turn from my soul misfortune, I beseech,
And all such tricks as those a *Dív* would teach.
That like to Káüs and *Z*uhák and Jam,*
Through pride no injury to me may come.
Of virtue should'st thou close to me the door,
My crookedness will but increase the more.
Ward off the power of the Dív from me,
So that destroyed my own soul may not be.

* Pronounced "*Jum.*"

My soul to that abode of bliss convey,
And guard me in the same especial way."
Day, night, a whole week he was standing there,
His body there and his whole soul elsewhere;
Sev'n days elapsed, and Khusru grew so weak,
The place of prayer he could no longer seek.
Upon the eighth he left the place of prayer,
In haste towards the king's throne to repair.
And all the Pehlaváns of Persia's host
At the king's doings were perplexed the most.
And they who honour won where'er they fought.
Each in his mind conceived a varying thought.

In the next few chapters are recounted the endeavours of the nobles to ascertain the cause of the king's retirement from the world and their remonstrances with him in the subject. He is, however, firm in his resolve, and Gív is sent to summon *Zál* and Rústam to render their assistance in the matter. Before their arrival Kai Khusru has a dream, in which he sees a vision of a Surúsh, or heavenly messenger. This event is related as follows:—

The seeing by Kai Khusru of a Surush in a dream, and learning from him of his own departure from the world.

His earnest supplication thus to pour,
He stood five weeks the Most High God before.
He did not sleep the dark night through from pain,
Till from its house the moon rose up again.
He slept himself, but not his spirit clear,
Which in this world was e'er to wisdom near
It seemed to him that in a vision clear
A heav'nly messenger spoke in his ear.
"Thou, king, beneath propitious star wast born,
And many a collar, crown, and throne hast worn.

Since thou hast now gained all of thy desire,
If thou could'st, hastening, from this world retire.
To God's pure neighbourhood to find thy way,
Here in this darkness do thou not delay.
In giving treasure, worthily bestow,
To others leave this fleeting world below.
He from misfortune's clutch may yet be free,
Who from the dragon's breath contrives to flee.
For thee whoever may have suffered pain,
Know that he did so in pursuit of gain.
On those who worthy are thy gifts bestow,
For thou remainest not for long below.
Choose them as one who's fitted for the throne,
One to whom even ants their safety own.
Yet do not rest when thou the world hast shared,
For destiny that meets thee be prepared.
Virtue like this in Lehrasp do thou know,
The kingship, throne, and belt on him bestow.
As thou from God has sought for such a grace,
Arise! As an immortal take thy place."
Many mysterious things beside he said,
Which, heard, the monarch to amazement led.
And when he woke up from his painful dream,
He found of water in the place a stream.
For he had wept, his face upon the ground,
And to his Maker praise was offering found.
And then he said: "If I in haste depart,
God will have giv'n the wishes of my heart."
He came and sat upon the throne as king,
And in his hand an unused robe did bring.
This worn, he rested on his ivory throne,
But had no collar, bracelet, or his crown.

Zál and Rústam, who had been summoned, now arrive, and admonish Kai Khusru, but without effect, for he announces to them that he has renounced the world, and his sole desire is towards God, Who has directed him through a heavenly messenger to prepare for his approaching death. *Zál* again remonstrates with him and accuses him of having been led away by the Dívs and Ahriman. This the king denies in his reply, and finally *Zál* repents the harsh terms he has made use of towards him. The king now directs a grand camp to be pitched in which all the heroes and celebrities assemble. In this he sits on a golden throne, and exhorts them all to fear God and not attach themselves to the world, informing them that he himself is about to die. He informs them that he will distribute his treasures among those who have undergone labours in his service and will name them to God. He will give the Iránis whatever precious things he has, arms, gold and treasure, and to every one who is powerful among them a Province. He directs them to deliver themselves for a week to feasting and himself prays for deliverance from this fleeting world, so that he may rest from his labours.

The feast is duly held, and Kai Khusru instructs Gudurz, the son of Kishvád, to observe what is going on in the world, both openly and in secret, for there is a proper time for expending as well as for amassing treasure, to look to the forts and bridges on the frontier of Irán that had been ruined during the wars with Afrásiáb, to provide for orphans, widows, and old men who were in need and did not proclaim their necessities, to expend money in the restoration of wells and give assistance to infirm people who had spent their money in the days of their youth, with any treasures that might be found in ruined and desolate towns. A treasure called *Arús*, in the town of Tús, accumulated there by Káüs, he ordered to be given to Zál, Gív, and Rústam. His robes, collars, chains, coats of mail and maces were given to

Rústam, all his horses to Tús, his parks, gardens, and certain named palaces to Gudúrz, his personal arms to Gív, with the remainder of his palaces, and all his tents and their contents to Faribúrz, with a special coat of mail, a gold crown, a helmet, and other things to Bezan as a souvenir. Finally he bade all the Iránis ask him for what they wished, and left them reddened with tears, and enquiring to whom he would leave the heritage of his throne. This he bequeaths to Lehrásp, whilst Zabulistán as far as the Indian sea, Kábul, Dambar, Maï, India, Bust, and Nimrúz are bestowed by royal patent on Rústam, Kúm, and Isfahán on Gív, and Khurdván, with the title of Commander-in-Chief and the right to wear golden shoes, on Tús. The king then bids farewell to his wives and hands them over to the care of Lehrásp, warning all that they must soon follow in his footsteps and die. He also dismisses his army, who promise to attend to all his wishes We now come to his final will in the following extract.

The going of Kai Khusru from the plain with his Pehlaváns to a mountain and his disappearance.

The king then bade Lehrásp himself begone,
And said to him as well : " My days are done
Go, on the royal throne to sit proceed,
And in the world sow but of good the seed.
Whenever of all trouble thou art free.
Of crown be thou not proud or treasury.
Know that the day to thee is dark and drear,
And that the way to God to thee draws near.
Do justice and e'er justice strive to see,
And every good man of the world make free."
Lehrásp in haste then from his charger leapt
And kissed the ground and loud in sorrow wept.

And Khusru said to him: "Now take thy leave;
Be warp with woof when justice thou wouldst weave.'
There went with him the chiefs of Irán then,
Wise nobles too, and all the valiant men.
Dastán, and Rústam, and Gudúrz, and Gív,
Bezan as well, and Gustaham the Niv,*
The seventh Faribúrz, son of Káüs,
The eighth the ever-celebrated Tús.
Band after band the army marching still,
From plain they moved up to the crested hill.
A week they stayed there till their breath they gained,
And moisture on their parched-up lips retained,
Wailing and mourning what the king had done,
For to him sorrow now the way had won,
Whilst every Mobed there in secret said
That none on earth such words had ever said.
When the sun raised his head above the hill,
From all parts crowding to the mountain still,
A hundred thousand men and women there
All to the mountain with the king repair.
The hill was full of wailing and of moan,
And boiling with the heat the hardest stone.
" How was it, king," cried everyone that came,
" Thy bright heart full of scars and smoke became?
Complaint if of thine army there arise,
Or this thy crown if thou dost now despise,
Tell it to us, but Irán do not leave;
New king to an old country do not give.
Beneath thy horse's hoofs dust are we all
Before thine Azargushasp prostrate fall.
Where are thy learning and thy wisdom gone?
To Faridún *Sarúsh* there came not one.
We all to God our praises will express,
On prayer in the fire temple lay great stress.

*Hero.

Perchance on us pure God may mercy show,
And cause thy Mobed heart on us to glow."
At this event bewildered grew the Kai
And from the crowd he bade the Mobeds hie.
He said to them: "As now here all is well;
On what is good with sorrow do not dwell.
With one accord to God show forth your praise:
Rejoice, God recognise in all His ways.
We shall together come, and soon, once more;
At my departure, therefore, be not sore."
And to the chieftains all he said in turn:
"Kingless ye from this hill must now return.
The road s long, waterless, and void of ease,
There is no grass there and no leafy trees.
The road to come and go ye should make light,
Direct your souls upon it tow'rds the right.
Not ev'ryone can pass along this sand
Without great power and a mighty hand."
Three of those heroes, then, of haughty look,
Hearing his words the monarch then forsook,
Dastán and Rústam and Gudúrz the old,
Remembering all things, in ambition bold;
Bezan and Faribúrz and Tús and Gív,
Would not turn back or there the monarch leave.
With him for one whole day and night they went,
With drouth were in the desert well-nigh spent.
Upon the road there came to view a spring
And to it hastened on Khusru the king.
Alighting by the limpid stream they met,
And gained their breath awhile and something ate.
Then to the margraves did the monarch say:
"To-night we go no further on our way.
Now let us speak much of past deeds of old,
For after this me no one will behold.
When the bright sun shall raise his standard grand,

The wave grows golden, violet the land,
For me of parting will have come the day;
May the *Sarúsh* be my friend along my way!
And would my soul now from this road depart,
I would at once tear out my darkened heart."
Of the dark night a portion had been spent,
Before his God the famous monarch bent,
With water washed his body and his head,
And from the Zandavasht in secret read.
The words on those famed wise men sadly fell
"I now for ever bid you all farewell.
When in the sky the sun displays his beam,
Ye none of ye shall see me but in dream.
To-morrow in this sand do not remain,
Although the very heavens musk should rain
Upon the hill a raging wind will blow,
Of trees each branch and leaf that shall lay low.
From the black clouds shall blow an icy wind,
And tow'ards Irán the way ye may not find."
Up from the hill the sun his head thus brought,
The nobles' eyes in vain their monarch sought.
In search of him they hurried from the place,
Down to the sandy desert turned their face.
Of Khusru then they found no single track.
As if of sense deprived then turned they back.

A snow storm coming on destroys some of the party, but Rústam, *Zál*, Gudúrz, and the others remain on the hill for seven days, at the end of which they become hopeless and go down, having found no trace of the king. When Lehrásp hears of the disappearance of the king he enquires of Rústam and the others what had been his wishes as to the succession, and they satisfy him that the throne has been left to him, and he accordingly ascends it. His reign is said to have lasted 120 years.

He builds a fire temple at Balkh. Of his two sons, Gushtásp and *Zarír*, he did not favour the former because his head was full of vanity. One day after drinking wine he demands to be nominated his heir apparent, but Lehrásp desires him to wait and be more prudent in his desires. Gushtásp on this leaves his father in anger, intending to go to India, where he thinks he will be favourably received. His brother follows him at their father's desire, and he goes back, at his request, but with the expressed intention of leaving the Court and of going away where he will not be discovered. He accordingly goes off alone at night and makes his way to Rúm (Constantinople) through the assistance of one Haishoi. He wanders about looking for work as a scribe, and enters the Kaiser's palace, where the other scribes send him away, assuring him there is no room for him. He now seeks employment from the man in charge of the royal horses, but is unsuccessful with him, also with a camel driver and a blacksmith, and is finally received by a peasant and remains with him for some months. About this time the Kaiser, with a view to procure a husband for one of his daughters, determines to hold a grand assembly of illustrious and wise men, for her to see and select from. This is accordingly done, and Kitayún, the eldest daughter, concealed among her female slaves in order that she may not be recognized, passes by them to make her choice. Failing to do so, another assembly is held of rich men, but of inferior rank, for her to select from. Among them is Gushtásp, on whose head she at once places her crown, and the Kaiser rather unwillingly agrees to the match, and tells him to take her away without treasure, throne, or signet ring. Kitayún and he go to the house of his host, who builds a residence for them and gives them handsome presents. Gushtásp now spends his days in the chase.

About this time also one Mírín, of Constantinople, sent word to the Kaiser that he was a man of rank, wealthy and brave, and desired to marry his second daughter. He is informed that he must prove what he is fit for by bringing the skin of a wolf that infests the forest of Fasikún. He consults his horoscope and finds that there would come from Irán an illustrious man who would become the son-in-law of the Kaiser, and then destroy two wild beasts who would make their appearance in Rúm. He discovers Gushtásp and proposes to him to undertake the slaughter of the wolf in the forest of Fasikún. Gushtásp undertakes the task and kills the wolf. Mírín reports the death of the wolf to the Kaiser, who inspects it and gives him his daughter in marriage. Another man of the name of Ahren now asks for the third daughter of the Kaiser, and on him he imposes the task of killing a dragon that lives in Mount Sakílá. In great trouble he goes to Mírín and finds out that it was Gushtásp who had killed the wolf, and after negotiations with his host Gushtásp kills it as well, and Ahren is allowed to marry the Kaiser's daughter. On a third occasion Gushtásp distinguishes himself in martial exercises before the Kaiser, who sends for him, and, discovering who he is, asks his pardon, and visits his daughter Kitayún, who has merely found out that her husband is of high rank, but only calls himself Farúkhzád. The Kaiser then directs all his people to obey Farúkhzád. He writes a letter to Alyás, the chief of the Khazars, to demand tribute; and threatens to send Farúkhzád against him if he refuses. Alyás proving obstinate, Gushtásp is dispatched, and notwithstanding an attempt on Alyás's part to conciliate him, as soon as he sees his great strength he attacks him and drags him before the Kaiser, who, with all his people, gives Farúkhzád a grand reception. The Kaiser now demands tribute from Irán, threatening Lehrásp with an attack by Farúkhzád if he refuses. Kálús, his envoy, is admitted to Lehrásp's presence, and is asked particulars as to who Farúkhzád may be. He describes him as like Zarír, and Lehrásp guesses that it must be Gushtásp. Zarír is accordingly sent to Rúm by way of Aleppo with a number of nobles from Irán, and being admitted to the Kaiser's presence recognizes Gushtásp, but pretends that he is a fugitive slave, and threatens the Kaiser with an invasion from Irán. The Kaiser declares himself ready to fight, and as Zarír has come as an envoy lets him go unharmed. He questions Gushtásp as to why he gave no answer to Zarír, and Gushtásp keeps up the deception of his being a fugitive slave, but offers to go to Irán to ascertain the king's desire. Being allowed to go, he proceeds to Zarír's camp, where he is joyfully welcomed by his countrymen, and sends a message to the Kaiser that Zarír and his army are ready to receive him and will enter into a treaty with him. The Kaiser proceeds to the camp, and discovering that the so-called Farúkhzad is Gushtásp sends him and Kitayún magnificent presents and accompanies them for two days on their way back to Irán, promising not to demand tribute from the country as long as he lives. On their arrival Lehrásp comes out to meet them, and gives up his throne to Gushtásp.*

After this in a dream Fardusi sees the poet Dakíkí with a cup of wine in his hand. He admonishes him to drink wine only, after the manner of Kai Káüs, for he had chosen a king on whom in this world destiny casts crowns and thrones, Mahmúd, the king of kings, who will be prosperous in every way, to whom princes will open their treasures, whose troubles will not increase up to the age of eighty-five years, and into whose hands all kings' crowns will fall of themselves. He tells him he himself

* At this point the second volume of Macan's edition ends.

had commenced this poem, and had composed a thousand couplets on Gushtásp and Arjásp before he died, and if these verses reach the king, his (Dakíkí's) soul will rise out of the dust and reach the moon. Fardusi announces that he will now repeat Dakíkí's lines, for he himself is still alive and Dakíkí has gone down to the dust.

He accordingly proceeds with Gushtásp's story by relating that Lehrásp retires to Balkh, to worship in the temple of Naobehár, which was then what Mecca is now to the Arabs. There he takes off his ornaments, clothes himself in the garb of a priest, and perpetually engages in devotion. Gushtásp thanks God for his elevation to the throne. Kitáyún, the Kaiser's daughter, whose real name was Náhid (Venus) gives birth to two children, one called Asfandyár, a warlike prince, and the other Bashotan. All kinds paid tribute, and he endeared himself to the hearts of all but Arjásp, the king of Túrán, whom the Dívs obeyed, and who every year demanded tribute from Irán. But why should one pay tribute to one's own equal? The story now proceeds to

The birth of Zardusht (Zoroaster) and the adoption of his faith by Gushtásp, Lehrásp and all the chiefs of Irán.

When after this some time had passed away,
A tree appeared upon the earth one day;
A tree with branches and abundant root,
From Gushtásp's hall up to his roof to shoot.
Wisdom its fruit and its leaves counsel good,
Who could e'er perish, nourished on such food?
Of feet propitious, *Zardusht* his name,
Who slew the Ahriman of evil fame.
"A prophet I," to the world king he cried:
"And I toward thy God thy foot will guide."

Bringing before him then a dish of fire,
"From Paradise, this," said he, "I acquire."
"Accept this!" did the world's Creator cry:
"Look on this earth and contemplate the sky.
Lo! without water was it made or mould,
And how I have created them behold!
Behold! By any else could this be done,
Except by me, who rule the world alone?
If, then, thou knowest I have done this all,
Creator of the world Me should ye call.
Of Him who speaks do thou the Faith believe,
From Him the road learn, and His laws receive.
Do what He says is lawful in His eyes:
Ever seek wisdom and the world despise.
The laws of his good Faith learn thou on earth,
For rule that has no faith is nothing worth."
Of this religion when the monarch knew,
A convert to its faith and laws he grew.
His brother, brave *Zarír*, of happy feet,
The elephant to slay who'd but to meet;
His sire, who had grown old, at Balkh apart,
To whom the world was bitter at his heart;
Illustrious nobles out of ev'ry land,
Physicians, heroes came on ev'ry hand,
Towards the monarch of the land all swarmed,
Girt with the *kushti*,* to the faith conformed.
The glory of their God thus shining clear,
From hearts of men all evils disappear.
Full of the light divine the *dukhmahs* grew,
And the seed growing no pollution knew.
And brave Gushtásp upon his throne took post,
And into ev'ry land sent out his host.
Mobeds on earth were scattered far and wide,
For the fire-temples grand domes to provide.

*The sacred thread worn by the Parsees.

The sacred fire of Mehr when first he placed,
With what good customs then the land he graced!
At ev'ry temple gate a noble tree,
A cypress tall, there Zardusht planted he
Upon that lofty cypress tree he wrote
To that good faith Gushtásp became devote.
And of that noble tree a witness made,
That justice would by wisdom thus be spread.
A few years in this manner passed along,
The cypress waxed, its waist grew thick and strong.
That lofty cypress so to grow began,
A lasso's length its girth would hardly span
As it grew tall, the branches o'er its head
Into a dome of fair dimensions spread.
To forty cubits high and broad it grew,
And earth no water its foundation knew;
On this a hall of pure gold did he found,
Its dust was amber, silver was its ground.
And they designed the form of Jamshíd there,
Who offered to the sun and moon his prayer;
Of Faridún, too, with bull-headed mace,
He bade them draw the portrait on the place.
And ev'ry chief of note was there designed:
Such proof of power, lo! where could one find?
When to completion rose that golden hall,
Jewels of price he laid upon the wall.
A fence of iron he around it laid,
And there his sitting-place the monarch made.
To ev'ry land he sent a message round:
"On earth where is like Kashmars'* cypress found?
This down from Paradise did God me send,
And say: From hence to heav'n must thou ascend.
Now to my counsel all of you pay heed,
Tow'rds Kashmar's cypress all on foot proceed.

*A village so named, where Zoroaster planted a tree.

The road to *Zardusht* do all embrace;
Away from Chinese idols turn your face.
Irán's king ever be by you preferred,
And on your loins do ye the *kúshti* gird.
To ancient customs no regard be paid,
But be contented with this cypress' shade.
Of the truth-speaking prophet by the grace
Towards the dome of fire turn ye your face."
Throughout the world then did the message speed,
To both the great in name and great in deed.
And ev'ry potentate at his command
Turned tow'rds the cypress then of Kashmar's land.
Fire-temples thus their Paradise they found,
And there Zardusht the evil demon bound.
After this manner when some time had passed,
The stars brought favour to the king at last.
Thus to the world's king said Zardusht the old:
"We in our faith to this would never hold
That tribute thou to China's chief should'st pay,
Nor is this of our faith or laws the way.
With this affair we none of us can hold,
For of our monarchs in the days of old
None tribute gave the Turks a single hour,
Nor in Irán have they or strength or pow'r"
Gushtásp agreed and hastened then to say:
"I, tribute too, will not tell them to pay."

The becoming aware by Arjásp, king of Turán, of Gushtásp's adopting the faith of Zardusht, and writing a letter to him.

When this the brave Dív heard the people say,
At once tow'rds China's king he made his way.
"O monarch of the world," to him he said,
"Both slaves and those who aye hold high the head
Are all obedient to thy high command,

And none before thy mighty spear may stand.
Except Lehrásp's son, this Gushtásp the king,
Against the Turks who now his host will bring.
His fell designs he openly arrays,
And tricks on thee like Ahriman he plays.
A hundred thousand horse are at my call.
If thou desirest, I will bring them all.
Come now, what he is doing let us know,
Nor fighting with him do thou terror show."
Now when the Dív's words to Arjásp were known,
The Turkí king came down from off his throne.
At once he summoned all the Mobeds there,
The words that Dív said to them to declare.
"Know that in Irán's land," to them he cried.
"God's glory and pure faith are set aside.
Late to Irán an ancient fool there came,
To gift of prophecy who lays a claim.
'For I,' he says, 'from heaven now appear,
From near the Lord of heaven I come here.
In Paradise I saw the Great God sit,
And He it was who Zandavasta writ.
And I have seen, too, Ahriman in hell,
But wandering about him could not dwell.
Thence for the faith the Lord God sent me down,
To him who of this country wears the crown
Of Irán's host he who the head has won,
And of king Lehrásp is the worthy son,
And in Irán the name of Gushtásp bears
Himself upon his loins the *kúshti* wears;
His brother, too, and Irán's General,
The horseman brave, he whom Zarír they call;
All now accept when of this Faith they hear,
And of the old magician go in fear.
Each one this Faith his own religion makes.
And the old road and laws the world forsakes.

And now by many vain and foolish ways,
He in Irán still as a prophet stays.
To write a letter now would it be well,
To him against thy rule who would rebel.
And it were well him many gifts to give,
For things not asked for gladly he'll receive
Tell him to turn back from this evil way,
And Paradise's Lord in fear obey.
Tell him that old impure man to expel,
And in our rites to hold a feast as well.
If then our counsel wise he shall accept,
Fast in our bonds his feet shall not be kept.
But if our word he look not on as right,
And our old hatred shall again excite.
Our scattered host we will assemble here,
To meet him a great army shall appear.
We in this matter to Irán will go,
And his ill actions in the land will show.
And driving him before us will abase,
And living on the gibbet him will place."
Of China then the heroes all arose,
And out of them two warriors he chose.
One Bí-darafoh* by name, a hero bold,
At heart intrepid and in magic old.
One Nám-kh'ást named, on magic ever bent,
Whose heart aye on destruction was intent.
A letter fair and dignified he wrote,
To him of faith accepted, king of note.
First, of the world's Lord, then, the name he took,
On all things plain and hidden who doth look.
"This letter as a king do I indite,
As is towards a king both fit and right,
To hero Gushtásp of the land the king,
Worthy the Kais' throne, whom all praises bring.

* Without a standard.

Of king Lehrásp the elder, chosen son,
Lord of the earth, and guardian of the throne,—
This from Arjásp, who China's heroes led,
World-conq'ring horsemen, warriors' chosen head."
In Túrki letters with the royal pen
He wrote a letter full of praises then,
And said: "Of the world's king O famous son,
Of king of kings enlightener of the throne.
Thy soul and body whole, fresh be thy cheek,
And may thy royal loins be never weak!
I hear thou goest on destruction's way,
And for thyself dark makest brilliant day.
An old deceitful man has come thee near,
And filled thy heart with terror and great fear.
He spoke to thee of Paradise and hell,
And in thy heart sowed evil seed as well.
Him and his Faith both dost thou now accept,
His way and laws hast with due favour kept.
The customs of thy kings didst thou forswear,
Of earth the great ones who before thee were.
Ere thou from thy old Faith didst loose thy hold,
Before, behind, why didst thou not behold?
Thou art the offspring of that happy king,
Who to a soldier's head the crown would bring.
Then has he chosen from his own elect
And before Jamshíd's seed did thee select.
And just as Kai Khusru, who longed for war,
Than other Kais thou'st had more honour far,
Greatness and kingship and prosperity,
Power and glory, too, and dignity.
With wealth-stored treasures, elephants arrayed,
With armies great and banners broad displayed.
These all to thee, O thou most famous king,
The mighty chiefs in friendly fashion bring.
And brilliantly thou through the world hast run,

In Ard'behisht as from the Ram* the Sun.
With lordship of the world has God thee graced,
And all the great beneath thy feet has placed.
Thou to the world's Lord hast not given praise,
Nor recognised his goodness in thy ways.
And after God of thee a king had made,
Thou through an old magician now hast strayed.
Now when the news of this came to my ear,
In bright day did the stars to me appear.
A friendly letter to thee now I send,
For thou a comrade art as well as friend.
When this thou readest, wash thy head and feet,
Show not thy face to him who brings deceit.
Off from thy loins do thou these bonds undo,
And thus with sparkling wine thy joy renew.
Cast not the rites of thine own kings away,
Earth's noble ones that were before thy day.
If thou accept this counsel wise from me,
The Turkománs shall do no harm to thee.
Of Kashán, of Turán, of Chín, the land,
Just as Irán is, shall be in thy hand.
I give thee all the treasure without bound,
That I have gathered with much trouble round.
Silver and gold, and steeds of varied hue,
And ornaments with gems embedded, too;
Then slaves on thee with wealth will I bestow,
All beauties from whose heads the locks hang low
But this my counsel should'st thou not accept,
In iron fetters shall thy feet be kept.
After this letter in a month or two,
Thy country will I ravish through and through;
I from Turán and Chín will bring hosts there,
Such that the ground their camp will never bear.
With musk I'll fill the Jaihún by and by,

*The constellation of Aries.

And with my musk the stream will render dry.
Thy decorated palace will I burn,
And root and branch thee will I overturn.
Your land will I consume with fire anew,
Your bodies pierce with arrows through and through.
Ancient of Irán's men those who may be,
These all I'll throw into captivity;
And those who no great price to fetch may sell,
Of them all heads will I cut off as well.
Women and children all will I bring down,
And will enslave them all in mine own town.
All of your land I'll render waste and bare,
Up from their roots your very trees will tear.
I now have told thee all I had to tell:
On this my warning letter ponder well."
When the king's Minister this letter read
Of the king's host before each chief and head,
He folded it and marked it with his hand,
And gave those old magicians of the land.
At once then Nám-khást read the letter through,
And Bí-darafsh then read the letter, too.
He spoke: "To Gushtásp, Lehrasp's son, now say:
'Why dost thou shed thine honour in such way?
If these my words from end to end thou hear,
That bad-faithed old man thou wilt not revere.
Him bringing to thyself thou here wilt burn,
And once again to thy old Faith return.'
If he as Ahriman should disagree,
Tell the Dastúr to bring him here to me.
Summon the wise men and the Mobeds there,
According to their rites a feast prepare.
Bid them to summon there a learned scribe
That letter's pleasing purport to describe,
And let him tell *Zardusht* that its reply
To Arjásp he must send immediately.

If of thy Faith the proofs thou bringest here,
To mine own Faith no more will I adhere.
Seeing its proofs in it will I believe,
But should they foolish be will not receive.
If what he says should false be in thy sight,
Let not thine heart derive from such its light.
Hear now from me this good and perfect word,
Behave not to the king thyself as lord.
Beware that what he says thou deem not true;
Him I as honourable do not view.
I find in his hand but hypocrisy:
'I am *Zardusht*,' he says, 'enough for me!'
Upon a gallows hang him upside down,
But of the matter speak thou now to none."
Upon their road the envoys then he sped,
As "Hasten on like smoke" to them he said.
Along with them three hundred horse he sent,
All bearing daggers and on war intent.
He said to them: "Now be ye wise in all,
And all together enter ye his hall.
When on the throne ye see him with his crown,
Before him then yourselves bend humbly down.
To kings as it is meet your prayer present,
Beyond the throne let not your eyes be bent.
Before him when ye there are seated down,
Turn both your faces tow'rds his shining crown.
My pleasant message thus before him lay:
Listen for answer to what he may say.
And when ye hear the answer end to end,
Kiss ye the ground and your way backwards wend."
The vengeful Bí-darafsh out from him went;
Tow'rds Balkh the noted was his standard bent,
With Nám-khást, blundering companion he,
Whom those who seek a name should ever flee.
On foot proceeding from Turán its town,

At Balkh they lighted at the palace down.
And as on foot before him there they went,
Upon his threshhold low their face was bent.
And when they saw his face his throne upon
More brilliant than the moon shone out that sun.
Before him then their humble prayer they laid,
As slaves to kings who mankind happy made.
Then to his hand the royal note they bring,
Written in Turkish letters by the king.
When the world's king the letter opened wide,
He shook amazed at what was writ inside.
He read the letter quickly to Jámásp,
Who acted as adviser to Gushtásp.
The generals of Irán whom they chose,
The Mobeds who had seen the world, all those,
And other Mobeds who were at his call,
The *Vasta**, laid he then before them all.
To Mobeds and the prophet this he read,
And to Zarír, the army's chosen head.
His brother was the general Zarír,
Who led the heroes of the army here.
He had been champion of the world for long,
For Asfandyár, the horseman, was too young.
Leading the host, he was its guardian, too;
With horemen's aid the world its refuge knew.
Of evil men the world he rendered free,
And in the combat the spear wielded he.
The story to his chiefs Gushtásp then told,
The great ones of Irán and warriors bold.
" Arjásp, of Chín and Turán general, he
Has such and such a letter sent to me."
To them the evil words he then displayed
Turán's king in his letter to him said.
He said to them : " In this what do ye see ?

*The Zandavastá.

What do ye say the end of this will be ?
Oh ! how unpleasant friendship is with one,
For whom true wisdom has so little done !
I from the seed of Iraj pure descend,
Him of a race in which magicians blend ;
Between us two how could peace ever be ?
And yet it had been this I hoped to see.
An honoured name whoever may possess
To anyone his words may well address."
Whilst by the king these words were being said,
Asfandyár, Zarír, the host who led,
Both of them swords drew from their sheaths and cried :
" In the whol world whoever may reside,
To him as prophet who will not assent,
And will to his commandment not consent,—
This happy king's Court who will not attend,
Or with loins girded to his throne not bend,—
The way of his good creed will not observe,
And this religion as a slave not serve,—
Our sword his soul shall from his body tear,
And a high gallows, too, his head shall bear."

The answer of Gushtásp to Arjásp's letter.

Zarír, the General of Irán's host,
The tearing lion who could valour boast,
" O thou of name," said to the king this word :
' If thou to me permission wilt accord,
Magician Arjásp, will I give reply,"
And king Gushtásp approved it by and bye.
" Well done ! " he said : " Arise, make thy reply,
A coal to burn up Khalakh's brave men by."
Zarír, Asfandyár, Jámásp, all three
With knitted brows, hearts stern as stern could be,
Went out and to Arjásp a letter wrote,
Fitting reply to his that they could quote.

With this in hand *Zarír* himself arose,
And took it there, nor would the letter close.
He read it to the king as there he bore;
Wondered the king Gushtásp still more and more.
Horseman *Zarír* himself, that learned one,
Jamásp, and Asfandyár his son,
The letter closed, he wrote on it his name,
The envoy summoning, who to him came.
"Take it and bear from me to him," he said,
"And on my road no more your feet be led."
"Now if the Avastá," again said he,
"An envoy's safety did not guarantee,
I would have made you from your dream awake,
And hanged you high upon the nearest stake,
So that that worthless one might learn this thing,
He should not lift his head before a king."
The letter down before them then he threw,
"For the magician Turk this bear with you.
Tell him," he said, "that this life soon will go,
And thou of blood and earth the want will know.
Thy soul shall wounded be and crushed thy pride,
Thy bones in dust be scattered far and wide.
Within a month, if God me should not fail,
I will put on my iron coat of mail.
Into Turán will lead my host for war,
And will destroy the land of Kargasar."
When the land's lord his speech had made complete,
The General summoned, he gave praises meet.
And said, the matter leaving in his hand:
"Lead them from Irán out and from this land."
The envoys by the Chinese General sent,
Out of the presence of the monarch went.
Despised and from the monarch's presence thrust,
Both were humiliated to the dust.
To Khalakh from Irán they further went,

But in Khalakh they did not feel content,
When from afar they saw the monarch's hall,
A black flag floating high above its wall.
From off their prancing beasts they 'lighted down
With blinded eyes and with their hearts bowed down,
Then tow'rds Arjásp on foot their way pursue,
Darkened their soul, their face of yellow hue.
They give him then that letter from the king,
The answer that from bold Zarír they bring.
A scribe the letter opened to his face,
And read out to that king of Turkish race.
And in that letter to the king was told
What was the purport of that horseman bold.
It had been written in a humble way,
For it was meant before the king to lay.
But we have heard and I have also seen
Such words to speak would have improper been,
Nor to be heard nor be to any shown,
Nor to be hid nor openly be known.
"Within a certain time," thus did it say,
"Tow'rds this fair land will I my host convey
For this not two nor four months does it need
Myself I with my lions will proceed.
Such trouble for thyself lay not in store,
For I will open lay my treasure door.
A thousand thousand warriors of fame
I'll bring experienced and of good name:
These all from Iraj spring, of kingly face,
Not, as Afrásiáb, of Turkish race;
All shining as the moon does in the sky,
All straight and tall, who would not tell a lie.
All worthy royalty and all renown,
Worthy of armies, treasures, and of crown.
All holding spears, the sword to wield who know,
Hosts to array and hosts to overthrow.

Each spear in hand, and with his saddled steed,
Upon whose signet rings my name you read.
All who religion practise and are wise.
Bracelets of pearl and ear-rings all who prize.
When on my elephant the drum they know,
With horses' hoof they'll lay the mountains low.
The world afflicts them not of lust with pain,—
Eager for war, they all have lions slain.
In day of strife when they put on their mail,
To heav'n to raise the dust they do not fail.
Its a hard hill upon their saddles leant,
By them the hill's head is in pieces rent.
Two horsemen out of those sought out for war,
Zarír, the General, and Asfandyár,
When they, of iron made, put on their mail,
Nor sun nor moon to reach their feet will fail.
When on their arms the mighty mace they raise,
Their very forms with dignity shall blaze.
When these before the army take their place,
Attentive, thou to them should'st turn thy face.
With throne and crown they shine as does the sun,
From fortune have their faces brilliance won.
Such is each warrior and General,
My chosen Mobeds are approved of all.
Think not the Jaihún with thy musk to fill,
For I my treasure doors will open still.
If at the Jaihún my sword's power arrive,
My mace shall thee in to the desert drive.
Thine elephant shall in the desert wail,
To boil nor shall the Jaihún's water fail.
If in the day of strife God deem it meet,
In fight I'll cast thy head beneath my feet.

The next Section relates to the assembling of Arjásp's army to the number of 300,000, under the leadership of an old Turk of bad reputation called Gurgsár, and two brother demons called Kahram and Andíramán. One Khashás was appointed to the advanced guard and Húshdív to guard the rear.

The next Section relates the gathering together of his army by Gushtásp and disbursing two years' pay to them. Then comes:—

The enquiring concerning the result of the war by Gushtásp from Jamásp according to star-divination.

There summoned at that time Jámásp the king,
Gushtásp's preceptor he in ev'rything.
Chief of the Mobeds, he all wisdom knew,
Light of the nobles and of Generals, too.
His faith correct, so pure was all he did,
That plain became to him all that was hid.
A knower of the stars, so worthy he
In wisdom on his footing none might be.
The king him questioning said: "God to thee
Has given Faith and a pure mind to see.
With thee in this world to compare is none,
All knowledge God has giv'n to thee alone.
Now must thou from the stars a reckoning make,
And tell me all the course that things will take.
What from the war will come and what its end?
Long life to whom below will God extend?"
Jamasp's old heart these searching words concerned,
And tow'rds Gushtásp with a stern look he turned.
And said to him: "Oh would that God the just
On me this skill and wisdom had not thrust!
Me with such knowledge did not God inspire,
What is to be the king would not inquire.
If I the king inform or do not tell,

The king of kings may ruin me as well."
"In God's name," then to him the king replied,
"In whom pure faith and wisdom e'er abide.
By Zarir's soul, that rider bold in strife,
And of Asfandyár, too, by the life,
Tell what thou knowest of this thing to me:
Thou knowest and I seek the remedy."
"O worthy monarch," then the wise man said:
"For ever rest the crown fresh on thy head!
Know, O thou brave one of the kingly race,
When in the fight strive heroes face to face.
Wherever may arise the cry and shout,
When thou would'st say the hills are rooted out,
Wherever valiant men may forward come,
And with the war-dust dark the air become,
The world turned azure wilt thou witness there,
Of fire full earth, and full of smoke the air.
Blows from the heavy maces such will peal,
As of a blacksmith's hammer on the steel.
The twang of bow-strings there shall pierce the brain,
With cry of war-steeds earth resound again.
The spheres shall all be rent in tumult wild,
The banners all with blood shall be defiled.
Sonless shalt thou then many fathers see,
And many sireless sons in like degree.
First Ardashir, that Kais' son of great name,
The brave son of a king of mighty fame,
Throws himself forward on his charger fleet,
And casts in dust down all who him may meet.
So many Turks will he to foot dismount,
That equal to them stars you will not count.
But in the end he will as well be slain,
The roll of honour will his name retain.
Then shall the king's son Shídasp in revenge,
His black steed forward urge him to avenge.

Sternly his vengeful sword shall he display,
And many men and many horses slay.
Fortune at last shall hurl him to the ground,
And naked there shall that crowned head be found.
And mine own son shall then come forward there,
And mine own girdle on his loins shall bear,
Avenging Shídasp, offspring of the king,
Like Rústam's self among the army fling.
Many of China's noted men around,
That lion hero casts down on the ground.
Then many a trouble happens in the fray;
This to the king of kings how shall I say?
The glittering Kávah banner on that day
The heroes of Irán have cast away.
Girámis sees, on horseback where he stands,
The sacred banner cast from loyal hands.
Bravely from off his horse's back he leaps
Lifting the flag, which in his hand he keeps.
The sword in one hand while he firmly holds,
The other has the flag of violet folds.
His foes thus overthrowing in the strife,
He roots up of those Ahrimans the life.
With a sharp sword and with a sudden blow,
Cuts off a hand of his a cruel foe.
Girámis with his teeth the banner holds,
That flag resplendent in its violet folds.
Beneath one hand then disappears the foe,
And none had ever seen more wondrous blow
But now a Turkomán with arrow thrust,
That crown and head of his lays in the dust.
But now Nastúr, the noble Zarír's son,
His horse, like a raging lion, urges on;
As victory again its face displays,
Against the enemy his hand will raise.
The chosen horseman after him comes on,

Naozár, the brave, ot the world-king the son.*
Full sixty of these foes he overthrows,
And as a Pehlaván his valour shows.
The Turks at last through him an arrow thrust,
And throw the elephantine form to dust.
At length upon the scene there will appear,
That horseman valiant whom they call Zarír.
He will come on, his lasso in his hand,
And with his Arab horse there take his stand.
His yellow breastplate like the moon will glow,
The host shall at the sight great wonder know.
A thousand warriors of the host he'll seize,
Will bind and to the king will send off these;
And ev'rywhere the king his face shall show,
Blood of his foes there shall in rivers flow.
Then fallen Ardashír will come to view,
Blackenened his cheek, his form of jaundiced hue.
Him will he sore lament and angry grow,
Excited, on his steed shall forward go.
He to the Khákán turns his angry sight,
Thou would'st have said he never had known flight.
When in the midst there he shall see Arjásp,
He'll speak the praises of the king Gushṭásp.
The ranks then of his foes he'll overthrow,
And from the earth on none his glances throw.
He now the Anjand of Zardusht recalls,
For royal aid on God alone he falls.
Fortune becomes at last of darker hue,
And thus that chosen tree is cut down, too.
And now one Bídarafsh approaches near,
And holds the violet standard tow'rds his spear;
The chosen hero tow'rds he dares not go,
But on his road in ambush crouches low.
Like raging elephant he'll bar the way,

* This is all described, as if the Mobed saw it in a vision.

And in his hand a poisoned sword display.
When from the fight the king turns back his head,
He from a feast returns, thou would'st have said;
At him that Turk an arrow then will throw,
Open to him himself he dare not show.
Of Bídarafsh then at the vile hand slain,
The free men's king shall not be seen again.
Saddle and steed he'll to the Turks convey,
Vengeance for him to whom first shall they pay?
Then shall the host that all men famous know
Like wolf and lion fall upon the foe;
Both with each other strive on ev'ry hand,
With heroes' blood is reddened all the land.
The faces of the heroes all turn pale,
The hearts of heroes tremble all and fail.
The army's dust shall up to heaven rise;
Nor sun, nor moon are seen by mortal eyes,
In glitter of the arrow, sword and spear,
As shining from a cloud the stars appear.
Then Bídarafsh, the foul one and the strong,
Like tearing wolf shall come and rage along,
With the same poisoned sword shall take his stand,
And many choice ones perish at his hand.
The bright Asfandyár shall then appear,
The army in support, with God him near.
On Bídarafsh a judgment storm shall light,
Bloody his robe, his soul still full of fight.
With Indian sword he'll strike at him a blow,
And half his body from the saddle throw.
He then shall seize upon his iron mace,
And cause his glory forth to shine in grace.
With one attack he'll scatter them around,
When scattered there, why leave them on the ground?
With his spear's point he then will choose them out,
Clean will destroy and scatter them about.

The Chinese General at length will flee
Before Asfandyár of high degree.
Fleeing, towards Turán his face he'll turn,
With broken heart and eyes with tears that burn.
With a small force across the waste he'll go,
The king victorious, destroyed his foe.
And now know thou, of kings the chosen head,
That nought shall happen but what I have said.
Words more or less from me thou shalt not learn;
Look not upon me with an eye so stern.
For but at thy command, victorious king,
I surely never should have said this thing.'
Much after this the king enquired as well
Of that deep sea and of that darkened well.
"I saw it not, from thee, king, to conceal;
If not, the secret why not now reveal?"
The king heard what the Mobed had to say,
And of his throne upon the corner lay,
Out of his hand his golden sceptre fell,
Thou would'st have said his glory passed as well.
He fell upon his face and senseless grew,
He spoke no more a word and no more knew.
When to his senses he came back once more,
He came down from his throne and wept right sore.
"This throne and place," said he; "why do I lack?
For ev'ry day to me becomes more black.
Now all my moons each his own way will take,
My horsemen brave, my kings will me forsake.
Fortune and rule why should I crave alone,
Or power, army or my crown and throne?
For those to me who are of all most dear,
My chosen troops, who are most famous here,
These from before me all will now depart,
And from my body tear my wounded heart."
He said to Jámásp: "If the thing is so,

At what time to the war myself I go,
I will not call my valiant brother here,
Nor fill my aged mother's heart with fear.
I will not bid him to the fight proceed,
But happy Guráz shall the army lead.
Hither my youthful Kais' sons will I call,
Dear as my soul and body are they all.
Them will I summon all before me here,
Before my flag they breast-plates shall not wear.
Why should the bright point of an arrow fly
Up to that stony mountain near the sky?"
Then to the land's king did the sage reply:
"O, thou of nature good, whose praise is high,
Should not the army now by thee be led,
With crowns of iron placed upon their head,
Warriors of China who to meet will dare?
Our pride, our Faith to us who back will bear?
Rise from the dust, and sit upon thy throne;
Let not the empire's glory be o'erthrown.
It is God's secret with no remedy,
The Lord of all the earth, no tyrant He.
In giving way to grief there is no gain;
What is to happen this will be again.
Now thine own heart do not thou further grieve,
In the Creator's justice but believe."

The history now proceeds to describe the preparations of Gushtásp and Arjásp for war with each other, and in the next section are recorded the deaths of Ardashir, Shíru, Shídasp, Girámi, Naozár and Zarír, Chiefs of Irán, with intervals between the combats. In the next Section is narrated the death of Bídarafsh at the hand of Asfandyár and the flight of the army of Arjásp towards the desert. On perceiving that Arjásp had gone, the leading men of the Turkománs approach Asfandyár on foot, throwing away their bows and war-suits, and beg for quarter. They offer to worship the sacred fires and adopt the new religion. The slaughter, however, continues until Gushtásp, hearing their cries, takes pity on them, and orders the Irání Chiefs to cease fighting. The king and army lament over *Zarír*, and put him in a coffin for burial. Thirty thousand Iránís are said to have been killed, and among them 1,166 men of note, while of the latter 1,040 also were wounded. Of the enemy 100,000 were killed, 800 being chiefs, and 3,200 wounded.

After this Gushtásp returns to Balkh with his army. He gives Hamái, who appears to have been his daughter, in marriage to his eldest son, for such was the custom in those days. The command of the army is given to Nastúr, and he builds a fire temple, to the charge of which he appoints Jámásp, and gives it his own name. He sends news of his good fortune to all provinces, and the Kaiser of Rúm, the kings of Sind and Barbar and the princes of India send him tribute. Asfandyár is sent out to convert everyone to the faith of *Zoroaster*. They are said to have adopted it, erected fire-temples, and to have written to ask for copies of the *Zandavastá*, which were sent. He then takes off his war belt and rests, and reports to his father that all people have submitted to him, and the whole world is prosperous.

Gushtásp now becomes suspicious of Asfandyár in consequence of Gurazú's calumniating him by saying he had a secret intention of rebelling against his father. He sends Jámásp for Asfandyár, who arrives and, notwithstanding his denial of the charge brought against him, is loaded with chains and sent off to the fort of Gumbadán in the hill country. After some time Gushtásp proceeds towards *Zábulistan*, with a view to promulgate his religion. Arrived there, he is received by Rústam and all his nobles, and these all embrace the new Faith, learning the *Zandavastá* and lighting fires. For two years Gushtásp is entertained by *Zál*. The tributary kings, however, hearing of the imprisonment of Asfandyár, although innocent, revolt against Gushtásp and go to Asfandyár in his confinement to keep him company. Arjásp also, hearing of these events and that Lehrásp was left alone at Balkh with only 700 fire-worshippers, determines to attack him, sends one Sitúh, a magician, to spy out what is taking place in Selstán, and reassembles his own army.

Fardúsi here goes on with his own history, having finished what had been written by Dakíkí, and which he pronounces to have been badly done.

Arjásp orders his general Kahram to attack the fire-worshippers, cut off their heads, and burn their houses, and if he finds Asfandyár in chains to kill him, too. Kahram accordingly proceeds to ravage the country, and the Turks arrive at Balkh, when Lehrásp, notwithstanding his age, defends himself vigorously, but is surrounded and cut to pieces, as are also the priests in the fire-temples; their blood extinguished the sacred fire, and we may understand, although it is not stated clearly, that *Zardusht* perished there as well.

The next section relates how Gushtásp's wife starts off alone to Sáistán and conveys the news of Lehrásp's death to her husband, with other details of the mischief done by Kahram. Gushtásp immediately assembles his followers and returns towards Balkh. The armies meet, and the Iránis are defeated, Farshídvard, the king's son, who commanded their right wing, being killed. Gushtásp takes fligh to a hill, where Arjásp surrounds him. Here the nobles kill their horses for food. Gushtásp consults Jámásp, who informs him he must release Asfandyár in order to save himself, and on obtaining permission starts off for the purpose, Gushtásp declaring that he will abdicate in favour of his son if he comes. Jámásp passes through the Turanían army by night disguised in Túrki armour, and being recognised by Núsh Azar, a son of Asfandyár, gains access to the latter, and with some difficulty persuades him, after he has been so badly treated, to have his chains knocked off and go to the rescue of his father and his sisters, Humai and Beh-Afríd, who are prisoners of the Turks. He leaves the fort with Bahman and Núsh Azár, and vows not to revenge himself on his father for his treatment of him if God gives him the victory, but to build fire-temples, erect caravanserais, dig wells and plant trees, and to serve God by converting to the Faith all who have no guide, and to slay all magicians. He finds Farshídvard wounded to the death and subsequently Gurázú and many other Iránis killed, and cutting his way through the enemy reaches Gushtásp on the mountain.

Gushtásp receives him with joy, and renews his promise to abdicate in his favour if he escapes. His troops reach Asfandyár, and preparations are made for a battle. Arjásp, terrified at the sight of the released Asfandyár and others, stands on a hill to witness the engagement, having, in anticipation of defeat, sent off a hundred camel loads of the plunder he had obtained at Balkh, with four of his sons who were younger than Kahram, on different roads. At this crisis a valiant Turk called Kargasár comes to Arjásp and offers to overthrow Asfandyár: he places him in command of his army offering him two-thirds of the world if he conquers. The Iranían army is arrayed with Gushtásp in the centre, Nastúr, *Zarír's* son, on the right wing, and Kardín on the left. On the other side Arjásp has the centre, Kahram the right wing, and the king of Chigil the left. Asfandyár throws himself against the right wing, and Kahram takes to flight; then he kills 125 of the most valiant of those on the left, crying: "This is how I avenge my thirty-eight noble brothers who are dead." Arjásp appeals to Kargasár, who shoots an arrow at Asfandyár, who pretends he is hit in the chest, and Kargasár draws his sword in order to put an end to him, but Asfandyár catches him with his lasso, ties his hands and carries him off to the Iranian camp, to be delivered to Gushtásp, with orders not to kill him till he sees how the fortunes of the battle go. Hearing this, Arjásp flees towards Khallakh with his nobles. The battle still continues, but when they know Arjásp has gone off, the Turks who have horses escape, and the rest submit to Asfandyár, who gives them quarter. Kargasár, in a costume of mourning, is fearful of his life, but when Asfandyár has rested for eight days after the battle, he is sent back to the camp bound. Asfandyár kills all the Turks that despoiled his army and plunders Arjásp's camp. After this he repairs to Gushtásp's camp and reports how he has avenged Lehrásp and Farshídvard. Gushtásp refers to his own promise to yield him up his kingdom, but Asfandyár refuses it and insists on going off to wreak his vengeance on the country of Turán.

The next Section contains the praises of king Mahmúd, under whose auspices the book is being written, and Fardúsi passes on to the account of the "*Haftkh'kán*," the seven tables or stations of Asfandyár; these are translated as follows:

The First Stage. The Killing of Two Wolves by Asfandyár.

The talkative Dahkán the table placed;
Of seven stages then the story traced.
He took up in his hand a cup of gold,
And thus of Gushtásp was the story told,
Of Rúïn-diz and of Asfandyár,
The route and intercourse with Kargasár.

As Asfandyár towards Balkh took his way,
His soul and tongue had bitter words to say.
Intent his way toward Turán to wend,
He left his sire, with Kargasár for friend.
He went on till two roads there came in sight,
And pitched tents with his army to alight.
He ordered there a table to be spread;
Wine, song and singers, too, they ready made.
Then came there all the warriors of the host,
At the king's table there they took their post.
He ordered broken-hearted Kargasár
To be brought out before Asfandyár.
He bade four gold cups filled up to the brim
Of wine to drink that they should give to him.
And said: "O thou whose fortune is no more,
To thee thy crown and throne will I restore;
And what I ask if thou wilt truly tell
All the Turks' land to thee I'll give as well;
This will I yield to thee with victory won,
And I will raise thee brilliant to the sun.
I will not trouble those to thee allied,
Relations ev'rywhere, thy son beside.
But falsehood with me if thou still maintain,
Favour with me that falsehood shall not gain.
Thy loins in two with dagger will I tear,
And all the people's hearts shall quake with fear."
Then said to him in answer Kargasár:
"O happy, fortunate Asfandyár,
Nothing but what is true to thee I bring:
Do therefore what is fitting for a king."
"Where is Rúín-diz," asked he, "to be found?
It is not of Irán within the bound.
How many roads has it and is it far?
And which roads to it the most easy are?
How many soldiers in it may there be?

What of its height thou knowest say to me."
Then said to him in answer Kargasár:
"O happy, fortunate Asfandyár,
Three roads hence to that palace access yield,
Which Arjásp now may call his battle-field.
One road needs three months, and the second two,
But there must be an army on it, too.
On it lie water, tent and many a town,
And nobles of Turán it two-parts own.
Upon that one that two months would endure,
The army there would hardly food procure.
Water for beasts or grass of any kind,
Or place to rest in there you will not find.
Upon the third for sev'n days must you strive,
At Ruín-diz upon the eighth arrive.
Lions and wolves and dragons there abound,
From whose claws safety none has ever found.
This will a woman, a magician, hold,
Than wolf more crafty, more than dragon bold.
Some to the moon she drags from sea below,
Or in a well will others headlong throw.
Desert and Símmurgh there, and icy breeze,
So that when blows a wind 'twill rend the trees.
When Ruín-diz itself shall then appear,
Such fort has never come to sight or ear,
Than the black clouds the ramparts loftier still,
And many troops and arms the castle fill.
Around a stream of running water flows,
At sight of which the soul bewildered grows.
And if the king goes hunting in the plain,
He in a boat must cross the place to gain.
A hundred years should he within remain,
He need bring nought whatever from the plain,
For in the fort is grass and bearing field;
And grinding mill and tree that fruit will yield."

When Asfandyár has heard the words he said,
He drew his breath awhile and bent his head.
He said: "There is no way of any sort;
Best in the world the road is that is short."
"Upon the sev'n-staged road, O monarch brave,"
Thus Kargasár to him his answer gave:
"By force alone no man has ever passed,
His life who did not give up at the last."
The hero told him: "If thou art with me,
My heart and strength are demon-like, thou'lt see.
But what will meet me first must thou now say,
To strive with it that I may know the way."
Replying, Kargasár to speak began:
"O thou heroic and most fearless man,
A male and female wolf first come to view,
Like a huge elephant each of the two,
With horns like antelope upon their head;
Lions to fight they by desire are led.
Like raging elephants their teeth are seen,
Their shoulders burly and their loins are lean."
Just as he was, still fastened with his chain,
The king bade take him to his tent again.
Upon his head the royal crown he had;
An audience tent prepared he and was glad.
And when the sun its crown above revealed,
Secrets no more from earth the heav'ns concealed.
Rose from the tents the sound of drums anew,
Iron the earth, the sky of ebon hue.
By the sev'n stages tow'rd Purán his way
He took, his army with him staunch and gay.
When the first station near him came in view,
He of experienced soldiers chose a few.
Of these Bashotan, e'er a watchful man,
Was set against the foe to guard the van.
He said to him: "The army hold in hand;

Of what says Kargasár I heedful stand.
I am the leader; should harm me befall,
'Twere wrong that ought should happen to the small."
Forward he came, his *khaftán** firmly wound;
His night-hued steed's girth then they tightly bound.
Across the horse his foot the leader laid;
The spheres had left their place, thou woulds't have said.
When near the wolves the General beheld
Tight like an elephant his thighs he held.
When the wolves saw the warrior face to face,
His shoulders, loins, and hero's grasp and mace,
Out of the plain tow'rds him their face they turned,
Two elephants who fierce for battle yearned.
The valiant hero promptly strung his bow,
Like a fierce rending lion growling low.
Arrows upon the demons smartly rained,
Whilst 'gainst the horsemen ambush they maintained.
Pricked with the arrows' steel they languid grew,
Neither of them without a wound came through.
To Asfandyár of bright heart thus 'twas known,
That they were wearied and had languid grown.
Out of its sheath he drew his glittering sword,
Drew in his head and on his reins pressed hard.
Their heads then with his sword he sheared away,
And with their blood he turned the dust to clay.
He lighted down from off his noted steed,
His sense of helplessness to God to plead.
From arms and body washed of blood the stain,
He sought a clean and pure place on the plain.
Upon the sand towards the sun he turned,
Dusty his face, his heart with sorrow burned.
" O righteous Ruler," thus his accents glowed,
"Strength, honour, skill, hast Thou on me bestowed.

* A garment worn above body armour.

In dust the wild beasts hast Thou overthrown,
Tow'rds good to me the rightful way hast shown."
Bashotan and the army came up there;
They saw him in the attitude of prayer.
At the heroic deed they stood amazed,
And in deep, earnest thought upon him gazed.
"Wild elephant or wolf shall we him name?
His heart, sword, hand, for ever be the same!
Glory be his and kingly dignity,
Justice his throne with royal majesty!"
The warriors of enlightened wisdom went,
And near his camp enclosure pitched their tent.
Grief was the portion sole of Kargasár,
When heard he how had sped Asfandyár.
A golden dinner-tray they spread to dine.
Food first they ate, and then demanded wine.
He asked him as he gave him wine-cups three:
"What say'st thou now? What marvels shall I see?"
He bade them bring him there his captive bound,
He trembling and with tearful face was found.
By Kargasár then was the hero told:
"O prince of lion heart and warrior bold,
At the next stage a lion thee will meet,
With him no crocodile could e'er compete.
Above the lion's road the eagles high,
Though there were many, would not dare to fly."
Bright-souled Asfandyár at him then smiled,
And said: "O fool, whom fortune has beguiled,
To-morrow with a lion shalt thou see
How brave a hero with a sword can be."
Ordered the king, as night usurped the day,
That from that place they should go on their way.
He drove the army on through that dark night
With bleeding eyes, his heart still full of fight.

The second Stage. The slaughter of the lions by Asfandyár.

The sun from out the sheet of azure blue
Put on brocaded robe of yellow hue.
The hero went then where the warriors go,
Battle with lions in the waste to know.
He bade Bashotan come before the rest,
And measureless good counsel him addressed.
He said: "I leave this army in thy hand,
And I myself prepared for war will stand."
And to the lions when he nearer drew,
Dark to those lions' hearts the world then grew.
One was a lioness, and one a male,
Bold so in fight that they would never fail.
The male came on: he struck him with his blade,
So that of coral hue his face he made.
From head to middle he was cut in two,
Of terror full the female's heart thus grew.
She, raging like her mate, her onslaught made,
And on her head came down the trenchant blade.
Fell down the severed head and rolled in sand,
Red with her blood became his form and hand.
With water washed his body and his head,
To the pure God above his prayer he said.
He said: "O pure, just Ruler of the land,
Thou hast destroyed these wild beasts by my hand."
Thither the army now had made its way,
Bashotan saw the lions as they lay
Each praised Asfandyár then as he spoke,
And on him many blessings all invoke.
The hero who had been their guide appeared,
Where the enclosure and the tents were reared.
A tray of dainty food they placed again
Before that king of kings of cleanly brain.

Then Kargasár he had before him brought,
Of evil fortune and of evil thought.
Of wine three cups he gave of ruby hue,
The captive's heart like demon's happy grew.
He said: "O thou of evil fate and base,
Say what to-morrow I may have to face."
He answered him: "O thou of lofty mind,
Be far from thee he who is ill inclined!
In haste like fire thou wentest to the strife,
And from misfortune hast escaped with life.
Thou know'st not what to-morrow will arise,
'Pity the fate that wakeful for thee lies.
Where hence to-morrow thou shalt forward go,
Than this a greater matter shalt thou know.
A dragon there shall come that to its maw
Shall with its breath the fish from ocean draw.
He with his mouth shall light up fire and flame,
And as the solid rock is made his frame.
Twere better from this road if thou withdrew,
To this my soul bears testimony, too.
In thine own matter there may be no fear,
But think thou of the host that's gathered here.'
"O thou of evil mark," he cried again,
"Thee will I drag and fasten with a chain.
And those sharp dragon's talons thou shalt see,
Shall not escape my sharpened sword and me."
He ordered them a heavy beam to bring,
Of heavy wood the hero made the thing.
A comely chariot of wood he made,
And all around it cutting swords were laid.
Above on this he laid a comely chest,
Which clear-brained carpenters made of the best.
And as the king sat there upon the chest,
Were yoked to it two horses of the best.
The king sat on the chest, and them to prove

Awhile upon the road the horses drove.
He placed a Kábúl dagger in his breast,
And laid upon his head a hero's crest.
All was prepared the dragon foe to meet,
And the world-seeker's labour was complete.
Black as a Zangí's face the earth was made,
And from the Ram the moon its crown displayed.
Sat Asfandyár on Shulak then, his horse,
His troops renowned behind him in their course.

The Third Stage. The Killing of the Dragon by Asfandyár.

The world upon the next day had grown bright,
The night's dark banner had been lost to sight.
The hero in his coat of mail was clad;
The host's command had then Bashotan glad.
He brought the chariot and the lion's chest,
And on it sat the monarch bold at rest.
Two valuable steeds were yoked thereto,
His course towards the dragon as he drew.
The dragon heard the chariot's noise from far,
And saw the prancing of the steeds of war.
Up from his place like a black hill he sped,
The sun and moon grew dark, thou would'st have said.
His eyes with blood-like flaming fountains grew,
And from his mouth blazed out the fire anew.
Like a black cave his mouth he opened wide,
And roaring, the advancing king still eyed.
When Asfandyár had seen the wonder there,
He held his breath and sought his God in prayer.
The horses both escape then sought from death;
The dragon drew them both in with his breath.
Chariot and horse both with his breath he drew,
And tow'rds the chest came on to fight anew.
When in his mouth was firmly fixed each blade,

Like a green sea the monster vomit made.
From chariot and swords great pain he knew
As his strength weaker and yet weaker grew.
Out of the chest the brave man took his stand,
A sharpened sword-blade in his lion-hand.
The monster's brain was shattered with the sword,
And poison-smoke rose from the dust and sward
By that smoke stupefied and whirling round,
Asfandyár fell senseless on the ground.
With a large force behind him at his need,
Bashotan then came forward with all speed.
Some harm has happened to him as he fears,
His heart is filled with blood, his cheek with tears
A wailing cry raised of the troops each man;
Their horses left behind, on foot they ran.
With every haste Bashotan forward sped,
Water of rose to pour upon his head.
The monarch opened presently his eye,
And hailed his haughty warriors with the cry:
" His poison-smoke it was that caused my fall;
No other wound have I from him at all."
Up from the earth he went towards the stream,
Just like a drunkard waking from a dream.
For new robes from his treasurer he sent,
And in the stream to wash himself then went.
The Great Creator then he sought in prayer,
Weeping in anguish in the dust fell there.
He cried: "This dragon monster who had killed
But one who with God's power had been filled?"
His army all their voice in blessing raise,
Whilst in the dust his head each humbly lays.
But Kargasár at heart with sorrow bled,
That Asfandyár was living who was dead.
Upon the water's edge the king's camp laid,
Around him all their tents the army spread.

He rose, by memory of his God inspired,
And for the wine and those who drank enquired.
He ordered them to bring there Kargasár,
Who weeping came before Asfandyár.
Three royal cups of wine he made him drink,
And laughed, and of the dragon bade him think.
He said to him : " In worth thou who dost fail,
Now look upon that dragon's twisting tail:
What shall befall me at the coming stage?
What greater trouble shall my mind engage?"
He said to him : " O thou victorious lord,
All good to thee may thy good star afford!
When thou to-morrow's journey shalt complete,
There to salute a sorceress will meet.
This force she has seen, many troops beside,
By none of which her soul was terrified.
When she desires she makes the desert sea,
And broad the sun on high can cause to be.
Kings when they name her but a *Ghoul* will call,
In youth by her ensnared do not thou fall.
Victorious with the dragon, turn thee back:
In dust turn not thine honoured face to black."
" O saucy cheek," thus did the monarch say:
" To see what I do till to-morrow stay.
I to that sorceress such harm will do,
That sorcerers with broken backs shall rue.
And through the victory of the only God,
Magicians' heads shall 'neath my feet be trod."

The Fourth Stage. The Killing of the Sorceress by Asfandyár.

And when its yellow robe put on the day,
Towards the East the world grew bright and gay.
He struck his camp, the army urging on,
And God, the bounteous Giver, thought upon.

Through the dark night the king his army led,
And when the sun raised up its golden head;
When the Ram's face was of a ruby hue,
Then equally the world was smiling too.
Of troops he gave Bashotan the command,
And took a gold cup full of wine in hand.
Of great price, then, he sought him a guitar,
And held a banquet, though prepared for war.
He saw a forest like to Paradise,
The sphere sowed tulips there, thou would'st surmise.
Through the thick trees of sun there was no trace;
Streams like rose water flowed in ev'ry place.
Alighting from his steed as it seemed fit,
He on a fountain's edge preferred to sit.
And when his heart with drinking wine was glad,
Upon his hand a golden cup he had.
With the guitar against his bosom pressed
He sang the melodies his heart loved best.
Asfandyár said in his secret mind:
"Wine and wine-drinkers now I never find.
Lions and dragons only do I see,
And from misfortune's claw am never free.
For from the world no profit e'er have I,
Or Pari-faces see with gladsome eye.
If I from God my heart's wish could obtain,
And He some fair form give to soothe my pain!
Of Asfandyár the sorceress heard the voice:
Like flow'rs in spring then did her heart rejoice.
Exultingly she cried: "The lion's there,
With gladness, song and wine cup in my snare."
Of wrinkled face that evil, ugly fright,
Enchantments in the dark began to write.
A fair young Túrki girl there to him went,
Chinese brocade her cheek, with musk for scent!
Of cypress stature and her cheek sun-fair,

Loose hanging to her feet her musky hair.
Forward tow'rds Asfandyár she pressed,
Rose-meads her cheeks, a flower in her breast.
And when upon her form the monarch gazed,
To brighter airs his voice and song he raised.
"O just and only God," he gladly cried;
"In hill and desert both art Thou my guide.
E'en now a Pari-face I sought to see,
Beauteous in form and a fair gain to me.
The just Creator gave me of my will;
Oh! may my soul and heart adore Him still!"
Musk-scented wine a cup she gave him, too,
So that his face assumed a scarlet hue.
He had a delicate small chain of steel,
This cunningly from her did he conceal.
Zardusht for this in Paradise had sought,
And on Gushtásp's own arm to bind had brought.
Upon her neck this chainlet fine he threw,
So that her body no more power knew.
The sorceress into a lion grew,
But instantly his sword the monarch drew.
He said: "Thou can'st not do me a despite,
Me with a hill of iron though thou smite.
Bring back thy face to what it was before,
Or to my sword thou yet shalt answer more."
An old hag hideous did the chain then show,
Whose face was black, and head and hair as snow.
Into her head a dagger sharp he thrust,
And head and body crumbled into dust.
The heav'ns were darkened as the sorceress died,
So that the world at her stood open-eyed.
A stormy black cloud covered o'er the sky,
That darkened of the sun and moon the eye.
The valiant monarch mounted on a height,
Like thunder growling, roared with all his might.

Soon did Bashotan there the army bring,
And cried to him aloud: "O famous king,
Before thy blow e'en crocodiles must fall,
Enchanters, lions, wolves and panthers all.
May'st thou remain still in thy lofty place;
The world will have occasion for thy grace!"
On fire was yet the head of Kargasár
At the fierce battles of Asfandyár.
Before the great Creator for His grace
The king awhile rubbed on the earth his face.
He pitched his camp within the forest round,
And laid a tray, where fitting food was found.
The executioner then bade the king
Thither that wretched man in chains to bring.
Him then at once near to the king they brought,
And when the eye of Asfandyár he caught,
Three royal cups of wine the king him gave.
With that red wine did Kargasár grow brave.
"O Turk of failing future," then said he:
"Behold the Enchanter's head upon yon tree.
Thou said'st she'd turn to sea the plain that's dry,
And to the Pleiades herself would fly.
At the next stage what wonder's there for me?
My measure from the Enchantress may'st thou see."
Then thus to him gave answer Kargasár,
As bowed he to Asfandyár,
"O hero who in time of war dos't rage,
A heavier matter meets thee at that stage.
Be thou more wakeful and have greater care,
Thou'lt see a hill whose head is high in air,
And a bird sits on it that is ruler there.
This the experienced the Símúrgh style;
A flying hill 'tis, seeking war the while.
An elephant 'twill take up in its claw,
And crocodiles out of the river draw.

To lift up these to much does not amount,
As sorceress and wolves them do not count.
He has two young ones of an equal height,
In counsel with him that will e'er unite.
If in the air with outspread wings he fly,
Its strength earth loses, sun its majesty.
Thou can'st with bird and hill strife not maintain;
If thou draw back, 'twill be to thee a gain."
Laughed Tuhamtan and said: "O strange to view!
I'll with my arrows pierce his shoulders through.
Into his form my Indian sword I'll thrust,
And bring his lofty head down to the dust.

The Fifth Stage. The Slaughter of the Símúrgh by Asfandyár.

And when the shining sun his back displayed,
And the East's heart thereby was harder made.
The warriors' chief his army forward led,
The Símúrgh's tale aye pondering in his head.
The whole night long he went on with it still,
When the sun shining came above the hill.
The lamp of time the earth made fresh and new,
And plain and desert took another hue.
He let the army with the General stay,
And horses, chest and chariot took away.
Like wind the monarch went on driving still,
And with its head in air perceived a hill.
Horses and chariot leaving in the shade,
His soul to thought again a prey he made.
When from the hill the Símúrgh saw the chest,
Behind which sounding drums and trumpets pressed.
He from the hill swooped as a cloud that's black,
Of sun and moonshine then there came a lack.
He wished to seize the chariot with his claw,

Just as its prey a panther in its maw.
His wing and feathers by the swords were struck,
And the bird failed in glory and in pluck.
Striving with beak and claw awhile distressed,
His strength forsook him and he lay at rest.
His young ones saw the Símúrgh with surprise,
Shouting and dropping blood out of his eyes.
In such a manner from the place they flew
The road the eye in shade no longer knew.
When languid from his wounds the Símúrgh fell,
In blood sank horse and chariot as well.
Out of the chest then leapt Asfandyár ;
Growling, he held his implements of war.
He cut him into pieces with his sword,
So helpless had become the crafty bird.
To the world's Maker then his prayer he made
In good and evil who had giv'n him aid.
'Twas thus he spoke : " Just Ruler of the heav'n,
To me who wisdom, strength and skill hast giv'n.
Thou the magicians' form hast cast aside,
In ev'ry good thing Thou hast been my guide."
Just at that hour the sound of blatant horn,
Bashotan's army coming, to his ear was borne.
Now for the bird the earth's face no one saw,
Nought but his blood-stained body and his claw.
From hill to hill there was of blood the stain,
Thou would'st have said indeed there was no plain.
With blood they saw the king's form was besmeared.
And all bewildered the moon's face appeared.
His praises sang the leaders all at once ;
Horsemen of war and heroes gave response.
" May the world-athlete now for ever be !
Of brilliant mind, alert and wise be he ! "
Such words when Kargasár had heard them speak,
His body trembled and pale grew his cheek.

His camp the monarch of the world then reared ;
The brave of bright soul round him all appeared.
They spread then fine brocade upon the ground ;
Demanding wine, they laid the trays around.
He ordered Kargasár then to be sought,
And him before the famous king they brought.
He gave him then three cups of sparkling wine,
And made his face like fenugreek to shine.
" O thou of evil mind and body, too,"
He said : " Behold what the world heroes do.
Lion, Símúrgh and wolf are no more seen ;
Nor dragon, fierce of evil claw, I ween."
With a loud voice cried to him Kargasár :
" O happy and renowned Asfandyár,
God and good fortune ever thee befriend,
The royal tree has come to fruitful end
To-morrow for a thing thyself prepare,
For which in battle men have not to care.
Of sword, mace, bow, thou wilt not think aright,
Nor see in battle or on road of flight.
Of snow a full spear's depth then there shall be,
And in time's face thou shalt a wonder see.
Happy Asfandyár, thou this should'st know,
Thou and thy army will remain in snow.
'Twould not be strange if thou should'st now retire,
And for my words no vengeance should'st require.
If thou would'st by another road then flee,
Of thine own army's blood thou wilt be free.
With a strong wind, this I can surely say,
The earth will rend and the trees fly away.
Towards the waste when thou shalt turn thy face,
At thirty *farsangs* is thy halting place.
The sand is heated and the earth and clay,
Nor locust, bird, nor ant will pass that way.
No drop of water on that road thou'lt meet,

The earth boils of the sun with fervent heat.
Upon the ground no lion passes there,
Nor swift-winged vulture hovers in the air.
No grass upon its sand or clay will stand,
Its soil, like tutty, is a flowing sand.
For forty *farsangs* in this way thou'lt drive,
The horse with no heart, and no man alive.
The host to Rúin-diz its way will trace,
Where thou wilt find an admirable place.
Its soil's according to thine own desire,
The castle's head might with the sun conspire.
Outside no animal its food can find,
And ev'ry horseman will be left behind.
From Irán and Turán should there arrive,
A hundred thousand who with daggers strive ;
A hundred years might they around it sit,
And arrows raining might pour into it.
Should there be fewer or should there be more,
An enemy could knock but at the door."
The Iránis heard what Kargasár had said,
And through them all were painful feelings spread.
" O king of noble race," to him they said :
" Be never thou into misfortune led.
If Kargasár has truthfully appealed,
For sure the matter cannot be concealed.
In this place we should be of death in fear,
Not to wear out the Turks have we come here.
Along this hard road thou thyself hast been,
And from wild beasts calamity hast seen.
None of the noted men or kings around,
Such pain to bear could ever have been found
As in these seven stages thou hast known,
To the Creator let thy praise be shown !
Victorious if thou would'st now retire,
And pleased and happy go back to thy sire,

And wreak thy vengeance by another way,
The cities of Turán for thee will pray,
As Kargasár himself may just now say,
In base contempt throw not thyself away.
The army's blood through thee be never shed,
For new tricks has this old sphere in its head.
Now that in victory we've been so gay,
Thy head thou should'st not to the winds betray."
And when the brave youth all their talk had heard,
The hero to the host these words preferred.
"On me such terror would ye now impress,
Nor open to yourselves its door the less?
Was it for counsel from Irán ye came,
And not to win yourselves a glorious name?
If this was all that ye could find to say,
Why did ye gird your loins upon my way;
But that from all this ill-starred Turk has said,
To trembling like a tree ye should be led?
Where are the king's gifts, counsels ye have known,
Your golden girdles and your crown and throne?
Where are your promises, your solemn oath,
By God and by your star of fortune both;
That now your feet so weary should have grown,
And your good counsels to the winds have flown?
Glad and victorious, do ye now go back,
And but to combat may I nothing lack.
For the victorious God is still my friend,
My good star in my bosom to the end.
None sees my equal in the manly strife,
Whether I take or whether give a life.
I'll to my foe my ev'ry skill display,
My manliness, my victory, what I may.
And ye, no doubt, the tidings will obtain
Of kingly dignity that I shall gain,
In manliness what to the fort I've done,

In the Lord's name of Saturn and the Sun."
When the Iránis opened then their eye,
They saw what rage could in his bosom lie.
Making excuses, to the king they went :
This fault to pardon would the king relent.
" Our souls and lives a sacrifice for thee ;
Such is our pledge and shall for ever be.
For thee 'tis thus our sympathy we show,
And of pain careless to the strife will go.
Of us, till for a hero we may lack,
Not one will hold him from the combat back.
Laid on the ground our heads before thee be,
The world, our wisdom, all be slaves to thee ! "
And when the king these words had heard them say,
From all that he had said he turned away.
And the Iránis praising then he cried :
" Virtue existing one can never hide.
Great victory if now we should obtain,
From troubles past we fruit as well shall gain.
We in our heart will not forget your pain,
Nor empty shall your treasuries remain."
Till day grew gray he went on talking still,
And a sharp wind then blew down from the hill.
Rose from the palace sounds of horn and flute,
And the whole army took at once their route.
Like raging fire they all then forward swung,
And the Creator's praise aloud was sung.

Sixth Stage. The Passing of Asfandyár through the Snow.

Above the hill when raised its head the dawn,
And night within the veil its head had drawn,
Its face before the sun did it conceal,
That shining brightly followed at its heel.

That mighty host then at the station met,
All bearing maces and with armour set.
Of springtime then it was a pleasant day,
The heart enlivening, and the earth was gay.
The tents and curtains the Kai ordered there,
And bade the tables and the wine prepare.
Sudden from off the hill a strong wind blew,
And terror then the mighty monarch knew.
Like raven's wing the world at once became,
And plain and mountain seemed to all the same.
From the black cloud keeps raining down the snow,
The ground is full of ice and fierce winds blow.
Three days and nights they blew the desert round;
And the wind's breath passed there beyond all bound.
The warp became the earth, the woof the snow,
The General helpless knew not where to go.
He with a loud voice to Bashotan cried:
"Our matter here to anguish is allied.
Bravely I faced the dragon's breath on earth,
Here manliness and strength are little worth.
In prayer to God now all your voices raise,
Call ye upon Him, and be loud in praise,
Perchance this evil soon may pass away:
On whom may any reckon who can say?"
Coming before God then Bashotan stood,
Who his great guide had always been for good.
Raising alike their hands the army there
Beyond all common bounds made then their prayer.
At once a gentle wind began to blow,
The cloud blew off, the air became aglow.
Their hearts when the Iránis could compose,
With thanks before God to their feet they rose.
Wet all the tents and the enclosures grew;
Though cold his feet and hands there no one knew.
The heroes there remained for three whole days;

The fourth, when earth with warmth was all ablaze,
The General his worthy ones all called,
And to them many good old tales recalled.
He said to them : " Your baggage leave behind,
And only warlike weapons bear in mind.
He than an Officer who is not less,
A hundred beasts of burden may possess.
On fifty let him water place, and food,
The rest bear what for sustenance is good.
Of baggage leave ye here what there is more,
For God has opened up for us a door.
He who of God commences to despair,
To him good fortune never will repair.
In God's strength will we overcome this day
The wretch who only idols doth obey.
And suddenly that fort shall ye possess,
With treasures all and diadems no less."

The seventh stage. The crossing of the river by Asfandyár, and his killing of Kargasár.

On head the sun its yellow veil had pressed,
And like the fenugreek become the West.
The warriors all their baggage quickly load,
And with the king go crowding on the road.
Of the dark night but little had passed by,
When a crane's voice was heard down from the sky
Astonished at the cry, Asfandyár
Sent quick a message back to Kargasár.
" Thou saidest here no water there would be,
No place for either rest or sleep for me.
From the sky now a crane's voice do I hear,
For water why hast thou put me in fear ? "
He said to him : " If here the beasts should halt,
They will find only water that is salt.

All other springs like poison wilt thou find,
Of birds and wild beasts only to the mind."
"In Kargasár," the General replied,
"Tow'rds vengeance only do we find a guide."
He at these words in haste the army drove,
And with his bounteous God in spirit strove.
Of the dark night one watch had but gone by,
When from the waste confused arose a cry.
The young king quickly leapt upon his steed,
From centre to the vanguard to proceed.
Before the army as the General drew,
A boundless sea there then appeared to view.
A dromedary in the caravan
A camel-driver drove on in the van.
The leader then was drowning in the wave;
The General stretched out his hand to brave.
And seizing on him from the mud withdrew,
That *Chigil** Turk a ghastly terror knew.
The evil Kargasár he bade again
To bring, distressed at heart, still with his chain.
He said to him: "O, vile as dust, and cheat,
Why crooked like a snake didst thou me treat?
I'd find no water here didst thou not say?
But in the sun's heat I should burn away?
Water as earth why didst thou represent,
And hast an army to destruction sent."
He answered thus: "The army's death to me
Would as the sun and moon great brightness be.
From thee but fetters can I never gain:
Why should I not wish for thee ill and pain?"
The General smiled, and opening wide his eye,
Of that Turk wearying, thus gave reply.
He said to him: "Small-witted Kargasár,
When I return victorious from the war,

* Name of a town in Tartary.

Of Rúín-diz I'll give thee the command,
Forbid that thou shouldst suffer at my hand.
If thou to tell me all the truth incline,
All of the kingdom shall be truly thine.
He who's thy son shall see no harm from me,
Nor any one who is allied to thee."
Now by the king when those words had been said,
They hope of life to Kargasár conveyed.
Astonished at his words he looked around,
And made excuses and then kissed the ground.
He said to him : " What thou hast said has passed,
Water's not land through thy crude words at last.
Where of this river is the ford, now say ;
Thou must point out to me the proper way."
" Winged arrows," said he, " when with iron bound
To pass through water there will not be found.
If from my bonds thou loose my feet as well
Over this river thou may'st read a spell."
Amazed at this the hero must remain,
And order them at once to loose the chain.
A dromedary holding by the head,
Into the river Kargasár then led.
In places where least water you could find,
Forward he went, the army marched behind.
Skins filled with air the General then bade
With great haste in the water to be laid.
These of each pack-horse by the side they tied :
At once the army reached the other side.
Army and baggage to dry land conveyed,
The right and left wings were then both arrayed.
Near to Rúín-diz they alighted then ;
The distance to it was but *farsangs* ten.
The leader of the warriors sat to dine,
The servants near him with full cups of wine.
He ordered them his breast-plate there to bring,

Sword, helmet, corslet for the valiant king.
He told them openly that Kargasár
Should be brought there to brave Asfandyár.
He said: "Thou'st rescued from an evil day;
But right and true words it behoves thee say.
When from his body I cut Arjásp's head,
And Lehrásp's soul to brightness has been led:
Of Kahram's self who Farshídvard has killed,
And has my army's heart with anguish filled,—
And of Andaríman, in conquest's gain
Who eight and thirty of our braves has slain,
My grandsire to revenge, with ev'ry art,
I cut the bodies from the heads apart;
Their graves I make of lions fierce the prey,
And to Irán's brave warriors' wish give way,—
Their hearts I with my arrows cause to bleed,
And captive all their wives and children lead,
Thee with this fort of mine will I rejoice,
Now what is in thy heart tell with thy voice."
Hardened then grew the heart of Kargasár,
And tongue and soul both urged him on to war.
He said "How long wilt thou such words repeat?
May justice thee with blessings never greet!
Evil to thee may all bad stars accord;
Thy body, too, be severed with the sword,
Thy bleeding form down in the dust be bowed,
The earth thy couch, nought but the grave thy shroud!"
Enraged the king grew at such speech again,
At Kargasár then with his muddled brain.
An Indian sword he struck upon his head;
His body to his loins in two was shred.
Into the river then the foe they threw;
And fishes as their food his body knew.
He leapt up on his steed from off the ground,
As his heroic loins he eager bound.

To look down on the fort he climbed a height ;
A massive iron castle came in sight.
Three *farsangs* high it was and forty wide,
Nor mud nor water could he see inside.
And so broad was the wall upon its crest,
With speed four horsemen there could ride abreast.
And when Asfandyár the wonder saw,
He from his breast a sigh was fain to draw.
"The fort is quite impregnable," he said ;
"A bad affair has to misfortune led.
Alas for all my battles and my pain ;
In this repentance is my only gain."
Around the desert as he looked again,
He saw two Turks that coursed upon the plain.
Four dogs they had along with them, and they
Such hounds were as in coursing seize their prey.
Came down Asfandyár to level land ;
A fighting spear he carried in his hand.
These from their steeds he with his spear unhorsed,
And from the plain above to go them forced.
"What is this famous castle ? " he inquired ;
"How many horsemen are there there required ?"
Of Arjásp many tales the men unfold,
In the fort's records all that was enrolled.
"Thou of the fort the height and breadth hast seen,
One gate is tow'rds Irán, and one tow'rds Chín.
A hundred thousand swordsmen it will hold,
All haughty horsemen they, renowned and bold.
These all Arjásp as his own slaves surround,
And all obedient to his will are found.
Food beyond measure is there stored up there,
All fair and good, if 'tis not in the ear.
Ten years if at the gates the king takes post,
Food there will be sufficient for the host.
From Chín and Máchín should he horse demand,

A hundred thousand more will come to hand.
Nothing from anyone he now desires,
For he has food and men when he requires."
He held his Indian sword: they spoke and then
He slew those haughty, simple-hearted men.

Asfandyár now gains entrance into the castle in the disguise of a merchant, determined, after finding that in consequence of its great strength it will take him years to subdue, to take it by stratagem. He accordingly has a hundred camels prepared, of which ten are laden with gold, five with Chinese brocades, and five with miscellaneous jewels and valuables. On the remaining eighty there are placed eighty pairs of chests, each chest containing one of his own warriors. On approaching the castle he is met by the Turanian nobles, anxious to buy, but refuses to display his goods until he is admitted into the presence of Arjásp, who receives him and assigns him a large building inside the castle in which to place his merchandise. Arjásp the next day questions him as to what people say in Irán of Asfandyár and Kargasár. Asfandyár tells him the various rumours afloat on the subject, and the conversation ends with Arjásp's saying that if an eagle passed the seven stages necessary to reach the castle they might call him a demon and not a man. Asfandyár remains some time selling for a *diram* what was worth a *dinár*, and is recognised by his two sisters, who have been set to perform menial services such as carrying water. They, however, keep his secret, and he proposes to the king to give a grand entertainment, which he is allowed to prepare on the inner ramparts, as well as to light a large fire. This he has arranged beforehand with Bashotan is to be a signal for attacking the castle with the whole army, and appearing at its head as if he were Asfandyár. The alarm being given, the Turánian troops issue with Kahram at their head, and a great battle takes place. Meanwhile Asfandyár opens the chests in which his warriors are hidden, and gives them arms and food, and divides them into three bodies, one to attack the interior of the fortress, one to go to the gates, and one to put an end to the chiefs whom he had intoxicated at his entertainment. Asfandyár himself goes with twenty men to attack the palace of Arjásp.

Clothed with cuirass then bold did he repair
To Arjásp's palace, with a lion's air.
In the *sarai** resounded there his shout ;
Humai, the noble, then came running out,
Her sister Beh-Afrid, too, did she bring,
He saw two veiled ones like the early spring.
Thus to his sisters did the hero say :
"Quick as the dust do ye two flee away.
Go to the market, where my way is, too;
Much gold and silver there is there to view.
And there remain ye till this fight is done,
My head is given or my crown is won."
He turned his face when he had said his say,
And vengeful tow'rds the palace took his way.
His Indian sword in hand again he drew,
And all the nobles that he saw he slew.
Such was the state of that illustrious place,
That to the palace he no road could trace.
With wounded there and dead men lying round,
The ground just like a troubled sea he found.
Awoke from sleep, Arjásp became aware
How great the noise: his heart was filled with care,
And from his couch of rest then leaping down,
Put on his *khaftán* and his Rúmi crown.
His mouth was full of sound, his heart of blood;

*The female apartments.

In hand a sharpened dagger, there he stood.
Held in his hand, then, the well-tempered blade,
The brave Asfandyár an onslaught made.
"From me, the merchant man," this was his cry:
"For many *dínárs* swords thou now canst buy.
A present here I bring thee from Lehrásp,
Which has been sealed with signet of Gushtásp.
If thou take this, thy heart will fill with blood,
And black beneath the dust be thy abode."
To Asfandyár Arjásp then clinging tight,
Beyond bounds went between the two the fight.
From blows of dagger and of sword they bled,
At times their middle and at times their head.
At last from wounds Arjásp so feeble grew,
No place from wounds free on his form one knew.
His elephantine body fell as dead,
And then Asfandyár cut off his head.
When Arjásp's life was thus brought to its close,
Up from the women's palace shouts arose.
Of the revolving sphere such is the style,
It honey gives, but poison, too, awhile.
Then on this fleeting world why fix thy heart?
Grieve not thyself: thou know'st thou must depart.
If thou a monarch or a warrior be,
The world is thus superior to thee.
Asfandyár with Arjásp finished all;
To Saturn rose smoke up then from the hall.
Then blazing torches bade he them to light,
And set the hall on ev'ry side alight.
The women to the eunuchs handed he,
And there was there no brightness more to see.
He placed his seal upon the treasure door,
And there remained to fight him no one more.
He to the stable came and mounted there;
An Indian sword grasped in his hand to bear.

Of Arab horses his selection made,
A saddle to put on his servants bade.
There went with him a hundred and three score,
Selected horsemen and all known in war.
When all his sisters were on horseback placed,
Forward the host from Arjásp's palace faced.
Of the Iránis some men of renown
Were in the fort with Sávah settled down.
"Out of the fort," he said, "when we shall go,
I and my warriors, to the plain below,
Against the Turks see that ye close the gate,
And may good fortune on me ever wait!
Whenever ye may be convinced that I
Myself have reached that famous company,
The sentry's cry should make the echo ring:
'The crown's renewed now of Gushtásp the king!'
If many of the army in their flight
Should reach this fortress from the place of fight,
The Turkish king's head from the sentry's post
Ye should throw down before the coming host."
He also bade them that the watchman there
Should from the fortress crying rend the air:
"Victorious is great Asfandyár;
The Turkish king's head he cut off in war."
Arjásp himself then in the dust he threw,
To brighten up Gushtásp's name and renew.
Hastened the hero forward once again,
Killing all those he met with in the plain.
Came from the fort a hundred and three score
Excited, shouting, to the field of war.
As to Bashotan's army he drew near,
From ev'ry mouth his praises rang out clear;
And with astonishment was moved the host
That such a youth such bravery could boast
When of dark night three watches past had flown,

The moon then sat upon its silver throne.
The watchman with a loud voice shouting cried:
"With victory is Gushtásp glorified.
Now may Asfandyár's youth never end,
Fortune, the heav'ns and moon him e er befriend!
For Lehrásp to avenge Arjásp's own head
He severed and himself to glory led.
In dust the king down from his throne he threw
Gushtásp's name and his fortune to renew."
When on this wise the Turks the shouting hear,
At once towards the sound they turn their ear.
Hearing the sentry Kahram dismal grew,
And at the voice his soul was dazed anew.
This hearing, to Andaríman he cried:
"In the dark night a voice one can not hide.
What say'st thou as to what may be this night?
Our counsel it behoves us to set right.
Who's dared his lip to open in this way
In the dark night just where the monarch lay?
Why jokes the watchman in the day of fight,
Of heroes' warfare making thus so light?
If in our own house be our enemy,
Then in the day may strangers also see.
For these ill words that omen ill contain,
Let us with mace of ill beat out his brain."
Still with those words resounds the sentry's cry
That Kahram's wakeful heart is wounded by.
And of such cries that echoed all around,
The haughty warriors' ears received the sound.
Exclaimed the host then: "There is too much sound
The sentry's cries are now beyond all bound.
First let us from the house drive out the foe,
And then this host shall our enchantments know."
But Kahram's heart the cry distressing now,
With a dark frown is wrinkled up his brow.

He to his army cries: "This host will bring
Great sorrow to my heart anent the king.
But now without a doubt return must we:
Thereafter know I not what there will be."
The nobles at his words were sore distressed,
And from the battle field at night all pressed.
Behind them came Asfandyár apace,
Clothed in his armour, with his bull-head mace.
As Kahram to the fortress gate drew near,
The host of the Iranis he saw there.
"And now with bold Asfandyár," he cried,
"To fight a battle what is left beside?
Now from their sheaths your swords must draw ye all,
And on your daggers with a message call."
But fortune on its brow now wore a frown,
And on the heroes looked Fate harshly down.
And the two armies, thus enraged again,
Blows on each other's heads began to rain.
Thus this went on until appeared the dawn,
And China's nobles' day had nearer drawn.
The warriors of Asfandyár came down
Upon that monarch's fortress of renown.
The severed head, then, of the king Arjásp,
Of him who shed the blood of great Lehrásp,
Before the army down they quickly threw,
And from the fight the Turks at once withdrew.
From the Turanian host arose a cry,
And all from off their heads their crowns laid by.
Then of Arjásp the two sons loudly wept,
As if on both of them the fire had swept.
The army knew to what the matter came,
And of the war on whom to cast the blame.
"Oh woe!" and "O thou leader brave!" they said
"O lion hero, who our hosts hast led!
He who has killed thee, may he too be slain!

With him may evil fortune e'er remain!
To whom must we give up our families,
Over our right wing, too, the flag that flies?
And as our monarch now has left the throne,
Be gone, our crown! Our army, too, be gone!"
From Khalakh to Turáz all full of pain,
Now naught but death the army needs again.
All forward pressed in death who would not fail,
Each wore his helmet and his coat of mail.
From battle field the tumult rose anew:
Like a black cloud the air then blackened grew.
In every place there lay a heap of dead;
From ev'ry one good fortune there had fled.
Heads from their bodies on the plain were hewn,
In other places hands and maces strewn.
Up to the castle gates were waves of blood.
His right hand or his left who understood?

The capture of Kahram, son of Arjásp, by Asfandyár and his placing him on the gallows.

When Asfandyár came forward from his place,
The general's feet held Kahram in embrace.
The warriors in such way mingled came,
Thou would'st have said their bodies were the same.
Of Kahram's girdle Tuhamtan laid hold,
And lifted him (Oh, wondrous to behold!):
Raised from the ground, him on the earth he cast:
The army sang his praises loud and fast.
They held him in contempt, his two arms tied.
The famous host was scattered far and wide.
He threw him on the ground as him he raised,
While his great deed the army loudly praised.
Maces were raining down as if it hailed,
Ground strewn with helmets, and grim death prevailed.
Fell heads from sword-storm as from trees leaves thrown,

One lost his goods, another won a throne,
By waves of blood the field was overflown,
One head 'neath hoofs lay, and one wore a crown.
None ever can the world's desire know well,
For what is secret it will never tell,
Then he who had a tall horse fled away:
Out of the dragon's mouth none found his way.
Of Chinese Turks but few were left behind,
But those who were of no repute they'd find.
Helmets and breastplates all away they threw,
And filled their eyes with blood-red tears anew.
Then running to Asfandyár they came;
Like the new spring their eyes were all aflame.
Their leader unjust blood to shed inclined,
The host towards injustice had a mind.
No quarter was to heroes there allowed,
And of the wounded there were slain a crowd
None of the Chinese heroes there were left,
Turán of all its princes was bereft.
Enclosures and the tents they bore away,
The dead men held the place as there they lay
At the fort gate they raised two gallows tall,
And from these gallows let two nooses fall.
Andarímán inverted there he hung,
His brother living from the gallows swung,
He sent his men to ev'ry place around.
Where you would say that people could be found.
With fire them all he ordered to burn down,
And in Turán he threw down every town.
Of horseman in Turán there was no trace,
No man of note remained there in his place.
A black cloud had arisen, thou hadst said,
And fire upon the battle field had shed.
And when of this the king saw every sign,
He called the leaders and demanded wine.

Asfandyár now writes to Gushtásp a letter announcing his victory, and receives a letter from him in reply, congratulating him on having avenged his grandfather, exhorting him to clemency, and directing him to return to Irán. Asfandyár, after distributing rewards to his troops, and burning and destroying Rúin diz, takes with him his sisters and 10,000 camels loaded with spoil. He hands over the command of his army to his three young sons, and returns by the road of the seven stages by which he had gone. He hunts on the the borders of Irán till his sons and the army overtake him; whence he proceeds to meet Gushtásp, by whom and by all the people he is joyfully welcomed, and fêted accordingly. The Section containing a description of these events ends with a forecast of the death of Asfandyár at the hands of Rústam.

Arrived at the palace, Asfandyár sees his mother Kitayún and declares to her that if Gushtásp, when he claims the fulfilment of his promise to yield him up the throne after he has avenged Lehrásp and found his sisters, does not fulfil it, he will place the crown on his own head, and partition out the land to the Iránís. She warns him against doing so, and he leaves her exclaiming against himself for telling his secret to any woman. Gushtásp hears of the idea of Asfandyár and summons his astrologers to consult with them on the matter. Gamrásp informs him that Asfandyár will meet his death in Zabulistán at the hands of Rústam. On the next day in a grand assembly of the nobles and others Asfandyár, relating his exploits, asks for the fulfilment of the king's promise. In reply the king directs him to proceed to Zabulistán and bring before him Rústam, who is the only man who is capable of opposing him, and that on his doing so he will not dispute the matter any more, but hand his power over to him. Asfandyár remonstrates, but finally submits to the king's command. He says that he requires no army to take with him, as when the hour of death has arrived one can not hinder it by force. His mother entreats her son not to go. He decides, however, that he must obey the orders of the king, and take his sons with him in order to train them, and goes off accordingly. Bad omens meet him on the road, and he sends Bahman as an ambassador on to Rústam to endeavour to persuade him to come to Court of his own free will to render an account of his alleged delinquencies in the way of not attending him, and being too proud and shutting himself up in his own distant territories, and to bring with him Zúarah, Farámúrz and others. On the road Bahman meets Zál, who does homage to him, but the former, desirous of carrying out his orders, insists upon being conducted at once to Rústam, who is engaged in the chase. To him Bahman delivers his message, and in reply Rústam reminds him of the great deeds that he has done for Irán, and refusing to go in a humble way without his army asks the king to come to Zábulistán and enjoy his hospitality. Bahman returns with the answer, and in the meanwhile Rústam consults Zuárah and Farámurz as to the situation, and the former assures him there is no fear of any unpleasantness, as Asfandyár is a noble and brave man. Bahman informs Asfandyár of what has occurred, and tells him that Rústam is coming as far as the Hírmand unarmed in order to meet him. Rústam comes across the river accordingly, and meeting Asfandyár salutes him amicably and the two embrace. Rústam begs that he will come and visit him, but Asfandyár replies that he must carry out the orders of the king, and Rústam must come with his feet in irons, as they will not dishonour him: the result will be that all blame in the matter will rebound upon the king himself, whom he himself is forced to obey against his own inclination. Rústam refuses to submit to the disgrace of putting himself in irons or that of having his hospitality refused. Asfandyár points out to him the orders of the king, and that he will be forced to attack him, for if he disobeys those orders his place in the next world will be in the fire. He invites him, however, to drink wine with him. Rústam accepts this invitation and retires, ostensibly to change his travelling dress, saying that he will await his summons to come and eat with him. Meanwhile Asfandyár sees his General Bashutan, and notwithstanding his advice does not summon Rústam to dinner, although the latter waits for him. When the hour is passed Rústam goes back to Asfandyár to reproach him for not having sent for him, and telling him that he has too high an opinion of himself and his position, reminds him of the grand deeds he (Rústam) has done. Asfandyár excuses himself by saying he had not wished Rústam to come so far on a hot day to fatigue himself. He then offers him a cup of wine and a place to sit on his left hand, which he refuses, as well as one on his right, which is offered instead. Finally a golden seat in front of the throne is given him, and he takes it angrily. Asfandyár begins to depreciate the antecedents of the family, bringing up the story of *Zál's* white hair, and his having been brought up by the Símúrgh, and Rústam replying stands up for them and magnifies his own deeds, and finally squeezes Asfandyár's hand until the blood gushes out at his finger nails. They drink and eat together, and each tells the other what he will do with him when they come to fight. On parting Rústam again invites Asfandyár to go home with him, but he replies by telling him not to sow a seed that will not germinate, and repeating the orders of the king. After mutual recriminations and threats Rústam returns home. Bashutan advises Asfandyár against the encounter with

Rústam, but Asfandyár will not give in. Rústam, arrived at home, sends for his arms, and Dastán remonstrates with him, saying that if he dies there will be neither earth nor water, neither high nor low in Zábulistán, and if Asfandyár perishes his glory will fade as well for having killed a king of Irán: that he had better bribe Asfandyár's army to retire. Rústam replies by pointing out the great deeds he had done, and that he is still a vassal of Irán: that he will not wound or kill Asfandyár, but will force him to come and accept his hospitality, and will afterwards take him back to Irán and seat him on Gushtásp's throne, which he will uphold with all his might. Zál answers him that he cannot speak in that light way of a king with an army at his back, and prays God to avert misfortune from them.

Rústam the next day puts on his armour and orders Zuárah to array his troops, whilst he himself goes on and crosses the Hírmand towards the Iránian camp. He mounts on to a height and announces his arrival to Asfandyár, who appears, and will not listen to Rústam's appeal not to force on a battle. The two then commence the combat alone, resorting after fighting with lances, swords and maces to their lassos, which they throw round each other's necks and pull against each other. Meanwhile a fight takes place between the Iránians and Rústam's army, and two of Asfandyár's sons are killed by Zuárah and Farámurz, and Bahman rushes up to Asfandyár in the midst of his combat with Rústam to tell him what has happened. Asfandyár reproaches Rústam, who disavows the slaughter, and promises to deliver Zuárah and Farámurz to be punished, but Asfandyár declares that this would be to avenge a peacock by killing the serpent, and the fight is continued with bows and arrows. Of these sixty wound Rústam and his horse Rakhsh: the former dismounts and flees to the top of a hill, while the latter crosses the river and goes back to the camp. Rústam refuses to mount Zuárah's horse, which the latter comes to offer him, and sends him off to Zál to procure medicine for his arrow wounds, and to try to save Rakhsh, acknowledging that even if he is himself cured he will be as weak as a new-born child. Asfandyár in the meanwhile taunts Rústam and exhorts him to do as the king had commanded. Rústam replies that it is too late in the day to continue the fight, and he will retire and try to get his wounds healed, after which he will be prepared to do what he is ordered. Asfandyár sees his ruse, but nevertheless lets him off for the night, and Rústam escapes across the river. The former returns to the camp, and sends his dead sons to the king in golden shrouds, reproaching him as the cause of their death.

When Rústam arrives his wounds are attended to, and he threatens to go away the next day to where Asfandyár cannot find him, but Zál recommends him to invoke the assistance of the Símúrgh. He goes up on to a high mountain and there burns three chafing dishes full of fire with a feather in it. The bird arrives, and Zál tells him the state of affairs, and at his desire Rústam and Rakhsh are sent for up to the hill. The bird closes the wounds and sucks out the blood, and after he has rubbed them with his wings Rústam regains his strength, and is ordered not to exert himself for a week, rubbing the wounds in the meanwhile with one of the bird's feathers dipped in milk. Rakhsh's wounds are also healed. The Símúrgh also tells him there would be no disgrace in bowing before Asfandyár, for if his hour had come he would disdain his excuses. Rústam would be provided with the means of excuse in any fight that took place after this. Rústam promises obedience, and is informed by the bird as a secret from heaven that whoever killed Asfandyár would become the prey of destiny and meet with misfortune both in this world and the next. The Símúrgh allows him to approach, rubs his head with his wing, and points out to him a tamarisk, of which he was to select the longest and most delicate branch and make an arrow of it; with this was bound up the fate of Asfandyár, and by that arrow he would perish. He was to try to induce Asfandyár by soft words, not to engage in combat but if he refused to listen the arrow soaked in wine was to be shot straight into his eyes. He was to remain perfectly calm when he did this and have no feeling of anger against his opponent.

Early in the morning Rústam prays to God, puts on his armour, and advancing, calls out to Asfandyár to awaken from his sleep. Asfandyár on appearing, taunts and threatens him, but Rústam obeys the Símúrgh's instructions and tries to soothe him. Asfandyár rejects his offers, although Rústam offers all kinds of treasure and inducement to him to put anger out of his heart. Rústam accordingly prays to God, and shoots the arrow into Asfandyár's eye, and the latter falls, and is picked up by Bahman and Bashutan. In dying Asfandyár calls Rústam, who is greatly distressed, to him, and tells him his death is not due to Rústam or the Símúrgh, but to the action of his own father Gushtásp in ordering him to go and destroy Nímrúz and Seistan. He hands Bahman over to him to take to Zábulistán and make happy there, and Rústam accepts the charge. Asfandyár sends touching messages to his father, mother, and sisters and dies. Zuárah tries to persuade Rústam not to accept the charge of Bahman, but he keeps his promise to Asfandyár. Asfandyár's body is sent to Gushtásp, who bewails him. The nobles, however, curse him and leave the palace. The mother and sisters of Asfandyár load his horse with reproaches and cover him with dust. Bashutan also puts their misdeeds before Gushtásp and

Jámásp, and Humai, and Beh-Afríd also join with the rest in charging Gushtásp with the death of Asfandyár, until he orders Bashutan to throw water on their *infantile fire.* Bashutan consoles the mother with the thought that her son had gone to Paradise, and she acknowledges the justice of God. For a whole year the habitations of Iran resound with lamentations, and for many years tears were shed over the arrow.

Bahman meanwhile remains in Zábulistán, being educated under the eye of Rústam. Rústam writes a letter to Gushtásp setting forth the efforts he had made to deter Asfandyár from the fatal combat, and Bashutan on the arrival of the letter bears witness to its truth. His heart accordingly becomes softened towards Rústam, and he writes him a letter acknowledging all his good qualities, and offering to bestow upon him more thrones and signets, more helmets and swords, in addition to India and Kanúj, which he already had. The message is conveyed to Rústam, and all his sorrow is changed to joy. In answer to Rústam's letter, he writes to Bahman, who in the meanwhile has grown tall, strong, and intelligent, to return to Irán. Rústam presents Bahman with jewels, slaves, and other valuable gifts, and accompanies him for two stages on his way back. On Bahman's return Gushtásp gives him the name of Ardashír.

The next Section contains a eulogy on Sultan Mahmúd, and commences the story of Rústam's being killed through the deceit of Shaghád. The account is said to be taken from an old book in the possession of one Azádah, of Marv. On the birth to Zál by a slave girl of a son the astrologers discover by the stars that when the boy grows up he will destroy the race of Sám, son of Narimán. He is given the name of Shaghád, and when grown up he is sent to the king of Kábul and appears to have become his son-in-law. Rústam was in the habit of exacting every year the tribute of a cow's hide from Kábul by way of acknowledgment of suzerainty, and the king was greatly disappointed at its being still exacted, notwithstanding the relationship thus established between them. Shaghád accordingly plots with the king of Kábul against Rústam, and the plan arranged is that a feast should be given at which the king should pretend to insult Shaghád, and the latter should go away to Zábulistán and complain. With the idea that Rústam would at once start to avenge the insult, they were to establish a hunting-ground on the way with pits filled with swords in them into which Rústam and Rakhsh might fall. The plan is carried out. The king goes out to meet Rústam on pretence of begging pardon for his offence with regard to the tribute, and entices him to the hunting-ground. Both Rústam and Zuárah fall into the pits, out of one of which Rústam, wounded by the hidden swords, manages to scramble and to kill Shaghád for his treachery, before he and Zuárah both die. One of the horsemen of the party escapes and informs Zál. Rústam and Zuárah and Rakhsh are buried; Farámurz leads out an army, kills the king of Kábul by casting him into one of the pits dug for Rústam, puts to death forty others of his idolatrous relatives, and burning the body of Shaghád takes his ashes to give to Dastán. Rudábah goes mad with grief, and is only prevented from eating a dead snake she finds in the water of the kitchen by one of her slaves; she, however, recovers her reason and eats proper food when it is put before her, and prays God to accord Rústam's soul a place in Paradise, and let him enjoy the fruit of what he had sown on earth. Finally Gushtásp gives up his throne and treasures to Bahman and dies.*

* This ends the 4th Volume of Mohl's translation.

Bahman, called Daráz-dast (long-hand) now mounts the throne and assembles an army in order to avenge Asfandyár, and invades Seistán. From the Hirmand he sends a messenger to Dastán, the son of Sám, who explains all the circumstances of the deaths of Asfandyár and his two sons and offers to give him up all the treasures of Dastán and Sám if he will forego his vengeance. The messenger gives the message and pleads for Zál, whom, when he comes in an attitude of humility, Bahman nevertheless loads with chains. Hearing of this on the borders of Búst, Farámurz assembles an army and marches against Bahman; in the battle that ensues he is wounded, and, being taken prisoner, is brought before Bahman, who hangs him head downwards on a gallows and has him shot to death with arrows. Bashutan now pleads with Bahman for a cessation of the burnings and plunderings that have been ordered in Zábulistán, as well as for Zál. Bahman repents and releases him from the captivity in which Rudábah is mourning for him, and has Farámurz buried.

Bahman (Ardashír) now marries his daughter, Humai, to his son Sásán, a connection which appears to have been allowed by the Pehlavi religion, and when she is six months gone in pregnancy seats her on his throne in the presence of his nobles and appoints as his successor her anticipated offspring, whether son or daughter. Sásán on hearing this is greatly aggrieved and goes off to Nishapur.*. The reason is not given, but it is presumably because he is to be superseded on the throne by his own child. He obtains in marriage the daughter of one of the nobles, and she bears him a son to whom he also gives the name of Sásán, and apparently dies soon afterwards.

* From the confused manner in which all this is told and what follows it appears not impossible that Bahman himself was the father of the child, and not Sásán.

Bahman dies, and Humái succeeds to the throne and reigns for 32 years. She gives out that she will rule in all equity and make her people happy. Her child is born secretly (no reason is alleged for this concealment), and, being given to a wet nurse, is alleged to have died. Eight months pass, and on the child's beginning to resemble the deceased king she orders a chest to be made for it of fine wood, which is covered with bitumen and musk, lined with Rúmi brocade, and otherwise adorned. The child is placed in it and is committed to the Euphrates, whence it is rescued by a washerman, and brought up by him and his wife. They give him the name of Dáráb, appropriating the pearls and other things that were in the box. The boy grows up into a noble and powerful youth and disdains his reputed father's occupation of washing clothes, and is accordingly brought up to a knowledge of the sciences and the accomplishments of a warrior. He at the point of the sword exacts from the washerman's wife a true account of the manner in which he was found in a box in the river, and makes her give him sufficient of what had been in the box to buy a horse and arms. He now goes to the Commandant of the frontier, when he is seen and admired by his own mother, who has organised an expedition against the Rúmís (Greeks) who were devastating the frontier. The Commandant is killed in battle, and one Rashnavád appointed in his place. Humai reviews his forces and is struck by Dáráb's noble bearing. A storm comes on, and both Rashnavád and Dáráb take refuge in an old ruin. The former passing by it hears a voice saying to the ruin, "Close not the eye of prudence, for thou shelterest the son of king Ardashír." His men enter and find Dáráb asleep; he is roused and comes out, and the ruin at once crashes together and falls to pieces. Rashnavád gives him a complete outfit, and assigning to him the command of the advanced guard, marches against the enemy, in the meanwhile summoning the washerman and his wife. Dáráb attacks the enemy and shows prodigies of valour, kills 40 priests (Jásalík, καθολικος), and brings a Cross that he had captured. On the next day the Greeks are completely routed, and send gifts and offers of tribute. On returning from the battle-field Rashnavád and Dáráb come to the ruin, where the washerman and his wife had arrived, and hear from them the full account of Dáráb's being found with the jewels in the box. A letter is written to Humái, who comes, and, recognizing her son, places him on the throne. The washerman and his wife are richly rewarded and resume their own occupation. Dáráb is said to have reigned twelve years. The first Section relating to his reign describes the building of the town of Dárábgadh, the finding of a deep lake among the hills and bringing of a canal from it to irrigate all (? the neighbouring) countries; it also notes the erection of a fire temple on the crest of the hills to which all the fire worshippers resorted. He sends his armies on all sides to clear the country of enemies and evil-designed men. The next Section relates an incursion of 100,000 Arabs into Irán under a leader called Shuäib; he is killed, his army dispersed, and many horses and other booty are secured.

At that time one Filkús* was king of Rúm, an ally of the king of Rús (? Russia†). Being informed by him that Dáráb was leading an army against him, he assembles an army at Amúríyah and advances. In three days two battles take place, and on the fourth day Filkús and his army take to flight, and the former's wife and children are taken prisoners, a part of the army only

* Philip of Macedon.

† Given by Mohl as Sus.

escaping to Amúriyah. Peace is now made with Filkús, who gives Dáráb his daughter Náhíd in marriage. She is sent together with the tribute (of which nothing has been said before) due from Rúm. The tribute is to consist of 10,000 golden eggs and other jewels of great value; each egg was to be of the weight of 40 *Mithkál.* Valuable presents are sent with her, and Dáráb conveys her to Irán. He soon discovers that her breath is bad, and is informed by physicians that there grows in Rúm a plant of the name of Iskandar, which will cure the ailment if rubbed on the palate. This is done and the breath is cured, but Dáráb cannot get over it, and sends her back to her father to Rúm, where she gives birth to Sikandar,* called after the herb by which her breath had been cured. The Kaiser takes from the first a great fancy to the child and to a mare that had thrown a foal on the same night, and treats the former as his own child. Dáráb after this had a son by another wife, who was given the name of Dara (Darius). When the child grew to the age of 12, Dáráb grew old and feeble, and, after nominating Dárá as his successor, dies. (We now come to the connection of the Greeks with Persia and the East.)

The death of Filkús and the ascension of Sikandar.

Just at this time when Filkús passed away,
Misfortune came to Rúm and heavy lay.
His grandsire's throne Sikandar then possessed,
Evil precluded, he e'er sought the best.
In Rúm a famous person then there dwelt,
In whom delight the whole of that land felt.
Both great and wise, Aristatlís† by name,

* Alexander the Great.
† Aristotle.

Alert, intelligent, and seeking fame.
He of pure counsel sought Sikandar's face,
And to unloose his tongue took fitting place.
He said to him : " O chief of happy fame,
Thou losest in this mode a glorious name.
I have been ev'rywhere that thou may'st say,
And need none on the earth to show the way.
Know this, most foolish that thou wilt appear,
If counsel of the wise thou dost not hear.
Earthy we are and to the earth were born,
And to the earth return at last forlorn.
If thou art good thy name will e'er endure;
Happy, of royal throne shalt thou be sure.
If ill thou doest evil shalt thou reap,
And no night on the earth shalt tranquil sleep.
Through goodness to a king is succour brought,
In bad days goodness may by none be sought."
Sikandar heard the words and much esteemed,
And prudent to him, too, the speaker seemed.
By his command he ruled his actions all,
In honour, combat, war and festival:
At ev'ry moment praising him anew,
And on the throne when seated ever knew.
One day it happened that an envoy came,
Upright of heart, an orator of fame.
From Dárá twas to Rúm the envoy came,
Tribute from ev'ry peopled land to claim.
When to Sikandar these words he addressed,
At that old tribute he was much distressed.
" Go now," he told him, " and to Dárá say:
The tribute's scent and hue have passed away.
The hen that laid the golden eggs has died,
And left no means the tribute to provide."
And when the envoy heard such words he feared,
And from Constantinople disappeared.

The leading of an army by Sikandar towards Irán and the preparation of Dárá for war with him.

Then did Sikandar call his host complete,
And these words that had passed to them repeat.
"The revolution of the heav'ns," he said:
"No man, however thoughtful, can evade.
All earth's face now must pass into my hand,
Its good and evil must I understand.
And now must all of you yourselves prepare
From country and from home your hearts to tear."
His grandsire's treasures thus he open laid,
And bade his army ready to be made.
Then of the horses in the desert found
The keepers drove in herds from all around.
Then all who were on foot on horseback rode,
And arms and money he on all bestowed.
At night in Rúm increasing uproar grew,
From town and palace of the leader new.
Behind Rúm's leader banners floated free,
Of azure lined and red embroidery.
On branching reeds did there the *Húma* sit,
"The loved one of the Cross" on which was writ.
Sikandar came to Egypt on the way,
With trump and drum, and army in array.
The king of Egypt with his vengeful host,
To meet him standing on the wall took post.
Two armies of each other came in sight,
Prepared for sev'n days face to face to fight.
Defeat upon the eighth on Egypt lay,
To them Sikandar had blocked ev'ry way.
So many captives were there on one way,
That powerless the captains' hands all lay.
Of horses, girths, and of the ponderous mace
Of golden Hindoo daggers and cuirass.
Of golden girdle and of silver rein,

Egyptian swords that golden sheaths contain,
Of *dínárs* and brocade so much was there,
And property the horses could not bear.
To ask for quarter many horsemen came,
Great men in war, and warriors of name.
Thence to invade Irán did he depart,
With hand of brave man and a lion's heart.
When Dárá heard that out of Rúm this band
Had been in movement set towards his land,
From Istakhar there started such a force
That their spears stayed the breezes in their course.
Tow'rds Rúm from Fárs to march was his desire,
And in that peopled realm to light a fire.
Over Euphrates when they came to pass,
The army in their count exceeded grass.
Along the bank through the cuirasses' sheen
The water of the river was not seen.
And when Sikandar heard the host was there,
To meet it on the road did he prepare.
Between the hosts two *farsangs* intervened;
Sikandar there his nobles all convened;
On ev'ry matter he with them conversed,
And all that Dárá said to them rehearsed.

The going of Sikandar on an Embassage to Dárá.

When his guides' words came to an end that day,
"No other counsel is there," did he say.
"But that as envoy I myself should go,
And more or less of him should seek to know."
Of royal gems a girdle then he sought,
A royal robe with choice embroidery wrought.
They brought to him a steed with golden rein,
His sword a golden scabbard to contain.
Ten of the Rúmi horsemen were his choice,
Who could both speak and listen to his voice.

From the host coming at the break of day
With ten interpreters he took his way.
And when that one of haughty mien he neared,
Alighting, he as suppliant appeared.
Near to himself him called Dárá the king,
Seated him down and asked of ev'rything.
The nobles stood around in humble pose,
And prayers for earthly blessings on him rose.
They praise him for his mien and lordly air,
And grand his stature and his grace declare.
As soon as he had sat he rose again
Sikandar's message rightly to explain.
First, blessings on the monarch he called down:
"For aye endure the head that wears the crown!
"O honoured one," Sikandar thus has said,
"To ev'ry place on earth whose will has spread,
I wish no warfare with the king this day,
Nor long in Irán's country to delay.
I wish to travel round the land awhile,
And with a sight of earth myself beguile.
Tow'rds rectitude and truth is my desire;
To lead Irán thou can'st alone aspire.
A little dust if thou begrudge me there,
Hand me not over, cloud-like, to the air.
In arms to come against me though inclined,
Thou knowest not my purpose or my mind.
If thou desirest war, then fight will I,
And without war this land will not pass by.
Choose for the battle now one special day:
Be firm, nor turn from thy desire away.
However great your army now may be,
I from your chieftains' war will never flee."
That heart and purpose Dárá knew aright,
And saw his eloquence, his grace, his height.
Dárá on ivory throne, thou would'st have said

Was sitting there with crown upon his head
He said to him: "What is thy name and race,
For thou hast ev'ry sign of royal grace?
In stature than a slave thou'rt more erect;
Thou art Sikandar's self, I now suspect.
With such a mien and stature for thine own,
The spheres have surely meant thee for a throne.
"Neither in peace nor yet in war," he said,
"Such act to do would any one be led.
Not few the orators at his gate found,
With crown of wisdom who might not be crowned.
Where is the monarch, of assemblies lord,
As his own envoy who would bring his word?
Such wisdom does Sikandar not possess
That he ancestral ways should thus transgress.
The message that my chief has giv'n to me,
That word, O king, have I conveyed to thee."
According to his rank and station there
A fitting place they now for him prepare.
The lord of Irán when a tray was laid,
"Bring here the hero" to those near him said.
At once then the ambassador was called,
And in the place for envoys was installed.
Finished the meal, the banquet they renew,
Calling for wine, song, and the singers, too.
Sikandar drinking luscious wine with zest,
Went on to place the wine cup in his breast.
And as the wine cups went on circling round
The taking of these passed beyond all bound.
To Dárá the cupbearer went to say:
"The Rúmi has those cups all borne away."
They both then ask him at the king's desire:
"Those cups for wine why dost thou now require?"
And the cupbearers said to him again:
"Those golden cups why dost thou now retain?"

Sikandar answered : "Thou of honoured name,
The cup as the ambassador's I claim.
Should such the custom of Irán, though, be
Take the gold cup to the king's treasury."
Then at his customs laughed, amused, the king,
And a cup full of jewels bade them bring,
And place it in his hand "a ruby red
In the same manner place upon his head."
Collectors of Rúm's tribute were at hand,
Who wandered ev'rywhere throughout the land.
They came from outside where the banquet lay,
And to the king took gracefully their way.
The envoy* as Sikandar's face he knew,
With praises to the monarch nearer drew.
"This is the Kaiser's self," to him he said,
"Who sits with mace and crown upon his head.
As soon to us as gave the king command,
We started off the tribute to demand.
Enraged, he treated us with great despite,
And with us then engaged in wordy fight.
Out of his kingdom when I took to flight
I urged the horses through the darksome night.
Any like him in Rúm we have not seen,
And he has boldly come upon this scene.
Now will his mighty army thee enfold,
Thy throne, thy crown as well, thy treasured gold."
And when the king heard what the envoy said,
He tow'rds Sikandar more attention paid.
Sikandar knew what in this secret way
To the world's ruler there they had to say,
He stayed till day was darkening into night,
And Westward sank what gives the world its light.
To the camp guard-house did he then proceed,
And boldly then approach his waiting steed.

*He who had been sent to Rúm to demand the tribute by Gushtásp.

To his own horsemen there around he said,
All men of name and to high fortune wed.
"Upon my horse must now my life depend,
If laziness he shows, all's at an end."
All urged their coursers to their utmost speed,
And fled before the monarch in their need.
When Dárá saw no more his crown and head,
He into darkness disappeared and fled.
A watchman summoning, he bade him go
At once to the encampment of the foe.
Gone him they found, good watch his heart had kept,
And of the king himself the fortune slept.
After him quickly Dárá horsemen sent;
A thousand brave men, seeking combat, went.
Like the wind coursing, followed they behind,
But in dark night his road they could not find.
The vanguard saw him and then turned them back,
Pain only finding on the weary track.
When to his own camp, thus, Sikandar came,
Scared were the Rúmi warriors of name.
At night they saw the king come, glad at soul,
And in his arms clasped, full of gems, a bowl.
His warriors he addressed: "As willows free,
At this good omen now rejoiced be ye.
The triumph of my life is in this bowl,
And the stars even lie in my control.
For I have reckoned up his army, too,
His horsemen than we hear are far more few.
Be for the combat now your swords all bared,
And for the desert be your heads prepared.
If in the fight your bodies suffer pain,
Both joy and treasure shall ye thereby gain.
The world's Creator coming to my aid,
The very stars in my embrace are laid."
Round him his nobles all applauding stand,

"May for the Kaiser prosperous be the land!
Devoted soul and body both to thee,
This shall our everlasting compact be:
That kings should be allied with thee is right,
In manliness and valour in thy sight."

The fight of Dárá with Sikandar, and defeat of Dárá.

From the crow's back raised up the sun its head,
Like brilliant lamp on earth its rays were spread.
The earth raised from its head its pitchy sheet:
Together Dárá's host began to meet.
Then from Euphrates' bank his host was led,
Thicker than grass upon the desert spread.
And when Sikandar heard the host had come,
Forward he led his troops to beat of drum.
With Hindoo daggers and cuirasses bright,
With horses and their girths prepared for fight,
With warlike weapons, warriors on each side,
Hills were as dust, the land like rivers' tide.
Two hosts opposing into line were brought,
And the sun brilliance from their daggers caught.
In the host's fronts the elephants advanced,
And brightly as the stream of Nile earth glanced.
With elephants in front, horse in the rear,
The heart forsook the soul, of death in fear.
Shouted for blood, thou would'st have said, the air,
And at its shouting earth stood boiling there.
With Indian drum and with the trumpets' blare,
The heart of ev'ry man was in despair.
With noise of horses and the leaders' cry,
And with the heavy maces rattling by,
A hill of war, thou would'st have said, earth grew,
With dust the sky assumed the *Zanzgis** hue.
For a whole week the warriors seeking fight,

* People of Zanzibar.

Stood of each other face to face in sight.
On the eighth day a dark'ning dust there flew,
So that the sun itself was turned to blue.
The army of Irán its face concealed,
And saw but dust upcn the battle field.
Dárá, the king, his face then turning back,
Warriors of fame all followed in his track.
The army to Euphrates' stream again
Came fleeing backwards from the battle plain.
Raging, Sikandar's army them pursue,
The one rejoiced, the other full of rue.
Sikandar on the river's bank again
Arrived ; countless Iránis there were slain.
Back from its edge he made the army stand,
None were to cross the stream, by his command.
Triumphant came he to the field of war,
Where with his chosen troops he was before.

The second battle of Dárá with Sikandar, and defeat of Dárá.

When Dárá from Sikandar fled away,
On no side did he let his horse delay.
From Irán and Turán the Chiefs he called,
Money disbursed and paymasters installed.
The army he restored by next full moon,
And filled his nobles' heads with wind full soon.
He crossed the river from this side again,
And ranged his army on the open plain.
Sikandar marched his army when he heard,
Left goods behind and to advance preferred.
When the two armies face to face then met,
For battle both the earth and age were set.
For three whole days the battle onward drew,
And with the slain the place too narrow grew.
Sikandar was victorious again.

His lofty star lit up of earth the plain.
His army fled, but Dárá in the fight
Preferred the dust to a disgraceful flight.
Of the Iránis many now were slain,
The monarch's fortune was reversed again.
Of sun and moon's assistance in the lack,
In pain he turned him from the battle back.
Like dust Sikandar then behind him came,
Oft calling on the World-Creator's name.
Before the host was proclamation made:
"O wretched men who from the path have strayed,
From me there is no fear of pain for you,
For with my army ye have nought to do.
Remain safe in your own halls evermore,
To God your souls and bodies giving o'er.
Although in blood your hands imbrued may be,
From Rúmis soul and body ye are free."
When to the army thus he gave his grace,
They to the Rúmis turned a willing face.
Sikandar came then to the battle ground,
And all the plunder there was heaped around.
This on the soldiers freely he bestowed,
And the whole army there in freshness glowed.
Awhile upon the battle field they stayed,
The king and soldiers there to rest delayed.
To Chehram did Dárá the king repair,
For of his treasures all the key was there.
There all the Chiefs in women's clothing came,
Heated, in anguish, full of grief and shame.
The father wailed, his son who could not see,
The son, his father lost, in misery.
In Irán ev'ry city full of woe,
The tears from ev'ry eye like hail would flow
To Itakhar from Chehram then he came.
Which was the boast of all free men of name

Envoys were then sent out on ev'ry side,
To ev'ry Pehlaván with name of pride.
The army gathered in the royal hall,
And there to sit they brought in chairs for all.
When Dárá sat upon his golden chair,
Warriors who served the king assembled there.
To the Iránis then: "O chiefs," he cried,
"Warriors of wisdom, lions in your pride,
What counsel is there now in this affair?"
He spoke and wept in anguish and despair.
"To die with good name were a better choice,"
He said, "than live while Rúmis all rejoice.
My royal ancestors while they were here
Have all exacted tribute ev'ry year.
Rúm was despised by us in every way,
But black all freemen's fortune is this day.
Sikandar in the kingdom rules alone,
And he has seized as well the crown and throne.
It will not so remain: soon cometh he
And our whole *Fars** a sea of blood will be,
Captive becoming child and man and wife,
Nor youth nor old man may remain in life.
In this if ye my friends will still remain,
This evil I may drive back and this pain.
This mob were of our nobles all the prey,
In fear from Irán's cities driv'n away.
We are the prey now, they the panthers are:
We are the fugitives in ev'ry war.
If back to back ye will all firmly stand,
We shall not fail to seize upon the land.
He in this war who cowardice displays
On his own soul but greater hardship lays.
No hope can in the world there henceforth be
That Rúm is as Zuhák and Jamshíd we."

* A province of Persia, often used to designate the whole country.

Thus spoke he, weeping, his heart full of rue:
His cheeks were pallid and his lips waxed blue.
His learned great men then arose at once,
Prepared, all ready with but one response.
Rose Irán's shout, but with a mournful ring.
" We would not have the earth without our king.
We all will turn our face towards the fight,
And for our foes make all the world too tight
For all our skirts together we will tie,
And gain the land, or in the dust will lie.'
Dárá to these words listened from the crowd,
And knew their hearts in war as mountains proud.
Money and arms he gave then to the host,
And all who in the land a name could boast.

The third fight of Dárá with Sikandar and the flight of Dárá to Kirmán.

Sikandar of his doings was aware,
That Dárá sat upon his moon-throne there.
His army from Irák he brought and pressed,
And in the name of God Almighty blessed.
His army neither middle had nor end,
Nor did for Dárá fortune good portend.
A force to meet him then the king prepared,
And many troops from Istakhar repaired.
Thou would'st have said, the earth these would not bear,
Nor for the heav'n was any passage there.
Drew up their lines the kings of either land,
With spear and mace and dagger in their hand.
The shout from the two armies one might hear
As if the spheres split of the sky the ear.
With blood of warriors was the land a sea,
And headless bodies seemed woe's plain to be.
Fathers for sons could no compassion find,
Nor were the heavens in revolving kind.

Night came and Dárá was defeated found,
To follow him his loins Sikandar bound.
To Kirmán fled away Dárá, the king,
His life in safety from his foes to bring.
To Istakhar in Fárs Sikandar hied,
Of kings the diadem, of Fárs the pride.
Then from the palace rose a mighty shout:
"O Chiefs, the road to me who should point out,
Protection those who now desire to take,
Of their own God should their asylum make.
All equally have shelter here with me:
Let them all know well-wishers who may be.
On all the wounded something I'll bestow,
Nor shed the blood of any as a foe.
To no-one's goods will we our hand extend,
But tow'rds enlightened ways our mind will bend.
As the Victorious gave us dignity,
Greatness and diadem of majesty,
He our command who now shall disobey,
'Twould be upon a dragon's neck his foot to lay.
All things upon the battle-field that lay,
At once be to the army giv'n away."
When Dárá to Kirmán proceeded on,
He saw two parts of Irán's Chiefs were gone.
Of sorrow from the army rose the sound
That no one with a crowned head could be found.
The great and wise ones he together brought,
All those who in the war with him had fought.
The Chiefs all weeping and lamenting came,
Their hearts with their ill fortune all aflame.
"Without a doubt," to them then Dárá said,
"Through me some ill fate hovers o'er our head.
Ruin of this kind none before has told,
Nor has one heard it from the wise of old.
Wife of Irán and child both captive made,

Sou's star-struck, bodies low by arrows laid,
Can *ye* not now some remedy invent,
That we may make our enemy repent ?
No country left us and no king, no crown ;
No wife, no children, treasure, or no town.
And should God's grace to us not now be giv'n,
Against us will to evil turn the heav'n.
The army with no pow'r to strike a blow,
Over our heads must soon the water flow."
With one voice they all shouted loud: " O king,
From evil fate we all are suffering."
Those of the mighty who alive remained,
All weeping bitter tears aloud complained.
" Sonless our sires, sons without sires, alas !
Through the revolving spheres this comes to pass.
Mother and sister, too, and daughter pure,
All these are in Sikandar's hand secure.
All those of thine whose faces have been veiled,
To tremble for thy life have never failed.
Treasures of great worth of thy sires as well,
That without blame to thy possession fell,
All fallen now of foes into the hand,
Offspring of nobles and Kais' treasure grand.
Now is there in delay for us no hope
That we with him in war might strive to cope
The cure with him humility alone ;
The crown of dignity remains with none.
Passing him by the spheres revolving go ;
This all who intellect possess must know.
Humility to him in yielding show,
And on thy words some pleasantness bestow.
And what may be the end now let us see ;
Fate's changes all beyond our thoughts must be.
And now a letter to him do thou write,
Make full of thought his soul devoid of light.

He who to wisdom his own tongue may sell,
By stratagem therefrom withdraw as well."
When these their words he heard he chose obey,
Of prudent monarchs as is e'er the way.

The letter of Dárá to Sikandar with regard to peace.

A scribe experienced the king then sought:
Paper and black musk, too, with him they brought.
A letter wrote he full of sorrowing wail;
With eyes that streamed with blood and cheek all pale.
From Dárá, ruler, son of Ardashír,
To Kaiser, who of lions has no fear.
Of God the praises were rehearsed at first,
Through whom we see good or with ill are cursed.
Again he said: "To us wise men 'tis giv'n
To pass by what has been decreed by heav'n.
In God we both are glad, in Him afraid,
At times on high, at times we low are laid,
From God all good is in the world revealed,
And He knows all, both open and concealed.
In him our refuge and to Him our praise,
Good is that monarch who may know God's ways.
No bravery we in the combat knew,
But all to whirling sun and moon was due.
What was to be to pained hearts now has come:
What can we now have from this azure dome?
To make a treaty if thou now consent,
And of war-seeking in thy heart repent,
Asfandyar's and Gushtásp's treasures here,
Bracelets and collars, ringlets for the ear,
The golden throne and crown of Kai Khusru,
Helmet, khaftán and golden girdle, too,
All from my treasury I'll send to thee,
From mine own sorrow though it wrung may be.
Ever thy friend I'll be in ev'ry fight,

Never delay thee or by day or night.
My friends by thee have all been captive made,
My sons and women in confinement laid.
'Twill not be strange if thou wilt send to me;
In the king's head revenge should never be.
Monarchs of dignity and lofty mind
In women nothing but reproaches find.
A victory thou'st gained: now greatness show,
For ev'ry good a greater good bestow
When that wise lord this letter shall have read
To the same views his judgment will be led,
'When on the hill,' then ask his friends around.
'The drum both Dárá and Filúks had bound.
Tow'rds Rúm and to the Rúmis with sharp sword
How did he act, that same ambitious lord?'
Now when Rúm's lord the truth considered well,
His iron heart grew as of wax a shell.
They wrote a treaty and then went away,
And to this staunch remained they many a day.
Wise growing, when thou pardon dost bestow,
And in no vengeful wise to rule shalt know,
Thou wilt not leave an evil name behind:
God's glory bright in thee shall see mankind."
Dárá a driver called for with his beast:
At once they brought it to him there in haste.
To him the letter gave the king and cried:
"Now with the wind together must thou ride."
Raging, at once then did the camel go
From Kirmán to Sikandar, still his foe.

Sikandar's answer to Dárá's letter.

Sikandar, when he read the letter, cried:
"With Dárá's soul may wisdom be allied!
Of his connections he who injures one,
Be it a veiled woman or a son,

Except a coffin's plank shall nothing see,
Or his head hanging from a branching tree.
From Irán no one hold I back in pain,
Nor treasure do I hope from them to gain.
To Irán to return if thou incline,
The country and its rule, the whole are thine
Now thy commandment will I not transgress,
Nor contrary to thine a thought express
Sikandar to that letter wrote reply,
Planting a tree in mead of dignity,
And said: "In glory may its fruit be won,
Pure from dark earth and from the burning sun!"
Dárá this answer read then with amaze,
And said: "Most wonderful are this world's ways."
At length he cried: "Than death is worse my doom
That I should gird my loins for him of Rúm.
I see not in the world a single friend,
And none but God will to my cry attend."

Dárá's letter to Fúr* of India.

As he nor near nor far could find a friend,
He wrote a letter then to Fúr to send.
Full of humility and grief and pain,
And first he praised the king in fitting strain.
"Wise, learnèd, and of lively soul," he said;
"Thou who of Hindoo peoples art the head,
Perchance by now the news thou hast obtained
Of what upon my head fate hath ordained.
Sikandar has from Rúm an army brought,
Of land inhabited he leaves us nought,
Nor throne nor crown, no relatives, no son,
No royal diadem and soldiers none.
If thou consent henceforth to be my friend,
That I myself from mischief may defend,

* Called Parus by European historians.

Such gems I'll send thee from my treasury
That treasure there no more shall lack to thee.
Thou in the world, too, shalt renown acquire,
And to the love of great men shalt aspire."
A camel with the pace of wind he sent
To Fúr straight, of Turánian descent..

The becoming aware by Sikandar of Dárá's letter to Fúr and the leading out of his army in pursuit of Dárá. The slaying of Dárá bv the hand of his own Dastúrs.

And when Sikandar in the matter knew,
What now the ruler had proposed to do,
He bade them sound aloud the shrilly flute,
Nor thundering drum nor Indian bells were mute.
From Istakhar he such a force conveyed
That in its course the sun an error made.
And when on that side Dárá came in sight,
The world with royal splendour grew more bright.
The soldiers shouted loud on either side,
No more the warriors could at rest abide.
Sikandar's host ranged in its usual way,
The ground invisible, the sky grew grey.
When Dárá on the road his army brought.
Eager no more his men the battle sought,
Broken in heart and weary of the war,
The fortune of Irán had fallen far.
They with the Rúmis will no longer close,
And like a fox the raging lion shows.
Those who were mighty then for quarter sought,
And were from zenith's height to baseness brought.
Dárá when this he saw turned round his face,
With loud cries fled away with quickened pace.
Three hundred horsemen with the king there came,
All of Irán, who were well-known to fame.

There were two high priests, to him very dear,
Who in the battle-field to him were near.
One of the Mobeds' names was Máhiyar,
The other one was called Jánúsiyár.
When profitless the thing before them lay,
And Dárá's fame and fortune passed away,
One whirlwind cried: "This man of fortune ill
The throne with crowned head never more must fill.
Strike we upon his form a dagger's blow,
Or with an Indian sword his head lay low.
Sikandar will to us give up the land,
And in his kingdom crowned shall we two stand."
The two Dastúrs went with him on the way,
For both his priests and treasurers were they.
On either hand they rode, on left and right,
A wind arose when dark became the night.
With dagger that Jánúsiyár possessed,
On the king's body struck he and his breast.
Prone lying, the illustrious monarch lay;
His army left him there and fled away.
Then to Sikandar coming, the Vazír,
"Victorious king," said, "and of wisdom clear.
Thine enemy we suddenly have slain:
No more the throne and crown with him remain."

Sikandar, having heard this, has himself conducted to Dárá's presence, and laments over him, placing his hand on his own thigh, and promising to avenge him on his murderers. Dárá invokes blessings on him for his compassion, and moralises on the unstability of human affairs. Sikandar promises to carry out all his wishes. Dárá bids him fear the Creator. He begs him to care for his children, his allies, and his women, and to marry his daughter, Raoshanak, who, he hopes, will present him with a glorious son to light up the fire of *Zardusht*, take the *Zandavastá* in his hand, observe the auguries, the feasts of Saddah, and the New Year, honour the fire temples, Ormuzd, and the Sun and Moon, to purify his soul and face with the water of wisdom, re-establish the customs of Lehrásp and the cult of the Kyanians, the successors of Gushtásp, and make religion flourish. Sikandar promising, he places his hand on his lips, and saying, "May God be thy refuge. I leave my throne, and am returning to dust. I give up my soul to God," dies. Sikandar builds a grand *dukhmah* for him, and having committed his body to it, hangs Máhiyar and Janusiyar on two gibbets opposite, head downwards, where they are stoned to death by the soldiers. He writes to Dárá's female relatives to condole with them, and to all the provinces to announce what has taken place and his own assumption of rule. He instructs them to strike coin in his name, to preserve the palaces and guard the frontiers efficiently, and to put down crime. They were also to send from every town a beautiful, wise, and modest slave-girl to serve in the royal *Zanánah*, to protect the Súfis in the exercise of their religion, and if anyone should be found to have been oppressed his oppressors were to be punished and even hanged. They should strengthen their hearts in justice and liberality, and place on their heads the crown of noble sentiments.

Sikandar leaves Kirmán and proceeds to Istakhar, where he is crowned. His reign is said to have lasted fourteen years. The praise of Muhammad and Ali, and of Sultan Mahmúd, with the recital of which the history of Alexander commences in some editions, is omitted in Macan's. Alexander ascends the throne, and makes a notable speech in which he ascribes victory and all good to God, and says that anyone who may have any complaint to make against him may present himself even at midnight and shall receive immediate attention, that he will ask for no tribute for five years except from those who consider themselves his equals, and that he will take nothing from those who possess property, but will give to the needy. He now writes letters to Dilárai, the mother of Raoshanak, and Raoshanak herself, calling on them to fulfil the compact made with him by Dárá on his deathbed that he should marry Raoshanak, and to send her to him with a fitting retinue for the purpose. Dilárai, as directed by Dárá, gives her consent, and Sikandar sends his own mother from Amuríyah to Isfáhán to receive his bride. When she arrives at Istakhar she is received with affection by Síkandar himself, who finds in her all dignity, sweetness, intelligence, and modesty. Síkandar's mother is here called by the name of Náhíd (Venus).

After this comes an account of a dream of Kaid, the king of Kanúj, in India, and its interpretation by a sage at his court of the name of Mehrám, who lived among wild beasts and ate only herbs found in the mountains, not associating with human beings. The dream which was repeated for ten nights, was that he saw a building like a tall palace, in which was shut up a large, furious elephant, and which had only a very narrow exit. Out of this the huge elephant came, notwithstanding its narrowness, without any trouble, but left his trunk inside. On the second night he saw in the same palace that the king had died and another was sitting in his place crowned with a beautiful crown. On the third night he saw four men pulling with all their strength, in different directions, at a linen cloth until their cheeks became blue with their exertions, and notwithstanding this the cloth was not torn. On the fourth he saw near a stream of water a man who was very thirsty, and over whom a fish poured water: the man leapt away from the water, but the water ran after him. On the fifth he saw a town of which all the inhabitants were blind, but nobody seemed to be at all distressed at the circumstance, and the town was full of opulence and trade. On the sixth he saw a town of which all the inhabitants were ill, and questioned one well-to-do who came amongst them, as to remedies for illnesses. On the seventh he saw a horse that had four feet and two heads grazing on a plain: it ate grass with its mouths, but it had no means of evacuation for the food that it had eaten. On the eighth he saw two men pouring water into three jars, two of which were already full of it, and the third empty, but neither did the latter grow moist nor the full ones overflow. On the ninth he saw a cow lying on grass in the sun, and near it a small thin, dried-up calf, from which the cow was sucking milk. On the tenth he saw a large plain with a spring in it, and a palace; the whole plain was overflowed by the water, but the edge of the spring was perfectly dry. To these enigmas Mehrám answered as follows:—

He warns him not to oppose Sikandar in battle. He had four wonderful things such as no one in the world had seen, viz., a daughter through whom his crown shone bright on earth, a philosopher who revealed to him the secrets of the earth, a renowned physician, and a cup the water in which could be made hot by neither fire nor sun, and which one could continue to drink without diminishing its quantity: by these four things he would be able to appease Sikandar. The house with the narrow entrance through which the elephant passed in his dream was the earth, and the elephant an unjust king, who had nothing but the name: in the next dream that king had quitted the throne and another sat upon it, as is the way of the world. The cloth that four men endeavoured each to appropriate, but which was not torn, was the Faith, of which all four desired to be the guardians: the first of the religions was that of the fire-worshippers, the Dehkáns the second, the Jewish religion of Moses the third, the pure Faith of the Greeks that implanted justice in the hearts of kings, and the fourth, that of the Arabs, which lifted from the dust the heads of men of intelligence, and all four, pulling in different ways, become enemies to each other. The dream in which a thirsty man fled from the water, which followed him, and a fish threw water on him was to be thus interpreted. There would come a time when a man who had drunk the water of wisdom would be despised, he would be degraded as the fish in the sea, whilst the head of the wicked would be exalted to the Pleiades; he would call the thirsty to the water, but none would answer him sensibly; all would avoid and abuse him. The city of the blind that was in a flourishing condition would be the world, when the wise would become the servant of the fool and despised, the tree of knowledge would bear him no fruit, but although he worshipped fools he would be sensible that he was acting a lie. In the sixth dream, where the sick man was asking after the health of the healthy, was to signify the time when the rich would despise the poor, who would beg from him in vain, and would neither be accepted when he offered to serve him for nothing nor bought when he offered himself as a slave. In the seventh dream of the two-headed horse was signified a time when men would obtain the smallest amount of nourishment and not be filled, when no poor man or one who sought for knowledge would obtain anything, and when men would be so selfish as to care for no one but themselves. By the dream of the three jars was signified a time when the clouds, though filled with moisture, would hide the sun from the poor, the rich would be friendly to each other, but the poor man's lip would remain dry. In the ninth dream, where a cow in good condition drank milk from a thin and miserable calf, it signified that when Saturn entered into Libra the world would have to submit to force, the poor and the sick would be in misery, and the whole world would ask of them, but would never open their own treasures nor relieve their sufferings. In the tenth dream, that of the dry spring surrounded by land overflowed by water, it signified that a king would appear on earth who would be wanting in wisdom, and whose dark soul would be full of regrets: through the evils brought about and the treasures accumulated by him the earth would become darkened. He would continually raise new armies in order to exalt his own crown, but in the end there would remain neither throne nor king. This was the epoch of Sikandar, to whom he must present his four marvellous things. He would ask for nothing more, and would pass on, for he was a wise man seeking for knowledge. The king leaves the sage, highly pleased.

Sikandar now leads his army against Kaid, and all the cities on the road open their gates to him. Arriving at the town of Míládá, and his troops taking possession of the country, he writes a letter to Kaid in order to enlighten his mind and point out to him that he (Sikandar) is the shadow of the victorious Master of the World, and kings who fear God repose in him, presumably to demand his submission. Kaid receives Sikandar's envoy amicably and sends him back with a letter in which he submits himself to his commands. Sikandar sends him back with an inquiry as to what are the four precious things he has in his possession that no one has ever seen. Kaid describes them, and Sikandar sends ten of his wise men to see them. Kaid shows them his daughter, and they write off glowing descriptions of her to Sikandar. Sikandar now tells them to return to him with the four wonderful things and to ask Kaid for nothing more. By Kaid's permission they are brought with a hundred of the most intelligent, eloquent, and soft-spoken Indians. Sikandar sees the girl and is charmed with her, and marries her according to Christian rites. He now puts to the proof the philosopher, the physician, and the cup. He sends to the philosopher a cup full of melted butter and tells him to anoint all his members with it, and rest himself until he has got over his fatigues, and he can then fill him with wisdom. The sage puts a thousand needles into it and returns it, and Sikandar has an iron disc made of them which he sends to the philosopher. The latter polishes the disc and returns it, and Sikandar puts it in a damp place, and sends it back when it becomes rusty. The sage rubs it with something that will prevent rust, and returns it. The sage is then sent for and tells him that by sending the butter he meant to indicate that he had more wisdom than the philosophers of the country. His answer, implied by the needles, was that the spirit of a pure man would pierce through bones and even stones as needles would, and that his soft words and understanding were finer than a hair, and his heart was not darker than iron. The king had answered that his heart had in the course of years become rusted with blood, and what could clean it? He had replied to him that if his heart had been bad from all eternity it could not become so again after he had polished it. Sikandar, greatly pleased with his answers, orders him valuable presents, and promises to abide by his precepts. In testing the physician Sikandar asks him what is the origin of the maladies that afflict men and make them weep. He is informed that they come from too much eating and drinking, and he would make up from herbs a medicine with which he had only to wash his body in order to attain to perfect health. This he prepares at the desire of Sikandar, who confers valuable gifts on him. The medicine prepared, Sikandar is washed with it, and attains such vigour that he takes to dissipation and does not sleep. The physician discovers this, and not content with Sikandar's answer to him that he is in perfect health, prepares another medicine for him. That night Sikandar desists from his dissipation, and the physician, finding from an examination of his tears, his usual method of diagnosis, that he has restrained himself, throws away the medicine and has a great feast, telling Sikandar, who asks why he has thrown away what had cost him so much trouble to prepare, that he knows he has not been dissipating. Sikandar on this presents him with a black horse and a purse of *dínárs*. The cup is now tested. It is filled with fresh water, and the water is drunk from morning till night without diminishing in quantity. On being asked the reason of this the philosopher informs him that it has been prepared for Kaid by learned astrologers from different countries, and is the result of much labour and knowledge, that it attracts moisture as the magnet draws iron, and thus never becomes empty. Sikandar now promises, having received the four precious gifts, never to demand from Kaid anything more. He also, for no reason given, determines to hide all his treasures in the mountains, and the faces of those who bury it are no more seen.

We now come to Sikandar's expedition against Fur, which is described as follows :—

And as the host to Fúr was drawing near,
He wrote a letter full of war and fear.
" Sikandar, Filkús' son, and king of kings,
To wisdom and to wealth who brightness brings,
To Fúr of India, ruler he of Hind,
Of lofty star, who leads the host of Sind."
He at its head invoked on God due praise,
Who ev'rywhere exists and ever stays.
" He to whom God victorious fortune gives,
With land and crown and throne e'er prosperous lives.
By Him abased shall he continue low.

On him the lofty sun confer no glow.
What that pure God has now on us conferred
On this dark earth, hast thou then never heard?
Glory and victory and fortune fair,
A royal diadem and throne to share.
Time passes on: my day will not remain,
Some other comes, of this the fruit to gain.
I strive that my name pure may linger here,
In this moon's circuit and this narrow sphere.
When they this letter bring thee on my part,
Fill full of justice thou thy darkened heart.
From off thy lofty throne on horseback ride:
Stay not to call a Mobed for thy guide.
Quarter demand from me: tricks do not play:
He who plays tricks can only cause delay
If thou depart from this command of mine,
To haughtiness or boasting shall incline,
When with my horsemen I shall come to fight,
Soon shalt thou wander in repentant flight.'
After these words had all been duly weighed
The scribe to finish it no more delayed.
To seal it then Sikandar's seal they brought,
And meanwhile one who knew the road was sought.
When the ambassador to Fúr's court came,
Talking of feast and breathing fire and flame,
That man experienced to him they called,
And near to him upon the throne installed.

The answer to Sikandar's letter from Fúr.

Fúr fierce that letter to peruse began,
And angry grew with that illustrious man.
Sharp answer did he then at once indite,
And in his garden planted tree of spite.
"Of the pure Lord of all," the heading said:

"We should be ever all in fear and dread.
We do not use these words by way of pride:
The boaster has no remedy beside.
Hast thou no shame when thou thus callest me?
Does wisdom give thy brain no modesty?
Had Filkús written this to Fúr to tell—
Now cease thy noise—thou might'st begin as well.
Art thou through Dárá thus becoming bold,
Of whom had had enough the spheres that rolled?
The strife with Kaid hast thou considered play:
Resolving that all kings shall be thy prey.
After this manner and with words so bold
None came to me ev'n of the kings of old.
I am a Fúr, and from a Fúr descend,
And to no Kaisers back my memory send.
When Dárá would have made a friend of me,
My heart was not one with his destiny.
My raging elephants to him I sent,
And with my tongue to friendship gave consent.
When of that slave he by the hand was slain,
The fortune of Irán turned back again.
And when of Dárá the earth's face was free,
From foes it was an antidote for thee.
If by a bad priest he to harm was led,
Why has all wisdom vanished from thy head?
Such ardour for this war do not thou know:
Such talk with me is but an empty show.
My raging elephants in war thou'lt see
In numbers to shut out the wind from thee.
On aggrandisement only set thy mind,
Thy nature that of Ahriman I find.
Do not on earth the seed of avarice sow,
But fear the harm of adverse fate below.
I in this letter good to thee desire,
And would with wisdom, too, thy heart inspire."

The arraying of his army by Sikandar for war with Fúr of India and making iron horses and horsemen filled with naphtha.

Now when that answer to Sikandar came,
He from his host selected chiefs of fame,
Who were both fitting and impulsive, too,
In knowledge old, although their years were few.
'Gainst Fúr of India he led such a host,
That only sea was seen, the land seemed lost.
On ev'ry side he such an army led,
Earth had no other king, thou would'st have said.
On hill and river and the hardest ground
With hearts of fire the warriors wandered round.
Moving, at once the host became aware
The roads were difficult and useless there.
A band arriving at a halting place,
Towards the monarch turning round their face,
"Rúm's Kaiser, China's ruler," all declare:
"This land thine army's weight can never bear.
Neither with thee will combat Fúr of Ind,
Nor China's Faghfúr nor the Lord of Sind.
Why dost thou thus thine army lead astray
To such a hopeless land in such a way?
In thy whole army no horse do we see
That will be fit to fight with energy.
If from this fight the army turn them back,
Nor horse nor foot will ever find the track.
Against the foe in ev'ry place have we
Up to the present time won victory.
Here lie before us only hills and streams,
And unfulfilled to each his own life seems.
Cover thou not our names now with disgrace:
With stones and water none in fight keeps pace."
Now at their words Sikandar was aggrieved,

And broke up the design that they conceived.
As thus to them he said: "Should rebels speak,
Such are the arguments that they would seek.
From Rúm to Irán till we came indeed
Nothing we saw but fertile land and mead.
Out of a hundred Rúm not one had lost,
And all accomplished at the smallest cost.
All Irán's cities now are in your hand:
What can ye better from your God demand?
To Dárá from his slaves there came this ill,
But ye unwounded are all happy still.
Without you on this road if I depart,
Behind me I shall leave a dragon's heart.
From me henceforward Fúr shall have no peace,
In fight, in feast, from him will I not cease.
With valour all earth's face will I lay low,
From him returning then to Rúm will go.
God and the host of Irán my allies,
Henceforth no Rúmi as a friend I prize."
With anger at this talk his spirit burned;
To make excuses then the army turned.
"We all the Kaiser's slaves are to command,
And yield but by his order any land.
Now will we strive, as horses are in vain,
To go on foot into the battle plain.
If with our blood the land become a sea,
With corpses filled the low-lands high may be,
None shall our backs see in the day of fight,
Though heav'n cast hills upon us in its might.
All we are slaves, and us dost thou command:
And would'st thou harm, our lives are in thy hand."
From them these words when great Sikandar knew,
For combat once again a plan he drew.
A hundred thousand from Irán arrayed
With implements of wăr he ready made.

Behind these Rumi leaders then he placed,
Armed with cuirass and all to battle braced.
Skilful in arm then forty thousand horse
Of Irán were all placed behind the force.
Behind, a space Egyptian horsemen filled,
All conquerors and with the dagger skilled.
Rúmis, Egyptians, and from Barbar men,
Footmen and horsemen, all arraying then;
Twelve thousand did the Kaiser there select,
All men of name, and battle that expect;
So that behind him, drawn up as a hill,
With them the plain and desert he might fill.
Astrologers and Mobeds then of fame,
Learnèd, experienced, behind these came.
Whilst with himself but sixty men he bore,
All longing, anxious for the day of war.
And when Fúr knew the army was in sight,
He chose a place well suited for the fight.
The desert with his army did he fill:
With feet of elephants 'twas like a hill.
For four *míls** long the army was aligned,
With elephants before it and behind.
Now to the world's king, speedily there came
Warriors from Hindustán of martial fame:
To him these elephants of war then say
That he should have his steed two leagues away.
No single horseman could with them compete,
Or would he do so there was no retreat.
For all their trunks were higher than the air,
And Saturn was their helper from the sphere.
Philosophers of Rúm at his command,
Made a wax elephant before him stand.
He said to them with pure and ready wit,
"Who brings a remedy for this that's fit?"

*A Persian measure of length.

The learned wise men then together sat,
And sought as remedies both this and that.
A band of blacksmiths they together brought,
And for the chiefs of them they eager sought,
An iron rider, iron saddle, too,
These with an iron horse they brought to view.
With copper pegs together they unite,
To horseman and his arms then set a light.
The army drive it on before them still,
With naphtha black its black inside they fill.
And when the stratagem Sikandar saw,
To his wise head it seemed without a flaw.
More than a thousand then on this same plan
He bade them there construct, both horse and man,
Of piebald, gray, and white steeds, too, I ween,
An iron army no one such has seen.
Within a month the thing was made complete,
And the artificer achieved his feat.

The iron warriors on horses filled with naphtha being set alight, the elephants of the Indian army take fright and fall back, and Sikandar and Fúr, meeting between the two armies, the former challenges the latter to single combat and the latter is killed. Seeing this, the Indian army throws down its arms. Alexander consoles them and promises to treat them well, and appoints one Surag, an Indian athlete, king in Fúr's stead.

Here occurs one of the anachronisms that render the Shah Namah so useless as a historical work, for Sikandar, some 900 years before the advent of Muhammad, is described as making a pilgrimage to the Kaabah at Mecca, here described as the abode of Abraham, where he worshipped God. Nasr Katib (?) who was in authority there, and who is said to have been a grandson of Ishmael, received him with honour, and informed him that the ruler of the land as far as Yaman was one Khazáah, having succeeded Kahtán, who came from the desert, and committed great oppression. Sikandar slays every one of the family of Khazáah and releases Yaman and the Hedjáz from his tyranny, raising up whatever worthy man he could find of the seed of Ishmael, and making everyone rich who had been found poor.

From Mecca Sikandar is said to have proceeded to Egypt in ships and boats made by his army from Juddah (Jiddah). There the ruler Kabtún receives him, and he and his army rest for a year. There he hears of Kaidáfah, the ruler of Andalusia (in Spain) and has a letter on silk written to him by a scribe, demanding tribute, and proceeding with his army, takes a fort belonging to a king of the name of Faryán. He goes as his own ambassador to Kaidáfah, and is recognised and hospitably entertained. A treaty is made that the land of Kaidáfah shall in no way be molested and no force sent against it. Sikandar then goes back to his own army loaded with valuable gifts.

After this Sikandar visits the city of the Brahmans and receives answers from them to various inquiries he makes. These are of the most uninteresting nature, as, for instance, whether what is seen or what is hidden predominates in the world, and if the dry land or the sea occupies the greater space. Asking them what they would desire of him, they ask him to close the door of old age and death and of course find that that is beyond his power. His next journey is one to what is called the Western Sea, where there were men who hid their faces as women, speaking neither Persian nor Chinese nor Turkish nor Pehlavi. He sees also a hill risen out of the water, shining and yellow like the sun, which he was prevented by the philosophers from approaching in a boat. When a party of Greeks and Persians entered the boat, it disappeared and sank. Then a piece of water is met with on the edge of which is a jungle of reeds as high as trees: of these the houses were made, and beyond is a deep sea, surrounded by a pleasant land smelling of musk, in which, when they attempted to sleep, they are tormented by snakes and scorpions, by crowds of wild boars with long teeth glittering like diamonds, and by a lion larger than a bull, which they cannot fight. Finally the reeds are set fire to, and so many pigs are killed that the road is blocked up with their bodies. Beyond this again the land of Abyssinia (Habsh) is reached, where the people, as black as crows, their faces and eyes like lamps, are armed with bones for spears. Numbers of these are killed and burnt in a big heap. At night come wolves with blue horns as big as buffaloes that kill many until they are slain with arrows. After this Sikandar arrives at the land of the *Narmpai*, or Softfeet, who had no armour or swords, but fought with stones, and were defeated. In their city, which had neither end nor side, the army are entertained at feasts, and rest themselves. Here he finds a hill as high as the stars, where the road is made impassable by a dragon, whose food is ten bulls every night. The creature is killed by poison and naphtha wrapped in the skins of five bulls, and by the army's arrows. Again he takes the army to another lofty hill, on which is a dead old man on a golden throne, who foretells to Sikandar that his time on earth has come to an end. Sikandar now visits the city of Amazons called Harúm, meeting on the road with a snowstorm. After a month's rest he endeavours to reach the water of life. Going forward, he reaches a city abounding in gardens and grand buildings. Selecting special men to accompany him, he takes forty days' provisions and chooses a guide, who appears, as far as the meaning can be made out, to have been Khizr, by which the Prophet Elias is generally understood. As they approached the fountain of life the Mussulmán cry of "Allah-akbar" resounded. Leaving their provisions behind them, they went on for two days and two nights. After this, three days in the darkness revealed two roads, and Khizr became separated from Sikandar, so that the former alone reached the fountain of immortality, washed his head and body in it, and returned praising the Creator. Sikandar then saw a lofty hill with pillars of aloe wood, on each of which was a nest with a large green bird on it. These called Sikandar up to the top of the hill, where he saw Saráfíl, the angel of death, with a trumpet. This he blew like thunder, and told Sikandar to prepare for the long journey he had soon to go from his earthly life. Coming down from the hill, the King heard a voice shouting that whoever lifted up a stone from the road should repent it, and equally so if he did not lift one up. Some did so and others not, and all came out of the darkness into light, repenting in various ways.

After a fortnight's rest they proceed Westwards, and on asking the people what wonders were to be seen, are informed of their oppression by Yájúj and Májúj (Gog and Magog), and build a wall to check their incursions. Then they see a hill of yellow rubies, lit up by a red jewel in place of a lamp. Here they find something with a human body and a wild boar's head, covered over with gorgeous vestments. A voice comes up from a fountain of salt water to warn Sikandar that his end approaches. On coming down from the mountain he is told of a tree that speaks, composed of two beings, one male and one female, the latter talking at night and the former by day. The ground is covered with skins of beasts. The tree also foretells his approaching end, that his mother and female relatives will not see him alive. After taking his army to China, where he proceeds as his own ambassador, he is received by the Faghfúr, who is given a letter from the Kaiser of Rúm demanding tribute, and answers that the king should not be exalted on account of his own greatness, for as Faridún, Sukáh, and Jam he must pass away. Sikandar is dismissed with rich presents. He now engages in war with the Sindis, who are defeated: many prisoners are taken from them; Sikandar thence proceeding towards Yaman and receiving gifts from the country before passing on to Babylon. On the road to this they come across a hill and a deep sea where there is a tract of country where nothing is to be got to eat but game, and there are hairy men with long ears, as broad as those of two elephants. These feed on nothing but fish, have only fish bones for clothing, and use their large ears to sleep on. They inform him of a well-populated country beyond, and are sent to fetch some of the inhabitants, who come to the number of seventy, and are richly decked with jewels. Sikandar visits the rich city, and goes on thence to Babylon, where he writes a letter to Aristotle, and receives an answer full of good counsel. He writes to the effect that as no man can remain long in the world, all being born to die, not even kings carrying away their honours and greatness with them, everyone should be careful not to shed the blood of traders, for that would bring curses on him at the Judgment Day, with other good advice. This counsel he impresses on his great men and nobles whom he summons for the purpose, and embodies it in a deed drawn up to the same effect. On the same night a woman is delivered of a child with a head like a lion's but with hoofs, which dies immediately after its birth. He enquires of the astrologers the meaning of the portent. He is told that he was born under the constellation of the lion, and as the child's lion head died first, so his kingdom would fall from him. He answers that there is no escape from one's own death, and falls ill on the same day. Knowing his end approaches, he summons an experienced scribe, and has a letter written to his mother, telling her not to be grieved at his death, but to bury him in Egypt, to pay 100,000 dinárs a year to his relatives, and if a son should be born to Raoshanak to make him king of Rúm. Other directions as to the manner of his burial are also given. They are to bring his bier out on to the plain, where the army mourn for him, as well as the Hakíms and other men. His wife and mother also lament him, with the Khakán of China, Fúr of India, and others.

There is now related the history of the dynasty of the Ashkáris, which endured some 200 years. They go by the name of the Murklu Tartáif, or Miscellaneous kings, from not being all of the same race, but derive their name from Ashk, the first of them. It is remarked that there was nothing of them remembered but their names, such as Shápúr, of the race of Khusru, Gudurz Ashkáni, Bezan of that of the former Kai monarchs, Narsi, Arsh, *Zû*, otherwise Ardván, and Bábak. This Bábak sees Sásán in a dream sitting on an elephant with an Indian sword in his hand; the next he sees a Fire-worshipper with three fires in his hand. This dream is interpreted to him by the wise men and the chief shepherd of the tribe to which he belongs by informing him that the latter was himself the son of Sásán and grandson of King Ardashír, who was called Bahman, and was son of Asfandyár. Bábak gives him an establishment and a horse and armour with his own daughter in marriage. To him is born Ardashír Bábagán, who is well brought up and educated. Ardaván, of whose origin nothing is said, hears of his perfections (he is said to be the Artabanus of the Greeks), sends for the youth in a manner befitting a prince, and looks on him with great favour. A slave girl of Ardaván falls in love with Ardashír, and the two run away towards Persia (Fars), pursued by Ardaván, who also writes to his son Bahman to seize Ardashír. One Tabák assists Ardashír with an army against Bahman. Finally, Ardaván is killed in battle by Ardashír, and two of his sons are imprisoned. From the prison they escape to Hindustán. The spoil from the battle-field being bestowed on the army, Ardaván is royally buried, Ardashír is married to his daughter, and founds a beautiful city.

Ardashír next becomes involved in war with the Kurds, defeats them in a night attack, and devastates their country. There now comes an extraordinary episode of one Haftvád, who grows powerful in consequence of the wealth he obtains from the spinning of a worm found by one of the women of his town in an apple that she ate. Finally, Ardashír himself, assisted by his son Sháhiri, becomes involved in war with Haftvád, but is defeated. A man of the name of Mehrak, Mishzád of Jahram, hearing that Ardashír has gone out against Haftvád, apparently seizes the opportunity to plunder his treasury. Ardashír consults his army, and becoming aware of the affair of the worm, and that it came from the brain of Ahríman as an enemy of God, proceeds against Mehrak, and disposes of him and his defendants with 12,000 men, and by pouring hot lead and tin upon it kills the worm. Mehrak is caught and put an end to, and entrance to the fort in which the worm lies is gained by a stratagem that he and his seven companions are traders; the attendants of the worm are made drunk, and both they and the worm are killed first, and afterwards Haftvád himself, being placed on a gallows and there shot. Ardashír Babagán is now enthroned at Baghdád, and reigns for 40 years and two months. In order to discover the whereabouts of Ardaván's treasures he demands the hand of his daughter in marriage. One of the sons who are in Hindustán is sent to his sister with a packet of poison, and a message that if she desires to be mistress of Persia she should give the poison to Ardashír. When she gives the poison the cup in which it is contained falls and is broken. Apparently Ardashír sends a Mobed to make away with her, but she begs her life on account of the child she is about to bear to Ardashír. The child, Shápúr, is in due time born and brought up by the Mobed for seven years, when, as the king bewails his fate in not having a son, he reveals to the king the circumstances of Shápúr's birth. The boy is placed among others of like age and similarly clothed, and picked out from among them by Ardashír. He and his mother are plentifully bedecked with jewels and the Mobed rewarded. Shortly afterwards an embassy is sent to Kaid Hindí to ascertain Ardashír's fortune, and is warned that in order that his reign may be prosperous his descendants should be amalgamated with the offspring of Mehrak. At this he is grieved, as it would be tantamount to bringing his enemy into his own house. Meanwhile, Shápúr grows up, and displays all kingly qualities. When out hunting one day he comes accidentally across Mehrak's daughter, and obtains her hand from the old man with whom she is living as a servant. In nine months Aormúzd is born to them. One day, when the boy is playing at Chaogán, the king coming from hunting sees him, discovers he is Shápúr's son by Mehrak's daughter, and acknowledges him with great joy.

After this comes a chapter in praise of the wisdom of Ardashír in the government of his kingdom, as follows:—

Now with the wisdom of king Ardashír
Store up your mind as ye the story hear.
Striving with might he to good customs led,
On all sides goodness both and justice spread.
When at his court his army multiplied.
He sent out people's guides on ev'ry side,

So that with ev'ry one who had a son,
He should not grow up without wisdom won.
The ways of war he taught and how to ride,
With arrow, mace, and poplar bow beside.
And when the boy to manly vigour grew,
With diligence he would the deer pursue.
From country to the palace when he came,
That palace known to all men by its fame.
Of its renown and of the court he'd write,
And palace both and hall would deck aright.
In adolescence war before him came
And he went out with pehlaváns of fame.
With him there always went a Mobed, too,
The business of the world who rightly knew,
And with each thousand one of note there went,
On guarding him and his affairs intent.
Each one in war who feebleness betrayed,
Or, in health weakly, in the strife delayed,
On this he would the king a letter write
On want of skill and failure in the fight.
And when the letter would peruse the king,
The messenger himself he'd forward bring.
In honour's robe he would the wise attire,
Bestow much treasure as he might require.
Then on the stupid one he'd cast his eye,
To feed his love for war who did not try,
Until his army reached such high degree
That its great breadth no star could even see.
Whoever good in counsel was appraised,
His head in the assembly high he raised.
A proclamation through the camp would ring:
"O men of note and warriors of the king,
He who would please the monarch in his mood,
And the soil wash of brave men with the blood,
He shall have robes of honour from the king,

And deeds of his renown shall all men sing."
He with his army the whole world adorned:
The shepherds, as their flocks sought war, were scorned.
But men experienced had he at his court:
Affairs of fools were never made the sport.
To skill in any point he who'd pretence,
All letters studied and true eloquence.
Of such a thing when any brought the news,
To give more pay the king would not refuse.
In wit and wisdom he who came off short
Of Ardashír went never to the court.
Those who wrote well would with the monarch stay,
The rest to officers would go away.
King Ardashír would ever praise those well
Who seemed in writing others to excel.
Writers, thou would'st have said, him riches brought,
And from his mind dispersed the pains of thought.
"Writers are to my soul allied indeed,
And all are kings to me in secret need."
When to some country officers would go,
The king said to them: "Count your dirhams low.
It is not right for cash to sell men's lives:
This fleeting world for none of us survives.
Seek ye for ev'ry excellence and truth,
Madness be far from you and lust of youth.
Connections carry not or friends with thee.
The army that I give enough will be.
Give money every month unto the poor,
Give to no evil-minded man your store.
If any land with justice thou endow,
With equal measure shalt be prosperous thou.
If any poor man down in fear shall lie
For gold and silver to sell life thou'rt nigh."
To court whoever went up to the king
For needful business or to ask some thing,

Approaching him, they all of them were strong,
To question officers for any wrong.
The king declared: "From wealth that I possess
May none rejoice and sorrow none the less.
Men of experience do I desire,
Young men approved, not given much to ire.
Young men of learning, too, who learning love,
Such should in old men's places sit above."
When anywhere his army went to war,
Wisdom went with it that could judge afar.
A scribe as envoy then would he select,
Gifted with wisdom, who could recollect.
A message would he send with smoothness rife,
So from injustice there should be no strife.
The messenger to enemies would go,
The secret things around him who would know.
If he were wise their speeches he would hear,
Grief and all pain would set down to bad cheer.
For this an honour-robe the king would find,
His pledge and mandate he would bear in mind.
Cash on the army he would so bestow,
That pain therefrom no man might ever know.
He had an Athlete with ambition fired,
Wakeful and wise, and one who ease desired,
A scribe of learning and of courtesy,
Soldiers' injustice who would ever see.
On elephant behind a man would ride,
Whose shout resounded for full two leagues wide.
"Illustrious in war," then he would cry:
"Repute and name ye who would reckon by.
Through you no poor man ought to suffer pain,
Nor he who has repute and cash, again.
Eat ye at ev'ry stage both, and bestow
Your praise that even humble men may know.
He who a worshipper of God may be,

Of all that may be his your hand be free.
He who may turn his back upon the foe,
Henceforth let Fate deal him its hardest blow."
To leaders he would say: " Be not too slack,
But in your forwardness the rather lack.
Always your elephants lead out before,
Stretch out advanced guards for four leagues and more.
Around your forces first let dust appear;
Of fame and combat when the times draw near,
Say to your army that is close at hand:
" Upon this battle-field why do ye stand?
Bring ye out to their hundred horses one,
A hundred of them ye may count as none.
For old and young men of you who are pure
I will from Ardashír a robe procure.
When horsemen from both armies forward move,
The horses from our side shall war approve;
All should not come and leave the vanguard bare,
However great your army may be there.
Both on the right and left wing do ye so,
That equal on both sides the warriors go.
Thus on the left wing and upon the right,
Do ye then gird your hearts up for the fight.
If from their centre they should then move back,
To come on from our van do ye not lack.
And if victorious, do your blood not shed,
And say the evil-minded foe has fled.
Should quarter ask thee any of the foe,
Quarter do thou, thy anger spent, bestow."

Much more advice, both for warlike and other purposes is now given in detail, but as this is only given as a specimen of the style, the thread of the history itself will now be resumed.

The Praising of Ardashír by Kharád.

On Ardashír's ascension of the throne an old man of the name of Kharád comes before him and praises his justice and other good qualities, wishing him prosperity, and this is followed by a Section on the faithlessness of time in such terms as these:—

If thou art humble or thou art a king,
For thy repose naught but dark earth they'll bring.
Where are those great men who were crowned and
  throned?
Where are those horsemen who good fortune owned?
All for their pillow have but brick or earth;
He's happy who to naught but good gives birth.
Enough for thee, King Ardashír, the sign,
If mindful thou shalt hear this word of mine.

Ardashír now admonishes Shápúr, and after taking a pledge from him dies.

The next Section contains his prayer to God and praise of King Mahmúd, and is followed by Shápúr's accession to the throne.

The reign of Shápúr was 30 years and two months. He sits on the throne and gives admonition to his chiefs and others. He announces that he will only levy one *dirham* in thirty from cultivators of the soil in order to provide pay for his army. and that he will convert his enemies nt o friends by taking nothing from them. All were to have free access to him to state their grievances, and experienced men would be sent out in all directions to keep him acquainted with the affairs of the world.

As the news of Ardashír's death spread, tumults arose on all the frontiers, from those of Kaidáfah to Rúm, and Shápúr prepared for war, and sent out light troops as far as the gates of Pálvínah, from which an army issued under the command of a Pehlaván of the name of Bazánúsh. Here Bazánúsh is taken prisoner with 1,600 other Rúmis, 10,000 having been killed, and the Kaiser sends an envoy to Shápúr to remonstrate with him on shedding so much blood, and agreeing to pay the usual tribute on condition that he leaves Pálvínah. Shápúr waits for the tribute and other presents and then retires to Ahváz. Here he builds a large town which he calls Shápúrgadh. In Khúzistán also he builds a large town called Kuhandiz at Nishápúr, taking Bazánúsh everywhere with him, and paying great attention to what he says. There was a river at Schustar so broad that no fish could cross it; this he suggests to Bazánúsh to bridge according to Rúmi art, and he completes it accordingly in three years. Shápúr crosses the bridge, and returning home rules with justice and judgment. When 30 years and two months have passed he abdicates in favour of his son Ormuzd, who reigns a year and two months without anything remarkable occurring. When he finds his death is approaching, he summons his son Behrám, and exhorts him as to his duty as a king. The admonition is written down by a scribe and placed before Ormuzd, and the king's red cheeks become of the hue of gold. Ormuzd mourns his father for forty days, and does not mount the throne.

The reign of Behrám, son of Ormuzd, lasts three years, three months and three days. He also commences his reign with exhortation to his Chiefs, and when his time comes sends for his son Behrám, and yields his place to him with due advice and dies. Behrám, son of Behrám, reigns for 20 years, and with the usual exhortation to his son Narsi dies. Narsi reigns for nine years, beginning with the customary advice to his Chiefs and ruling wisely and justly. He is succeeded by his son Ormuzd, who also reigns nine years. He dies without leaving a son, and the throne is unoccupied for some time, but the Grand Mōbed discovers that one of the king's wives is *enceinte*, and she in due time, forty days after Ormuzd's death, gives birth to a son, who is named Shápúr Zu'laktáf. A wise Mobed, of the name of Shahrúi, takes charge of affairs for some years, and the country prospers under his rule. In five years the young king becomes so intelligent as to order a second bridge to be constructed over the Tigris; wise men are appointed to him as teachers, and he becomes skilled in all royal accomplishments. He fixes his residence at Istakhar after the manner of his ancestors. After some time Táir of the Ainánis (the name is given as Ghassáni in Mohl) assembles an army of Rúmis, people of Fárs and Bahrim, Kurds, and Kádessians against Ctesiphon, plunders the country, carries off Nushah, the king's aunt, a prisoner, and marries her. In a year she bears a daughter, to whom the name of Málikah is given. When he is twenty-six years of age Shápúr leads an army against Táir, whose army is defeated and takes refuge in a strong fort in Yaman, where it is besieged. Málikah sees and falls in love with him, and sends her nurse to offer to deliver up the fort to him if he will marry her. Shápúr accepts the offer gladly, and Málikah, having intoxicated her father and his chief men, opens the door of the fort and goes to Shápúr's tents, while she admits his army into the fort, where they wreak their vengeance on their enemies. Next morning Shápúr sits on a throne with Málikah opposite him and sends for Táir, who has been made prisoner. Táir warns him that Málikah may do to him as she has done to her father, but he orders him to be executed and his body burnt in revenge for his carrying off Narsi's daughter. He also orders the arms of the Arabs to be cut off from their shoulders, thus earning his nickname of Zu'laktáf (lord of the shoulders), and returns to Fars.

Shortly after this, being in bad spirits, he sends for astrologers and consults them as to his future. He is informed that a terrible trial is in store for him, which nothing can avert. He resigns himself, and sets himself to rule with justice, but takes a fancy in his head that he would like to see Rúm and all its grandeur. Having entrusted his kingdom to a Pehlaván, starts off with a number of camels laden with merchandise and arrives at Rúm, where he is entertained by the Kaiser, but is betrayed by an evil-dispositioned Iráni, and is sewn up in ass's skin and imprisoned in a small, dark room in the palace, the key being given to a woman with orders that she is to give him a little bread and water so that he may not die too quickly. The Kaiser himself at once starts off with an army and devastates Irán, the people of which had no information as to whether Shápúr was dead or alive. Numbers of the people became Christians, and went to the Bishops. The young girl to whose charge he had been delivered, was of Iránian descent, and was greatly distressed at the sufferings of Shápúr sewed up in the ass's skin, and begs him to confide his secret to her. He binds her by an oath on the soul of the Messiah and the sorrow of the Cross not to reveal it, and begs her to bring him some hot milk with which to soften the ass's skin. This is effected in a fortnight, and Shápúr is freed from his confinement in it. After this she procures two horses from the stables, and the two escape together to Irán, where, in the province of Khúzistán, they are given shelter by a gardener for three days. Having ascertained that the chief Mobed lives not far off, he sends for some seal earth, on which he impresses his signet and sends it to the Mobed, who recognises that the hidden man must be the king, and sends word to the Pehlaván of the region to announce the great event. An army at once assembles, and Shápúr makes his arrangements, and obtaining good information as to the doings of the Kaiser, who is engaged, with his army scattered about, in drinking and hunting, makes a night march to Ctesiphon, sets fire to the Kaiser's camp, and makes a prisoner of the Kaiser himself. He reproaches him for his brutal treatment of him when he came only as a merchant, and demanding restoration of all the property he has carried away from Irán, and the restitution of the places he has ruined, sends him back to prison in fetters with a piece of wood through his nose like the bridle of a camel. Shápúr now advances without delay to the frontier of Rúm. Here he is met by Zánus, the Kaiser's brother, and completely defeats him, so that neither Bishops nor crosses remained. The Rúmis, disgusted with the Kaiser and his brother, place one Bazánúsh on the throne, and he writes deprecating the anger and vengeance of Shápúr, who thereupon pardons the Rúmis and summons Bazánúsh to his presence. Bazánúsh goes as he is directed, with sixty ass loads of silver and other offerings, accompanied by a hundred nobles. Shápúr receives them graciously, and assigns them places according to their rank. He demands from Bazánúsh by way of reprisals, for all the injury done to Irán, three times a year a tribute of 100,000 Rúmi dínárs, and that Nasibin should be ceded to him. Bazánúsh agrees, and a treaty is accordingly drawn up, and Shápúr returns to Istakhar. The inhabitants of Nasibin, however, object to the cession of the town for fear of Shápúr's abolishing Christianity, and reintroducing fire worship, and Shápúr, retorting that it was impossible to believe in a religion of which the Jews had killed the prophet, sends an army against them and reduces them to submission. He gives the slave girl who had released him the name of Dilafrúz Farúkhpai, and esteems her above all his fair women. The gardener also is well rewarded. The

Kaiser remains in chains in prison and finally dies there, and his body is sent in a coffin to Rúm. A town is built in Khúzistán for the captives whose hands and feet he had cut off, and is called Khurram Abád. Another town, Firúz-i-Shápúr, is built in Syria, and a third near Ahváz, which is called Kinám-i-Asírán (dwelling of the prisoners). Thus fifty years of his reign passed away, and he had not his equal on the earth.

About this time Máni, the Chinese painter, comes to Shápúr, claiming the gift of prophecy, but is confounded after disputation with a Mobed, and, having his skin flayed off him, the skin is stuffed with straw and hung up at the gate of the town.

Shápúr reigns with justice and prudence, and nominates his youngest brother Ardashír his heir-apparent during the immaturity of his own son, giving him the usual good advice, and in another year dies. He is succeeded by Ardashír, who reigns twelve years, and hands over the government to Shápúr's son Shápúr. The younger Shápúr gives the usual admonition to his nobles and succeeds Ardashír. He had reigned five years and four months, when one day he went out hunting, and whilst he was asleep a great wind arose, and blew down his tent, the pole striking and killing him. He is succeeded by his son Behrám, who reigns for 14 years. He opens his reign with the customary address, and dies after a long illness, leaving no son, but a younger brother of the name of Zazdagird, and a daughter. The former succeeds him on the throne. He despises wise men, and thinks nothing of Governors and guardians of the frontier, all tenderness and justice being expelled from his heart. He receives no ambassadors, to whom his Ministers have to say he is not disposed to do any business. This went on for seven years, when a son was born to him, who became the celebrated Behrám Gúr. Zazdagird reigned altogether 30 years. On the birth of Behrám the best astrologers are summoned to cast his horoscope, and predict that he will be a great and glorious king and master of the world. They assemble and advise his father to find a place where the child will receive good instruction. He sends out men in all directions to find who is well instructed, eloquent, and an observer of the stars to educate Behrám. When a number of wise men are assembled from all parts he selects one Manzir, an Arab, from among them for the duty, and hands over Behrám to him. Manzir has him fed on the milk of four wet-nurses till he is four years old, and continues to tend him till he is seven, when he demands to be placed for education among wise men. Astonished at the boy's precocity, he sends for three learned Mobeds from Súristán, one to teach him letters, the second how to hunt, and the third to instruct him in the duties of administration as a king. He remains under them till he is twelve, and becomes perfect. He then desires to dismiss his masters, and they are sent away with fitting gifts. He now sends to the desert for horses to select from, and chooses two from among them. He objects to Manzir looking after him too carefully, and insists on being provided with a beautiful woman who should calm his passions and, inspiring with the worship due to God, should be his guide to all that was good. Four beautiful Rúmis are accordingly brought, one of whom plays the lute and is called Ázádah (the free or noble one). One day he goes alone with her to a hunting place mounted on a dromedary. They see four gazelles or deer, and he asks Ázádah which he shall shoot, and she tells him to make a female of the male and a male of the female. He should urge on his dromedary when a deer fled before him, and shoot a ball with his cross-bow, so as to make it lay its ear on its shoulder, and when it lifted its foot to its head he should pierce head, ear and shoulder with the same ball, and she would then call him the light of the world. He immediately shoots off the horns of the male deer so as to make it appear a female, and then sews together with one arrow the head, the ear, and the foot of another. Ázádah takes compassion on the deer, and bursts into tears at his inhumanity, whereupon he treads her underneath the feet of his dromedary, and puts an end to her. After displaying his skill in hunting other animals Behrám returns, and has a drawing made of himself and his feats. He still, however, has to complain of the surveillance he is kept under by the king, but Manzir promises to supply him with any money he may require, and advises him to serve his father diligently, and he follows the advice. One day, to the annoyance of his father, he falls asleep during some festivities, and is ordered to be confined in his palace as if it were a prison. Just at this time one Táinúsh comes as an envoy from Rúm, and Behrám complains to him of his position. Táinúsh begs his release from his father, and he goes away, and is hospitably entertained by Manzir in his own palace. Some time passed after this, and Zazdagird becomes disturbed as to the fate of his kingdom, and assembles astrologers and others to consult as to the probable time of his death. They advise him to go to a spring at Tús called Sáo, where his fate will be decided. Just at this time he appears to have been taken with a bleeding from the nose, which, although healed by the physicians for awhile, breaks out again. He is informed by a Mobed that it is because he has forsaken the way of God, and is advised to go to the spring of Sao by way of the lake of Shahd in a litter. He does so, and the bleeding, which has been going on intermittently all the while, ceases on his putting some of the water on his head and calling on the name of God. When it ceases he becomes presumptuous and makes light of the matter. Just then a monstrous creature comes up out of the fountain, which he orders his people to catch. When they can not do so, he proceeds himself to put a saddle and bridle on the creature, which submits quietly till he tries to put on a tail strap, when it kicks him on the forehead with both its hind hoofs, and kills him, and disappears in the water. The body is embalmed and taken back to Fárs. After his death the Chiefs and others whom he had treated with contempt assemble together and dispute as to who shall be put upon the throne, and finally fix upon one Khusru, a valiant man of good family, whom they accordingly declare to be king. Behrám, on hearing this, engages Manzir to assist him, and ravages the country. The people of the neighbouring countries, learning that the throne is vacant, and there is no one worthy of it, commence to make incursions into it and to aspire to the dignity. The Iránis on this apply to Manzir for assistance through one Júánúi, but he refers them to Behrám as their rightful sovereign. Behrám receives him graciously, and sends him back to Manzir, whom they invite to come with Behrám and take possession of the country. Behrám and Manzir now hold counsel together, and 30,000 Arabs are dispatched into Irán and come to Jahram. Here an assembly of the notables of the country is held, and Behrám is finally elected king. Some of them object on account of the iniquities of his father Zazdagird, and he proposes that the crown shall be placed among lions brought for the purpose, and that whoever has the hardihood to take it from among them shall be king; otherwise he threatens them with Manzir's army. This is agreed to, and Behrám kills two lions with his mace, and seizing the crown places it on his own head. He is then acknowledged king by Khusru and all the nobles. Behrám's reign lasts 63 years. On mounting the throne he returns thanks to God, professes himself a follower of the religion of Zardusht, pardons the Iránis the offences they have committed and remits all outstanding taxes, amounting to 93,000,000 *dirhams*. He sends envoys abroad to gather together those whom Zazdagird had exiled, and distributes dresses of honour to the Mobeds, the nobles and others. After settling himself down firmly on his throne he engages in hunting and ball play.

He goes out one day, when an old man with a stick in his hand addresses him, and informs that there are two men in the town of the names of Baráhám, who is a rich Jew, and Lambak, a poor water-carrier. The former is reported to be avaricious and stingy, and the latter generous and hospitable. The king thereupon causes a herald to make proclamation that everyone should be careful of how he drinks the water; and waiting till evening, himself goes to Lambak's house as a stranger, and is very hospitably entertained by him, both that evening and for three days. After this Behrám goes to Baráhám's house and demands shelter, but answer is brought to him that the owner is a poor Jew, who cannot afford to give him anything. On Behrám's saying that he will sleep at his gate, he admits him on condition that he is not to ask for anything, but carry away any litter his horse may make, and pay for anything broken. He is admitted on agreeing to this, and the Jew gives him nothing, but lets him look on while he eats his own dinner, and similarly with wine that he drinks after it. As he does not carry away the dirt of his horse when he goes the Jew reminds him of it, and he wraps it up in a silk handkerchief he has and throws the dung away, the Jew immediately taking possession of the handkerchief. He goes back to the palace, and next day sends for all the Jew's property, and after making handsome presents to the water-carrier gives the Jew four pieces of silver as capital on which to begin business again, leaving everything else to be plundered.

There is now told a story of Behrám's killing two lions

in a wood, and an old cultivator of the name of Rehr Bídád witnessing the affair, and asking him to remain there for awhile, whilst he brought for him milk, honey, and wine, as many lambs as he might require, and showing him trees that would give him as much fruit as he wanted. He thus entertains him hospitably. The old man tells him he resembles a king, and Behrám on leaving him presents him the wood. Another anecdote is told of him that the head of a village, whose name is Keirúi, comes to him boasting of his capacity for drinking wine, and is allowed to take seven cups full of it. He rides off, and finding the wine had got into his head, alights from his horse and lies down in the shade. A crow plucks out his eyes and kills him, and Behrám, shocked at what has occurred, forbids the use of wine to the whole world, Pehlaváns as well as citizens. A year passes during which his order that wine is not to be drunk is in force, but Behrám cancels it in consequence of discovering its effect upon a young cobbler in overcoming a lion, &c.* His orders are that everyone may drink according to his own measure, and reflect what may be the result. When wine has exhilarated anyone he should go to bed, in order that he may not suffer for it.

One day the king goes out hunting, but sees no game, and arrives when very hot at a beautiful, well-cultivated place, where he would like to rest, but the people of which only stare at him without offering him shelter. He remarks that a place like that ought to be peopled by nothing but wild beasts, and he wishes that all the streams in it might become pitch. The Mobed he speaks to immediately goes to the place and tells the people that the king makes all of them lords, so that there shall no more be servants and masters. A shout of joy arises from the castle, and the young people in the place immediately set

*This relates to a matter that is not fit for translation.

to work to cut off the heads of the old men, and all attack and kill each other. The people desert the castle, all cultivation is neglected, the streams remain without water, and the trees wither away. The next year the king again goes there, and shocked at the state of affairs, orders the Mobed to take money out of the treasury and have the place repeopled. He goes and finds out the cause of the desolation, and discovering an old man in it whom he makes the head of the place, provides him with funds to set everything to rights again, assisted by the neighbours with asses and cattle. On Behrám's coming to the place in the third year he finds it flourishing, and enquires from the Mobed how it has all been brought about. Thereupon he praises the Mobed, and declares he is worthy to wear a crown, and gives him a robe of honour and other valuable gifts. After this he goes out to hunt again, and as he is returning is overtaken by night, and halts at a village near which there is a mill. The villagers had lighted a large fire, and on one side were seated the chief men and on the other the girls, crowned with chaplets of flowers; they were half intoxicated with joyousness and wine, while they sang the praises of the king to the accompaniment of music. One of them raises her voice above the others and sings: "Let this be a memento of King Behrám, who has glory and form and face and goodness. The whirling sphere is at his feet, There drop drops of wine from his face; the scent of musk comes from his hair. He hunts only the lion and wild ass; hence they call him Behrám Gúr." The king advances and calls for wine from his cup-bearer, and summons some of the singing girls. Four come forward named Mushk-i-náz (pure musk), Mushknak (little musk), Náztáb (brilliant fair one), and Susanak (little lily). They turn out to be the daughters of the miller, and he takes all four of them to wife. The next week Behrám goes hunting again, and is met by a man who desires a private interview with him, and on this being granted, tells him that as his fields were being irrigated a hole was formed in the ground and a noise as of cymbals issued from it, indicating the existence of a treasure. Labourers are thereupon called to dig up the place; and the treasure, of great value, of Jamshíd and the old kings is discovered. Out of this he distributes a year's pay, and has a great entertainment.

The following week again Behrám goes to hunt, and having a pain in his stomach goes to a merchant's house, whom he pays some money to, and tells him to bring some old toasted cheese and almonds, but his host brings him a roast fowl instead. In the morning, after Behrám has slept, the merchant has a dispute with his apprentice (*shágird*) for having bought for a *dirham* a fowl that was not worth nearly so much, and the latter informs him that he will pay for it himself. He then brings 200 almonds, and has them toasted for the guest, and makes a feast of lamb, sugar, saffron, and other delicacies, finishing with wine. He then goes away, telling the host that Behrám will be wanting him, and rebuking him for having grudged him the fowl as too dear. Behrám then mounts his throne, summons the merchant before him with his apprentice, and enriches the latter with his master's property, while he condemns the merchant to serve his own apprentice.

Next comes an account of Behrám going into Turán in the springtime, when all is fresh and green, with a thousand horsemen. He sees a dragon with hair on its head and breasts like a woman, and kills it with arrows, finding inside it a young man whom it has swallowed. He takes the body to a house on the plain, where he sees a woman, and asks for hospitality, which she gives him. She prepares water for him to wash with, abusing secretly her husband for doing nothing. In the morning she makes him kill a lamb to entertain her guest with. She prepares a meal for him of boiled lamb with vinegar and greens from the brook (?watercress), as well as a roast leg. After he has eaten, he asks her to tell him stories of the king, and hearing of the manner in which those about him commit wrong to extort even five or six *dirhams*, he lies deep in reflection and cannot sleep. He grieves that people will not see the difference between clemency and justice, and determines to be hard in his treatment. When the woman goes to milk her cow she finds the milk has dried up, and knows that the king has grown unjust, and that that is causing the milk to dry up, musk to lose its perfume in the musk bag of the deer, adultery and hypocrisy to make their appearance, soft hearts to become hard as rocks, wolves to devour men in the desert, the wise man to become a fool, and the egg under the hen to become addled. As she is telling her husband this, Behrám overhears her, and prays to God that if he ever gives up doing justice he may cease to occupy the throne. On the instant milk begins to come from the cow's udder, and a meal is prepared for the king. He sends his whip to be hung up on a tree in front of his palace to see what people say of it. His host sees that all the passers by salute it, and knows that his guest has been the king himself, and comes and begs pardon of Behrám, who presents him with the land, and bids him give up his profession as a gardener and exercise hospitality. The king again goes to the chase. Amongst the falcons employed is one called Túghri, which the Khákán had sent him with other valuable gifts. As they come to the bank of the Jaihún Túghri is let fly and comes to a garden where there is a palace, and by the side of some water in it an old man sitting with his three daughters, surrounded by slaves and all kinds of beautiful things. The old man recognises the king, and hopes he will enjoy himself in the garden. The king is in trouble because Túghri has disappeared, but the bird is soon found, and the old man then makes his daughters sing, play the lute and dance to please the king. Finally the king marries all three of the girls, who are sent off in litters, while he remains enjoying himself with wine for a week. After this he goes out hunting again, and commences by shooting a wild ass. Going on, he sees two fierce lions in front of a wood, and shoots them as well. He goes on and finds a wood full of sheep, which on enquiry turn out to belong to a rich jeweller. The jeweller has also a daughter who plays the lute, from whose hand alone he will drink wine. The king enquires for the man's house, and is directed to a village, where he will hear the sound of the lute. The king goes off there alone in royal apparel. Meanwhile Rúzbeh, his Minister, laments with the nobles the way in which the king is going on accumulating women in his palace: he has been informed by a eunuch that there are 930 young girls there, and the king is wearing himself out. Meanwhile, the latter goes to the jeweller's house, and gains admittance on the plea that his horse has fallen lame. The jeweller prepares a feast for him, and his daughter Arzui brings water and serves, and after the meal sings to him at her father's desire. The king is enchanted with her, and demands her of her father Mahyár in marriage, who gives her her choice, and she at once accepts Behrám, who gives his name as Gushtásp. The usual marriage rites are performed. In the morning the whip is put up outside Mahyár's door as a sign that the king is there. The king's retainers appear, and Mahyár discovers who has been his guest, and is bewildered that he should have taken the liberties he has with the king of kings. He sends his daughter with humble offerings to make excuses. The king receives her and her father graciously, and she is escorted to his palace.

The king goes hunting again with Rúzbeh, and remains for a month in the hunting ground, enjoying himself with hunting and wine. After this he starts to return, and finds on the road a castle (*shársán*), the owner of which lives in a ruinous house, and tells him that through ill-fortune he has neither cow nor ass nor clothes, and no spirit left in him. He finds the house full of the droppings of sheep, and can get no place to sit down in, and when he asks for some hot milk and bread is answered that he must imagine that he has dined and go away, for there is no food to give him. Behrám asks him whence come the droppings if he has no sheep, and is answered that the night is dark and his head is bewildered with his words. He is asked to find another house; why did he come to that of a wretched man who slept at night on the leaves of trees? Even when asked only for a little fresh water the old man says he will find it a couple of bow-shots beyond the gate. He gives his name as Farshídvard, and declares that he has nothing, and when asked why he does not try to procure bread and a bed, says that God may find it for him, and begs him to leave a poor man alone, and weeps bitterly. Behrám passes on, and finds a man cutting thorns with a hatchet, from whom he asks who is the master of the soil. He informs him that Farshídvard is really a very rich miser. Behrám sends him with a hundred horsemen and a leader called Behrúz to point out where Farshídvard's sheep and camels are, and a list of large herds and flocks is accordingly made out and sent to the king, who thereupon orders everything he has but the gold he may have buried to be seized and distributed.

Behrám once more goes out to hunt wild asses, and by way of proving his valour decides not to shoot them with arrows but attack them with his sword. He kills several of them, and when remonstrated with for his foolhardiness in going to a forest full of lionesses with cubs, says that heroes of old did not make their reputation with bows and arrows, but with swords. Returning from the forest amidst the applause of the Court, he has an entertainment, and afterwards proclaims by a herald in his camp that no one must be despoiled or injured in any way in hill or island* under severe penalties. As a result the desert became like a bazár full of merchandise. The next day he goes to hunt wild asses, and shows his dexterity in their chase. He forbids the sale of them on that plain to merchants, and has gold rings made to fasten to the ears of those that are caught and released, to the number of 600, but allows them to be given away. On returning to the palace he gives entertainments for the army to enjoy themselves for a week, and, having proclaimed what he proposes to do in order to secure the happiness of all people and punish the wicked, he goes to Baghdád, where he amuses himself for a fortnight, and thence goes to Istakhar, where he distributes treasures, to the great discontentment of Rúzbeh. He for the most part enjoys himself with the chase and in drinking wine.

News having been spread about in the world that Behrám had given himself up entirely to pleasure, and kept no proper guard against invasion, the Khákán is emboldened to make an attack upon Irán. Behrám, notwithstanding, continues to amuse himself, but at last hands over the administration to his brother Narsi, and starts with a small body of 6,000 men with some of the best of his Generals. Meanwhile an army arrives from Rúm, and is received honourably by Narsi. All the nobles advise that everything should be done to stave off pillage by sending ambassadors to the Khákán and China, but Narsi scorns the idea. They, however, send one Humái to the Khákán offering submission. Rejoiced at this, he

*Mohl's translation seems faulty here.

makes valuable presents to the envoy, and advances his army to Marv, proposing to await there the arrival of the tribute from Irán. At Marv he sits down to enjoy himself, and Behrám has in the meantime disappeared from sight. Behrám, is, however, on the look out and busy night and day making his preparations, sending out spies in all directions. He advances without baggage to Adargushasp and thence moves on rapidly to Aml and Gurgán to the town of Nisá, marching with every precaution, and as far as possible at night. Arriving near Marv, he meets one of his spies, who informs him that the Khákán is careless, and enjoying himself with hunting at Kashmíhan. He advances from that place to Marv and attacks at daybreak, and before he is hardly awake the Khákán is taken prisoner by Khazraván. The Chinese at Marv are all killed. The rest are pursued by Káran, the Persian, for 30 *farsangs*. When Behrám returns to his camp he divides the spoil among his army, and returns thanks to God for his victory.

He now rests himself and his army at Marv, and decides to attack Bukhárá. Reaching the Amu in a day and a night, he crosses the river Jaihún and the sands of Farab, and overthrows all the Turkománs in Mái and Margh, devastating the country. The inhabitants accordingly come to Behrám, and deprecate any further harshness on his part, as the fault was that of the Khákán himself, and offer to pay tribute. He is moved by their words and stops all further bloodshed; imposes a tribute on the country and passes into Farab. Before returning to Irán he erects a boundary mark on the borders of the two countries, and appoints a man from his army of the name of Shuhrah as king of Turán.

Behrám now writes a letter announcing his victory to his brother Narsi, and it is received in Irán with great rejoicing, the nobles and Mobeds praying for forgiveness for their fault in applying to the Khákán. After establishing a fire-temple at Azar Abádgán, he repairs to Istakhar, restoring the bridges on the way. He also makes provision for the poor and widows and orphans. He goes on to Ctesiphon and relieves Narsí of the Government. He now writes instructions to his officers as to their conduct towards the people, and promises not to levy taxes for seven years, and great rejoicings and feastings are carried out. (Here ends the 5th vol: of Mohl's translation).

The king now sends for the envoy from the Kaiser, after having dispatched his brother Narsí as Governor to Khurásán. The envoy is reported to be one of Aflátúm's (Platu's) followers. He apologises for having kept him so long waiting for an answer. The envoy gives a salutation of the Kaiser and says he has been instructed to put seven questions to the king's wise men and obtain their answers. The first question is as to what is the inside and what is the outside, and the answer that the outside is the heaven and the inside the air. The second question as to what is above and what is below is answered by saying that what is above is the splendour of God, which is not contained within the limits of the world; what is above is Paradise, and what is below is the hell for the wicked who are bold against God. What has many names is wisdom. One calls it love (*mehr*) and another reliance (*vafá*), for if wisdom fails there is nothing left but pain and oppression. The eloquent man says it is truth, the man of good fortune cleverness (*zíraki*). It is at times patience and sometimes secrecy, for words remain permanently with it. Thus the names of wisdom are many and beyond all measure, and there is nothing superior to it. The question What is the most despised thing? is disposed of by saying it is the stars, which are beyond count, and the notation of the world. The sage is astonished that any trust should be laid on the rays of Mercury, and there is nothing more contemptible than astrology. The envoy of the Kaíser acknowledges that he is conquered. He exhorts Behrám not to ask God for more than he has, for he has the whole world in his hands, and his minister surpasses all the Mobeds in knowledge. Behrám is greatly pleased and bestows valuable gifts on the Mobed. The latter asks him the next day what is the most mournful thing, at which men should mourn the most, and what is the most profitable thing, from which men derive most power. He answers that the sage will always be great and powerful, and the ignorant more vile than mud and undeserving of any happiness. After some further philosophic reflections, the envoy acknowledges that with such a king on the throne as Behrám and such a Mobed, it is right that tribute should be demanded from Rúm, for the latter is the king. The next day the envoy is dismissed with rich presents.

The next Section contains a long admonition given to all his nobles on the practice of justice and their conduct in general, and then follows an account of Behrám's dealings with Shangal, king of Kanúj, which is translated from the original as follows :—

The going of Behrám to the king of India with his own letter.

The wise Vazír said, rising on his feet :
" O ruler, thou whose justice is complete
The world fears evil men no more this day,
And hardship from the land has passed away.
Shangal of India there remains alone,
His soul from justice who aside has thrown.
To China's border from the Hindoo's land
Full of thieves' terror still he lets all stand.

He stretches tow'rds Irán his hand for ill,
Which thou beneath thy care should'st shelter still.
Thou king, he but the keeper is of Hind:
Why should he tribute claim from Chín and Sind?
Reflect on this: a remedy seek out,
Lest what is ought but well should come thereout."
Then full ot thought, when this he understood,
The world seemed to him as a darkened wood.
He said: "This matter secretly I'll do,
Nor leave it open for the world to view.
His army will I now see all alone,
The manner of the monarch and his throne.
As an ambassador to him I'll go,
And will not let the Persian nobles know.
Do thou, O Mobed of faith pure and right,
A letter full of wrath but love indite."
Then with a scribe the minister retired
When there was no one who was not required.
On small things and on great consulting then,
They brought together paper, musk, and pen.
The letter counsel of the best contained,
Of wisdom full, that God's praise first maintained.
The letter's heading first from God gave praise
To him who would himself to glory raise.
The Lord of Being and Non-being He;
All things are mortal, He alone must be.
Of things He gives His servant everywhere,
Be he a slave or crown deserves to wear,
Than wisdom nothing can one greater call,
That ever lights the path of great and small.
He by intelligence who is made glad
To the world never does what may be bad.
He who good prizes never will regret,
Ill none from wisdom's water tasted yet.
Wisdom saves man from all calamity:

May none by evil overtaken be!
This is of wisdom ever the first sign,
That man to evil fears him to incline,
That his own self he may know inwardly
And seek to see the world through wisdom's eye.
For wisdom of all monarchs is the crown,
The ornament of all men of renown.
"Thou thine own measure hast not understood,
But deeply hast thy soul imbrued in blood.
As monarch of the age if thou me view,
For good and bad am I the model, too.
Where is the justice that thou dost as king?
On ev'ry side there lacks some little thing,
For kings to make incursions is not right,
Or with the evil-minded to unite.
Thy grandfather to us his service gave,
Thy father to our kings was as a slave,
And none of us to this would e'er agree
That India's tribute now delayed should be.
Consider what of Chín's Khákán became
When out of China to Irán he came.
He gave to plunder all that he had brought,
And turned from evil that himself had wrought,
In the same manner acting there I view
Thy tricks, thy glory and religion too.
Weapons have I in war to take a part,
Wealth and a host with me that have one heart.
Before my warriors thou can'st never stand,
In Hind, too, leader there is none at hand.
Of thine own strength thou still art unaware,
And with the river would'st thy brook compare.
Behold now, an ambassador I've sent,
Noble and learned, too, and eloquent.
Or send the tribute or prepare for war,
And close tight places that now narrow are.

On him my salutation ever be,
Whose warp and woof are sense and equity."
And from the air's breath when grew dry the sheet,
'Twas folded by the scribe and made complete,
The heading that the scribe wrote was correct :
" From the world's king of brilliant intellect,
The lord of fortune, and the lord of pow'r,
The generous Behrám Gúr, the conqueror,
The crown who has received from *Zazdagird*
In Khurdád month and on the day of Ard.
To Shangal, lord and General of Hind.
From the Kanúj river to the bounds of Sind
The charge of all the land who doth assume,
And levies tribute from *Sakláb** and Rúm."
A seal he placed upon the letter there,
And bade as for the hunting place prepare.
None of the army must his secret know
Except the nobles that with him would go.
Of the Magicians'† river past the strand
Forward he went of Hindoos to the land.
When he came near to Shangal's audience hall,
Gate, screen and palace, he looked on them all.
It raised its lofty head up to the air :—
Of many arms was heard the clatter there.
Horse, elephants stood there the gate around,
Of Indian drums and horns was heard the sound.
Amazement to his heart the palace brought,
And he remained there standing deep in thought.
He said to those the screen who guarded round,
To guards and the attendants that he found :
" From the victorious Behrám Gúr, the king,
As envoy to this Court I message bring."
Running the keeper of the gate was seen,
Towards the king himself from near the screen.

*Generally taken for Russia. † Probably the Indus

He ordered them to raise the palace screen;
According to his rank he passed between.
With graceful gait as Behrám forward sped,
Crystal the roof appeared above his head.
His drawers were silver and the body gold,
With many costly jewels in each fold.
He saw his brother sitting lower down,
And resting on his head a jewelled crown.
Seated his Councillors to guide appear,
And by the throne his own son standing near.
Forward to Shangal as he came alone,
He saw him sit on a luxurious throne.
The steps were crystal of that throne of gold,
Where sat that king magnificent and bold.
The king approached the throne and made his prayer,
As a long time he stood before him there.
They seated him upon the golden chair,
And summoned from the Court his comrades there.
Sitting, he loosened of his lip the chain,
And, "O thou lofty monarch" said again,
Quickly he loosed his tongue and said: "I bring
A letter from Behrám, the conqueror king.
On silk and in Pehlávi it is writ,
This to the king of Hind would I submit."
And when he heard he bade the letter bring,
And at it wondered much the noble king.
"My tongue I'll loose if thou wilt order me.
Greatness and fortune ne'er without thee be!"
"Speak on," in answer to him Shangal said
"For God pours blessings on the speaker's head."
He said to him: "That king of royal birth,
No mother bore one like him on the earth.
To whom the nobles all their tribute pay,
And, hunting, lions are an easy prey.
His sword when in the combat seizes he,

The desert must become of blood a sea.
He's generous as spring clouds in the skies :
Dínárs and treasure does he all despise.
He sends a message, India's king to greet,
In Pehlávi written on a silken sheet."

The taking by Shangal of the letter from the hand of Behrám and his giving an answer to it.

Sent for and heard the letter, then the king
Remained in sheer amazement at the thing,
And when the happy scribe had read it through,
Became the king's cheek of a jaundiced hue.
"O man of haughty words," to him he said :
"Be slow of speech : be not to rashness led.
In this does thy king arrogance display :
As of thyself, this also seems thy way.
Tribute from Hindustán should one require,
No man of wisdom will with him conspire.
Should he of treasures speak or of his host,
Or town or country's ruin should he boast,
Kings are like cranes, and as the eagle I,
Or as a river to the dust when dry.
None with success have with the planets fought,
Or from the heavens name and glory sought :
Than idly talk 'tis better to be wise,
Lest any knowing man should thee despise.
Nor courage, knowledge, land dost thou possess,
And thou of kingliness hast even less
Treasures are hidden here throughout my land :
To these my ancestors ne'er stretched a hand,
Horse-armour, breast-plates have I treasured more ;
And open should my treasurer the store,
On elephants he'd have the keys to lay,
Nor furious elephants could draw away.
Of swords and breast-plates should I take account,

The stars in number would to less amount.
Beneath my army's weight the earth will groan,
Of raging elephants and of my throne.
It will, if all who call me king you count,
To thousands multiplied by thousands mount.
Mine are the jewels of the hill and sea,
The world itself owes its support to me.
Fountains of amber, musk, and aloes, too,
Treasures of camphor that is fresh and new,
With medicines for ev'ry man that ails
Or on earth's face from any harm that fails,
All these my land produces manifold,
Be it or gems or silver, or e'en gold.
Now eighty monarchs who with gold are crowned
At my command have all their girdles bound.
In all my land, its hills, its rivers, wells,
No demon has his road, nor ever dwells.
From Kanúj West as far as Irán's bound,
Thence on to *Sakláb* and to China round,
Nobles and great men all beneath my hand,
To worship me in helplessness they stand.
Rulers in Hind, in Chín, in Khatan, all
Upon no other name but mine may call.
All these both of my crown are full of praise,
And to extol my service voices raise.
In my abode Chín's Faghfúr's daughter, too,
Will in the world my praises e'er renew.
I have by her a lion-hearted son,
Who by his sword the mountain's heart has won
From Käús down to Kai Kubád his day
None of this land had anything to say.
Three hundred thousand men, my glorious host,
Of me as their own king would ever boast.
Besides of my allies twelve hundred, too,
Hidden from me a secret never knew.

Father to son all are to me allied,
Before me all in Hind on foot abide.
And in the forest when the lions fight,
They at their voices their own fingers bite.
Had it of freemen ever been the way
With savage haste ambassadors to slay,
I should have from thy body shorn thy head,
And thine own robes would bloody tears have shed."
Behrám said to him then: "O monarch, know,
A prince should not the seed of rashness sow.
My king has bade me: Go to him and say,
'If thou art wise seek not the crooked way.
Two learnéd men now of the court produce,
Talkers, of speech who have the ready use.
If all these men of wisdom and of sense
This man should pass by in intelligence,
I with your land will nothing have to do,
For with the wise words are of value, too.
Or else amongst those valiant in the field
If there are those who know the mace to wield,
A hundred horse from Hindustán select,
To fight with one of us who may elect.
Thy marrow and thy valour if these prove,
For tribute from thy land we will not move.'"

The ordering of a feast by Shangal for Behrám and Behrám's exhibiting his skill before him.

When Shangal heard this, to Behrám he cried:
"To valour is thy wisdom not allied.
Awhile descending, undo thou thy chain:
Why dost thou utter all these words in vain?"
A pleasant hall for him they now prepare,
And bring together all that's needed there.
Then until noonday Behrám took repose—

When the world-lighting crown on high arose,
By order of the king within that hall
Prepared a feast the willing servants all.
Before Shangal as they a tray prepare,
He ordered one to call the envoy there.
He was from Irán envoy of Khusru,
Though eloquent yet to state business new.
Those of his comrades of such rank as they
He bade bring forward to the envoys' tray.
The way then to the table Behrám led:
He closed his lip and stretched his hand for bread.
Bread eaten, then a meeting they arrayed,
For music, wine, and singers calls they made.
Out of their food was spread of musk the scent,
On carpets of brocade laid as they leant.
And when the nobles were by wine made glad,
Care they abandoned and were no more sad.
Two men who well with demons might compare
He bade display themselves in wrestling there.
When two men fitted for the work were found,
At once around their loins their drawers they wound.
With force against each other these two went,
Roaring, their limbs around each other bent.
The glass cup in his hand when Behrám raised,
With fumes of wine his brain within him blazed,
"O king," he said to Shangal, "Give command,
That of my drawers I should tie tight the band.*
When with a strong man I to wrestle go,
Or sleep or drunkenness I no more know."
"Arise," then Shangal laughing to him said,
"Nor hesitate, thrown down, their blood to shed."
Then rose up Behrám as became a man,
And from his lofty height to bend began.
Then anyone whose loins around he clasped,

*Preparatory to wrestling.

As him a wild ass that has tightly grasped,
He threw him on the ground so as to break
His bones, and from his cheeks the colour take.
Shangal remained in wonder at the sight
Of shoulders, strength, and such commanding height:
Calling in Hindí on the God of grace,
Gave him than forty others higher place.
With luscious wine intoxicated all,
They went out from the gem-bespangled hall.
When its silk robe of musk had donned the sphere,
Rested both young and old from their good cheer.
From wine turned back in eye and heart the Kai,
Then Shangal sought his chamber by and by.
When golden grew the sheet of musky scent,
Its face the bright sun showed in its ascent.
The king of Hindoos then his steed bestrode,
And mace in hand towards the open rode,
Down with the king they bow and arrows brought.
Pleasure awhile in riding there he sought.
Behrám then mounted at the king's command,
Holding the royal bow fast in his hand.
He said to Shangal then: "O mighty king,
Horsemen from Irán many now I'll bring,
Who, if the noble king the word shall say,
With mace and arrows all desire to play."
Thus answered Shangal to him: "Arms and bow
A true support to horsemen one should know,
Now with thine arm and hand of mighty blow,
Do thou unloose the stall and string thy bow."
Roaring and urging on his rapid steed,
Thus Behrám Gúr strung up his bow with speed.
Opened the thumb-stall, thence the arrow flew,
And with one shaft he struck the target through.
Praise from all lips resounding echoed far,
Of horsemen of the plain, of men of war.

The suspicion of Shangal with regard to Behrám and his keeping him back from Irán.

Shangal of Behrám doubts began to show:
"This presence grand, this arrow and this bow
Are not an envoy's, as it seems to me,
Or Hindoo, Turk or noble though he be.
Himself should he be king or Chief of might,
That I should call him brother now were right.'
Then laughs the monarch and to Behrám says:
"O thou renowned and full of princely ways,
With all this strength and all this archer's art,
No doubt a brother of the king thou art.
Thou hast Kais' dignity, a lion's strength,
No simple hero art thou now, at length."
"O King of India," Behrám to him cries:
"Envoys as bastards do not stigmatise.
No king am I, of Zazdagird the seed:
To call him brother, that were crime indeed.
Of Irán but a simple stranger I;
No knowledge I possess nor dignity.
Now send me back, for distant is my route,
And the king's anger must not find me out."
"Do not be rash," Shangal to him replied:
"For I have many words to say beside.
Be not thou urgent hence too soon to go;
To go in too great haste thou wrong should'st know.
Stay with me here, nor let thy heart repine;
Seasoned if thou desire not, drink new wine."
He summoned there his Minister at last,
And of Behrám much talk between them passed.
Then this good man, his relative, he told:
"With thee in secret I this converse hold.
Of Behram's relatives should he not be,
Or of the Pehlaváns of high degree,

To wise men's hearts 'twere matter of surprise,
For no one on such flimsy tales relies.
Go, tell him mildly that he here should stay,
And from Kanúj he must not go away.
And thou should'st tell him this with cunning art:
If I should tell him, he would fear at heart.
Go, say to him whatever may be best,
Whatever suits to set his heart at rest.
Speak to him right things that may him advance,
With India's king his honour to enhance.
And now towards him when thou goest hence,
Observe thou well his fine intelligence.
Say his the land that may most pleasing seem—
With India's king art thou in great esteem.
In any place where spring may ever bloom,
Where the streams waft of roses the perfume.
At Kanúj never fails good fortune's breeze,
And twice a year give fruit the laden trees.
Gems are there there and treasured money, too;
Where there is treasure, hearts need never rue.'
After this manner all thou knowest say,
When face to face thou meet'st him on the way.
When all this has been said, his name enquire;
Knowing his name, my heart gains its desire
If thus he grow obedient to my will,
My glory will through him wax greater still.
Soon of our host shall he have the command,
And in our favour shall he rule the land."
This came th' experienced Minister to say,
And spoke to Behrám, pointing out the way.
And then of Behrám he his name enquired,
Else incomplete the answer he required.
As Behrám heard, the colour of his cheek
Was changed, to think what answer he should speak.
"O gifted man," at last Behrám replied,

"Abate not thou in both these lands my pride.*
Irán's king I will not deny for gain,
Although my poverty should cause me pain
The customs of our Faith are otherwise;
Its honour as our road and mode we prize.
From his own king he who may turn his face
Errs on his road to take a higher place.
Increase he does not seek who may be wise,
Evil or good before him equal lies.
Where now is Faridún, the crown who wore,
Upon whose back the age its fortunes bore?
Why should those great men of the kingly race
Kaikhusru, Kaíkobád, not leave their trace?
Again, the young Behrám, dost thou not know,
Who in his selfish way would have things go?
Away from his command should I be led,
Bravely he'd heap the whole world on my head.
There would be left no longer Hindustán;
He'd draw the Magic land's dust to Irán.
It would be better if I hence should flee,
And that my face the conquering king should see.
My name thou askest: it is Barzüí;
The king, my sire and mother gave it me.
To Shangal be my answer whole conveyed:
In a strange land have I too long delayed."
The Vazír took the answer that he made,
And to the king what he had heard conveyed.
Frowning the king's face grew at this reply.
He said: "The right road he is passing by.
For him I now will make up a new plan,
To end the day of this victorious man."
There was a wolf in the king's land so high,
That he would stop the wind from passing by.
Out of that forest shade the lion fled;

*Literally: "Do not make my face yellow."

No vulture flew in heaven overhead.
If India all to it had turned its ear,
Its loud-toned voice 'twould in the forest hear.

The combat of Behrám with the wolf at the wood of Shangal and his killing of the wolf.

"O man approved," he then to Behrám cried:
"All will succeed to which thy hand's applied.
There is a forest near this town of mine,
To which with anxious care I e'er incline.
For like a crocodile a wolf within
Tears out the lion's heart, the panther's skin.
Now it behoves thee to the wolf to go,
And his skin through and through with arrow sew.
Now should its old repose regain the land,
O conqu'ring hero, through thy glorious hand,
Near me shall be reserved a place for thee,
Along with this illustrious company.
So that henceforth in Hind and China's lays,
For evermore may all recite thy praise!"
"O thou of pure intent," Behrám replied:
"To go with me must I now have a guide.
And when in God's strength I his form shall see.
His very robe in blood submerged shall be."
Shangal a guide procured him for the road,
To where he knew it in its lair abode.
The guide went with good heart upon the way
To where the wolf, of blood the shedder, lay.
He told him much that of its lair he knew,
Its height, its breadth, and its huge body, too.
Showing the place, he turned; Behrám in haste,
With graceful movement tow'rd the forest paced.
Behind on combat with the wolf intent.
With girded loins a few Iránis went.
When from afar these all its height surveyed,

The forest and the lair that it had made,
Each one then said to him : "O king, beware,
Of manliness the terms thou passest there.
Brave as thou art, O monarch, in thine ire,
With hill and rock to fight none may aspire."
'My king no leave has giv'n,' to Shangal say,
'And this is not a reasonable way.
If at thine order I should do this thing,
Would strip me of my dignity my king.'"
"If God the pure," in answer he replied,
"For me in Hindustán earth would provide.
How elsewhere could to me my death be brought?
The very fancy is beyond all thought."
The youth then to his bow the string made fast,
Thou would'st have said his life aside he cast.
And raging then towards the wolf he came,
Resigned to death, his heart with rage aflame.
The royal bow he held fast in his hand,
And from his quiver drew a poplar wand.
Arrows he then began to rain like hail,
All with one aim ; the wolf began to fail.
Its time had come. This when he came to know
Dagger he took in hand in place of bow.
With this he cut off from the wolf its head,
And "In God's name who has no fellow," said.
"It is from Him such strength that I have won :
By His command shines in the sky the sun."
Oxen and carriage he bade bring him there,
Out of the wood the dead wolf's form to bear.
When Shangal from afar then saw the beast,
The hall he with brocade decked for the feast.
And when the glorious king sat on his throne,
Before him seated was Behrám alone.
Then ev'ry one with blessings raised his voice,
Great men of Hind and China's warriors choice.

As each Chief there with gifts before him went,
They cried to Behrám all with one assent:
"The deeds of great men all unworthy thee,
No eye is fit thy glorious deeds to see."
Shangal rejoiced, but yet at times in woe,
At times a harsh face or a stern would show.
In water and dry land a dragon there,
At times would lie in river or in air.
Elephants he drew in with his breath awhile,
Or waves rose from him high as in the Nile.
Then Shangal to sharp-witted comrades said,
His secrets those who carried in their head.
"I at this lion-envoy still remain,
At times in gladness and at times in pain.
To be my aid if only he would stand,
In Kanúj he'd be chief and in the land.
And if towards Irán he now should go,
Kanúj from Behrám soon would ruin know.
With such a servant, such a master, too,
This land would not retain or scent or hue.
As all night long I brooded on the thing,
I thought on him another trick to bring.
I thought him to the dragon I would send,
And him he'll not escape from in the end.
If he to combat with the dragon came,
I in the matter should incur no blame."
This said, he summoned there Behrám the bold,
And many tales of valiant men he told.
"The soul-creating God," to him he said,
"Has from Irán's fair land thee hither led,
That Hindustán from evil thou should'st free,
As fitting for renowned men it would be.
There now before us is a painful thing,
At first that pain and then would treasure bring.
When thou hast done this, then no more delay,

But happy, to thine own place take thy way."
Shangal then answering, the king replied:
"There is no way thy counsel to avoid.
I will not pass from thy command awhile,
Although the heav'n revolving should not smile."

The killing of the dragon by Behrám.

"A dragon is there in our land," said he,
"And for long past a great calamity.
On land and river he can come and go,
The crocodile with swinging tail o'erthrow.
Could'st thou for this some remedy prepare,
From this misfortune India to spare,
Thou India's tribute then would'st bear with thee,
And the whole country would to this agree.
With tribute thou would'st India's presents bring,
Aloes and swords and ev'ry kind of thing."
"O monarch," then to him Behrám replied,
"Who dost o'er India in thy rule preside,
Of pure and just God I by the command,
Will cut this dragon's feet from off the land.
But where his lair is as I do not know,
The straight road thither thou to me must show."
Shangal sent with him one the road who knew,
And bade him point out there the dragon, too.
With thirty dagger-bearing horse of name,
All nobles of Irán, he onward came.
Up to the river he drove on his way,
And saw in darkness where the dragon lay.
He saw that twisted form in anger lie,
Where blazed the fire that sparkled from his eye.
Then Irán's warriors shouted at the view,
And at the dragon all excited grew.
All to Behrám exclaiming said: "O king,
As on the wolf, now look not on this thing.

Disperse not Irán's cities to the wind,
Lest in this land thy foes rejoiced thou find."
To the Iránis Behrám thus replied :
"To Him who's just our live's we should confide
Should mine hour in this dragon reach its end,
Will cut it short no valour nor extend."
He chose an arrow, the bow ready made,
In lion's poison had that dart been laid.
Then right and left, as in a horseman's war,
Upon the dragon arrows 'gan to pour.
Its mouth he pierced through with his points of steel,
And soon the poison's torment he could feel.
Four shafted darts he struck upon its head,
And from its body blood-mixed poison shed.
Its body through those arrows languid grew,
With blood and poison earth was washed anew.
Quickly he drew his poison-tainted sword,
And through and through the dragon's heart then bored.
Through neck his sword and battle-axe he thrust,
And cast its lifeless body in the dust.
And when the dragon's matter was complete,
Composed he forward went the king to meet.
Of justice pure he to the Ruler cried :
"This noxious dragon Thou hast now destroyed.
Were it not so, then this who could have done?
Thee in all ill thy slaves depend upon."
And thence returning to the king of Hind,
To him who had arrayed the hosts of Sind,
He said : "Of God Almighty the decree
Has set the monarch from this conflict free."
This Shangal heard, and sorrowful he grew,
When Behrám and his quarry came to view.
He bade them bring a cart and bullocks there.
From wood on to the plain the form to bear.
On Irán from the great and righteous Lord,

From Hindustán they all their blessings poured.
May equal horsemen e'er produce that land,
To fight with dragons who may dare to stand!
To men of stature and such dignity,
Only in princes one may equals see.

The king, enraged at Behrám's exhibition of prowess proposes to his Courtiers to kill his supposed envoy, but they show him the enormity of such a proceeding, which would call down upon him the vengeance of Behrám. He spends the night in reflection, and next day offers his daughter in marriage to Behrám under the impression that he is an envoy. He agrees rather hesitatingly, thinking of the dignity of his throne, and asks that the bride chosen may be one worthy of homage. The king gives him the choice of three, and he chooses one called Sapínûd. They spend a week there in enjoyment, and Sapínúd shines by Behrám's side as wine in a crystal cup. The Faghfúr of China, hearing of this, writes to Behrám, informing him that Sapinúd is a relation of his, and inviting him to come and visit him. Behrám is displeased at the haughty tone of the letter, considering that he had put a slight on him as king of kings, and declines the invitation. After this he informs his bride that he intends to leave Hindustán, and she consents to accompany him, and proposes a time for their flight when the king will be engaged in festivities. They start accordingly, and when they arrive at the Indus he orders some Iráni merchants who are on the trade route not to appear to recognize him. He crosses the Indus with Sapínúd, and Shangal, who has pursued them here, catches them up and taunts Behrám with having deceived him, but Behrám confesses who he is, and they part mutually satisfied, Shangal returning to Kanúj and Behrám to Irán. The latter is joyfully received by his subjects. The day after he reascends his throne a grand assemblage is held, and he exhorts every one as to his proper duty, and shows them it will be their own fault if they allow themselves to be oppressed by any one without complaining to him and getting redress. He goes to Adargushasp and returns thanks for God's mercies, and instructs Sapínúd in the faith of Zartusht. Behrám, at Shangal's desire, now writes a new treaty of friendship, and Shangal also comes to visit him in company with seven kings, those of Kábul, of Hind, of Sind, of Sandal, of Jandal, of Kashmír, and of Múltán, in great state. Behrám goes as far as Nahraván to meet them, and entertains them. Shangal sees his daughter and they weep tears of joy together. Shangal writes a letter announcing that Behrám shall be Rajá of Kanúj after his death, and after two months of enjoyment returns to Hindustán.

Behrám was troubled about this time with the predictions of the astrologers that he would live for sixty years, but in the fourth twenty he would die. He had laid out his life before him so that the first twenty should be passed in amusement, the second in executing justice and judgment in the world, and the third in serving God, that He might be his guide. He orders the Vazír to count his treasury and ascertain how much he has to spend, and on being told that he has enough to last for the remaining twenty-three out of the sixty-three years of life promised him, he determines not to levy any more taxes. He sends Mobeds to each town to be mediators in all disputes, but receives letters from them to say that the youth of the period despise the valour of the great, that their hearts were filled with the desire of riches, and they respected neither the Mobeds nor the king. Accordingly for each province just and wise administrators are appointed, who are provided with means for being generous, and ordered to remain in their offices for six months to levy money, during which the king received it, while during the other six months he spent it, but the receivers were not to profit by it in any way. The object of this was to prevent men out of employment from shedding blood and involving others in evil, but his agents wrote him that justice had disappeared from the world, those who had the money would not pay taxes, and oppression prevailed. He appointed administrators full of justice in each province to carry out the laws of God against all who shed blood, and, remembering God's generosity, distributes a year's pay. After some time has passed he enquires whether there is anything hurtful that is injuring the country, and finds that the effect of his gifts is that no one would observe old customs and follow the right road: agriculture had ceased, cattle were dispersed, and grass was growing up in sown fields. He issues orders that people should only labour to the middle of the day, and devote the remainder to sleep, rest, eating and enjoyment. If a man had not seed or cattle, or if his crops were injured by the weather, he should be benevolently assisted from the treasury. If locusts devoured the crops, the owner should have compensation given him. Nothing is to be demanded from waste land, and any one demanding rent from such should be buried alive, and there should be no place for him to dwell in. These orders were issued under Behrám's seal throughout the land. The Mobeds reporting to him that the poor complained of their hard lot while the rich were enjoying themselves with eating and drinking to the sound of pleasant music, he writes to Shangal to send him 10,000 Lúris who play the lute and sing, in order to make agriculturists of them, and when they come gives each a bullock, an ass and corn for the purpose, stipulating that they should play and sing to amuse the poor: they, however, eat the bullock and the corn and present themselves at the end of the year with yellow cheeks. He accordingly tells them to make the most of the asses they still have. They accordingly wander in the world singing and playing, to steal day and night.*

Sixty-three years having thus passed over Behrám's head, his treasurer comes to tell him that the treasury is empty, and he tells him to look for no more, but give up the world to Him who had created it: heaven would pass away, but God would remain and be their Guide to happiness. The day after this, in the presence of the nobles and a large crowd, Behrám hands over the crown and other insignia of royalty to his son Yázdagird and is found dead in his bed the next morning. The chapter winds up with the usual moralising as to the fickleness of fate that carries off such a worthy king as Behrám.

The reign of Yazdagird lasts for eighteen years, and is passed in happiness, as his rule was just. It commences with the usual exhortation and admonition to his nobles, and when he feels his end approaching, he nominates his son Hormuz as his successor. After this he lives only a wee

The reign of Hormuz only lasts a year. Pirúz, his elder brother, jealous that Hormuz should have been preferred to him, applies for assistance to Fagháních, king of Chaghán, who gives him an army of 30,000 men on condition that the towns of Tarmad and Vísah are ceded to him. In the fight that ensues Hormuz is taken prisoner, and out of kindness only deposed and sent away to his own house. The reign of Piruz lasts eleven years. After addressing his Courtiers in the usual moral strain, he governs for a year with wisdom and justice. A drought comes on, and lasts for seven years. So many people and animals die that there is no room left to stand. He distributes corn to great and small, and orders all those who have granaries and beasts to sell their grain and animals at whatever price they choose, threatening death

*These are presumably our gipsies.

to any owner of a granary through whose fault in not opening his store any one may die. All are ordered out into the fields to pray to God, and at last, in the month of Farvardin in the eighth year, favourable rain falls, and after the scarcity has disappeared Pírúz ascends the throne and lives happily. He builds the castles of Pírúzrám and Badán Pírúz, which was afterwards called Ardabíl. He bestowed *dirams* on the army until he went to war with the Turkománs, the army in this being led by Hormuz and followed by Kubád. There is apparently some confusion in this place, and it is not clear whether a son of Pírúz who is here mentioned as the eldest, wise and a fruitful branch, was now seated on the throne, or Balásh, or who was Khushnaváz, who now appears, and is mentioned as writing a letter to Pírúz accusing him of a breach of treaty, and sending it with an envoy. Pírúz replies that the Turkománs have advanced to the Jaihún whilst Behrám had fixed the boundary at the river Tarak, and that he will bring his army and leave not even the shadow of Khushnaváz on the earth. Khushnaváz prepares his army, and puts on the point of a lance Behrám's treaty fixing the boundary at the Jaihún, sending another envoy to remonstrate with Pírúz against his provocation of an unjust war. Neither side listens to the other, and Khushnaváz, appealing to God, digs a trench twenty cubits in breadth round his camp. The army of Pírúz proceeds to the attack, Khushnaváz makes a feigned retreat, and Pírúz himself falls into the trench, and none of those with him escapes alive but Kubád, who is put in golden chains. The whole of Irán is thrown into grief. Balásh mourns for forty days and then ascends the throne. He reigns for five years and two months, after pronouncing the usual allocution to the the nobles and receiving their benedictions. Pírúz, when he left for the war, had left as guardian of the throne and of Balásh, a man of Shiraz, Governor of Kábulistán, Zabulistán, and Ghazni. His name was Súfrai. He writes a letter of encouragement to Balásh, and proceeds to Marv, writing a letter to Khushnaváz full of threats of sword and vengeance. An answer is sent reiterating the charge of breach of treaty, and preparation is made for war. Baigand is chosen by Khushnaváz for the battle. At sunrise it commences, and the latter, seeing that fate is against him, takes to flight, pursued by Súfrai. Many are killed and wounded, and Khushnaváz flees as far as Kuhandiz. Súfrai does not halt for the spoil that is brought to him, but pushes on, and is met by a messenger from Khushnaváz to say that he submits to his fate, and will restore the prisoners and all taken from Pírúz and carry out the compact made with Behrám. The message is brought before the army, and Súfrai advises that peace should be made, and Kubád's release effected, as well as that of the Grand Mobed Ardashír and other prisoners. This is agreed to, and on his messenger's return Khushnaváz gladly carries out the agreement. Kubád and the other prisoners are restored and the army returns to Irán with great rejoicing. Balásh now gives up the throne and crown to Kubád. The reign of Kubád lasts 43 years. He addresses the usual exhortation to the Court and people. He has no Vazír, but Súfrai manages all affairs of State until the king attains the age of 23. Súfrai then asks leave to return to Shiráz. People then begin to whisper against him that all have become his slaves, that his wealth is greater than that of the king himself, and that the latter has only the title. Kubád's ears are thus poisoned against him, and he sends for Shápur, a descendant of Mehrak, from Rai, an enemy of Súfrai's, and orders him to Shiráz to put Súfrai in chains. Súfrai in vain sets forth all that he has done and suffered for the king, but is at last put to death by the advice of the

Grand Mobed. A great outcry rises in Irán at this outrage, and the whole people seek out Jámásp, the youngest brother of the king, and place him on the throne, handing over Kubád himself in chains to Razmehr, Súfrai's son, who, however, does not kill him, as they had hoped, but professes himself his slave, and takes off his chains. The two take flight together with five others who are in Kubád's confidence, and go towards the town of Heitál. Arriving in the country of Ahváz they alight at the house of a rich citizen, to whose daughter he gives a ring of value, and promises to ask for it back when he has had his revenge. Remaining a week, he goes to the king of Heitál, who promises him an army on condition that if he is victorious he shall cede Chaghán to him. An agreement is made, and receiving 30,000 men from him Kubád returns to Irán, where he had left the daughter of the rich man (Dehkán), and finds that during his absence a son has been born to him. He enters the house joyfully and names the boy Kasrá. He starts towards Ctesiphon with his army, taking his wife in a litter. The nobles meet him and beg pardon for their fault, which he condones, and Jámásp, who is only a child of ten years, is removed from the throne. The management of affairs is handed over to Razmihr, and all is conducted with justice until Kasrá, who has in the meanwhile been educated by wise men, grows up. He carries an army to Rúm, which becomes like a ball of wax in his hand: the country is desolated, and two cities, Hindíyá and Fárikín, claim protection from him. He teaches them the *Zandavastá* and the true Faith, erects fire-temples in them, and establishes in them the Náorúz and Saddah festivals. His capital is fixed at Madáin, and to a city founded between Ahváz and Fárs, with a hospital. The town is called Arash, and now goes by the name of Halván, where canals are made and the country becomes the abode of peace and repose.

He adopts the Faith of Mazdak, who becomes his Minister and treasurer. At this time drought and famine occur, and the people go to Mazdak for bread and water. He refers them to Kubád, but goes to him himself, and puts this question to him : "A man has been bitten by a snake, and another man has an antidote for the poison, but will not give it to the one who has been bitten: what does this man deserve ?" The king replies that the man is a murderer and deserves to be killed. Mazdak returns to those who are clamouring, and he tells them to wait till the morning, when he will show them the road to justice. When they come he goes to the king and asks him what is due to one who refuses bread to a man who is fastened up with a strong chain, so that he dies: the king answers that he is a murderer for not doing what he ought. Mazdak now tells the people to go where there is corn hidden and take it, and if its price is demanded to pay for it. He himself gives up what he has of his own in the city, until not a grain was left in the city or in Kubád's granaries. This is reported to the king, and blame attributed to Mazdak, who is sent for, and explains that he merely told the people what the king himself had said. Kasrá is put out by what has been done. Many questions are asked and replied to, and he finally says: "The rich man is the same as the empty handed one : no one should have in excess, for the rich man is the warp and the poor the woof. Any excess of the rich man is unlawful, and riches and women should be common property. I will make this right, that the Faith may be purified." He finally treats rich and poor alike, and adheres to the faith of Mazdak. One day a great number of the same belief assemble together, and he has his throne taken out into the open plain in order to receive them. Mazdak now addresses him and says that Kasrá is not of this faith, and a declaration in writing should be taken from him that he would renounce his evil ways. Five things make one avoid what is right, viz.: hatred, envy, anger, revenge, and want. If these things are overcome, the way of the lord of the world will be made clear. Women and wealth destroy the faith. Envy, avarice and want come from them and consort with anger and vengeance. The demon turns the head of the wise. Having said this he seizes Kasrá's hand, to his amazement, and the latter angrily snatches it away from him and turns his eyes away from him. Kubád laughs and asks him what he knows of the faith of Kasrá, and he answers that secretly he is not in the right way, and is also not of his religion. The king asks Kasrá why he deviates from the true faith, and Kasrá promises to answer in six months. Kasrá now sends for men whom he knows to be learned, and who could assist him. One was to go to Ardashír to induce the aged Hormuz to come to Court, and one to Mihr Azar to bring him with 30 of his friends. All assemble together and consult, and all give their views to Kasrá. The next day all meet together at the palace to talk of the true faith, and a Mobed says to Mazdak that he has proposed that women and riches should be held in common, but if that were to be how would the father know his son or the son his father? If there is no distinction between men who would serve and who exercise power, when a man died to whom would his house and his fortune go, for king and artizan were to be equal? The world would become a desert. Who would be the masters and who would be the paid servants? If all had the treasure, who would be treasurer? No founder of a religion had ever broached such ideas. Kasrá approves of the Mobed's words, and all the assembly cry out that Mazdak was destroying religion and should not remain with the king. The king disapproves of Mazdak's views, and hands him and his adherents over to Kasrá, who hangs him alive on a gibbet and kills him with arrow shots.* When Kubád has reigned for forty years, he tires of life and writes a letter, in which, after writing the praises of God, he moralises on the gradual approach of old age and death, gives up his throne to Kasrá, and dies. He is placed in the *Dukhmah* by the Mobeds, his letter is read to the assembly, and his heir apparent is placed on the throne. The reign of Kasrá, or Naoshírván, lasted 48 years. On ascending the throne he gives a long exhortation to his people to be thankful to God, and to obey His will. Whoever executed justice would be happy in himself and be free from all evil thoughts; they must not put off till to-morrow the affairs of to-day, for one may pluck roses one day and the next they will have faded—when in health they should think of sickness and pain—remember that the day of death follows life, for we are like the leaves before the wind. avoid jealousy, for there is no medicine for it. When passion takes possession of the head, there is no need to show what is folly. The man without occupation who talks much is respected by no one. Lying is for feeble people, and one can only weep for them. A wise man has no need of amusement, &c. When these exhortations were all finished, the assembly were left in astonishment. He proceeds to divide the world into four portions, the first Khurásán, the second Kúm and Isfahán, with Azar Abádghán, Armenia as far as Ardabíl and Gilán, the third Fárs, Ahváz and the land of Khazar from East to West, and the fourth Irák and the country of Rúm. All previous kings had a third or a fourth of the crops, but it was fixed at a tenth by Kubád. Kashrá gave up even the tenth. The land was measured and distributed. An impost was levied on the *dirham* of produce in such a manner as not

*Here an extraordinary account is given of Mazdak's followers being planted in the ground like trees with their feet upwards, and of Mazdak being sent to see them before he is himself hanged.

to distress the villagers (*Dehkan*): those who had no cattle or seed at the proper season were assisted from the treasury, and nothing was charged for uncultivated lands. Liberal terms were also given for fruit-bearing trees and date palms. There appears also to have been a kind of graduated income tax on those who possessed means but had no land to cultivate, at from four to ten *dirhams* a year, payable in instalments, from which fathers of families were exempted. Other regulations follow as to the officers who were to supervise the registration and collection of imposts. Over the face of the earth were scattered experienced men, so that nothing might be concealed from him, and justice so prevailed that the waste was tilled, great and small slept safely in the desert, and wolves and sheep drank at the same water.

The next Section is entirely taken up with an account of the justice he has set himself to carry out, and recommendations to those who are under him to do the same in a Pehlavi letter sent round to all the king's officers. After this comes a description of the measures taken by a Mobed of the name of Bábak, who has charge of the army, for a review of the forces, in the course of which the king displays his skill in warlike exercises, Bábak watching him and giving him orders. He afterwards apologises for having drilled him like a common soldier, but the king applauds him for his honesty and straightforwardness, and informs him that he has sent a letter to his Pehlaváns exhorting them to educate their sons for military service and become masters of their hands, stirrups, and reins, as well as learn how to wield the mace and sword, bow, and arrows, for no one, though a descendant of Arish, was of any use unless he had been taught. He has also sent out inspectors to hold reviews for forty days so that everything may be ready in case any is attacked. The next Section relates how the king summons together all people desirous of seeing justice established and how he addresses them on the subject. The people applaud his sentiments and go away contented. The whole earth blooms like the garden of Irán, and his fame spreads to Rúm and India. Other kings became convinced that they could not resist Naoshírván, and resigned themselves at once to the payment of tribute, and sent offerings of money, slaves, and other gifts. The heaven, in turning, did so with love for the king of Irán.

The king now determines to make a tour in his empire. He follows the route of Khurásán, Gurgán, Sari, and Amal into the hilly country, and seeing all its beauties gives praise to God. A man says to him all would be a Paradise if the Turkománs were prevented from pillage and murder. He thereupon directs his ministers to select able men from India and China and build a wall to prevent incursions into Irán. This was not to be carried out by forced labour, but every one was to be duly paid for his work. The wall is built so as to completely shut out the desert with a strong iron gate, and the sheep are guaranteed against attack from the wolves. Guardians are placed in all the country, and when all is in security he takes away his army.

The king now punishes the Alánis, and Balúchis, and the Gílánis. He sends an envoy to the Alánis to say that their incursions into Irán will be tolerated no longer. Seeing the hopelessness of resistance, they give in and repair to his camp with offerings, and he orders a large town to be built in the desert they had made with land for cultivation round it and an enclosing wall to keep their enemies out, whilst they pursue their new avocation in place of the plundering by which they had hitherto lived. After this he proceeds to India, where all the nobles present themselves ready to obtain his help. They are well received and he then proceeds against the Balúchis, who had depopulated the frontier* by their plundering incursions. He severely punishes them and brings peace and comfort into the land. Thence he marches to Gílán, where the people submit themselves to him and give 300 hostages for their good behaviour, and goes on to Madáin (Ctesiphon). Here he is met by Manzir, the Arab, who demands his aid against the Rúmis, who are encroaching on the desert. He sends, as the Suzerain of the Arabs, a message to the Kaiser, threatening him, and the latter sends an evasive answer, and Naoshírván provides Manzir with 30,000 horse to assist him, and informs him that he will write to the Kaiser. This letter is given in the next Section, and threatens the Kaiser if he interferes with the Arabs. It is sent to the Kaiser by a discreet and valiant envoy, and answered to the effect that no Rúmi has ever paid tribute to the family of the Kais, but on the contrary he will demand tribute from Irán, and his forces will ravage its plains from one frontier to the other. He dismisses the envoy with the words: May the Messiah and the Cross protect thee! Naoshírván receives the Kaiser's letter, waits for three days to take counsel with the Mobeds and wise men, and then advances with the standard of Kávah to the temple of Ázargushasp, when the Zandavastá is produced and worshipped, and after writing a letter to the army to be on their guard during his absence, he proceeds towards the enemy. Shirúï, son of Behrám, commands the army, Farhád the left wing, and Ustád, son of Pírúz, the left. Gushtásp is in charge of the baggage and Behrám of the centre of the army. The king threatens to cut in two any one who plunders fruit trees or treads down cropped fields or commits any other act of oppression. These orders are proclaimed through

*They are wrongly called the people of Kachh (Kutch).

the army, and Naoshírván goes through the ranks and confirms them himself. He attacks the fort of Shúráb, situated on a rock with deep water alongside of it, and beats down the walls with his catapults and carries off all the rich men and those who are distinguished for valour and wealth. He next attacks Aráish-i-Rúmi (the ornament of Rúm), which contains the Kaiser's treasure, and destroying it, distributes the treasure to his army, pardoning the inhabitants. He next defeats the army of Farfúrius (Porphyry) sent against him, and takes possession of Kalínius (?) and Antákiah (Antioch), the latter being given up to him without opposition. His prisoners and the Kaiser's treasure are sent off to Madáin, leaving the people of the country, who were not sent, in a new city called *Zíb-i-Khusru*, near Antioch, which] he has built for the purpose. He leaves the charge of the town and troops in the hands of a Christian governor. Farfúrius reports to the Kaiser all that has happened, and the latter sues for peace, offering to pay tribute, sending a philosopher of the name of Mehrás as an ambassador. Mehrás makes a prudent speech, and the matter is settled by the annual tribute from Rúm of six bullocks' hides filled with pieces of gold being fixed and a treaty being made that Rúm should in no way interfere with Yaman. Naoshírván now retires to Syria, where he remains some time, and then, leaving Shirúi, Behrám's son, in command of the country, with an order to him to demand the tribute regularly from Rúm, and not allow it to fall into arrears, marches into Armenia.

The history now proceeds to relate the birth to Naoshírvan of a son, who is called Núshzád, by a Christian woman. This boy grows up like a cypress: he knows of hell and Paradise, of the doctrine of Esdras, and the Messiah and the Faith of Zardusht, and becomes a Christian. His father confines him accordingly to his own palace. Naoshirván on his way back from Rúm becomes ill, and unable to hold audiences, and news is taken to Núshzád that he is dead. He rejoices at this, issues from his place of confinement, assembles Christian and other troops, takes possession of the surrounding towns, and goes so far as to levy tribute from Ahváz and Shustar. The governor of Madáin, Rám Barzin, sends information of all this to Naoshírván, who writes to him to send an army, to proceed with all gentleness and with no injury to his person, to make a prisoner of Núshzád, as Naoshírván will not harm his own blood. Rám Barzín prepares an expedition against Núshzád, who assembles an army of Christian priests (*Jasalík*, καθολικος) and others, with one Shamás at their head, and notwithstanding the warnings of one called Pírúz the lion that he cannot hope to resist his father, arms himself and stations himself in the centre. After a success at first in overthrowing the left wing of the Iránis, he is wounded by an arrow, after declaring that he holds to the faith of the Messiah, whom the glory of the Creator has not abandoned, although he may have been killed, for from the earth he has attained to the loftiness of the pure God, and that he is not afraid to die, as there is no antidote to this poison. He now confesses to a Bishop (*sakaf*) that he has done wrong. He sends a message to his mother to bid her not to grieve for him: that he only desires a Christian tomb without camphor, musk or amber; and thereupon he dies. He is lamented by both sides, and is buried by his mother. The Section curiously winds up with an exhortation to believe in Ali.

Naoshírván now has a dream. Here Fardusi utters a warning against treating dreams lightly, for they contain prophesies, especially when a king dreams them: the stars hold council with the sphere and the moon, and their words being spread abroad bright souls see in their dreams all things that are to be like the reflection of fire in water. Naoshírván sees a royal tree grow up before his throne which charms his heart: he sends for wine, music and singers. But there sits in this delightful place a boar with sharp teeth, and it prepares to sit down at the banquet and asks to drink out of Naoshírván's own cup. The interpreters of dreams, whom he sends for in the morning, cannot explain it, and he sends out wise men in all directions to find someone who can. One Buzúrjmihr is found, who undertakes to do so, but refuses to speak except to the king himself, and proceeds with one of the men sent out by Naoshírván towards Marv. On the road Buzúrjmihr falls asleep under a tree, with his head covered with a piece of cloth. His companion sees a snake come out of a wood and remove the cloth from Buzúrjmihr's head; then smelling him from head to foot the snake hides himself among the leaves of a tree. Arrived at the Court, Buzúrjmihr is brought before the king, and tells him with reference to his dream that there is a young man among his supposed wives. These are paraded before him, and he fails to detect a man among them, but Buzúrjmihr insists on their coming unveiled, and a young man is found among them of the stature of a cypress and a face as one of the royal race. He is found to be the brother of one of the king's seventy women, and the two are then and there hanged by the executioner by the king's order in the female apartments.

Buzúrjmihr is richly rewarded and enrolled among the Councillors of the king: his fortune increases every day, and the king is rejoiced at having him.

The king now gives seven entertainments to the Mobeds, of whom there were seventy at his Court; each of these is set forth separately. Buzúrjmihr at the first of these descants on duty, especially that of kings. Ambition, avidity, and useless words are inveighed against; honesty, humility, and the fear of God are inculcated. The assembled Mobeds are delighted at his noble sentiments, and salute him with new benedictions. He impresses upon them the necessity of not turning away from or disobeying the king, who is the dispenser of justice, and warns them of the power he possesses, both to do good and to inflict punishment. The assembly breaks up ful of his praises. In another week the king gives a second entertainment, and the assembled Mobeds and others question him on various points. The last of these is: "By what is a man rich, and who in the world is poor and loaded with trouble?" His answer is: "He is rich who is content with the gifts of the Lord of heaven, and there is no misfortune greater than covetousness." In another week a third entertainment is given, and four others at the same interval after each other. All are full of the same description of questions and answers on points of morals and conduct, and quite devoid of historical value.*

The story of Mahbúd, Vazír of Naoshírván, is now related. He was intelligent and honest in his intentions and of good counsel, and was honoured by the king. He had two sons, who waited on the king when he went to pray. The King would only eat what Mahbúd or his sons provided for him. The nobles of the Court were jealous of Mahbúd, especially one old chamberlain of the name of *Zurán*, who was constantly on the look out for an opportunity to irritate the king against him and his sons. Mahbúd was aware of this, but paid no attention to the wretched man's proceedings. One day a Jew brought Mahbúd some money to value, and the two contracted a friendship for each other, and he began to frequent the palace. *Zurán* spoke to him one day secretly about magic and incantations, and told him not to men-

*At this point the 3rd Volume of Macan's edition ends.

tion it to anyone: that he must perform some magic rite in order to free the world of Mahbúd, for such was the state of affairs that he seemed to consider the world was made up of Naoshirván and himself alone. The Jew bids him inspect the dishes provided for the king and ascertain whether there is any milk in them, for he had only to look on the milk, from whatever distance, and he would see Mahbúd and his sons no more in life. A certain honest and intelligent woman in Mahbúd's house always prepared the king's food, which was carried to the king by Mahbúd's sons. One day as the sons were taking in the dishes Zurán begged that he might look at them in order to see their colour. They allowed him to look, and at the same moment the Jew cast a glance at them, and afterwards told him that the tree he had planted was bearing fruit. The dishes were taken in to the king, but before he tasted them Zurán rushes in and tells the king that the cook has mixed poison with the food. The young men at once taste the food and fall down dead, and the king orders Mahbúd to be executed, his palace to be razed, and all his property to be pillaged. Zurán for some time had high renown in the palace of the king. The king himself was grieved for Mahbúd. It so happened that when a number of horses were collected for the king to go out hunting wolves he saw among them two branded with Mahbúd's mark on them, and was greatly affected at the sight. Shortly afterwards Zurán and the Minister were talking in the king's presence about incantations and magic, which the king disregarded. Zurán, however, mentioned that magicians could convert milk into poison by merely looking at it. Remembering what had taken place on the day when he had had Mahbúd killed, he begins to suspect Zurán, and on questioning him extracts a confession of the truth from him, and subsequently from the Jew as well. The nobles, Mobeds, and Chiefs of the army are called, and the confessions being repeated in their presence, the two men are strung up to two gibbets before the camp and then and there put to death with arrows and stones. The king now searches for and discovers a daughter of Mahbúd, and three men, and hands over to them all the property of the two executed men.

The next Section descants on the justice of Naoshírván and the excellence of his rule, and relates the foundation by him of the city of Súrsán on the road to Rúm, after the plan of other towns of the same kind already existing in the country. In this he settles the prisoners he had taken from Barbar, Rum, and other places that he had destroyed, as well as the many hostages, and those from Gílan and other devastated countries, and makes the place like a Paradise.

Hearing nothing but the praises of Naoshírván, the Khákán desires to acquire his friendship, and consulting his Ministers and nobles determines to send him valuable presents by an intelligent and eloquent messenger. His route lay by Heitál, where an army had been gathered together that extended as far as the Jaihún. Hearing of the proposed alliance between China and Irán, a man whose name is Ghátkar, General of the people of Heitál, fears that it will be a cause of terror to his country, and determines on preparing an expedition in order to cut off the Chinese envoy, and does so accordingly. Only one Chinese horseman escapes the massacre. The Khákán immediately is intent on revenge, and assembles at the Gulzáriún river an army and treasure from Balkh, Heitál, Shakmán, the Amú, Khatlán, Tarmad and Vísáhgadh, and crosses the Tarak. On the other side Saghd and Káshán come together to Ghátkar at Bukhárá. For seven days a battle rages between the two armies, and on the eighth the army of Heitál suffers a great defeat, and sees the uselessness of further resistance under their present circumstances. The people accordingly elect Faghánísh, a descendant ot Khushnaváz, king. Naoshírván learns what the people of Heitál have done, and assembles Ardashír, the Chief Mobed, Shápúr, Gazdagird, the scribe, and other wise Councillors, and describing the state of affairs consults them as to what should be done. All recommend that he should not advance out ot Irán but merely prepare for war, for fear that if he leaves the country the Rúmis might seize the opportunity of invading it. Naoshirván is of a different opinion, and determines to lead an army into Khurásán, not to demand tribute from the Khákán or Heitál, but to clear the world of the evil disposed, and rule with justice. The assembly agree, and declare they will be ready to fight as soon as the king orders them. When the king is ready to start he collects a large army, and marches to Gurgán, and the Khákán continues to boast of what he will do against him, but when warned by an intelligent man of the seriousness of the task, consults his Vazír, and determines to send a letter by ten eloquent Chinese professing his desire for friendship with Naoshírván. The envoys are well received and entertained with hunting and festivities for a month. One day he holds a great gathering when the envoys of Barda, India, Rúm and China are all present, and exhibits his large army and his own skill in martial exercises, which they all admire. Nasohírván now writes an answer to the Khákán's letter, in which, after speaking slightingly of the people of Heitál, and of the Faghfúr's treasure and power, he says with regard to the proposal for friendship that he has no desire to fight, and sends also a message by his envoys. These return to the Khákán, and give him their impressions of the person, power and wealth ot Naoshírván. The Khákán, hearing this magnificent description, withers away and becomes like the flower of the fenugreek. Distracted with care, he consults his Court, and with their approval offers to give one of his daughters to Naoshírván. The offer is sent by three members of his own family, and Naoshírván agrees to send Mihrán Sitád to choose among the Khákán's daughters, with instructions not to take one born of a slave, but a princess, grand-daughter of the Faghfúr as well as daughter of the Khákán, if she is as handsome as she is of high rank. Mihrán proceeds on his errand, and is graciously received by the Khákán. He is allowed into the female apartments and finds five girls, with the face of *Paris*, sitting on thrones, four of whom have crowns and are covered with jewels, and the fifth without any ornaments. He chooses the last one, and she is finally accepted and dispatched with great pomp with Mihrán, all the country en route being decorated and offerings being presented. She is received at the palace with great honour, the people assembling on the road, throwing money down from the balconies, musk and amber being poured upon her, dishes with aromatic scents spread about, drums and trumpets filling the air with sound, the horses' manes steeped in musk and wine, sugar and silver cast upon her feet, flutes and lutes resounding. The king is astonished at her beauty, and invokes the name of God over her, and prepares a throne for her in an apartment worthy of her. The Khákán hears of this, and leaving Saghd, Samarkand and Cháj, sends his crown to Kachárbáshi. The world is rejuvenated by the justice of Naoshírván. All the people of the surrounding countries assemble at the Gulzáriú, and determine to present themselves before him with gifts. Headed by Fagháních, they prostrate themselves before him and pour benedictions, and Naoshírván himself ascribes all his power and happiness to God. He now returns in triumph to Irán, and finds peace and plenty everywhere, with waste lands cultivated and valleys and plains abounding with cattle and sheep, full of fruit trees and houses filled with children. An envoy from Rúm soon makes his appearance with the tribute of six bulls' hides filled with pieces of gold and other gifts. Naoshírván receives these, and then proceeds to Azargúshasp in order to return thanks to God. Thence he returns to Madáin, taking his new Chinese bride with him.

The next Section treats of the justice of Naoshírván and the enjoyment of ease by the world under his laws, and is translated from the original as follows:—

Discourse on the justice of Naoshírván and the finding of rest by the people of the world through his laws.

When Kasrá mounted proudly on his throne
And one with fortune found himself alone,
A very Paradise the world to view,
Replete with justice, wealth and beauty, too.
The whole world was at rest from any strife,
From all injustice and from taking life.
The earth renewed with God's light spread around,
Both hands of evil, thou had'st said, were bound.
None knew to plunder or invade the land,
And none tow'rds evil to stretch out his hand.
The world subservient to the king became,
And back from crookedness and darkness came.
If anyone strewed money on the way,
Thieves from such riches all would run away.
On land and water money and brocade,
In shining day at sleeping time were laid.
And yet from fear and justice of the king,
No robber cast his eye on anything.
The world like Eden was adorned again,
And full of riches were the vale and plain.
Around to ev'ry land they letters wrote,
To ev'ry Chief and ev'ry man of note.

There merchants both from Turkey and from Chín,
From *Saklab** and from ev'ry land were seen.
Plenty of musk and Chinese silk were there.
Embellishments that Rúm and Hind prepare.
Irán grew like an Eden to behold;
Its dust was amber and its bricks were gold.
Now tow'rds Irán the world its face addressed,
From aimless talk and sorrow it had rest.
The air, thou would'st have said, shed tears of rose,
Mankind from pain and doctors had repose.
In due time fell upon the rose the dew,
And want of rain no cultivator knew.
Of grass for beasts the world then did not fail—
With flow'rs and palaces filled plain and vale.
There ev'ry brook would as a river run,
And melon-gardens as the Pleiads shone.
They in Irán taught many a foreign tongue,
Knowledge was bright enlightened souls among.
Merchants around from ev'ry place and strand,
Turkey, Rúm, Chín, and from the Hindoos' land,
Their praises of the Guide would never cease,
The beasts with grass abounding found increase.
Knowledge and learning all there who possessed,
And orators to the king's palace pressed,
With Mobeds rare, the learned and the wise,
Whilst from the fear of harm the wicked flies.
The sun would with its rays the world adorn,
And from the palace would a voice be borne.
" All ye the world's king's subjects who abide,
The evil that ye suffer do not hide.
He in his work who has experienced pain,
Shall by its measure treasure, too, obtain.
This to the palace ruler do ye say,
That he of me may then demand your pay.

*Russia.

And if a creditor put forth his hand,
His debt from one who's needy to demand,
Be labour's hand as empty as it may,
My treas'rer from his store the debt shall pay.
If on another's wife one cast his eye,
And to the palace then her husband hie;
Only the stake or dungeon shall he know,
With the pit chains, on stake an arrow's blow.
When anywhere they find a horse has strayed,
And at my gate a Dehkán* plaint has made,
Let them its blood shed and on that field slay,
And he who suffers bear the flesh away.
Thenceforth his rider on his feet shall go,
And penitence at Azargúshasp show.
The army's roll his name shall no more know,
And under foot shall they his dwelling throw.
He in whom fault, or great or small, is seen,
Or he be worse than he has ever been.
The king with him will not be intimate;
He wishes none but true men at his gate.
He who this way may not approve, in short,
'Twere better should he not be at my Court."

The giving of advice by Buzúrjmihr to Naoshírván and his discourse on good deeds and words.

The king one day sat joyful on his seat,
His nobles wise in audience to meet.
He talked there smiling with an open face;
Buzúrjmihr on a throne then took his place.
One blessing he invoked upon the king,
That made his heart bloom like the gladsome spring.
"O ruler of the pleasant face," said he:
"May the fault-finder have no words for thee!

* A villager.

Auspicious king of kings, with victory,
Ruler with wisdom and prosperity.
A Pehlavi letter I to thee addressed,
On royal paper on a roll impressed.
I gave it to thy treas'rer, that some day
To read it he before the king might lay.
I see that heaven's slow-revolving sphere.
My secret will not open to thine ear.
When a man rises from the festive board,
In hand he lays his own life for the sword.
From his own land he clears out ev'ry foe,
And frees himself of demons from the woe.
King he becomes of earth and regions wide,
And meets with pleasant words on ev'ry side.
Treasure lays by, and round him many a son,
For many days, he counts his hopes upon.
And though in pain here there may be the poor,
Good name and riches he collects the more.
Lawful, unlawful he collects around,
And not a hundred years his being's bound.
Dust he becomes and fruitless all his pain,
He to his foes leaves all his wealth again.
Of son or crown or throne he cannot boast,
Of kingly hall or of his wealth or host.
When his wind-searching at the last is o'er,
No one on earth will then think of him more.
After this manner as time passes by,
Two things alone will in men's memory lie.
These are soft words and ev'ry act that's pure,
These, aye, will last while earth and sand endure.
Dust, wind and water, sunshine in the sky,
Good name and pure words never can destroy.
After this way it is that time goes round;
Happy the virtuous man who's modest found.
And if thy soul should not approve the thing,

Commit thou any fault no more O king.
Do no one injury, but profit all,
This of religion is the way and call.
Let my memento be these words I've told;
And I believe they never will grow old!"
The bright soul of the monarch thus awake,
Request for many more words did he make.
"Who is the happy man," he then enquired,
"Whose heart is glad, and sighs has not required?"
"The man who has no sin," thus did he say,
"Whom Ahriman has never led astray,"
He asked him of the Demons' crooked way,
And His true road who o'er the world holds sway.
He answered him: "'Tis good God to obey;
In both worlds pow'r can He alone display.
The gate of ill tow'rds Ahriman must go,
For of true worshippers he is the foe.
Bless'd in the world is he of lofty mind,
Whose pure robe full of modesty you find.
When wisdom of his body is the guard,
To live a life of ease is his reward.
Whilst he shall righteousness and truth retain,
Of vice the door he will not strike in vain.
All things from which his body profit knows,
Will after death be of his soul the foes.
Sorrow to these two things he'll not accord,
Which of the scabbard's are or of the sword.
Hear not the words of one of crafty mind,
Though bright of soul him wicked you will find.
Impenitent should he the next world know,
Here may he linger on, still full of woe.
He who gain grudges by another won,
Let him be silent and with hopes have done.
Wisdom he knows not for his soul to prize,
Nor will he hear the counsel of the wise."

"And who among the great," the king enquired,
"The measure of the good may have acquired?"
To him replied he: "He who is most wise,
And who beyond desire himself can rise."
"Wisdom," the king asked then: "in whom's revealed,
For wisdom's mostly in mankind concealed?"
"Obedient to a Demon," he replied.
"He is who from God turns his heart aside,
Who to the wicked's rule will never bow,
The snare of wisdom, of the soul the foe.
Ten lions in pow'r are there, demons too,
Who wisdom and the souls of men subdue."
"Who are the demons ten," then questioned he,
"Whom it behoves us evermore to flee?"
"Both Greed and Want," he to the king replied,
"Are demons strong and haughty in their pride.
Revenge and Anger, Envy and Disgrace,
Slander, Impiety, a Double Face;
Such are the nine: Ingratitude the last,
For benefits, and God aside to cast."
"And of these ten," he asked, "of mischief full,
"Which of the demons is most powerful?"
"Avidity," the sage to him replied;
"This fiendish tyrant longest will abide.
You never see this demon satisfied:
One thing obtained, he asks for more beside.
And Want is he in grief and pain you find,
With yellow cheek and altogether blind.
Pass king beyond this, thou wilt Envy see,
Physician needing, ever pained is he.
Should he a man find, safe from harm and whole,
The very sight will irritate his soul.
The next Disgrace, a cruel demon, too,
With sharpened claw who e'er has ill in view.
Next Vengeance demon, who is full of spite,

In man a sudden shouting to excite.
For generous to none, he shows no grace,
A cruel demon with a frowning face.
The next is Slander, falsehood his delight,
Who never says a single word that's bright.
Tale-bearing demon next, of double face,
In whose heart fear of God there is no trace.
Between two men he strife and discord throws,
And strives on till he union overthrows.
And the next demon's the ungrateful fool,
Good men to know himself who cannot school.
To him are modesty and judgment small,
'Twixt good and bad no difference at all."
Further the king the sage to ask began :
" As demons struggle with the heart of man,
What does the world's lord to his servants send,
Themselves against the Dívs' hand to defend ? "
The pious man to him thus gave reply :
"O king of knowledge and of dignity,
Wisdom's a breastplate 'gainst the Demons' swords,
And to man's heart and soul a light affords.
For wisdom stores up words out of the past,
With knowledge nourishes the soul at last.
May wisdom as its guide thy soul still know;
The way is very long thou hast to go.
With what's good nature called it should appear
That hearts with it of demons have no fear :
The good heart's with the world contented found,
Nor of desire the gate will wander round.
But words of hope to thee will I now say,
Thy heart to gladness that may point the way.
For full of hope is always found the wise,
Nothing but gladness he in time descries.
At no time fear of evil will he know,
The arrow's path he chooses, not the bow.

Contented with the treasure he may gain,
His body he will give no further pain.
He who for treasured dirams does not care,
Time passing to him will be ever fair.
He on God's service who is fully bent,
With pain or wealth or losses is content
From God's commandment will not turn aside
And in his nature ill will not abide.
By this mark, too, will virtue in him dwell,
That nothing tempts him God's own way to sell."
" Who is there on this road," the king enquired
"To show the way towards the good desired ? "
"The way of wisdom," thus he gave reply,
" No doubt all other knowledge passes by,
And disposition good will leave a man,
Honoured through life in this his little span.
And of all qualities most firm I see,
With one's own fortune to contented be.
And of these hope the mildest is, again,
And all becoming, to have rest from pain.
And of these qualities avidity,
The worst, with wealth that ne'er content will be "
" Which quality," the king asked, " is the best,
And most advancing for a man confessed ? "
" Knowledge is best," the sage to him replied :
"The wise man's greater than all men beside.
Rashly the wise stretch not their hand for gain,
But hold their persons ever free from pain."
Of his foe's strength the monarch thus enquired ·
How would he seek for aid that he desired ?
Thus gave he answer : " Evil deeds to do,
Of the bright soul and wisdom is the foe."
The righteous king then of the sage enquired :
" Is birth or breeding to be more admired ? "
Answered the king then of his road the guide :

"Above birth breeding far is dignified.
Whilst breeding ever makes all life more gay,
Of birth there is not very much to say.
Birth without virtue is despised and low,
The soul with breeding will more vigorous grow."
He asked the soul to brilliance how to raise,
And of the body how the arts to praise.
He said: "I will repeat from end to end,
If thou from point to point thy ear wilt lend.
A gift from God alone is wisdom still,
Free from all care, remote from ev'ry ill.
If learnèd men but in themselves believe,
One's virtue from them one must not receive.
The working man who is good-natured, too,
Despised is never in a wise man's view.
Justice, good manners, generosity,
By wise men with good birth combined will be;
Greatness and power and the righteous way,
Will through bad temper always lose their sway."
And once again then Kasrá to him said:
"O man of note, by prudence who art led,
By luck is greatness or by effort gained,
By rulers who have throne and crown obtained?"
"Fortune and talent," then the sage rejoined,
"Are with each other, so to speak, combined
Body and soul are but as one revealed,
The body visible, the soul concealed.
The body, too, is giv'n to man to strive,
If it is warm and fortune is alive.
But greatness is by effort not attained,
Unless good fortune as a guide is gained.
The earth is like unto a tale and wind,
A passing dream to carry in one's mind.
When one awakes, it is not seen by eye,
Or good or ill if one regards it by."

Again, of hidden things would he enquire:
"Who is it that the wise man should admire?"
"The king," he said, "the throne who may adorn,
And to whom vigour by good fortune's borne.
If he is just, as well as of good name,
In speech and act he will secure his aim."
"Who's needy in the world," he asked again,
"Who has bad days and never has a gain?"
He answered him: "The poor man who is vile,
On whom nor his desire nor Eden smile."
He asked: "Who is unfortunate, of pain
Who ever has to weep and to complain?"
Thus answered he: "It is the man who knows,
And through whose acts his cheek still pallid grows."
"Who is content," once more he would enquire,
"In whom for increase there is no desire?"
He answered him: "For this revolving sphere,
He who cares not nor has affection here."
He asked him also: "Who would best suit me?"
He answered: "He who would the gentlest be."
"And who is gentle," he of him would ask,
"At angry men to weep whose is the task?"
"Only observe the man," thus did he say,
"Who from fault-finders turns himself away.
His to be modest and to gentle be,
His wisdom, judgment and propriety."
"And who," he asked again, "is of mankind
He who is blessed with the most hopeful mind?"
He said: "He who's the most inclined to hear,
And quickly to learn wisdom turns his ear."
The monarch of the world then asked him, too,
Of good and evil hidden what he knew.
"Of knowledge such as this," he answering said:
"Much may be spoken from an empty head.
All they have said to this earth you may trace;

I know not what is in another place."
Then Kasrá said: "What cities mostly thrive,
And what the profit from them we derive?"
"Each prosperous place," to him then answered he,
"From the king's justice gains prosperity."
He said to him: "In any giv'n event,
What man's alert and most intelligent?"
Who in the world is there among mankind,
Who will from learning the most increase find?"
Thus gave he answer: "An old man that's wise,
And who knows what has passed before his eyes."
Kasrá then asked him: "Who has most delight,
And ev'n in gladness holds his back upright?"
He answered: "He by fear who's not oppressed,
And who of gold and silver is possessed."
He asked: "In what does praise for me abound?
And who with men the most approved is found?"
Thus gave he answer: "He who need conceals,
With all desire and envy that he feels.
Revenge and envy in whom hid remains,
He in the world most approbation gains."
To the long-suffering man the king then said:
"Who wears the crown of patience on his head?"
He answered: "He whose hope is dark as night,
And yet whose judgment as the sun is bright.
And he, again, whose days to live are few,
And a great enterprise who has in view."
He asked: "Whose heart is so oppressed with grief,
That satisfied with life he seeks relief?"
He said: "From off his throne he who may fall,
And of good fortune has no hope at all."
The king of lofty rank enquired again:
"Whose wretched heart through me is full of pain?"
He answered: "He who wisdom has not won,
The rich man also who may have no son."

"Whose is the wretched heart," the king then said,
"Though sitting warmly still of harm has dread?"
He said to him: "A pious man and wise,
Above whose head a foolish ruler lies."
He asked: "Who does his fate the most deplore,
With a good name and wealth in ample store?"
"He who," he said, "falls from a lofty place,
And nothing's left him but his lordly race."
Again king Naoshírván sought his reply:
"O man of brilliant soul and seeing eye,
Without a name and rank whom dost thou see,
Who love deserves and generosity?"
He said: "The man who has much evil done,
The wretch from no one who support has won."
He asked and said to him: "Now tell me true;
Repenting, who the past will truly rue?"
"Upon the day of death the king," he said,
"Who the black helmet places on his head,
With fearful heart repentant aye is he,
To God ungrateful lest his soul should be:
Also for many things that he has done,
For those ungrateful ones around the throne."
He asked and said: "Thou, wisdom who hast found,
Virtues within each other who hast wound,
What knowest thou to bring the body gain,
And access to the hearts of all attain?"
Thus then he answered: "When the heart is sound,
Seeking for nought but pleasure is it found;
And when through pain and sorrow it is weak,
In hope for health restored it still will seek."
He said: "Good man, what greater is than hope,
Explain to me and tell me now its scope."
"Where there is ample dignity," he said,
"The hope is, there may be of want no dread.
And where of indigence there is no dread,

No word except for heart's wish need be said."
Once more he said then to his trusty guide:
"What care, then, is there for the heart beside?"
The sage him answered: "There, at any rate,
Wise men to him who seeks might indicate.
One is lest evil fortune may be sent,
And harm may come to him, though innocent.
He fears a friend against him who conspires,
And who his life, his blood, his skin desires.
Third, from a king unjust he fears a blow,
Worthless from holy men who does not know.
How fair would fortune's revolution be,
Could one a wise friend and preceptor see.
A brilliant world as well as righteous king,
No greater blessing could the heavens bring."
Of faith and righteousness he then enquired,
May none to crooked methods be inspired!
"Hold fast to men of faith, O king," he said,
"From whom God's memory may not have fled.
To demons' methods who not drawing near,
Of the pure God of earth have ever fear.
Those who to God's command obedience pay,
None must there be who would their Faith betray."
And for a king he made enquiry then,
Who could assume command of holy men;
Of those of happy fortune who were known,
Who on the earth were worthy of a throne.
He said: "To justice those who may incline,
In wisdom, industry, and virtue shine."
Again, of ancient comrades questioned he,
To dwell and speak with whom he might agree.
To this the sage replied: "In any friend
Justice and generosity should blend.
Others to please, he will not wish thee ill,
And in hard times he will assist thee still."

"Who has most friends," he asked of him again,
"With blood and skin who e'er would him sustain?"
He said: "From the true-hearted none would part,
Except the bad men who would grieve the heart;
Nor yet him whose caresses never cease,
Whose kindly actions ever tend to peace."
He asked: "Of enemies who has the more,
And who on him the greater hatred pour?"
He answered: "He who is of lofty mind:
Whom to reproach he might be more inclined."
He next asked: "Who is, then, a constant friend,
Parting from whom in bitter tears would end?"
He answered then: "The true companion he,
Who wounds not and who fears not pain for thee."
He asked: "What thing, then, will for ever last,
And still continue after all is past?"
He answered him: "An action that is good,
Is never absent from a true friend's mood."
Kasrá then asked him: "What is there most bright,
And on men's heads that is a crown of light?"
He answered thus: "It is that wise man's soul,
Which over its desires has full control."
"O lord of love," the king to him then said,
"What is there broader than the sky o'erhead?"
He answered him: "A king whose hand is free,
And that man's heart who God's true slave may be."
"What is most honourable," then he said,
"With which a wise man may lift high his head?"
"O king," to answer thus the sage began,
"Give thou not treasure to an impure man;
For with ungrateful men to have to do,
Is into water unburnt bricks to throw."
He asked him then once more: "What is that pain
Through which one loses the desire of gain?"
And then he answer gave to him: "O king,

May thy heart ever be as early spring!
A king, bad tempered, he who serves through pain,
Desires not body, life, or treasures' gain."
He asked him then: "What marvel dost thou find,
Beyond whose measure cannot rise the mind?"
Then to the king did Buzúrjmihr reply:
"All full of wonders is the whirling sky.
First see a man to whom wealth may be given,
Whose crown may rise to the black clouds of heaven.
His right hand from his left nor knoweth he,
Nor what is stint from generosity."
Another, from the movement of the sky,
Will say the stars predict both how and why.
The heavens him will but to hardship guide,
For him nought but misfortune will provide."
He asked: "What is the heaviest thing that's known?"
And he replied to him: "Of sin the stone."
Another question then the king preferred:
"Of ev'rything that may be done or heard,
What is most shameful or the most to blame,
That all the world would give an evil name?"
"'Tis avarice in kings," the sage replied,
"And to oppress the innocent beside.
The man of opulence who grudges food,
Stints clothes and nourishment in stingy mood.
Women of modesty who make not choice,
In speaking who have not a gentle voice.
Those worthy men who may be rash in deed,
And tow'rds the humble harshly may proceed.
Without cause he who is devoid of truth,
Towards a king or ev'n a worthless youth."
"What on the earth," he asked, "is of things best;
Open be it, or hid among the rest,
So that a man may it as breastplate take,
Or with that thing his soul more brilliant make?"

He said: "In Faith he who shows energy
Will nothing in the earth but blessing see.
Beside this, on him God will praise bestow,
The man of learning God will always know.'
Kasrá said to him: "By great men or king,
To do or leave undone what best the thing?
What to withhold is best and what command,
Or what as vile to let loose from one's hand?
What were it best from taking to hold back,
To seize at once or be in taking slack?"
He answering said: "Of passion be thou ware,
When eyes, thou know'st, are waiting for thee there.
Again, beware thy soul to keep alive,
And whilst thou canst, tow'rds evil do not strive.
With vengeance set aside and new hope won,
Thy soul will brilliant shine as does the sun.
In doing wrong whatever taste thou gain,
Reject the flavour; from the wrong refrain."
Praise to the lord both of the moon and sun,
That with Buzúrjmihr and the king I've done.

In the next Section is related the sending of an envoy by the king of India with the game of chess and valuable gifts of many sorts. The chess-board is laid before the king by the envoy, and he is desired to set before his most intelligent men the task of naming the different pieces, of settling their moves and their places, of knowing the footmen, the elephants, the army, the Rúkh (roc or castle), the horses, and the movements of the queen and king. If they discovered these the Rájá would willingly pay him tribute, or otherwise not, as they would be inferior to the Indians in wisdom. The two sides were respectively of black ivory and teak wood, and being told they were meant to represent a battle, the king asks for seven days in which to solve the problem. The nobles and

Mobeds, the Councillors of the king, all study the subject in every possible way, but in vain, and Buzúrjmihr undertakes the task. He gives a day and a night to it, and succeeds, and the king calls together the envoys and the Court to see the play. The king is placed in the middle, and the army arranged about him on either side, with the fighting footmen (the pawns) in front. At the side of the king is placed his clever Minister (the queen) to point out the way in the fight. The fighting horses* are on the right and left hands of these (the bishops), and the war elephants on both sides of these again. All the assembly are amazed at Buzúrjmihr's skill, and the envoy from India is greatly put out. The king presents Buzúrjmihr with a bowl full of jewels and a horse and saddle.

In the next Section is related the invention by Buzúrjmihr of the game of *nard*. Two ivory dice were made with teak-coloured figures on them. A field of battle was made like that for chess, on which the two sides were arranged face to face, the two armies being placed in eight portions (? squares) for taking a town. The field being dark, and the battle-field four-sided, there are two powerful kings of good disposition that march together, neither oppressing the other, at whose command the army is arrayed for sharp combat. When two catch one alone the two defeat the one. If on the field of battle either of these kings passes beyond the other, the fight taking place sometimes on the hills and sometimes on the plain, the armies of the two kings meet together (to see) who is defeated. (A most unintelligible explanation). The king is bewildered, and orders 200 camels to be laden with the tributes of Rúm, China, Heitál, Makrán, and Irán, and sends for the Rájá's envoy, and talks much to him of knowledge, and writes a letter to the Rájá, acknowledging

*Mohl has elephants here, and his original of this passage must have varied from this.

the receipt of his gifts and the chess, and sending in return Buzúrjmihr's new game of *nard*,* with the condition that if his Brahmins cannot discover the rules of the game the same number of camel loads of gifts are to be returned. Buzúrjmihr himself accompanies the caravan, and explains the game. The Rájá asks for seven days for his assembly of wise men to find out the rules of *nard*, but on the 8th day they acknowledge that they can make nothing of it, and Buzúrjmihr explains it. The Rájá makes rich gifts to him, and sends him back with 2,000 camels laden with them and the tribute, with a letter extolling the king and his envoy. Buzúrjmihr returns to Irán, and is received with all honour.

There is now related the story of Jamhúr, Rájá of India, and his son and his nephew Talhand, and the invention of chess.

There was a king of India of the name of Jamhúr, possessed of riches and an army of renown greater than that of Fúr. He resided at Sandali, and his subjects were happy under him. He had a wife worthy of him, and from her was born a son who was called Gao. The king dying while his son was still a child, his brother Máï, who was worthy of a throne, was made king, and married Gao's mother, by whom he had a son of the name of Talhand. When this child was two and Gao seven years of age, the king died, and the people elected their mother to reign over them as queen. She entrusts her sons to two virtuous Mobeds for education, and when they dispute as to who is to inherit the throne she assures each of them that it is his. When they grew up each was consumed with jealousy of the other, and the people and army were divided as to who should have the crown. The mother appears to side with Gao, but not content with this or the opinion of the nobles, they hold an assembly,

* Probably backgammon or drafts.

which their respective preceptors address, each on his own pupil's behalf. The assembly desire to discuss the question in their absence, and the whole nation is divided. The two princes decide to resort to force to assert their claims. When the respective forces assemble Gao sends one of his nobles, an eloquent man, to Talhand to remonstrate with him, but without success. He then consults his preceptor, who advises him to give up to his brother all his treasures, but not the throne and crown and the royal seal. Gao accordingly sends to him another honourable man to argue the matter out, in order to prevent war between them, but still in vain, as Talhand is obstinate. The two sides accordingly decide on war, and after several messages to and fro, Gao proposes that they should lead their forces to the seashore, and there dig a trench filled with water, beyond which the defeated side could not pass, that no blood should be shed, and the defeated should be made prisoners. Talhand and his army agree, and a fight takes place on the seashore accordingly after the trench has been dug. Looking from his seat on his elephant Talhand sees the world in confusion like the waves of the Nile; the wind turns against him, he finds no rest from the wind, the sun, and the sharp swords, and no way of flight, and lays himself down on his golden saddle and dies.* Gao receives with great grief the news of his brother's death, and leads away the combined armies, after preparing a grand coffin for the corpse. The mother of the two princes, hearing of her son Talhand's death, in despair sets fire to his palace, and prepares a funeral pyre on which to burn the body. When Gao meets and embraces her she at first accuses him of his brother's death, but at last demands to see how he died on his elephant, and says that unless that is made clear to her her tender soul will be consumed with the fire

* What was the cause of his death is not apparent.

of grief. Consulting his preceptor, the latter advises him to assemble a number of learned and ingenious men from Kashmír, Dambar and Margh and Máí, and consult them as to the river, the trench, and the field of battle. They assemble, and the preceptor draws out the plan of a field of battle similar to that which had lately taken place.

The field of battle is described as having 100 squares, on which foot and horse soldiers in two ranks were to move. The king was in the centre, having on one side of him his preceptor (the queen). At their side were two elephants, that raised a dust dark as the waters of the Nile. Beyond the elephants were two dromedaries ridden by men with pure intentions, and beyond these two horsemen ready for battle, and this rank was ended by two valiant *Rúkhs* with lips foaming with blood. Before and behind these were foot-soldiers ready to aid the others in battle, and if one of these traversing the board arrived at the other side he took his place as a preceptor to the king.* (As a pawn becomes a queen in the modern game). The king could only move one square at a time: the elephants moved three squares and overlooked their field of battle for two *mils*. The dromedaries could also advance three squares, as well as the horsemen, but in the latter two squares were in a direct, and one in an indirect line. The *Rúkhs* could traverse the whole board. When anyone saw the king in the battle, he cried to him with a loud voice: "O king, beware!" (equivalent to "Check king"), and the king had to move from his square as long as he could until the horse, the elephant, and the troops blocked his way completely, and he died of fatigue and thirst. The game was produced before Talhand's mother, and she only found relief from her troubles in contemplating it till she herself died.

*The ten pieces in a row, in place of eight as in modern chess, account for there being 100 in place of 64 squares.

As Naoshírván was in the habit of consulting sages and physicians, he now determined on sending one Barzúi, a well-known physician, to Hindustán to bring him a wonderful grass he had read of in an Indian book, which if spread upon a dead man would resuscitate him. He prepares three hundred camel loads of gifts and dispatches him with them to the Rájá. The latter, having read the letter that accompanied these, gives him every assistance, and he goes through all the mountains in his search, but cannot discover the wonderful plant, although he tries many. Having failed in this he asks those who were with him to take him to one wiser than themselves, and they introduce him to an old sage, who informs him that he himself has failed, and also that he must look upon the matter in another light. The grass must be considered a wise man, and the dead one an ignorant one, who would be revived by knowledge. There was a book in the king's treasury called *Kalílah*, which he would advise him to obtain, and he would be resuscitated by its contents as the corpse was to be by the grass. The king on his asking him for it allows him to read it chapter by chapter, and he writes down each from memory until he has transcribed the whole, and he then sends it to Naoshírván, and himself returns to Irán loaded with the Rájá's gifts. The book is then translated into Pehlavi by Buzúrjmihr, subsequently in the time of Mamún into Arabic, and in that of Nasr into Persian by his Minister Abúlfazl. After this it appears to have been put into verse by the poet Rúdaki. Shortly after this Naoshírván goes out to hunt, and is separated from all his attendants but Buzúrjmihr. A jewelled armlet falls off his arm, and is picked up and the jewels swallowed by a black bird that flies down and sees it, while the king is asleep, the sage in the meanwhile doing nothing in his amazement at the tricks of fate. The king on awaking perceives his loss, and suspects Buzúrjmihr, and the latter responding to his enquiries only by sighs, is imprisoned in his own house. He has a nephew, who was a servant of the king, and one day he asks him in what manner he served the king, that he might instruct him how to do it better. The man informs him that he had that day had a mishap with the king and spilt some water on the floor. Buzúrjmihr instructs him how to pour water on the king's hands, neither too fast nor too gently, and he obeys his instructions the next time he does so. The king observes this, and finds that it is Buzúrjmihr who has taught him. The king sends him to Buzúrjmihr to ask why he who had attained to such great dignity should lower himself instead of trying to advance still higher, and the sage, when asked, insists that he is better off than the king himself. Naoshírván on hearing this throws Buzúrjmihr into a dark dungeon, and asks him again through the same man how he fares there, and the sage once more gives a similar answer. Still further enraged, the king has a box made for him with nails pointing inside, and has him put in, so that he can neither rest nor be free of torture. A third time the sage is asked the same question, and gives the same answer. A wise man, who could understand what the sage said, and an executioner are now sent to him to tell him that if he does not send an answer pleasing to the king the executioner would show him what the day of judgment meant. Buzúrjmihr replies that neither the good nor the bad would remain here long, neither those who possessed thrones nor those who led lives of misery: that it would be an easy matter to give up such a life, while the hearts of kings would still be full of fear. On this answer being reported to Noashírván, he releases him and restores him to his own palace. After this the Kaiser sends Naoshírván a letter and presents with a locked box, and promises to send his tribute if he can, without opening the box say what is in it. Thereupon Buzúrjmihr is released from his constraint with honour in order to discover the secret. He consults the stars, and washes his eyes with the water of intelligence, for his eyes were darkened through his troubles. He bids his servants observe everyone whom they may meet and question him as to who he is. The first is a woman, who says she has a husband and child, the second one who has a husband but no child, and the third one who has neither husband nor child. He reflects on these events, and goes to the king, who assembles the nobles, the Mobeds, and the wise men at his request, that he may tell the contents of the box in their presence. Buzúrjmihr hears the message from the envoy from Rúm, and reveals to the assembly that there are three pearls in the box, one pierced, one pierced on one side only, and the third not pierced at all. When the box is opened the contents are found to be as he describes them. The king fills his mouth with pearls, and is grieved that he should have punished such an innocent and faithful servant. Buzúrjmihr now tells him what had happened when his jewelled armlet disappeared, and shows that what had occurred was decreed by fate, and gives him advice as to how he should reign.

The next Section describes the manners of Naoshírván's rule. One day a Mobed says to him that he sometimes passes over a fault without blaming him who has committed it, and at others makes a man responsible, although he has an excuse for his fault. The king tells him that when a man confesses his fault he is like a sick man and the king as his physician. Another Mobed says to him that a general went secretly from Gurgán, and going into a wood slept there for some time, but having nothing with him was obliged to return in order to rejoin his baggage. Naoshírván remarks that he required no escort, for he who had charge of an army did not care for himself. On another telling him there was a man there whose wealth exceeded that of the king, he said: "Good! This man is the crown of my kingdom. I am the guardian of his treasure and his life, and will labour that they may increase." Another told him that they had brought several unweaned infants among the prisoners, and he answered that they were to be returned to their mothers, happy with the gifts he would bestow on them. They wrote to him that there were a hundred rich Rúmis who were desirous of buying back their relatives. He told them to let them be ransomed for a cup of wine, for it was with the sword that he would take their jewels, their slaves, their chests of gold and silver. He was told that there were two rich merchants who for two thirds of the night allowed no one to sleep for the noise of drunkards and music. He told them not to trouble themselves, but to enjoy themselves and to do no harm to anyone. Someone wrote that the king of Yaman had said in his audience hall that Naoshírván, whenever he opened his mouth, began to speak of the dead and thus filled with sadness the happy souls of the living. He answered that every wise and well-born man did so, and he was not a true friend who did not bear him in mind. Several pages are now filled with the replies of Naoshírván to questions asked him or remarks on events reported to him. Amongst them are several to prove his generosity and justice. On being told that Jews and Christians were his enemies, double-faced, and worshippers of Ahriman, his reply was that an intolerant king would never become great. He orders money plundered in war to be repaid and enunciates many excellent moral maxims; finally, when he is assured there has been no such worthy king since the days of Kayumúrs, he gives thanks to God that things should be as He desires. The Section ends with praise of Mahmúd. The next two Sections are taken up with the advice he addresses to his son Hormuzd in a letter, and wise answers he gives the Mobeds to questions on many topics. There is nothing more in these than has been already noted in Buzurjmihr's advice to Naoshírván himself. The next Section relates the preparation of Naoshírván for war with the Kaiser. It commences by his sending a letter to the latter on the death of his father, in which he reminds him that all men are mortal, and ends by offering him whatever assistance he may require in the way of troops, arms, and treasure. The Kaiser, being a foolish youth, does not pay the envoy sent with the letter any special attention or endeavour in any way to gain his friendship, and after his ministers have consulted sends a curt and almost defiant answer to the letter, winding up with saying that when he had need of him he should be his king, as he was to him only a memory of his father. The envoy returns home with gifts hardly worthy of his rank, and recounts what he has seen and heard to Naoshírván, who indignantly prepares for war, swearing by the most holy God, by the sun and moon, by Adargushasp, and by his crown and throne that he would destroy the glory of Rum. He leads from Madáin an army such that the green waters of the river were agitated by the sound of his clarions. The Kaiser, hearing of Naoshírván's advance, undertakes the siege of Aleppo—300,000 Iràni horse sieze on Aleppo, and catapults are erected on every side: 30,000 Rúmis are taken prisoners in a fortnight, and they finally dig a trench into which water is admitted. This puts a stop to the advance of the king and his army. Sakíla is meanwhile occupied by Naoshírván. As this state of affairs continues for some time, the Iráni army seems to have run short of money by 300,000 dirams. In this difficulty the king sends for Buzúrjmihr and orders gold to be brought from Mázandirán, but the latter points out that this will take a long time, and recommends the taking up of a loan from the rich men of the neighbouring cities. The king agrees. A cobbler agrees to advance the money, and in weighing it out sends a message to Buzúrjmihr asking him to appoint his own son to a place among the royal lawyers. Buzúrjmihr communicates this wish to the king, but the latter refuses to entertain the idea, and sends back the money the cobbler offers to lend, being unwilling to borrow from such a source, for fear of the influence that would be gained by such a man when he himself was dead and his son succeeded him. The money must be found elsewhere. After this envoys arrive from the Kaiser with apologies and offerings. These were brought by forty Rúmi philosophers at the rate of 30,000 pieces of gold each, who agree to pay the usual tribute and make excuses that the Kaiser is young and inexperienced. Naoshírván receives them graciously. Being sent to his minister to pay their money, the latter demands from them 1,000 pieces of gold brocade besides, which they consent to give. After this the king returns to Ctesiphon.

Hormuzd is now chosen as heir apparent to the throne, the king being then seventy-four years of age, and having six sons, of whom Hormuzd, the eldest, is said to have been dignified, learned, handsome, and full of affection for the people. The Mobeds now assemble by the king's orders, and Buzúrjmihr asks Hormuzd what renders bright the spirit and soul and the body healthy, and he answers that knowledge is best of all things and gives safety and restrains the power of Ahriman. Then come patience and liberality, which give men a good name and repose, and amiability towards everyone in good and ill, with the performance of justice towards others, so as to obtain peace with oneself. Buzúrjmihr now asks him a number of questions to test his character and disposition, and the king listens to all the answers Hormuzd gives to them until far into the night. The replies are found satisfactory, and the deed by which Hormuzd is nominated heir-apparent is duly drawn up. A eulogy of Naorshírván follows this, attributable, apparently, to Fardúsi himself, and a letter from Naoshírván full of good counsel to his son, as to the manner in which he should reign and conduct himself towards his subjects, and as to the ceremonies to be observed on his death. This includes the erection for his body of an elegant mausoleum (*kákh*) in a place where men should not pass and vultures should not fly.* He was to be embalmed with camphor, and his body was to be dressed in royal robes of brocade, with a crown of musk on his head. An ivory throne was to be placed there with a crown upon it, with whatever cups and gold utensils he was in the habit of using, with 20 cups full of rose water, wine, saffron, musk, camphor, and amber on his right hand and on his left. The blood was to be cleaned out of his stomach, which was to be filled with camphor and musk. After this no one was to see him. His family were to abstain from feasting for two months, as due in the case of a king's death. All were to obey Hormuzd, and only breathe as he desired. All wept when this letter was read, and Naoshírván lived but one year more.

After this is related a dream of Naoshírván's, as follows :—

The night had once obscured day's brilliant rays,
He slept while still engaged in prayer and praise ;
There in a vision saw his spirit bright,
A sun arising in the dead of night.
Of forty steps a ladder from its head,

*This is not in accordance with the usual method of the fire-worshippers, who expose corpses to be eaten by vultures.

Up to the utmost height of Saturn led.
On ladder from Hijáz it rose aloft,
Its movements all were delicate and soft.
The world from Káf to Káf it rendered bright,
In mourning's place brought ev'rywhere delight.
Nor near nor far was there in heaven a place,
That from its light did not derive some grace.
On ev'ry side around its brilliance shone;
In Kasrá's palace it was dark alone.
At midnight as he leapt up from his sleep,
Silence withal he forced his lip to keep.
Off from its face the veil the sun then threw,
And to his side he Buzúrjmihr then drew;
Nor did the monarch from the sage withhold
The mystery that to him the dream had told.

(This prophesy is altogether omitted by Mohl, and is so unlike the usual style of Fardúsi, that it is probably an unauthorised interpolation).

When Buzúrjmihr these words had heard him tell,
The dream from first to last he pondered well.
Thus then he said to him: "O prosperous king,
There is a mystery hidden in this thing."
"Tell me the very truth," then Kasrá said:
"From fear the soul has from my body fled."
And Buzúrjmihr to him thus answered soon:
"O thou of wit beyond the sun and moon,
Thy dream since I have learnt from end to end,
To hear its wondrous answer now attend.
Henceforth not forty years shall pass away,
Before an Arab man shall take his day.
The way of righteousness shall he embrace,
And from all crookedness avert his face.
The Faith of Zardusht he shall overthrow,
If tow'rds the moon his finger point he show.

Split into two halves then the orb shall be,*
And in the strife his back shall no one see.
Jews, Christians, in their place shall not remain,
Nor the old Faith its footing shall regain.
On the high throne three steps shall he ascend ;
In speech wise counsel to the world shall lend.
And when this transient world he leaves behind,
By treasured words shall he be borne in mind.†
Joy in him earth from age to age shall find,
But the king's hall shall *not* go to the wind.
Thereafter shall to thee a grandson come,
Who elephants shall have and kettle drum.
Against him from Hijáz he'll lead a host,
Though neither arms nor vessels he may boast.
From throne down to the dust him shall he throw
And never more shall earth such warriors know.
Rites of the *Saddah* all shall pass away ;
Fire-temples all shall he in ashes lay.
Nor fire nor sun shall men thenceforth adore,
And warriors' fortune than dreams be no more
This to Gushtásp Jámásp himself has said,
As from this road and mystery he fled."
These words from Buzúrjmihr when Kasrá knew,
His changing face assumed another hue.
The whole day long his face betrayed his pain,
And anxious still at night he slept again.
And when three watches of the night had sped,
There fell upon his ear a voice of dread.
"The world entire has broken down," that cried,
And one "The hall has broken down" replied.
The king's heart leapt up from its proper place,
Nor head nor foot of that thing could he trace.

*Referring to an alleged miracle performed by Muhammad.

†Presumably a prophesy of the Koràn.

Then as to Buzúrjmihr he gave a cry,
From out the broken hall there came reply.*
And as the learned sage this saw, at once
"O monarch Naoshírván!" he gave response:
"Know this, from thine own hall this voice is borne,
That moon-face of its mother has been born.
A two-horsed horseman even now is seen;
Who says, 'Azargushasp, destroyed has been.'"
A horseman, swift as dust, to cry that came,
Of Azargushasp cold had grown the flame.
At this the king's heart was so deeply grieved,
That constantly a deeper sigh he heaved.
And to the king did Buzúrjmihr then cry:
"At this, O king, why should'st thou mourn and sigh?
When fate has driv'n thee from the earth afar,
What feast can please earth and what mourning mar?"
Uttered the words, the monarch quickly slept,
He died and over him the whole earth wept.
Buzúrjmihr, in earth's veil his face to hide,
After the king within a month, too, died.
He went with but this memory left behind;
Do thou this warning ever bear in mind:
As cruel was to him the whirling sphere,
Nor love nor justice do thou look for here.

The reign of Hormuzd, son of Naoshírván, lasted for twelve years. Before commencing the history of the reign Fardusi gives a practical address to the month of Tamúz (July), and then proceeds with his recital as if it had been spoken by an old man of the name of Mákh, a warden of the frontier of Haír (Herat?). He makes Hormuzd address his chiefs in the usual manner as to the glory of his ancestors, and what he will do for the benefit of his people, in an address that put fear into the

*This is unintelligible.

hearts of the rich, tore in two those of tyrants, and rejoiced those of the wise and the poor. Governing for a short time well until his power was established, he subsequently departed from the right way, and destroyed those who were innocent and had lived in safety under his father. There were three men who had been ministers under his father named Izad Gushasp, Buzúrjmihr, and Máh Àzar, whom he wished to destroy at once for fear of their turning against him. He commenced by throwing the first into jail in irons, with no one to wait on him, no friend, no clothes, and no food. Izad Gushasp sent a beseeching message to the chief Mobed for food and linen to make a shroud. The Mobed orders his cook to send some food to the jail, and himself goes to the prisoner, with whom he converses as to the king's evil disposition. Izad Gushasp explains to him his last wishes with regard to his property, and asks him to tell Hormuzd of all the trouble he had endured in the time of his father and to have mercy on him, as he was innocent and generosity became a king. Meanwhile one of the king's agents, who had been in the prison and heard what was said, ran and informed the king, and he at once sent to the jail and had him put to death. The Mobed went and told the king what Izad Gushasp had said, and he betrayed no particular displeasure, thinking all the while how he should do away with him. When the Mobed went to the usual audience he bade him sit down at table, as he had found a new cook, and the Mobed did so, being convinced that his death by poison was intended. Then the king, after the manner usual with kings when they wish to honour a guest, handed him with his own hand a bone with poisoned marrow in it, and insisted on his eating it, notwithstanding his remonstrances. The Mobed obeyed, and knowing he had been poisoned, ran to his own palace. Then the king sent a confidential man to see if his plan had succeeded, and the Mobed sent him back with a message that he was about to make a complaint to a Judge, before whom they would eventually appear face to face, and that his evil deeds would bear fruit in misfortune to himself. This was reported to the king, who, too late, repented what he had done, and the Mobed died, to the regret of all.

The king then proceeds to destroy Behrám Azarmihán and Simáh Barzín. When he questions the former with regard to the latter in an assembly of the court before the throne, as to whether he is a bad man or a worshipper of God, he orders him to answer that he is an evil intentioned man and of the devil's seed. He agrees to do so and more. This accordingly takes place, and Simáh Barzín is sent to the thieves' prison and made away with on the third night. Behrám now offers to give him some important advice, urging the services he has rendered to his father. Hormuzd sends for him at night and makes him kneel before his throne. Asked what the advice he has to give is, he tells him there is a box in the treasury with a Persian note in it written on silk in his father's handwriting which he should look at. The box is sent for, and the note read: It is to the purport that Hormuzd would be an unequalled king for twelve years, and after that the world would become full of confusion, enemies would appear from all directions, the army would be scattered on all sides, and his enemy would cast him down from his throne; he would be blinded in both eyes and afterwards killed. The king, enraged, sends Behrám to prison, after the latter has told him he is the offspring of a Turki woman and the race of the Khákán and not of Kaikobád. The next night he has Behrám killed by the executioner in the prison. After this Hormuzd remains at Istakhar for two months, as the air there is pleasant, and afterwards for three months at Isfahán.

During the winter he is at Ctesiphon, but always in terror of what had been foretold in the note. In consequence of this he changes his habits, prays three times in the night, does no injustice and sheds no blood, and every morning causes a proclamation to be made by a herald that if a horse should enter a cultivated field or any man into an orchard, the horse's feet and ears would be cut off and the man's head placed on the stake. He travels about for two months, enquiring into everything, and the peasants all praise him. He has a son of the name of Parvíz, who is also sometimes called Khusru. The prince's horse, having strayed into a field and the owner making complaint, the king orders the tail and ears of the horse to be cut off and the damage he had done estimated, that it may be recovered from Parvíz in the proportion of a hundred to one. The nobles entreat that the horse should not be mutilated, but are not listened to, and the sentence is carried out. When the king had gone out hunting one day, the son of one of his generals saw a vine full of fruit and ordered his servant to pluck some of the grapes and take them to his palace. The owner threatening to complain to the king, the young man took off his belt studded with jewels and gave it him; the owner declared he did him a favour in accepting it, for if the king had known of it he would have taken his life.

When ten years of the reign of Hormuzd had passed, the voice of his enemies arose from all the countries round. From the direction of Herát there came against him Sávah with an army of 400,000 men and 1,200 fighting elephants, and ordered him to repair the roads and bridges for his passage. On the other side advanced the Kaiser of Rúm with 100,000 men, and re-occupied the territory that Naoshírván had taken from him. Others came up from the country of the Khazars and Armenia as far as Ardabíl, with other horsemen armed with spears from the side of the desert under Chiefs such as Abás and Mur, who devastated the country from which Hormuzd drew his tribute. Hearing this, the king repented of having killed the Mobeds, for he had no longer good Councillors around him. He assembles his Ministers to consult them, and is told that the most pressing danger is from Sávah. His army when reckoned amounts to 100,000 men, with which to oppose Sávah. With regard to the Kaiser he determines to give up the towns taken by Naoshírván, and thus gets rid of his enemy on that side. A numerous army is sent into the hills in the country of the Khazars. Advancing towards Kharád, their army is defeated, and many of them are killed when they bar the way towards Armenia, so that there only remains Sávah to encounter. By the advice of Nastúh, an attendant, he summons Nastúh's father Mehrán Sitád, to his councils, and ascertains that it was he who when he was sent to the Khákán of China for a wife for Naoshírván, chose out of five of his daughters the only one who was a princess by birth and not a daughter of a slave. The Khákán had consulted his Mobeds on the occasion, and they had foretold that there should be born to his daughter and the king of Irán a son like a lion, who after he succeeded his father on the throne would for some time reign badly, but would afterwards repent. At that time there would appear against him a bold king who would bring with him a strong army of Turkománs, but one of his Pehlaváns of the name of Chúbínah would beat and destroy their army. The Khákán's daughter is accordingly given to the king. Having related this tale, the old man dies. Search is made according to the description given of Chúbínah by the old man, and a man of the name of *Zád* Farúkh, who is in charge of the king's stable, points out that the description can only apply to a Pehlaván called Behrám, to whom the command of Barda and Ardabíl has been given. This man is accordingly immediately summoned, and on arrival is admitted to audience by Hormuzd, who recognises in him the marks pointed out by Mehrán Sítad. He advises the king not to hesitate to attack Sávah even with 10,000 Iránis, saying that if such a small army is defeated by the hosts of Sávah there will be no disgrace in it. The nobles remonstrate, but the king appoints him to command his army. He chooses of them 12,000 men of the age of forty, and appoints Zalán Sínah to lead them, and Kandá Gushasp to bring up the rear, and exhorts his army. When the king asks why he has only chosen 12,000 men of forty years of age to fight he points out that this was the number chosen on previous occasions, and a commander is often embarrassed by having more in the field, and that men of forty are experienced men, who think of their wives and families, and are not easily discouraged, whilst young men are impatient and rash, have not wives and children or lands, and do not distinguish between what is of value and what is not, and are happy if they are victorious, but run away if they have the worst of it. Hormuzd, satisfied with his answer, gives him a royal standard, and he starts for the war, taking with him by order of the king a young scribe of the name of Mehrán. After he has left, the king consults his chief Mobed with regard to him. The latter is confident that he will be victorious, and is only anxious lest when he becomes so he should turn against the hand that has raised him. The king puts the question aside for the moment, but from remembering what has been said and from another circumstance it seems unnecessary to relate, sends a man after him to tell him to halt his army and come back to him. This Behrám refuses to do, until he can return victorious, and the king lets him go on. He conducts his army as far as Khúzistán. Here he cuts in two one of his army who deprives a woman of a load of straw she is carrying without paying her, by way of warning to others, and the army moves on without daring to do any damage on the way. Behrám leads on his army to Dámghán. Hormuzd, being full of anxiety on account of Sávah's army, orders Kharád Barzín to go secretly and ascertain the number and quality of the enemy's forces, who led them, and who were their warriors. He also sends with him a letter and presents worthy of a king, and tells him to inform Behrám on the way that he is about to play a trick on Sávah and bring him into his net. Kharád Barzín proceeds accordingly, and endeavours to persuade Sávah to take his army to Herát. Sávah enters the plain of Herát and encamps on the bank of a river. A Turkomán vidette sees Behrám's army and reports to Sávah, who sends for Kharád Barzín, and accuses him of treachery. Kharád puts him off by saying he need not fear any treachery, as it is only a small frontier patrol, and he will send and ascertain. He, however, returns to his own tent, and makes preparation for flight. Sávah orders the Faghfúr (according to this his son) to go with an escort to the camp of the Pehlaván and find out who he is and why he has come. He goes, and Behrám shows himself to him, and tells him he has come from Baghdád by order of Hormuzd to bar the road to the army of Sávah, of which he has heard. The Faghfúr returns and reports to his father, who immediately sends for Kharád Barzín, but finds he has escaped. Sávah dispatches a message to Behrám Chúbínah to warn him that he could only have been sent with a view to his own destruction against one who had no rival in the world, for if a mountain opposed him he could trample it down with the feet of his army and elephants. Behrám only laughs and answers him that if Hormuzd seeks his death he must perforce submit.

This is reported to Sávah, who sends to ask him what he really desires, and receives for answer that if he wishes to be at peace with the master of the world he will receive him as a guest, and will send to Hormuzd to meet him half way and become his friend, but if he has come to fight he has thrown himself into the jaws of a crocodile.

Sávah returns a message that he could gain no glory in fighting, and if he would come under his protection he would provide for his army and bestow great riches on him. This message being delivered, Behrám sends back a defiant answer on the part of himself and his king, who has sent a banner to him which shall be the signal for his (Sávah's) death in the day of battle. At this answer Sávah is enraged and leads his army to the encounter. Behrám advances with his back to the town of Herát. Sávah perceives that from the position chosen his own army will have too narrow a front to be able to deploy, and sends another message to Behrám, pointing out the danger he is incurring, and offering to give him power and his own daughter if he will give up the fight. Behrám returns a defiant message, which is repeated to Sávah, whose face becomes black with anxiety and he begs the Faghfúr not to deliver battle till the next morning. The armies then retire to their respective camps. After discussing the war with his army, Behrám retires to his tent and dreams that his army has been beaten and the road for his return to court cut off. Calling to his warriors for assistance, as he is alone, he awakes, terrified at his dream but tells no one of it, and dresses himself. At this moment Kharád Barzín arrives, having escaped from Sávah, and warns him to beware, as Sávah's army is of great size. Behrám tells him his business is with nets, and he does not understand maces and arrows, but as soon as the sun rises he will show him how to fight. Accordingly, at sunrise, he posts 3,000 men with Izad

Gushasp on his right wing, and an equal number with Kandá Gushasp on his left; in the rear was Zalán Sínah, and in the centre Hamdán Gushasp. Behrám erects two mounds of ten cubits in height on each of the two roads towards his camp by which his men could escape, to prevent flight, and notwithstanding the warnings of the chief Scribe and Kharád Barzín, prays to God and engages, the two Scribes mounting on a distant height to see the battle. Sávah has magic practised in front of his army and fire thrown into the air, but it has no effect on Behrám and his Iránis. Sávah attacks the left wing like a wolf against sheep, and it begins to give way, but Behrám rushes and overthrows these Turkomans, and asks if his men are not ashamed of themselves. Letting them see that he has blocked up the road for flight, he exhorts his men to fight valiantly. Sávah brings his elephants to the front, but these, being wounded by flights of arrows, turn back and throw their own army into confusion. Sávah is sitting on a hillock on a golden throne, but Behrám shoots him with an arrow adorned with four eagle's feathers, and when he falls cuts off his head. The foe flies in confusion, many being killed in a narrow defile through which they have to pass. Behrám makes Kharád Barzín assist in looking after the wounded and seeing who have been killed. One Behrám, a valiant man of the seed of Siávash, brings a Turkoman with red hair, in tears, who turns out to be a sorcerer. The sorcerer's head is cut off and Behrám praises God. The Grand Scribe now comes and praises Behrám, who sends a letter to the king with news of his victory, and with the heads of Sávah, his eldest son, the Faghfúr, and his chiefs and their banners, to Herát, where at the moment Hormuzd is sitting awaiting news in despair, and asks for orders as to maintaining the war against Parmúdah, Sávah's son, who had determined to continue fighting.

Hormuzd bows down in thankfulness to God, and sending for 100,000 *dirhams* from the treasury distributes one-third each to the poor and the fire-temples, and the remaining third to men in order to rebuild the ruined caravanserais in desert places. He also remits all taxes for four years, sends a letter to Behrám with a silver throne and other valuable gifts, and makes him governor of the country from the frontier of Hitál to the Jaihún river. He also orders him to continue the war against Parmúdah. Parmúdah advances with the remnant of his army to and beyond the Jaihún, sending all his treasures to a fort of the name of Avázah. A battle-field is selected two stages from Balkh, where the armies halt at a distance of two farsangs from each other. Parmúdah determines to make a night attack. An astrologer having told Behrám not to fight on a Wednesday, as that would be an unlucky day for him, he goes into a garden to enjoy himself. Parmúdah hears of this and sends 6,000 men without lights to surround it, but Behrám orders Zalán Sínah to make a breach in the garden wall, from which he and Izad Gushasp and a number of his bravest men issue on horseback. They attack the besieging force, another breach is made, and the Turkománs are driven back, leaving the plain covered with their dead. Behrám, returning to his camp, now himself meditates a night attack, and surprises the Turkománs, who with Parmúdah take to flight, pursued by Behrám, who overtakes them. Parmúdah now shuts himself up in the castle of Avázah and offers to write a letter of submission. Behrám surrounds the castle, buries the dead and their arms under a heap of stones, which was thenceforward called Behrám Tal, and writes a letter to Hormuzd announcing his victory. He sends out Izad Gushasp and Zalán Sínah to slay all the Turkománs they can find, and on the third day sends a message to Parmúdah pointing out the hopelessness of further resistance, and recommending him to come out and ask for quarter, and sit no longer in the castle like a woman beating her cheeks with her hands, at the same time offering to intercede for him with the king. Parmúdah replies that he will address the king himself as a king, and not his servant. Behrám sends news of this to Hormuzd, who rejoices and sends a reply that the Khákán Parmúdah is his friend and is under his protection in the country where he is, and to this he invokes God as his witness. He writes to Behrám at the time to direct Parmúdah to come to his court with such of the plunder as he may think worth sending. He also calls for the names of the Iránis who may have distinguished themselves, with a view to rewarding them. When these letters arrive Behrám sends them to the castle, and Parmúdah comes out with his army, paying no regard to Behrám, but addressing him as an inferior Behrám, enraged at this, strikes him with a whip, and puts him in chains in a small tent. Kharád Barzín, hearing this, declares he is mad, and goes to the chief scribe, and both go together to Behrám to remonstrate with him. Behrám sees he has done wrong and has Parmúdah's chains taken off and remains with him till he mounts his horse and starts off to go to Hormuzd. He begs him not to mention to the king what has happened, but the latter says he must do so, although he cares nothing for it himself, as it affects the king's honour. Kharád Barzín, afraid that Behrám may kill Parmúdah, manages to restrain him, and Behrám goes off meditating vengeance in his heart. He orders the Mobeds to go to the castle to see what riches there are left in it. They do so, and make out a list of valuables accumulated from the time of Arjásp and Afrásiáb, such as the jewelled girdle of Siávash, which Kai Khusru had given to Lehrásp. Some of these things he appears to have appropriated to himself and not to have recorded in the list. Parmúdah arrives at the palace of Hormuzd, and dismounts from his horse, the king waiting to see if he does so. Hormuzd receives him graciously and assigns him a dignified lodging. On the eighth day he prepares a banquet, at which he seats Parmúdah in the seat of honour. The treasures are all produced, and the king asks Izad Gushasp what he thinks of what Behrám Chúbínah has accomplished. He answers that in an entertainment of which the tale was such as this the table must be ill-bred (*bad áyín*). This arouses the suspicions of the king, and his soul becomes a prey to anxiety.

Just at this time a drómedary arrives with a letter from the Chief Scribe to say that the Pehlaván (Behrám) had carried off two pieces of stuff from Zaman, two shoes embroidered with pearls and two earrings that had belonged to Siavásh and Parmúdah, when questioned, does not seem to have denied it. Hormuzd is very angry and asks if Behrám has become a king that he could not do without gold earrings. He takes an oath from Parmúdah that he will be faithful to him, and dismisses him with rich presents, accompanying him on the road for two stages.

Behrám, hearing of this, goes to meet him, and makes excuses for himself, offering gifts which the Khákán refuses to receive. He accompanies him for three marches, and is then dismissed by a message without being once spoken to, and goes off to Balkh in great anger.

Hormuzd now writes Behrám a letter of reproach, sending him at the same time a woman's dress and a spindle and cotton, a blue robe of hair, red drawers, and a yellow veil, and telling him he will no longer consider him a man. Behrám receives these, and is indignant that he should be thus rewarded. Putting on the woman's dress, he summons the chiefs of the army and shows himself to the indignation of the army, which refuses to serve the king any more. A fortnight elapses, and he comes out into the plain and sees a very beautiful wild ass, which he pursues leisurly, so as not to heat his horse. He comes to a narrow place, which the ass passes through and then perceives a palace, up to which he rides and enters, throwing his reins to Izad Gushasp, who has followed. Izad tells Zalán Sínah, who has also come up armed, to enter the palace and see what has become of Behrám. Zalán Sínah enters and finds a crowned woman like a cypress sitting on a throne with Behrám seated on a golden throne before her, with a number of beautiful slaves around them. Behrám and the woman are conversing, and the latter orders one of the slaves to tell Zalán Sínah that he has no right to enter there, and that he must go before his master, who was about to go. She entertains Behrám at a feast in a beautiful garden. The horses are then brought round, and Behrám says to her in going: "May Mushtar be the companion of thy crown," and she in reply wishes him victory, and that his heart may be patient and of good counsel, for he is the leader of Turán and Irán, the king of heroes and lions; the throne and crown of Irán are his, and the world has its support in him: that he shall subdue the world with his dagger from the black earth as far as the East. They say many things in secret that no one else knew of. When he left the garden it appears as if he wept blood, and his speech and answers seems altogether changed; it might have been said that his head had risen to the Pleiádes. The wild ass appears again and acts as a guide to him out of the forest. He returns, but says nothing to the army of what has occurred, or to Kharád

Barzín when he questions him, nor does anyone dare to enquire of him.

The next day he spreads a carpet of Chinese brocade in his palace, places chairs in it of gold and covered with gold brocade; as well as a throne of gold on which he seats himself with a royal crown on his head. The Chief Scribe informs Kharád Barzín, saying that he has grown bold and insolent. The latter tells him the matter must not be taken lightly, but they must go and inform the king, who should not have insulted Behrám, as he had, by sending him a women's dress, and Behrám had evidently conceived the idea of a crown for himself. By a ruse they manage to escape, and Behrám sends a hundred horsemen after them with Zalán Sínah, who brings the Chief Scribe back in chains. On being questioned the latter throws the blame on Kharád Barzín, who had frightened him for his life as Behrám had assumed the state of a king. Behrám tells him that may be, returns him what has been taken from him, and bids him reflect on what he will have to do but not to run away again. Kharád Barzín goes secretly with all haste to the king and tells him all he has to say, every word of which is engraved on the king's heart. Consulting a Mobed on the subject, he hears that the wild ass might have been a demon that lured Behrám from the right way and the crowned woman a magician who had pointed out to him the way to a crown and throne of power. He would never be obedient again, as he carried in his heart the insult he had received. The king had therefore better seek for some means to bring back his army from Balkh, for all the army thought the crowned woman was the destiny of Behrám. Shortly afterwards there arrives from him a basket of bent swords. These the King sends back with their points broken, and Behrám shows them to his army. They curse the king, and Behrám if he ever returns to his court. Behrám sees that they are estranged from the king, and asks them to enter into an understanding with him, making arrangements that no letter from the king might reach them and put an end to his designs.

He asks them what they propose to do to save their lives, and begs them to say all they have to say. He has a sister of the name of Gurdiyah, who, hearing what her brother says, grows angry and goes to the assembly determined to say what she has to say. Hearing her voice Behrám remains silent, and she asks them what they intend to do and why they are silent. Izad Gushasp remarks that they cannot contend against the whole world, but that if she desired to fight they would support her. Behrám considers that he means to steer a middle course between the two sides, and asks Zalán Sínah what are his secret ideas. Zalán Sínah boldly urges him to accept the crown and throne offered him. Asking Behrám, son of Behrám, and Kandá Gushasp, they support him. Behrám receives from the Chief Scribe the enigmatical answer that if God the just bestows anything it is useless to strive against it. Finally Kandá Gushasp tells him that he who would seize dates must not fear prickles. His sister is much grieved at these speeches, but does not open her lips to speak until Behrám asks her her opinion, when, disapproving of what has been said, she cries to the Chief Scribe that although the throne has often been vacant no subject has ever stretched out his hand towards it, and it is not right that a stranger of no lofty birth should possess it. She then relates what has taken place at various times. She exhorts her brother not to let passion rule his reason, and not to give to the winds what his ancestors had accomplished, ending by hoping her woman's words might not have to be recalled at some future time. Behrám bites his lips and the assembly is amazed at a woman speaking so, and *Zalán* Sínah declares that the career of the Kais is over, and her brother, whose humble servants they all are, shall be king of Irán. They need not think of Khusru Parvíz. Gurdíyah replies that a black demon has cast a snare on his road, and retires weeping to her own place. They admire her spirit, but her words only make Behrám more eager for the throne. He calls for wine and singers and music, the nobles drink to his health, and disperse in the dark night, heated with wine.

Behrám now writes a letter to the Khákán, promising that he will do no injury to his country, and if he becomes master of the world will act towards him as a brother, and beseeching him not to think of vengeance and not part Irán and China. The Khákán rejoices when the messenger arrives with this letter, and at once answers it favourably, sending presents to Behrám, who now distributes money to his troops and chooses a Pehlaván from among them to receive charge of the government of Khurásán, Nishápúr, Balkh, Marvand, Herát. He goes to Kai and strikes coin in the name of Khusru Parvíz, which he sends by a messenger to show to king Hormuzd, with a letter, in which, after reciting the matter of Sávah, Parmúdah, and the battle he had fought, he declares that as long as Parvíz lives he will, under his orders, convert mountains into plains and the plains into streams of the blood of his enemies, and that he will serve him, and no other, as king. By this he hoped to induce the king to put Khusru Parvíz to death, and he would then root out the race of Sásán from the earth. Hormuzd is greatly agitated on the receipt of the letter, and when he sees the coins struck in his son's name becomes suspicious of him, and instructs a man to get rid of him. The man agrees to put poison into his wine some night when he is intoxicated, but his chamberlain, getting wind of the design, informs Khusru Parvíz, who quits his father's court at Ctesiphon in the middle of the night and goes to Azar Abádghán. Here the nobles assemble around him, Sám, son of Asfandyár, from Shiráz, Pírúz from Kirmán, and others offering him their services. Khusru replies that if they will swear a solemn oath before Azargushasp to protect and stand by him he will remain in the country in confidence on them. They do so, and Khusru sends out agents everywhere to see what his father says of his flight and what more he proposes to do. Hormuzd at once imprisons Gústaham and Bandúi, Khusru's maternal uncles, and others of his adherents. Having done this, he consults Ayín Gushasp, his minister, as to what should be done with regard to Behrám, and he offers to be sent to him in fetters, as he was his enemy and that would please him, but the king refuses and sends him against him with an army in order to test his loyalty. Ayín Gushasp leaves and goes to Hamádán, accompanied by a fellow townsman who was in prison and who asks to be allowed to accompany him. The king gives him this companion, warning him that he is a scoundrel and a murderer. In Hamádán he consults a woman, who is an astrologer, as to whether he will die in his bed or by an enemy's sword. As he is speaking to her this man passes by, and looks at him, and the woman tells him his life is in this man's hands (cursed be his marrow and skin !). At this moment he remembers an old prophecy made about himself that he will die by the hand of a poor neighbour who will be in want and who will join him on a long journey, and writes a letter to the king to acquaint him with what has happened, and beg him at once to cut off the head of the messenger who brings the letter, the man whom he has saved from prison. The latter has his suspicions and breaks open and reads the letter, and returning cuts off Ayın Gushasp's own head, which he carries off to Behrám, telling him it is that of his enemy. Behrám retorts that on the contrary it was Ayín Gushasp's intention to reconcile him to the king, and proceeds to hang him head downwards on a gibbet in the face of the army. The troops that had come with Ayín Gushasp now mostly join Behrám, while some go to find Khusru and others return to the king. All scatter like a flock of sheep that has lost its shepherd. When the king hears of the death of Ayín Gushasp he in grief refuses to give audience to anyone, and loosing his appetite and sleep, gives way continually to tears, and his rule becomes despised. Bandúi and Gústaham and other prisoners release themselves from prison, and the two former arm themselves and march against the palace, where, having on the way fraternized with the king's troops that are marching against them, they seize and throw Hormuzd off his throne and burn out his eyes, leaving him alive and plundering his treasure. Such are the revolutions of destiny! The reign of Khusru Parvíz lasts for thirty-eight years. Gústaham at once sends news to Azargushasp to Khusru of what has occurred. Afraid that Behrám might forestall him, Khusru goes at once to Ctesiphon, taking with him troops that assemble from Barda and Ardabíl. The nobles assemble and seat him on an ivory throne, giving him a collar and crown. He sees the king, his father, with a cold sigh. In ascending the throne he declares to all the worthies who are assembled that he will rule with justice and will injure nobody, and they invoke blessings upon him. Visiting his father, Khusru bewails his miserable condition, professes himself his slave, and vows that he will do whatever he desires. Hormuzd desires of him three things, first, that every morning and night he should gladden him with the sound of his voice ; secondly, that he should send him one of his grand horsemen who bore the signs of old wars upon his person to speak to him of the fight, and some wise man who knew tales of the old kings to tell him, to be written down in a book, and thirdly, that his uncles should no longer see the world with their own eyes, and he would requite him for the sorrow they had brought upon him. Khusru reminds him that Behrám has become a powerful Pehlaván with a large army, and if he (Khusru) does his uncle any harm he will find no resting place on earth, but he will send him constantly old scribes who shall recall the past for him, as well as horsemen who can talk to him of war and feasting, but as for the rest he must resign himself to his fate. He will take vengeance on Bandúi and Gústaham for himself and give them without a shroud to the dogs to eat. He, however, does not tell this secret to anyone.

Behrám, in amazement at what has occurred, begins to talk of war with Khusru, orders the drums to beat, and his standard to be displayed, and boldly leads his army to Nehruán. Khusru sends out spies of experience to ascertain what Behrám is doing, how he sits at the time of giving audience, whether he remains in the van of his army or on one side, and if he goes out to the chase. They come and report that the army are all one with him, and when he marches he is sometimes in the centre and sometimes with either wing: that he gives audience after the manner of kings and hunts with panthers, and fights like a king. He also reads the book of *Damnah.** Khusru remarks to his own minister that such being the case he has a long business before him. He assembles a counsel of Mobeds and others and proposes to them that when he meets Behrám's army he should himself call Behrám forward and propose peace to him, and if

*Kalilah and Damnah, the Anvar-i-Suhaili.

he will not agree that he should be prepared to fight. To this all who are present agree. Khusru leads out his army from Baghdád to the desert, and orders Bandúi and Gústaham to put on their iron helmets, and when the two armies approach each other Behrám comes riding forward with Izad Gushasp on his left and Azar Gushasp and Zalán Sínah with three Khakains. The three agree that when they see Khusru's face they will bring him either dead or alive to Behrám. They meet at the spring of Nehruán, and the two armies look on to see how the Pehlaván would meet the king. When they approach each other in full array Behrám, after speaking insultingly of Khusru to those about him, urges forward his piebald horse, and Gardúi points out to Khusru which he is. After some preliminary talk with Gústaham and others, Khusru calls to him that he will treat him and his army as guests, and call him General of Irán and pray to God for him. Behrám answers that he will erect a high gallows and hang him upon it with his hands tied, and he will have a bad time of it with him. Khusru, perceiving that his thoughts are still fixed on the throne and crown, answers him that it is not the way of kings or of high-bred horsemen to abuse a guest at a feast, nor of Arabs or Pársis for 3,000 years, and he fears evil days are before him; that he is ungrateful and a sinner before God. As Kasrá was his grandfather and Hormuzd his father, whom did he consider more worthy of the throne? Behrám replies that he is of evil omen and unfit to be a king, that the Iránis are hostile to him and will tear him up by his roots, strip him of his skin, and throw his bones to the dogs. Khusru tells him it will be better for him to cast out anger from his heart and call on God and base his intellect on justice, but he will ask God as to his thoughts of greatness. He takes off his crown and dismounts and prays to God not to give his dignity and crown to a slave, but to give victory to his army. If he obtains his heart's desire he will lay his crown before Àzargushasp, give charity to God's worshippers, repeople cities that have been ruined by injustice, will make every prisoner of the Behrámis worship God and delight the hearts of the Mobeds. He rises from prayer and again reproaches Behrám, on which Behrám retaliates in like manner and claims that he alone is fit to be king from the sun to the back of the moon. In this manner both Khusru and Behrám proceed to bandy words with each other to the end of the chapter.

One of the three Turkománs accompanying Behrám now approaches Khusru and throws his lasso and catches him by the head, but Gústaham cuts the cord with his sword and releases him from his danger. Bandúi now strings his bow and shoots an arrow at the man, but he turns aside, and Behrám asks him why he did so when he was there. He then goes back to his camp. His sister, hearing that he has returned, comes running to him and asks him what he has done to Khusru. He tells her that he should not be reckoned among kings, as he is neither a wise man nor a warrior. His sister again comes and reproaches him for his folly in desiring to be king, saying that no one can obtain the throne but a man of good fortune, intelligent, of a bright heart and full of justice. Behrám replies that this may be right, but the matter has gone too far, and his heart and brain are sick with desire. On the other side comes the young king when he had passed the bridge of Nehruán. He sends for the chiefs and seats them on fitting thrones, and informs them that he has determined to make an attack at night, having seen Behrám and discovered that neither he nor his officers have any intelligence, and considers him a senseless youth. He bids them accordingly to be mounted and ready by nightfall, and warns Gústaham and Bandúi as well. After some talk with Gústaham and Gardúi, the latter tells him not to go into the fight, as the enemy will become aware of their secret preparations to attack. He agrees, and chooses to be with him and assist him, Kharád Barzín, Gústaham, Shápur, Andián, Bandúi, Kharad, Nastúh, and other suitable men. They mount a height whence the fight will be visible, and he offers to reward those who do their duty. Meanwhile one of the enemy overhears what is taking place, and goes and warns them to be on their guard, for there is to be a night attack. Behrám accordingly selects 6,000 men from his army to attack Khusru at daybreak, led by three valiant Turkománs. Khusru calls on his warriors to assist him and charges these three men, one of whom aims a blow at him with his sword, which Khusru wards off with his shield. Behrám and he then meet, but Behrám's weapons fail of effect. The fight goes on till sunset, and Takhvár, who has been sent by Khusru to send away the treasure and the baggage, comes and reports that it has passed the bridge of Nehruán, and Khusru proposes to Gústaham to flee, as he has only ten men and the enemy are in strength. He goes towards the bridge, pursued by Behrám. He stands on the bridge and demands his bow of Gústaham, and keeps back the enemy. Behrám comes on with his lasso, but his horse is struck by an arrow, and Behrám is dismounted. He retreats with his army from the bridge, and Khusru makes the best of his way to Ctesiphon, and relates to his father what has occurred. Hormuzd advises him to go to Rúm and get assistance in money and troops from the Kaiser. He tells Bandúi, Gardúi, and Gústaham to prepare, for they must give up Irán to the enemy. Just then a black dust and a dragon standard, such as Behrám had at Nehruán, appear on the road, and Khusru rides away in haste. Seeing Gústaham and Bandúi riding along slowly he points out that Behrám is close upon them. Bandúi tells him not to trouble himself about Behrám, for he is still at a distance, that he will come and give the crown to Hormuzd and sit by him as minister, and will have a letter written to the Kaiser to put him in confinement when he arrives, and send him back. Khusru reproaches them as he rides off. The two go into the king's hall and in revenge kill Hormuzd. By the time Behrám comes up they make their escape and rejoin Khusru, who sees their confused state but says nothing to his warriors, and orders them to leave the highway and march through the desert. Behrám now sends an army of 6,000 men in pursuit of Khusru, who obtains something to eat and drink at a caravanserai (*rabát*) and sleeps there. A cloud of dust is seen approaching them, and in order to save Khusru Bandúi puts on his clothes (probably not the gold crown, ear-rings, and belt that Fardúsi mentions) and remains in the place while Khusru makes off like the wind. The pursuing force think Bandúi is the king, as he sits on the balcony, and as soon as Bandúi sees this he comes down and puts on his own clothes and tells the son of Siávash when he comes up that Khusru is wearied out with travelling, but when the sun rises will go with him to Behrám. The chief consents to wait. The next day he says Khusru has been engaged in prayer and it has grown too hot for him to go out, but he will come next morning. The young chief is doubtful what to do, but being afraid of the difficulty he will get into with Behrám if anything happens to Khusru agrees to wait. The next day he tells Siávash's son that Khusru has gone off to Rúm and offers to go to Behrám and tell him what has happened. The latter thinks it will be better to take than to kill him. Behrám is naturally very angry at having been duped, and puts Bandúi in chains. He calls a meeting of his officers, and putting them in mind that *Z*uhák and Khusru had killed their fathers in order to gain the throne, offers himself as king. The council one after another speak and urge on him to take the throne, with the exception of one who appears rather doubtful. Behrám then says that someone of the descendants of the Kais should come forward and assume the royal belt, even the speaker himself. The others, however, all rise and with their hands on their swords hail Behrám as king. Behrám declares that he will cut off the hand of anyone who draws his sword, and leaves them, and the assembly scatter. Behrám sends for pen and paper, and tells a scribe to write an agreement from the people of Irán that Behrám is worthy to be king. The night passes in reflection and anxiety, and the next morning Behrám sits on a golden throne and all the grandees sign the agreement that has been prepared and seal it, calling God to witness that he should possess the throne from generation to generation. Yet even those who were his connections were wounded at heart at his becoming king.

Bandúi for seventy days was kept in prison by Behrám, his jailor being Behrám, son of Siávash. Bandúi endeavoured to persuade him that within two months an army would come from Rúm and cast fire on Chúbínah's throne and crown and break all the jewels on his head. Behrám answers that if the king would promise him his life he would listen to his advice, and would swear a solemn oath that if Khusru came with an army from Rúm and would guarantee him life and freedom from injury, he would not listen to the words of the Iránis. He accordingly brings the *Z*andavastá and swears Bandúi upon it, and now tells him that he will set a snare for Chúbínah and destroy him, and he should not be called king. Bandúi assures him that when Khusru comes with his army he will do anything he asks him, and will pardon his faults, even to giving him his crown. He persuades him to release him from his chains. Behrám informs him that he has made a plot with five men to kill Chúbínah when he is playing that day at *Chaugán*. He sends for a coat of mail and puts it on under his coat, but a woman who is in love with Behrám Chúbínah sends to tell him of this, and warn him to be careful. Behrám goes to his namesake and discovers the coat of mail and cuts off his head. When Bandúi hears of this he puts on the mail and takes flight from the town with the relations of the dead man, and goes to Ardabíl, collecting men on the road. Behrám tells the woman to look after Bandúi, but is informed that he has already fled, and repents that he did not kill Bandúi at once. Bandúi meanwhile escapes with a small force to Musíl, the Armenian (?), who persuades him to remain with him until he hears how Khusru fares in Rúm, and whether there is to be peace or war.

Khusru arrives with difficulty at Bablah (? Babylon) on his way to Rúm, and is received by the chief men of the city. A letter comes from Behrám to tell the chiefs not to let any army that comes there go free, for he will send men to them from time to time with all speed. This letter is at once shown to Khusru, who is rendered anxious by its contents. On the Euphrates Khusru meets with a caravan under the leadership of one Haris, son of Háris, who kills a cow and provides him shelter. With assistance from this man and another merchant he comes across he proceeds to the town of Kárván, the gate of which is closed to him. He remains outside for three days and on the fourth sends in to ask for food and friendship, which are given by three bishops (*iskulá*) and apologies made for their fault. He is allowed to put up in a palace there, and remaining in it for some days writes a letter to the Kaiser. He goes on to a town called Mánúi or Mínúi, where the Bishop and monks receive him with presents, and he remains for three days. On the fourth he goes on to a town called Varígh, in which there is a hospital (*bimársán*) and cross. He finds an old monk in a monastery who studies the stars, and tells him he is a slave of the king of Irán, carrying a message to the Kaiser. The monk tells him he knows he is the king himself and how he comes to be there, informs him he will obtain arms and an army from the Kaiser as well as one of the daughters of the royal house in marriage, and in fifteen days will be a king, but will be put to pain by one of the name of Bastám, whom he will call his uncle, and whom he must avoid. He accuses Gústaham of being the man, as his mother had called him Bastám, and the monk confirms him in saying so. Gústaham swears that he will always be true to him, asking him why he believes a Christian's word. Khusru acknowledges that he has never seen any evil in him, and leaves the monk and goes into the town, where the great men give him a good reception. A horseman now comes from the Kaiser to bid him welcome to the town and tell him to ask for whatever he desires, and saying that he will neither eat nor sleep till he has provided him with an army. Khusru orders Gústaham, Bábúi, Andyán, Kharád Barzín, and Shápúr to go in grand array to Rúm to the Kaiser, to talk to him in a friendly way and play with his men at archery and *chaugán*, and not allow themselves to be defeated. They were also to write a letter with which the Greek philosophers could not find fault, and to speak for him with a honied tongue as regarded a treaty and alliance. They accordingly go to the Kaiser, who sends to meet them and prepares a palace for them. He receives them in state, and they present the letter, which is full of the reputed power and excellence of the king of Irán, and asks for assistance. The Kaiser agrees to give him everything he requires, even to his own eyes, and calls a scribe to write a favourable reply. This is at once sent off with a horseman, and delivered to Khusru. He then consults with four philosphers, who remind him that if Khusru receives the royal crown he will raise his head to the moon's height and demand tribute from Rúm, and that he ought to pay no attention to what the Iránis say. The Kaiser thereupon sends off another letter to Khúsru, according to what the philosophers have said. Khusru sends back an answer that if the Rúmis will not listen to him he will apply to the Khákán, and when his envoys return he will not remain long in that town. He tells the Iránis not to break their hearts at the answer, for God is his friend, and he will be brave. This letter he sends to the Kaiser by the hand of Takhvár. On receipt of this letter the Kaiser consults his Minister and an astrologer, and the latter informs him that Khusru will reign 38 years, and, on the Kaiser asking him what answer he shall send to him, points out that if Khusru has to go to the Khákán he will never forego his hatred to him. The Kaiser, being helpless, decides to send troops to Khusru, and writes a letter to say he has consulted his Minister, and will send him an army called in from various quarters. He reminds him that in the time of Hormuzd and Kaikubád the Iránis had laid waste 39 Rúmi towns and carried off their women and children captives; it was no wonder that the Rúmis resented this, but nothing should now be said about it, but he must consent not to demand tribute from Rúm as long as he was king, and in return they would be friends and brothers, binding themselves by treaty that Rúm and Irán should be as one country. He offers him his daughter in marriage and agrees to send him troops and money. Receiving this letter, Khusru lays it before the Iránis, who agree it will be best to get rid of all old enmities. Khusru accordingly answers the Kaiser's letter that as long as he is king he will demand no tribute, will send no army into Rúm's territory, and will restore the captured towns. He asks that the Kaiser's daughter shall be handed over to Gústaham and the other Courtiers who had gone to Rúm. All enmity, he declares, has passed away, and Rúm and Irán have become one country. The letter is written with his own hand and sealed with his own seal, and is given to Khárshíd Kharád to convey to the Kaiser. When the letter reaches the Kaiser, he orders a talisman to be made. A fair woman was to sit on a luxurious throne, surrounded by her servants, with slaves all around, weeping and in silence, and from time to time raising her hand and brushing away her tears. The enchanter (*nairang-sáz*), makes a figure of a woman with long ringlets, whom everyone looks on as a mad woman (*shíftah*) full of light, with red cheeks and eyelashes like a spring cloud. When it is placed the Kaiser goes to see it, is astonished, and summons Gústaham, telling him he had a daughter like the spring, whom when she arrived at a marriageable age he had married according to Christian rites to an ambitious relative, and sent her to the young man's palace, and his soul rose to the sky. She was now sitting there in grief and pain, and the bright day had grown dark to her; she spoke no word and did not listen to his counsel, and the new world had grown old through her sorrow; he should address words of wisdom to her and see if she would open her lips to him. Gústaham goes, and the deceitful talisman salutes him with prayer. He offers good advice to the mourning woman, and says to her: "O daughter of the Kaiser's race, a wise man does not cry out at what justice does. The flying eagle is not exempt from death nor the tiger in the wood nor the fish in the water." All the Pelahván's talk was so much wind, for she had neither soul nor tongue, but continued brushing away the tears with her finger. Gústaham is astonished, and the Kaiser sends for him and asks what he thinks of his daughter, for whom he is grieved. He answers that he has given her much advice, but she would not listen to it. The next day he sends to her Bábui, Andyán, and Shápúr to see if they can get an answer out of her to make him happy. The result is the same, and she does not answer a word to their advice. They report this to the Kaiser, who now sends Kharád Barzin, with a strong man from his palace.* He stays some time and regards well her face and head and crown, but still gets no answer, although the talisman salutes him (*burdash namdz*). He is astonished that her servants should not speak if she is silent, and if these are real tears she sheds, why her hands and feet do not move. He comes to the conclusion that it must be a talisman's philosopher, and goes to the Kaiser laughing and says that this beauty (*màh*) has no intelligence, and the Rúmis have made a talisman, which Gústaham and Bábúi had not made out. When the king heard of it he would laugh. The Kaiser now says he is suited for the customs of the Khusrus; that he has a house in a wonderful palace, one than whose measure nothing higher can be conceived, and when he sees it he does not know whether it is a mere talisman or made by God.† When Kharád Barzín hears this he comes back to his old place (?) and sees a horseman standing close to it, and comes and tells the Kaiser that the horseman is made of iron, which a learned man would call a loadstone (*maknàtis*), that a Rúmi had set up on an Indian horse: whoever read of

* The whole story of this talisman is quite incomprehensible.

† This is equally vague with the story of the Talisman.

it from the books of the Hindus would rejoice and be of clear understanding.

Kharád Barzín now explains to the Kaiser that the religion of the Hindus is to worship the bull and the moon. The rest of the Section contains nothing historical, and is only remarkable for quoting the saying of Christ that if a man take away thy coat or strike thee on the cheek, it is not right to be angry. When the Kaiser hears the moral advice it gives, he approves of it and bestows praises on the speaker, and gives him money and a crown, saying: "May the land of Irán prosper through thee!" The Kaiser now sends his daughter and an army to Khusru. The former's name is Mariam, and she is said to have been learned and intelligent. She brings as dowry many rich vestments, jewels, carpets, brocade, bracelets, collars, crowns, four gold litters with golden hangings covered with jewels, and forty others of ebony, 300 beautiful female attendants, 560 clever slaves, 40 European slaves, 4 Rúmi philosophers, horses, robes, and many other fitting things. He also writes a letter praising Gústaham, Shápúr, and Bábúi, and accompanies the procession for three stages. He bids farewell to Mariam, telling her not to ungirdle her waist till she sees Khusru in the land of Irán. He sets his brother Nyátús in command of the army. The army with him at its head goes by way of Varígh. Khusru comes out to meet the army smiling like a rose in spring, embraces Nyátús, goes to Mariam's litter and kisses her hand, and, remaining with her for three days, marches on to Azar Abádghán. Here he remains a fortnight whilst troops come in to him from all quarters, and the command is given to Nyátús. He moves on by way of Khan, just to where the Armenian Musíl is. Here his uncle Bandúi meets him with Músíl, who kisses his foot and stirrup. At Azargushasp he enters the fire-temple and worships, and the army collects round to assist him. When Behrám hears of Khusru's arrival, he has letters written to Gústaham and the other chiefs with Khusru to say that nothing but evil has been brought about by the house of Sásán and enumerating the bad deeds of several of them: that he is not afraid of Rúm or its king, and if they will come to him their dark souls should be rendered bright. The messenger that conveys this letter finds the road closed and takes it and the presents he is entrusted with to Khusru himself, who writes an answer as if from Gústaham and the others to say that though they are in speech with Khusru, they are at heart with him, that when he brought his army there they would draw their swords and kill the Rúmis, that Khusru will tremble when he sees his army and will flee away from him like a fox. He gives this letter to the same messenger and money as well, and tells him that when Chúbínah's day arrives he will make him independent of the world. Behrám receives the letter and prepares to start notwithstanding the remonstrances of his chief men, and goes off to Azar Bádghán. An encounter now takes place between the two forces. Nyátús, Gústaham, Bandúi, and the king mount up on a hill to witness the fight, and Khusru prays for victory. One Kút, a Rúmi, makes his way to Khusru and asks him to point out Behrám, in order that he may give him a lesson in war and warriors' ways. He points out a warrior on a piebald horse, and tells him not to run away when he advances to fight, lest he should have to bite his lip from shame. Kút goes to the attack, and Yalán Sináh warns Behrám, who draws his sword. The Rúmi slips, and Behrám cuts with his sword through to his breast. Khusru sees Behrám's blow and laughs, whereupon Nyátús rebukes him for levity in battle, but Khusru tells him he is not laughing at his death, but at what Kút had said just before as to his having run away from a slave, for there was no shame in running away from a slave who could give such a blow. The body of Kút is now sewn up in linen after musk has been poured into his wound and sent to the Kaiser, and the Rúmis weep at his death. The Rúmis now making an attack, many of them are killed. All the dead are heaped together and form a mound, which they call Behrám Chid. Khusru is disappointed with the Rúmis and orders them not to be used in the next day's fight, for their iron swords were like wax, and says he will himself lead on his Iránis instead. The next day a second fierce battle takes place, in which after various encounters Khusru himself is saved from Behrám by an angel, who, after rescuing him, disappears, and Mariam, who has lost sight of him, is consoled. A third battle now takes place. Behrám strikes Khusru in the waist with an arrow, and a slave comes forward and draws the arrow out of the brocade. The king then uses his spear (it is not quite clear against whom) and it breaks in two, whereupon Khusru strikes his enemy's helmet with his mace, and the head of the mace breaks off in the helmet. On seeing this his army acquire fresh vigour, and Behrám turns back. The Rúmis and Iránis both advance to the attack, and separate the two forces. and Bandúi, advancing between them, proclaims that the king forgives all who have committed a crime against him. When this sound is heard in the darkness of the night all hear it, and Behrám's men gird their loins to go away, and when the sun rises the plain is found to be bare of men, and no one is found in Behrám's tents but himself and his companions. Behrám, seeing this, advises flight, and calling for 2,000 camels, on which they load all their valuable property, all retreat. Khusru, finding the army gone and the tents empty, sends Nastúd in pursuit with 6,000 chosen men. Behrám, in his flight, comes to a deserted village, his heart full of repentance, and enters the house of a widow, whom he asks for bread and water. This is given, and when the barley bread has been eaten they ask for wine, which she gives them in the head of a pumpkin cut off. She tells him she has heard of a fight between Behrám and the son of Hormuzd, from which Behrám has fled without an army, and everyone laughs at the idea, for no one thinks much of him. He lies down for the night with his coat for a night-robe and his breast-plate for a pillow, but cannot sleep. He collects whatever force remains with him and they march on and come to a cane-brake, in which men are cutting canes. They ask him why he has come that way, as there is a large army in front of him. Behrám knows this must be the king's army, and sets fire to the canes, in which some are killed and others burnt. When he sees Nastúd he rides at him and catches him with a lasso and binds his hands. Nastúd begs for quarter, and Behrám granting it, tells him to go to Khusru and tell him all he has seen. Behrám now proceeds to Ria and subsequently to the Khákán. Khusru writes a letter to the Kaiser describing all that has occurred. When this letter reaches him the Kaiser returns thanks to God and bestows charity and food by the ass-load. He writes an answer to the letter with valuable gifts to be sent by four philosophers, and when Khusru hesitates to put on some of the Christian clothing that is included with them, for fear of looking like a Christian, his guide (?) tells him that religion does not consist in wearing a particular kind of clothing. He accordingly puts it on for fear of displeasing the Kaiser, and shows himself to his followers, the wise among whom understand this is done by way of humouring the Kaiser, while others conceive that he has secretly become a Christian. The next day Khusru gives an entertainment to which the Rúmis are invited.

Nyátús, apparently offended at Bandúi's sitting by the king, considering it an insult to the Messiah, throws down his bread and leaves the table on seeing the cross and the *báj* (?) together. Bandúi pushes him (?) away. Khusru is angry when he sees this, and says to Gústaham that Bandúi is not fit to eat at the table with a king. Nyátús goes and puts on his armour in order to break up the feast and all the Rúmi horse go to Khusru to resent Bandúi's act in striking a worshipper of God (? *báj*) on the face, and demand that he shall be given up to them, or else there will be an uproar. Khusru becomes angry and says no one can hide the faith of *Yazdan*, for from Kayumúrs and Jamshíd to Kai Kubád none has ever heard of the Messiah. He will not give up the faith of his forefathers and turn to that of the Messiah. Mariam now interferes and has Bandúi sent to Nyátús with ten horsemen to ask him if he has not seen what the Kaiser had done with Khusru, although he knew he would not give up his old religion, and bids him embrace Bandúi and say nothing that may not be pleasing to him, or render useless all the trouble the Kaiser had taken. Nyátús takes Mariam's advice, and is reconciled to Bandúi, and Khusru approves of what he has done, and Nyátús tells him to keep to the faith of his ancestors. Khusru now reviews the Rúmi troops, gives Nyátús and them handsome presents, and sends them back to Rúm. He himself goes to Azargushasp and spends a fortnight in reading the Zandavastá, and presents large offerings to the temple with gifts to the poor. Thence he goes to the Dív (?) city, and spending many days in the hall that Naoshírván had built, constructs a large palace there, and seats himself on his grandfather's throne. He sends for one scribe and has a decree written to the Iránis after the style of his ancestors. He gives Khurásán to Gústaham, and patents sealed with the golden seal to

Shápúr with a robe of honour and servants, another patent to Andyán with the city of Kirmán, with another province to Gardúi, the city of Cháj to Bábúi, the keys of his treasury to the son of Takhvár; he puts all the Chiefs under the command of Kharád Barzín, and gives robes of honour to all those of the army who had remained with him in his day of trouble. He makes proclamation, telling the people not to call on any other name but God's, not to be revengeful or shed blood, and not to engage in evil deeds. If any of the humble ones complains or is treated unjustly by the army, the oppressor is to see the gallows. His treasurers in every town are ordered to give food and clothing to all who are in want of them. The world through his justice became a Paradise, and for all this Parvíz was to be praised.

In the next Section Fardúsi laments the death of his own son, mentioning his own age as 65, and his son's as 38. When Behrám arrives at the city of the Turkománs and finds the Khákán, he is met and received by 10,000 chosen horsemen. The Khákán questions him and Izadgushasp and Zalán Sínah as to the fatigues of their journey and the fight with the king. Behrám tells him that if he will not befriend him he must go to Hindustán to get away from Khusru; but the Khákán assures him he will care for him more than for his own connections. Behrám takes an oath from him to this effect, and the Khákán bestows all kinds of valuable presents on him. He informs him that he is in the habit of giving 1,000 *dinars* to one Makátúrah because he is a greater fighter than himself. Behrám offers to free him from him, and the Khákán agrees. Behrám tells him to refuse him the next morning when he comes to demand money, and not to laugh or open his eye to him. The next day when Makátúrah comes he does so, and pays no attention to him. Makátúrah is enraged, and asks him why he has suddenly been treated with such contempt, and Behrám answers him that he will not allow this kind of thing to go on as long as the Khákán keeps faith with him. Makátúrah draws an arrow from his quiver and shows it to him as the mark of his power. Behrám gives him back an arrow and tells him to remember him by it, and Makátúrah leaves the Khákán. The next day he comes to the Khákán in full warlike array, and Behrám prepares himself in a similar manner. After the usual mutual speeches against each other a combat takes place between them, and Makátúrah is killed. The Khákán accordingly bestows valuable gifts on Behrám.

Just at this time there appear to have been numbers of wild beasts in the hills of China, and one in particular with a body larger than a horse, with two black locks on its head like ropes, its body yellow, and its mouth and ears black, its claws like a lions, and with a roar that sounded beyond the clouds. They called it Shír kapí, and it kept the whole country in terror. The Khákán had a beautiful daughter like the moon, and of whom her parents were so fond that they grieved if the sun shone on her. This animal kills her one day when she goes out with her companions, to the intense grief of her parents. The mother is desirous of getting Behrám to avenge her on the lion, and the Khákán invites him to an entertainment and asks if he will undertake to get rid of the monster. Behrám agrees, and manages to do so by shooting it with arrows and afterwards cutting it in two with his sword. The Khákán and his wife go into the forest and see the dead beast, and shower praises on Behrám. The Khákán of China sends a hundred purses of *dirhams* to him, with slaves and robes, and gives him his daughter's hand, and all the horsemen declare themselves his slaves. Khusru hears of the doings of

Behrám, and writes to the Khákán to remind him of Behrám's having struck him with a whip, and asks him to send him back in chains, otherwise he will send an army from Irán that shall render the day black in Turán. The Khákán answers that he is breaking no treaties in being friendly with Behrám, and sends the messenger back in haste. On receiving this the king summons the Iránis, who advise him to select some wise old man to send to the Khákán to remain until the matter is settled, as it would not be easy to cry down Behrám when he had become the Khákán's son-in-law, but soft words must be made use of. Behrám, on hearing of the letter, goes to the Khákán and asks him to send him with an army to seize on Irán and Rúm and make him king of them both, after cutting off Khusru's head, and thus root out the seed of the Sassanides. The Khákán sends for old men of counsel to consult, and obtains from them an answer that as Behrám has many friends in Irán he should hear him on the matter. In the end an army is prepared, and the command of it given to two men of the names of Chínúi and Zangúi to go into Irán, where, as soon as the news is heard, Kharád Barzín is also ordered to prepare an army. Treasure is lavishly spent on the preparations, and when Kharád Barzín crosses the Jaihún he selects another route towards China. Arriving near the palace of the Khákán, he selects an eloquent man to go forward and announce to him that an envoy has come from Irán. The Khákán opens out the road, and the envoy addresses him as directed by the king. Kharád Barzín reminds him that he is related to Khusru, and the Khákán orders presents and a suitable lodging to be prepared for him. Kharád says to him that Behrám is of evil nature and worse than Ahriman, and in the end will break faith with him, as he already had with the king of Irán; he should send him to the king and exalt the latter's head to the moon. The Khákán tells him not to speak in that way, as he is not one to break faith; and on Kharád's reminding him that the king is more to him than Behrám, says that Behrám is his son-in-law, and he cannot break his pledge to him. Kharád now begins to think out some trick, and goes to the Khátún, and looks about for some one who may influence her. He comes across a certain person (*kad khuda*) and asks him to assist him with the Khátún, but he tells him it is of no use, as Behrám is her son-in-law. There was a Turkomán of the name of Kalún, whom all the rest despised, a relation of Makátúrah, who hated and cursed Behrám because he had killed Makátúrah. This man is sent for and money given to him, as well as clothes and food. Gaining access to the Khátún on the pretence that he is a physician, he cures her daughter of some illness. She pays him money and gives him brocade robes, and tells him to ask for whatever else he desires. Behrám takes an army to Marv. The Khákán issues a proclamation (for what reason is not evident) that if anyone goes to Irán without his seal he will cut his body in two. Kharád Barzín remains two months, and hears of these secrets, and summons Kalún, and, pointing out to him how prosperous he now is in comparison with what he was, says he has a fearful business for him to undertake. He will get a seal of the Khákán which he must take to Behrám. He must put on a black *púst*ín (a woollen coat) and take a knife with him, and tell Behrám he has a secret to tell him from the Khákán's daughter. which no stranger must know, and when he finds him alone he must drive the knife into him and run away. If they kill him he will at least have had his own revenge; if he escapes he will have bought the world and given its price, and Khusru will make him famous. Kharád Barzín gets the Khákán's seal from the Khátún and gives it to Kalún to take to Behrám. Kalún gains access on pretence of telling Behrám a secret from the Khákán's daughter, and stabs him with the knife. The people about seize him and push and beat him with their fists till midnight, but he will not open his lips to say who has put him up to the deed, although his bones are broken. Behrám's sister comes to him, weeping, tearing her hair, and lamenting. Behrám repents at not having listened to her advice, and tells Zalán Sínah to look after his sister and attend to her advice. He sends his salutation to Gardúi and bids him avenge him, and to make his *dukhmah* on Iráni soil. He also sends for a scribe to write a letter to the Khákán begging him to look after those he leaves behind. He embraces his sister. She makes him a silver coffin, covers his body with brocade, and pours camphor upon him. The Section winds up with the advice that as such is the course of this perishable world it is better not to grieve but to drink wine day and night, to have one's heart full of song and one's lip ever smiling. The Khákán hears of what has happened and knows it is the work of Kharád. He burns Kalún's fields and his two sons, and plunders all his property. He seeks everywhere for Kharád Barzín, but does not find him. Kharád returns to Khusru and relates all that has occurred, and Khusru in his joy at getting rid of his enemy, gives gifts to the poor, informs the neighbouring kings and sends robes of honour to the fire temples, fills Kharád Barzin's mouth with jewels and gives him 100,000 *dínars*.

The Khákán now sends his own brother to Gardíyah, Behrám's sister, and demands her in marriage, but she refuses to decide anything till her four months of mourning for her brother are over. She calls her friends together and consults them. She finally selects 1,160 horsemen to return with her to Irán, as she feels herself a stranger where she is. They all profess themselves her slaves. Zalán Sínah and Àzargushasp elect to go with them, and they start at night with 3,000 camels, Gardíyah going with them armed with breast-plate, sword, and helmet. As soon as he hears this the Khákán sends his brother in pursuit with instructions to try soft words with Gardíyah at first, but, if she will not give in, to make a graveyard of them at Marv. Tabrag, the commander of the force, comes up with her and tries to persuade her that the Khákán is anxious to avenge her brother. Gardíyah says: "Here am I ready to throw my horse on a raging lion." After further altercation she, with Àzargushasp and Zalán Sínah, attacks the Chinese and defeats them, and the whole plain becomes a river of blood. She then writes a letter to her brother to tell him what has occurred, and that she is being pursued by an army, but has defeated them and will wait for his answer on the Amúi. Khusru is now free of anxiety, since Behrám is dead. He says to his minister one day: "The slayer of my father is continually passing before me, and is my relation; how long shall I suffer secret anxiety?" On the same day he has an entertainment and shuts Bandúi up in prison and orders his hands and feet to be cut off his body, that he may no more be able to shed the blood of the Kais. They do so, and he dies. Khusru then sends a messenger to Gústaham to summon him immediately. Gústaham, hearing what he had done to his brother, rends his clothes and throws dust on his head. He knows that Khusru wishes to kill him to avenge his father, and recalls his scattered army, and goes to the forest of Nárvan. He meets Gardíyah, and the two lament together with Azargushasp and Zalán Sínah over the deaths of Behrám and Bandúi. He tells them how Khusru cut off Bandúi's feet, and asks them what hope they can now have from him, for the willow bears no fruit, and he would do even worse to them. When he saw Zalán Sínah from a distance he would fly into a rage and revive his hatred. If they would remain with him there they could consult together in every matter. She agrees to his advice, and, being mollified by his talk, the thoughts of Behrám no longer distress her heart. He (? Gústaham) tells Zalán Sínah to marry the woman. (Here follows a few sentences the meaning of which it is difficult to interpret with regard to this proposal).

Some time passes and the soul of the king is more and more troubled with regard to Gústaham. In a rage one day he says to Gardúi that Gardíyah has married Gústaham, and they consult together on the subject. Khusru says he has sent many troops to Amil to exact vengeance, but all had been killed or wounded. When Behrám strayed from the right way Gardíyah still was his friend. It was the right thing to do now to write a letter to her and ask her what she could think of to set matters to rights and to put an end to this misery; if she could bring Gústaham under a stone (? kill him) she would bring his heart and house into her own hand. He would bestow a province on whomever she desired, and to all this he would swear. Gardúi says he is her devoted slave, and agrees to send someone to advise her and enlighten her dark understanding. He would send his own wife to his sister for the purpose, and the thing would soon be managed for him. Khusru is greatly rejoiced, and a letter is accordingly written to Gardíyah, and Gardúi's wife is sent with it, and the matter ends with the smothering of Gústaham in his bed. Gardíyah writes to Khusru to inform him of what has happened. He sends for and marries her and exalts her above every one in his palace, and gives rich presents to all her companions, The next Section relates how Gardíyah displays her skill in martial exercises before the king in the presence of Shírín, his well-known queen, so that everyone is astonished at her prowess. In the next Section is related how a cup with Behrám's name upon it, used when wine is being drunk at a feast, is thrown away and Behrám cursed. Khusru says that Rai must now be trodden down under the feet of elephants. His Vazír remarks that Rai is a great city, and God would not approve of this proceeding. The king says there must be for some time a governor (marzbán) of evil disposition in Rai with crooked green eyes and large teeth. All the Mobeds are amazed that such an idea should have entered his head, but a man of this description is one day brought to him, at whom the people are all disposed to laugh. The king inquires as to his evil deeds, and is told that he is never at rest from them; that he does the contrary to whatever he says, and is altogether false; that he always breaks his pledges. He is sent to Rai, and washes from fear of God his heart and eyes, and commits all kinds of atrocities, and threatens to burn any place in which he sees water or grain or a cat in a house. All flee from their houses from fear of him, and the whole city is ruined. Gardúi is informed of this miserable state of matters, and thinks of some remedy. He tells his sister to speak to Khusru about it, and she dresses herself in a ridiculous fashion and gambols round the garden like a child so as to amuse the king, who asks her what she would like as a reward. She answers that she would like Raí to be given her, and the vile man who is there recalled. He agrees to do so, and tells her to send some pure man there and recall the other one. The world, after five years of rule, now prospers with him. He sends 12,000 horsemen to Rúm to prevent anyone coming thence from destroying Irán. He also sends 12,000 to Zábúlistán and the same number towards the country of the Aláns in order to defend them from enemies; another 12,000 are sent to Khurásán in order to keep every one out of the country from Heitál to China. In the sixth year of his reign a son is born to Khusru from Mariam, the Kaiser's daughter; one name, that of Kubád, being whispered by his father in the child's ear, and the other, Shírúi, openly given out. The king consults an astrologer, who prophesies that the earth will be terrified by him and the army will not bless him, as he will stray from God's way. The king, grieved at this, gives audience to no one for a week, and does not go out hunting. The nobles enquire the cause of all this from the Vazír, and Khusru shows him the horoscope! The Vazír cheers him by saying all must submit to fate, and the king sends a letter to the Kaiser announcing the child's birth. The Kaiser replies, and the whole country is decorated in honour of the event and rejoices. The Kaiser dispatches a caravan of 100 camels laden with presents, a golden jewelled peacock for Mariam, and quadruple tribute, with forty Rúmis, headed by a leader of the name of Khángí. The king goes out to meet them, and Khángí kisses the ground before him, uttering the usual complimentary blessings on the king and his son. He also asks for the *dár** of the Messiah, that his Faith may shine in the world and the fast of Sunday (*yakshambadi*) may be observed by all worshippers, that all who sorrow may rub their face on it (?) and burn scent (? incense) upon it: that the kingdom may be relieved from raids, and all enmities may cease. On hearing this Khusru praises him, and prepares a suitable lodging for him into which all necessaries are taken, and Khángí remains there a month, after which Khusru writes an answer returning thanks, and saying with

* What this precisely means it is impossible to say, unless it is the crucifix itself.

regard to the Christian Faith and Sunday observance that he knows no better religion than that of Hushang, which is full of justice, goodness, and love: that he knows no fellow, son, or wife to God. With regard to the *dár* that he requires, in every Faith that is well established, and to which intelligence is a guide, who can say that he whom he calls sorrowful (? the Man of Sorrow) and who died as a prophet on the *dár* was the Son of God? If he was His Son, he has gone to His Father, and that he should not fret for that piece of wood. When some foolish requests come from the Kaiser, old men laugh at the letter. The *dár* of Jesus was not worth so much trouble that king Ardashír should put it in his treasury. The whole country would laugh at him if he sent a piece of wood to Rúm, the Mobeds would think he had become a Christian, or had become a priest for Mariam's sake. He might ask for anything else he wished. All the presents sent for him and Shírúi were approved. He fears that when the latter grows up he may do mischief to Rúm. He has heard from Mariam that she has magnified his crown, is striving for the Messiah's faith and listens but little to his words, but is happy in this new royal tree (her child). The letter ends with the usual blessings. The treasury is opened, and first 160 *paidávasi** are filled with jewels and a tight seal placed on each, the value of each being 100,000 *dirhams*. Broçade, 500 pearls of fine water, and many other presents are enumerated as sent, to the extent of 300 camel loads, to the Kaiser, while Khángí and the Rúmi philosophers are rewarded with robes of honour, money, &c.

The story of Khusru and Shírín is now related, and is said to have been written at first in six times 10,000

* Described as pieces of 5 dinárs, but it must mean something else. as a coin could not hold jewels.

couplets. One day Khusru goes to hunt in state like the ancient kings, with over 300 nobles with golden bridles, 1,060 footmen, with spears, 1,040 with swords, 700 falconers, 300 horsemen with chítahs (hunting leopards), 70 trained lions and panthers in chains, with their mouths fastened up with golden chains, 800 pairs of dogs, 2,000 minstrels, with tents, camels, horses, &c., and 200 slaves with lighted chafing dishes of incense. With the king went 300 young men on horseback, in robes of red, yellow, and violet, and Kávah's banner. When Shírín hears of the king's coming she appears on her terrace in a musk-scented dress (*piráhan*), with red brocade and many jewels on her person, and a royal crown on her head, weeping, with the tears running down her cheeks. She addresses the king and asks (why it does not appear) where are the love and the tears of blood, to which the sight of Shírin was a physician, where is all that turning of day into night, with weeping eyes and smiling lips, where are all his pledges and oaths? Khusru hears this and sees Shírín and sends forty honourable Rúmi slaves to take her to his palace, and goes on to hunt. After this he returns to the town, which is decorated for him. He goes to Shírín's palace and kisses her feet and hands and head and calls on the Mobeds to perform the ancient customary marriage rites. The nobles and the whole city, hearing of the coming of Shírín to the palace, are much troubled, and do not go near Khusru for three days. On the fourth he sends for them, and asks them why he has not seen them for so long. All are silent and look to the Mobed, who makes a long speech, the purport of which is not very clear, but apparently objecting to Khusru's taking Shírín because she is a stranger. He gives no answer, and is told they would come for it the next day. The next day a dish covered with warm blood is produced, from which all turn away their faces in disgust. He asks them whose blood it is, and why it is placed before him. The Mobed replies that it is foul blood, at which every one is disgusted. Saying this, they (? who) lift it up and pass it from hand to hand, and clean it from the blood with water and earth. The dish purified, the Mobed fills it with wine and pours musk and rosewater into it, and the dish shines like the sun. Khusru remarks that the dish looks quite different, and the Mobed answers that good has come out of bad and by his order paradise had been made out of hell, as good deeds come out of bad. Khusru says that Shírín in the town had been like that ill-savoured dish, but that now she had become wine in his palace and was scented with his scent; that Shírín had acquired a bad reputation through him, and had not sought friendship with those who were above reproach (*purmáyah*). On this they invoke blessings on him, and say that she is the sun on earth whom he makes the moon. Shírín grows jealous on account of Khusru's paying more attention to Mariam than to herself, and kills her with poison, but she keeps the secret. A year afterwards Khusru gives her the golden sleeping chamber in the palace. When Shíruí is ten years old he is delivered to learned men to be educated. One day the Mobed finds him with a book in which he had written the story of Kalílah, and the dry foot of a wolf that had been cut off on his left hand and those of a bull and sheep on his right. The Mobed is vexed at this gruesome style of game and at the boy's evil propensities, for he had seen his horoscope. Khusru is informed, and his rosy cheek becomes pale. When 33 years of his reign have gone he becomes so vexed with his son that he makes him a prisoner in his own palace.

The next Section relates the making by Khusru of the throne called Takdis. A description is given of how the different kings one after another had added to it, but Khusru desires to make an entirely new one, and the manner of its construction and the jewels lavished upon it are given in full detail in the whole Section. There follows this an account of what took place between Khusru and the minstrels Sarkash and Bárbúd. The latter, coming to know that the king favours Sarkash, is jealous of him, and wishes to supplant him, and comes for that purpose to the palace. Sarkash tries to bribe the porter not to allow him access to the king, and he does so. Being turned back, Bárbúd takes his lute to the king's garden, and goes to the gardener, whose name is Mardúi. The king used to remain there a fortnight at the New Year, and on this occasion Bárbúd gets the gardener to let him go into the king's entertainment. He sits under a shady cypress to which the king is in the habit of coming. A Pari-faced cupbearer comes and presents the king with a cup of wine. The singer comes and sings a royal song with a sweet voice, at which all are astonished. The king tells them to find out the singer, but they are unable to discover him. The king takes another cup and the singer strikes up another song, and they search for him with lamps under the trees in vain. The same thing happens when the king takes another cup of wine, and Khusru tells them to find the singer, that he may fill his mouth with pearls. On hearing this the minstrel comes down from the tree and goes to the king and kisses the ground. The king asks who he is, and he answers that he is his slave who lives in the world only by his (the king's) voice. The king is delighted at seeing him, and tells Sarkash that he is like colocynth while Bárbúd is like sugar, asking him why he has kept Bárbúd away. He listens to him till it is time to sleep, and fills his mouth with pearls, and Bárbúd becomes a chief minstrel. Many great and small pass away and he (? Fardúsí) does not wish to wake from his sleep. When this book comes to an end he will not die, for he has sown the seed of words, and whoever has intelligence will praise him even after he is dead.

The next Section describes the building of the city of Madáin by Khusru. Khusru sends men to Rúm, India, and China, and brings 3,000 clever workmen, out of whom he selects skilled men to build what will not be injured by rain or frost or sun. The rest of the Section contains interesting details of the building of the town, and is followed by another Section describing the magnificience and greatness of Khusru. After this, however, Khusru turns aside from justice and takes to plundering the property of his subjects, and has no other thought but how to amass greater wealth for himself, so that the people all begin to forsake the city. There was one man of the name of Guráz in whom he seemed to place all his confidence, but who had a demon's head for injustice, and a second of the name of Farúkhzád, who was dear to Khusru and allowed no one near the king. Guráz sets him at variance with the Kaiser and incites the latter to seize upon Irán, a matter in which he would assist him. The Kaiser accordingly assembles an army and proceed to the frontier. Knowing that Guráz has incited the Kaiser to take this step, Khusru treats the matter lightly and sends for Guráz to an assembly of the chiefs, and writes a letter to him accusing him of deceiving the Kaiser; that he is to remain still until Khusru begins to move, and then, with his own army, go to the assistance of the Kaiser, who, when he sees armies moving in different directions, will change his mind; he (Khusru) would then come to his assistance in Irán and take all the Rúmis prisoners.* He sends a crafty man with this letter in

*These instructions are perfectly unintelligible, and are perhaps meant to be so.

such a manner that he may fall with it into the hands of the Rúmis and be taken to the Kaiser. If they take him to the Rúmi commander and he is questioned he is to say that he has a letter for Guráz, and allow it to be taken from him. The messenger acts accordingly, and when he reaches the Kaiser the latter conceives from the letter found on him that Guráz means to destroy him by a trick, and withdraws his army. Guráz, hearing this, writes to the Kaiser to know why he has done so, and receives an answer assigning the Kaiser's suspicions as the reason. Guráz makes many excuses. Khusru now writes to Guráz to know why he has not come to court when summoned, and declaring that the army he has is friendly to the Kaiser, and ordering him to send it to him. Guráz is full of anxiety and chooses 12,000 horsemen, and orders them to be of one accord and remain for some time on that side of the river and not be in a hurry to move. The army goes to Karach-i-Ardashír (?) to see what orders the king would give. Khusru sends a message by Farúkhzád to ask why the Kaiser has been allowed to penetrate to the frontier. The army are terrified from fear of what the king may do, and do not divulge the secret. A messenger favourable to Guráz comes to them to tell them not to fear, as the king has seen no open fault in them; that they are in reply to ask who suspected them, for they were all under one sheet. The chiefs give an answer accordingly, and Farúkhzád returns to Khusru and reports. Khusru sends him back with an order to the army to send to him whoever may be guilty and has been deceived by the Kaiser, otherwise they should all see the gallows and the well. The army, hearing this message, do not dare to open their lips, and remain silent. Farúkhzád tells them not to fear the king, for his army is absent abroad, and he has no great man with him to improve his fortune;

they need not be afraid of him, but might abuse both him and the king. All rise and begin to utter abuse, and Farúkhzád goes and reports to Khusru that the army have all combined together and he fears for his life. Khusru knows that that crooked speaking one would bring water and blood into the river (?), but from fear of his brother says nothing. Farúkhzád also knows that Khusru laid the fault of the army on his shoulders, and is told so by an intelligent old man, who tells him that until he produces another king he must not go any further; that he should place his son on the throne. Shortly after this Farúkhzád meets Takhvár, and relates all the evil he knows of Khusru. They arrange to go to the prison and bring out Shírúi. He (Farúkhzád) says that if Khusru's fortune changes for the better there will be no Pehlaván left in Irán, but all will be disposed of on the gallows or in a well or by chains. He brings his army to the encounter, and the general (not specified) meets him and is killed. The army of the king is scattered, and Takhvár comes to the prison and calls to Shírúi, but the latter does not know why he has come. Takhvár says to him that if he is not in league in the matter he should show some manliness, and if not there are fifteen brothers of his who are worthy to be king. Shírúi stays weeping in his place. Farúkhzád is in the palace and allows no one to pass in. The king becomes aware of what is going on, and orders the watchmen of the city up to to the palace, giving them as watchword the name of Kubád. As night comes on there arises a tumult in the city. Shírín is alarmed at the noise and tells Khusru to listen to the cries of the watchmen. He tells her that they must go off during the darkness of the night to the Faghfúr of China or Makrán or Máchín to ask for troops from the Faghfúr, making their way by some pretext. As his star was not in the ascendant, this could not be managed, and he is in difficulties. Shírín tells him he must strike out some new idea, or the enemy will make his way towards the palace. He sends for two Indian swords and a Rúmi helmet, with a quiver, arrows, and a golden shield, and goes while it is still dark into the garden about the time that the crow awakes, and sits among the saffron and narcissus with a sword under his knee. The enemy at sunrise come to the palace and finding it empty plunder the building. The two (Khusru and Shírín) are in a cave in the garden. When the day is half over the king becomes hungry, and he tells a gardener, who does not know him, to go into the bazár and buy him some meat and bread for a goblet (*shákh*) that he gives him. He goes to a baker and asks for bread in exchange for it. They go to a jeweller to value the goblet, and he asks who would dare to buy it, for there was such a goblet in Khusru's treasury. Where had he stolen it from? All three now go to Farúkhzád, who runs with the cup to Shírúi. Shírúi threatens to cut off the gardener's head if he does not say where the cup comes from, and he accordingly says the person from whom he got it is in the garden; that he had sent him to sell it in order to buy bread. Shírúi at once sends 300 horsemen to the edge of the river. Khusru, seeing them, withers away and draws his sword. Seeing the king they all retreat weeping and report to Farúkhzád, who goes with men from the palace and finds Khusru alone, and asks him what will happen to him in the end if he kills a thousand men. All Irán is his enemy. He reminds him of what an astrologer had told him, that he would die between two hills at the hand of a slave, one a golden and the other a silver hill, and that he was sitting there with his heart in two, the sky above him being golden and the earth like iron. An elephant is brought and he sits on it full of sorrow, and is taken out of the garden. Kubád (Shirúi) now orders that he be sent to Ctesiphon, and that no harm should be done to him. He is placed in charge of Galínúsh with 1,000 horsemen. This takes place when his reign has lasted thirty-eight years, and Shírúi only lives eight months. Such is the way of this tyrannical world, from which faith can never be looked for.

Shírúi ascends the throne, and is extolled, as usual, by the heroes of Irán. He promises to reign with justice and refrain from all deeds of Ahriman. He decides to send Ashtád and Kharád Barzín to his father, as chosen by the Iránis, to make excuses to God for his sins, and if he agrees to do this he himself will engage to employ himself with doing justice and not in breaking the hearts of the poor. They were to tell the king that the fault of his misfortunes did not lie with his son or the Iránis, but with himself for turning aside from the way of God, first, because it was not right that a son should shed his father's blood or be an accessory to such a thing, to shock the hearts of the righteous; secondly, because the earth was full of the treasure that he had toiled to amass; thirdly, that he had scattered all the nobles of Irán, some to China and some to Rúm. Again that the Kaiser had given him his daughter and an army and asked him for the cross (*dar*) of the Messiah for Rúm, in order to refresh the land and he had not given it. He had taken away their property from the helpless, and killed two of his uncles. He should now demand pardon from God for all this, in order that He might take him by the hand. The two men start off for Ctesiphon, and find Galínúsh on guard with all his men armed and ready. Khárád Barzín asks him why this is necessary, as Shírúi is sitting quietly on the throne, and tells him he has a message for Khusru from Kubád. Ashtád informs him the message is to ask why he makes much of the rebellious ones.

Galínúsh goes to Khusru to ask him, and he smiles and says: "If he is king, who am I? Why am I in this narrow jail?" Galínúsh repeats this, and they go to him respectfully and deliver the message. Khusru replies that the message that has been brought from his evil-disposed son has come from a few badly-disposed criminals who wish to deprive the family of all good fortune and that none of the stock may enjoy any happiness, that the crown and throne should go to the unworthy and the royal tree should be destroyed and that all his friends should become enemies. They then give him the message in full, and after some words of good advice he answers that his father Hormuzd had become enraged against him through the words of a slanderer, and when he heard of it he had left Irán on a dark night, and as his father wished to poison him he had fled away, both from him and from Behrám, when he brought an army against him. When his uncles Bandúi and Gústaham shed his father's blood he was not slow in avenging him, and cut off Bandúi's hands and feet, and Gústaham was also killed. He had not shut up his son in a close prison, but behaved to him as the old kings had, and had not denied him hunting or conversation or singers, only nominally imprisoning him in his own palace, and had otherwise treated him well. With regard to what he said as to his imprisoning people, such had been the case under old kings as well, and the Mobeds would tell him no one who was God's enemy should remain alive in the world, and he kept them in prison so as not to shed their blood. As to taking people's property he had only demanded the usual tribute and taxes. The wealth he has acquired had been taken from his enemies who were scattered abroad and is all left behind for his son: for if he has no wealth he will have no army and even the humble will not desire him as a king. After giving a good deal of advice he says with regard to the Messiah's *dar*, he has thrown an old piece of wood into his treasury which was of no profit to him, about which the Christians have cried to him. He was astonished that such a man as the Kaiser, surrounded by wise men and philosophers and Mobeds, should call one who had been killed a God or desire a piece of useless dry wood. It had suddenly disappeared from his treasury; it had become the Messiah and was no longer in the world.* With regard to what he had said as to repentance, God had placed the crown on his head and he had accepted it gladly. When God demanded it he had given it up, and would answer to his God and not to a boy. He tells Kharád at the same time to bid farewell to Shírúi for ever, and both the envoys to take their leave and say nothing but what they had heard. He goes on to name various kings and heroes of Irán and recall their deeds and accomplishments. When the angel comes to take away his life, he will surrender it easily. Many days will not pass before the king and the army will give each other to be killed, fire will be cast into every land, fathers will be slain by their sons and sons by their fathers. As his kingdom and greatness had come to an end, what were milk (or a lion) and rule to him? Ashtád and Karád Barzín, hearing these words, are pricked to the heart, strike their hands on their own heads and cheeks, and repent what they have said; they rend their garments, pour dust on their heads, and depart weeping to give the message to Shírúi, who says to his army that he who is not grieved at his father's woes is worthy of the gallows, and he could call him nothing but evil-dispositioned. He orders his cooks to prepare all kinds of nice sweet dishes and lay them before Khusru on golden tables, but Khusru refuses to eat anything except at

*This passage is unintelligible in the original.

Shírín's hands (probably for fear of poison). Shírín was his only companion, keeping up his spirits but herself trembling like the leaves of a willow in the breeze, whilst Khusru passed his days for a month in repentance and had no pleasure in life.

Bárbíd, hearing of this, comes from Chehram to Ctesiphon in great tribulation. He sees Khusru and pours out his lamentations on his lute, and finally cuts off his four fingers and burns his musical instruments. The army, fearing that if there are two kings by the reconciliation of father and son some harm will come to them, assemble together at the palace, and Shírúi, knowing that he will be a slave in their hands, sends them away, promising to seek for a man to put an end to his trouble. A man is found on the road with two blue eyes and yellow cheeks, a dry body covered with hair, and his feet dusty, with a hungry stomach, who goes to Farúkhzád and undertakes to kill the king. Farúkhzád commissions him to do it, but to tell no one, and promises to pay him and cherish him as his son, and gives him a sharp dagger. Khusru is afraid of his object when he sees him and asks him who he is, and he answers that he is a poor man without a friend in the town. Khusru tells a waiting boy to bring him a bowl of water with musk and amber and a new robe. This he puts on and draws a new sheet over his head so as not to see his murderer, and the man fastens the door and stabs him to the heart. When the people know that Khusru is no more, those who were his enemies enter the prison and kill his fifteen sons. Hearing of this, Shírui sends twenty guards to take care of their wives and children. He sends word to Shírín calling her a sorceress, and bidding her not to tread the hall in such seeming security but to come to him. She is enraged and refuses to look on the murderer of his father even from a distance. She sends for a scribe and makes him draw up a list of her property. She takes out some poison she keeps in a box and sends a message to Shírúi to say that he ought to be ashamed of himself for sending for her. Shírúi sends back word, insisting on her coming and looking on his crown to see if it becomes her. She refuses to come alone and he sends fifty men for her. She puts on blue and black clothes and goes to him and sits behind a curtain. He sits on the other side like a chaste person and proposes marriage to her, saying he will make her more exalted than his father did. She tells him to do her justice and then her life shall be in his hand, and she will not delay her answer. To this he consents, and she accuses him of having called her a sorceress and appeals to the nobles who are with him to say what they know of her. They all speak well of her, and she says there are three things a woman should have; firstly, modesty, and property with which her husband may adorn her house; secondly, that she should bear him a son; and thirdly, that she should have a good height and a face to carry off her dress. She had four sons, who were now under the earth. Saying this she draws the sheet off her face, a face like the moon and with hair like musk, and says this is her only sorcery. All are astonished, and Shírúi says if he has her for a wife it is enough from Irán. She answers that she desires him to hand her over all her property and to sign the list in the presence of that company. Shírúi does so at once, and she rises and goes to her own house, where she frees her slaves, gives them all her property and whatever else she has to the poor, and bestows something on the fire-temple for the New Year and Saddah feasts. She then sits in the garden, and, calling her people, exhorts them to fear God, and only to speak the truth, and asks them what fault they have had to find with her since she became mistress there, and all cry out loudly in her praise. She then tells them that that wicked murderer of his father had sent a message to her that his soul had become darkened (without her). She had answered that she was the slave of the Creator. She now sends a message to Shírúi that she has but one wish left, viz., that the door of the *dukhmah* may be opened for her. She goes in and lays her face by the side of Khusru and swallows the deadly poison, and placing her back against the wall dies. Shírúi orders another *dukhmah* to be made for her. In a short time he himself is poisoned, and his son Ardashír sits on the throne.

Ardashír, son of Shírúi, reigns for six months only. He addresses the usual exhortation, and promises to follow the rules of former kings, to exalt the worshippers and draw oppressors into blood. He hands the command of the army over to Pírúz, son of Khusru. When Guráz hears what has taken place he sends word to Rúm, and to Pírúz, son of Khusru, that the fortune of the house of Sásán has become dark, and he should gird his loins, to collect both young and old and rid the world of Ardashír. If he let this be known he would dip the dagger of revenge in blood. He himself would bring such an army from Rúm as to darken the world to his eyes. He must ponder his words well and not despise what he was doing. Pírúz, reading the letter thinks what would be most to his own advantage and consults the chiefs, who advise him not to listen to Guráz, but to write to him not to set aside the word of God or allow the devil to prevail over him, for the world was happy under the rule of Ardashír, and he should not raise a greater disturbance. On this Pírúz writes to Guráz: "May there be no general in the world like thee!" Enraged at this, Guráz prepares his baggage and army, and Pírúz sends a dromedary to summon Takhvár, who advises him not to try to avenge the ancestors of Irán, but listen to what Guráz says. Pírúz becomes very anxious at this state of affairs, for Ardashír was continually sending for him, as he was an eloquent man. He goes to an entertainment with wine and music, and becomes intoxicated, and drives out Ardashír's friends. When he and Ardashír are alone he strangles him, the king's reign having lasted for six months.

Guráz, hearing of the death of Ardashír, at once makes a raid on Ctesiphon. The nobles meet and Pírúz asks whom they have chosen for king, and Guráz answers that they will see a new and wise king upon the throne. and telling them what a king should be, says that if he were once to be a king and happily sit on the throne of gold in grand clothing it would be better than slavery for 300 years with treasures scattered, that his son would sit after him, and wear the royal crown; he would sometimes feast, and sometimes fight and hunt down his enemies. His eldest son asks him secretly which of them would be king; he tells him not to make too sure, but to collect treasure, for if one of the royal seed should come he would not remain long there. The younger son says he is worthy of rule and treasure, but if he were without treasure he would only remain with difficulty; that he must hold the world by bravery, for no one is born a king. He approves this speech, and collects his army at the court, and gives away money and dresses of honour. In two weeks nothing remains of Ardashír's treasure. He is guilty of great extravagance and splendid living, and all the chiefs turn against him. He goes to sleep drunk. The world is ruined by his injustice, for he sheds blood unjustly, and thinking of nothing but gold would sell the world for a *dínár*. All the world abuse him and wish for his death. One Shehrán Garáz plots with the army and offers to lead them if they will support him against a man who is neither of the seed of the Sásáns nor of the Kais, and they agree. One day when out hunting he shoots Guráz in the back with an arrow and it comes out at his naval. A fight ensues in the darkness and indiscriminate slaughter succeeds, a great many being killed and wounded.

A girl of the name of Purándukht, and the wife of the king (?) was the only one left of the seed of Sásán. The nobles elevate her to the throne. She gives the usual promises to make the poor rich, to drive all bad men out of the country, and rule according to the customs of the kings. Pírúz is brought before her, and she has him tied on a horse without a saddle, and with a halter round his neck, and apparently a lasso tied to the stirrups of horsemen. The horse thus driven constantly throws him down, until blood flows from his skin and he is at last killed. Purán rules kindly, but in six months is ill for a week and dies.

She is succeeded by Mordándukht. It does not say who the latter woman was. She makes the usual promises and threats and dies in four months.

She is succeeded by Farúkhzád, who only reigns one month. He is poisoned by a slave of the name of *Bíhunar*, with whom, apparently, he at first falls in love and throws into prison for not acceding to his wishes, and subsequently releases. Enemies now appear on all sides, and the throne of Sásán is overthrown by the ill-deeds of the Iránis.

She is succeeded by Yazdagird. He declares himself to be a son of Naoshirván. Nothing particular is recorded of him. In his reign the Amír of the Faithful, an Arab, makes an incursion into Irán, and Yazdagird collects an army from all quarters, and orders Rústam, a son of Hormuzd, and an astrologer, to proceed against him with an army. The war proceeds in Káúsí for thirty months. He ascertains from a study of the stars that the Arabs will be victorious for 400 years. He writes accordingly to his brother that an envoy has come to him to say that the country from Káüsí to the mouth of the river (?) will be given to the king. Thence how far will they open the road and where is there a market for buying and selling? He will look no farther than this, but not looking for the crown will accept a heavy tribute. He will obey the orders of the king and give him hostages if he demands them. Some of the nobles who are with him, such as Galbúí Tabrí, Armaní (?), Mahui Surán, and these chiefs will not look at these terms, but insist on the mace and sword. If he strive manfully, and make the world too narrow for the enemy, yet who knows what is ordered by fate? When he reads the letter he must arrange to send an army and advance to Ázar Abádghán, and bring all the horses he has to Ázargushasp, as well as all troops he can from *Z*ábúlistán. He is to mention all he says to his mother and salute her. If anyone brings bad news of him they are not to grieve overmuch, for in this transitory world he who collects wealth suffers pain. They must always pray to God and praise Him, for he (the writer) is in difficulties. He must do all he can to preserve the king, for there is no other one left of the royal race. He describes the state of affairs as all turned upside down, the son hating the father and the father the son, the unskilled slave becoming a king, and descent and dignity being of no use, there being no faith left in the earth and all inclining to oppression. No one knows the secrets of the stars nor that the state of affairs is likely to last a long while. His brother must continually watch the king and devote himself to the war. When the letter is sealed it is given to a messenger to take to his brother with all speed.

Rústam now sends a letter to Sa'd Vakás, the Arab

general. He first inquires who is his king, and who he himself is and what are his customs, and on whom he relies for support, and goes on to describe the power of the king of Irán. Asking if he is not ashamed to desire to possess the throne of Irán, he bids him send an eloquent, learned, and experienced envoy to him to say what are his intentions, so that he may inform the king of his wishes. He should not go to war with such a king as the grandson of Naoshírván, for the end of it would certainly be disastrous to him. The letter is given to Shápúr, son of Pírúz, and delivered by him to Sa'd Vakás. The latter receives him and tells him the words of Rústam, and writes an answer in Arabic, with the superscription of God and his prophet Muhammad. He exhorts him to embrace the right Faith, which will give happy rule in both worlds, as Muhammad would intercede for him for the pardon of his sins. The paper is sealed with an Arabic seal. Sa'd's envoy takes the letter to Rústam, and says that if he accepts the Faith, peace be to him! Rústam gives the letter to a reader, and bids him say that if Sa'd were a Sásán with a crown it would be a simple matter to meet him in war or at a feast. If Muhammad were there in person, and he were to adopt the new religion, it would be a hard thing for him. As the day of battle was not a time for talk, the envoy should go back and tell Sa'd that it would be better for him to die honourably in battle than to utter crudities. Rústam now orders his army to prepare. A fight takes place that lasts for three days. The Iránis are distressed for want of water, and take to eating dry mud. Rústam and Saíd draw to one side from the battle. The former wounds Sa'd's horse with his sword and Sa'd falls, but, Rústam's eyes being blinded with dust, he strikes him with his sword on the helmet, and Rústam falls. This is not visible to the army, but they go to see and find him covered with dust and blood. The Iránis now take to flight, many are killed and many remain thirsty on the field. The army goes to the king and the Mussulman army advances to Baghdád where the king Yazdagird is, and thence onwards to Karkh. Farúkhzád, son of Hormúzd, advances in anger from the Arúnah river, and coming to Karkh, delivers an attack, thinking there are no spearmen left there, but they suddenly come out from Baghdád and kill and wound many men. Farúkhzád goes to the king and tells him, as he is one man and the enemy numbers 100,000, that he should flee to the forest of Narún and there assemble a new army. He gets a new idea, and assembles a meeting of wise men and nobles to consult. Farúkhzád proposes that he should go to the forest of Narún, as his servants and all his slaves are at Ámil, and turn back when he has got together an army, and fight. The army approve, but the king says he would prefer battle to disgrace. With this the nobles agree and ask him what pledge he gives them. He tells them that anxiety ruins the heart and they had better go to Khurásán, where he has many troops and Pehlaváns, and where the Túrki nobles and the Khákán of China would come and praise him; that he would form an alliance with them and marry the daughter of the Faghfúr; that a large army would come to his assistance with the nobles of the Turkománs and Mahúi, the guardian of the frontier. Farúkhzád warns him not to trust too much to men of evil disposition, and the king replies that no harm can come from the experiment. Accordingly, early the next morning, they start from Baghdád towards Khurásán, the army all crying out that they are his slaves and desirous of accompanying him, but he decides it will be better for them to remain. Farúkhzád leads on the army to Raí, and having rested there proceeds by Gurgán on the way to Búst. When the king proposes to proceed to

Marv he writes to the guardián of the frontier, Mahúi Súri, to prepare his army to fight; that he will not stay more than a week at Nishápúr but move on to Marv, and will write to the Khákán and the Faghfúr of China for troops, following his letter up in person. He selects another intelligent envoy to send to Mahúi Súrí, and writes another letter to the Margraves of Tús, to tell them what has befallen him. Mahúi receives the messenger and says that no one dares oppose the Arab in fight, inasmuch as fortune favours him. The king grows full of anxiety at this proceeding of his enemy, and Mahúi, seeing him in this state, in haste sets up the throne of desire and adopts another tone towards him, and writes to one Bejan, an ambitious man of Samarkand, to tell him that the king of Irán has arrived without an army at Marv, and if he will come he can acquire his throne, crown, and treasure, thus avenging his ancestors. Bejan tells the messenger that if he goes to assist Mahúi his affairs there will go to ruin. He, however, arranges to send Barsám with 10,000 men to Marv. An army arrives in a week from Bukhárá at Marv. The king is unaware that Mahúi is his enemy, when a horseman comes to him at dawn to say that an army of Turkománs has arrived, and asks what he proposes to do. He is bewildered, and puts on his breastplate. The two armies are drawn up face to face and the king charges, and they all turn their backs to him. It was Mahúi's intention that the king should be taken prisoner, but he shows great bravery, and only turns back, pursued by Turkománs, after he has killed many in the main body of the army, and hides himself in a mill that he sees, the Turkomán horsemen searching for him. The miller, to his amazement, finds him sitting there, and asks him why he has come there. The king tells him he is one of the Iránis, who has fled from the army of Turán. The miller gives him some barley bread, and as he is eating it gives information to some of Mahúi's men. Mahúi sends the miller to cut off his head on pain of losing his own, and having none of his race left alive. His chiefs hear this and cry out against him, and a Mobed of the name of Rádúi tells him that to kill a king or a prophet will bring evil upon him and his son, and is supported in what he says by a holy man of the name of Hormuzd Kharád Shehrán, and Mehronúsh. The last reminds him of what has happened in the days of former monarchs in consequence of such deeds, and lately to Bandúi and Gústaham, and bids him go and beg pardon of the king or fear the anger of God if he does such a deed. The Mobeds go on in the same strain until nightfall, but have no effect upon him. He sends for other learned men from the army and tells them that if Yazdagird is allowed to live an army will collect round him and he himself will come to harm. One man tells him that if he kills the king, the deed will be avenged and will cause sorrow right and left. His son also warns him that an army will come against them from Chín and Máchín, and the face of the earth will become too narrow for them, and if the flag is removed from his skirt they will root him and his army out of the earth. Notwithstanding this, he orders the miller to make away with Yazdagird, not allowing a drop of blood to touch his clothes. The miller most unwillingly goes in and stabs him with a dagger in the middle. Mahúi's horsemen all go and see him and take off his clothing and ornaments, leaving him on the ground. All the nobles curse Máhúi and wish him the same fate. Mahúi has the body carried off and thrown into the water during the night, but it is seen there, and bishops and monks come to see it from all quarters, and after lamenting draw the body out of the water. A *dukhmah* is made for him in the garden. His wound is dried with camphor and other things, and his body wrapped in brocade. The rest of the Section is composed of the remarks of various people on Yazdagird's death and moral reflections.

The bishops, priests, and monks of Rúm carry the body out of the water and mourn for the dead, and prepare a *dukhmah* for him in the garden. Mahúi sends and kills all who have had any hand in these proceedings and plunders their land. Looking round the world he sees no one left of the seed of his ancestors. He calls all the faithful ones (*rázdar* ?) and says to the Mobed that the days of shame and strife have passed away; that he has neither name nor honourable descent, but he desires justice. There was a name on the ring of Yazdagird. They had not tamed him with the sword. All the country of Irán was a slave to him, although they had scattered his relatives. There was another secret remedy: why did he shed the blood of the world's king? All night he was full of anxiety: God knew in what state he was.*

A councillor says to him: "This has all occurred and the world is filled with the noise of it. Now review all thou hast done, for thou hast worn through that *zanár* bound round thyself. He has now gone into his *dukhmah* in the earth, and the dust has become a medicine for his spirit. Assemble all the experienced men and speak good words to them. Say that the king gave thee this crown and ring. When he knew the Turkomán army had come, he called thee in the darkness of the night and said to thee: 'Whence has arisen this noise of strife? Take this crown and ring: they may be of use to thee some day. I have only one daughter in the world. Do not give up my place to the enemy; preserve this in remembrance of me.' I have this hereditary crown from the

* These seem to be all incoherent ravings, for there is no connected sense in them.

king, and will sit in his place by his command. By this trick lighten up thy affair: who is to know whether it is true or false?" Hearing this, Mahúi says: "Good: thou art my Minister, and there is no one greater." He summons all the Chiefs and discourses to them on the subject. The army knows that it is not true, and it would be right to cut off his head for his impudence; but a Pehlaván says that is his affair, whether it is true or false. Hearing this, Mahúi seats himself on the royal throne and gives away the land to the nobles, so that the stars even wonder at him, and takes other measures to curry favour with the people. He gives Balkh and Herát to his elder son, and sending troops in every direction and placing an experienced man of the name of Garsívan over them, orders him to Bukhárá. He says that he must seize on Samarkand and Cháj by order of King Yazdágird, and must demand them from Beján with the sword of vengeance, for the fortune of the lord of the land had become obscured through him.

Beján, hearing of Mahúi's assuming the throne, and having sent the seal and ring round, in order that people might obey him, moves towards the Jaihún, and learning what has taken place in the mill, orders his army to assemble again. When he approaches Bukhárá he spreads his army over the plain and the desert, and makes them wait till Mahúi should come to that side of the river in order that he might avenge the king on him. He asks whether Khusru has left no son or daughter with whom he could ally himself, and is informed that the whole race is extinct. He now marches against Mahúi Súri, who is terrified when he sees his army. Beján arrays his army and is about to lay an ambush for the Iránis, when Mahúi comes forward from the centre of his own forces. Beján sees him and his standard. He orders his General Barsám to move his troops to one side from the centre, for fear Mahúi should be frightened and move off to the Jaihún. Barsám does so, and takes his forces as far as the sand of Faráb. Finding him with his stirrups heavy in the sand, he strikes him with his dagger, and seizing him by his belt throws him out of his saddle. He then ties his hands. His companions come up to him, and tell him he ought to cut off his head. He refuses, because Beján is not aware that he has been caught. Beján now hears of it and rejoices. They plunder his baggage and strip Mahúi, who, when he sees Beján, loses his wits and casts dust on his own head. Beján asks him why he killed the king, and he answers that there is nothing for an evil doer but death and reproach, and he should therefore cut off his head and throw it before the people. Beján replies that he will do so, and first cuts off his hand and says there is no equal to that hand in wickedness. He then orders both feet to be cut off, sc that he might not move from the place: then follow his ears and nose, and he is placed on a horse. Orders are then given to place him in the warm sand until sleep comes to him through shame. A herald goes round the camp, saying: "May all be like Mahúi who do not grant a king his life!" On Mahúi's death a great uproar takes place in Merv, and Guráz and his three sons are all burnt in a fire. Beján also goes mad.

This concludes the historical part of the Sháhnámah, but there is still a Section that relates to the date at which it was written. Its purport is as follows: When I arrived at the age of 61 years the heavens bowed themselves down before my poem. For 35 years of this transitory world I underwent much labour for the sake of treasure. As I threw my labour to the winds, there were not 35 gains for me. Now that my age has approached 80 years my hope has been given to the wind. The story of Yazdagird has come to an end on the day of

Ard in the month of Safand Armuz. As five times eighty have passed from the Hijra (Hejira) I have told this royal history.

From this it appears that the book was completed in A.H. 400, about corresponding with A.D. 1020.